# THE POWER POLICY OF MAINE

**Lincoln Smith**

# THE POWER POLICY OF MAINE

Berkeley and Los Angeles • 1951
UNIVERSITY OF CALIFORNIA PRESS

UNIVERSITY OF CALIFORNIA PRESS
BERKELEY AND LOS ANGELES, CALIFORNIA

CAMBRIDGE UNIVERSITY PRESS
LONDON, ENGLAND

# PREFACE

*My interest in the hydroelectric power of Maine goes back to 1927, when I discussed it as a high-school debater. My side maintained that the Fernald law was unconstitutional and economically unsound—but we usually lost the decision. Since then my views have, I hope, become more mature; but they have not fundamentally changed.*

*This study emerges from my doctoral dissertation. The scope of the investigation has been expanded from state to regional power policy and administration. The study assumes that policy is determined by law, its administration and judicial interpretation. Because of the broad scope of this phase of Maine's power policy, relatively little attention has been paid to the economic effects of this policy on the communities of Maine and New England. That would be another complete study in itself.*

*The objective has been to provide a study in political and legal history relative to the principal subject, to concentrate on polishing one facet of regional politico-economic policy, considering Maine's power policy in perspective as part of a New England regional problem in the formulation and administration of a vital and dynamic scheme of control.*

*The Honorable Harvey D. Eaton of Waterville, Maine, and the Honorable George C. Wing, Jr., of Auburn, Maine, made numerous suggestions on several phases of this study; they have both been very patient in answering questions both in interviews and by letter. To Commissioner George E. Hill of the Maine Public Utilities Commission and the Honorable W. B. Skelton, president of the Central Maine Power Company, are due also my sincerest thanks for great assistance rendered.*

*To the following persons I am deeply indebted for kindnesses of many different sorts: Mr. Leonard W. Labaree, Mr. Francis Coker, and Mr. William H. Dunham, Jr., of the faculty of Yale University; and Professor John M. Gaus of Harvard University. The latter, as director of the research project embodied in this book, made many fruitful suggestions for its carrying out.*

*At the Sterling Memorial Library and the Law Library of Yale University, also at the Maine State Library at Augusta and at the library of Bowdoin College, I met with nothing but cheerful coöperation.*

*Much of the data for the revision of the original form of this study was obtained at the library of Securities and Exchange Commission in Philadelphia in 1945–1946. Commissioner Sumner T. Pike and Commissioner Robert E. Healy, together with several staff members of the Public Utilities Division, were very helpful. The Honorable Charles Evans Hughes, Jr., kindly lent some of his father's private papers dealing with certain legal matters involved. Professor James C. Bonbright of Columbia University gave the manuscript a critical reading, suggested new lines of approach, and very graciously helped to make some of the necessary new material available.*

*Certain staff members of the Federal Power Commission in Washington and in the New York regional office obtained pertinent data on obscure points. Mr. Harold Gerrish of the Maine Public Utilities Commission, Mr. Justice Edward F. Merrill of the Supreme Judicial Court of Maine, Mr. E. W. Morehouse of the General Public Utilities Corporation, and Professor Edward C. Kirkland of Bowdoin College gave invaluable assistance.*

*Thanks are extended also to the students in my proseminar in regional administration in the University of California at Los Angeles for thought-provoking questions which emerged when parts of this material were tried out on them. To my parents and my sister, and to certain friends in New Haven, I am indebted for encouragement and searching criticism, and for patience shown on numerous occasions when I forced the conversation into channels relating to my consuming interest.*

*To the Press Committee of the University of California at Los Angeles, and especially to the chairman, Professor William Matthews of the English Department, I am grateful for the interest and enthusiasm shown in the study. For important editorial advice I am greatly indebted to Mr. W. H. Alexander of the University of California Press, and for infinite pains in shaping the manuscript for printing to Miss Genevieve Rogers of the same institution. An attempt has been made to incorporate major developments into the manuscript while going through the Press. I also appreciate the kindness and encouragement of several friends in Los Angeles, especially that of Dr. and Mrs. William C. Pomeroy, Dean David F. Jackey, and Professor Malbone W. Graham.*

LINCOLN SMITH

# CONTENTS

# CHAPTER I

## The Great-Pond Ordinance

The first landmark in power legislation for New England was an ordinance adopted by the general court of the Massachusetts Bay Colony in 1641, and amended in 1647. The original act was more nearly an organic law than an ordinance because it was embodied in a number of "Common Liberties," including the right of free speech in courts and town meetings, freedom of emigration, and free fishing and fowling.[1]

> Every Inhabitant that is an howse holder shall have free fishing and fowling in any great ponds and Bayes, Coves and Rivers, so farre as the sea ebbes and flowes within the presincts of the towne where they dwell, unlesse the free men of the same Towne or the Generall Court have otherwise appropriated them, provided that this shall not be extended to give leave to any man to come upon others propertie without there leave.

This law did not originally provide for public ownership of great ponds; that would have contravened the Colony's charter grant, which prohibited the enactment of laws repugnant to those of England. The law merely declared a public right of uses or license for specific purposes. The concept of public ownership of the pond itself was written into the ordinance by judicial interpretation many years later.[2] The original ordinance merely permitted free fishing and fowling in these waters. The principle was limited to householders residing within the town, and they could not trespass on the property of others to obtain access to the privileges.[3]

Max Farrand has well described the nature of these "Liberties":[4]

> The Liberties were partly a declaration of general principles, such as later became familiar in bills of rights, and partly specific provisions of

positive law. They were apparently compiled from the Scriptures, Magna Charta, and the statutes and common law of England, and intended for the guidance of the General Court in framing laws and of the magistrates in applying them . . . .

Unless some further evidence is brought to light, doubt may exist as to whether the Liberties were ever formally made law. The records of the General Court are far from satisfactory at any time, especially in comparison with our modern meticulous and repetitious forms, but even these records are lacking for a part of the particular period.

While no official records exist to prove that the "Liberties" were enacted into formal law at this time, a notation of Governor Winthrop that they were revised, amended, and presented in the court is strong, if not positive, evidence.[5] But there is no doubt of their validity a few years later. According to Mr. Justice Savage, the general court affirmed in 1644 that the body of "Liberties" was the "chief civil power of the commonwealth."[6] And Whittlesey offers, as evidence that the ordinance was sanctioned by the general court, the fact that this legislative body authorized Joseph Story in 1812 to prepare a new edition of the *Colony and Province Laws,* which appeared in 1814 and included the great-pond ordinance.[7]

The colonial ordinance of 1641 can be understood only from the perspective of its English background and the common-law principles involved. The law in England concerning the sea bottom and tidal waters clearly recognized the title to be in the sovereign, not for his own benefit but for the benefit of his subjects at large:[8]

> The title of the sovereign in the sea bottom within the limits stated (from ordinary highwater mark to an imaginary and arbitrary parallel one marine league, or three miles out to sea) was accompanied by exclusive authority and jurisdiction in the waters over it, and was held not for his own benefit but for his subjects at large, and for the subjects of all states at peace with him; he held it in trust for public uses established by ancient custom or regulated by law, among the most important of which were navigation and fishing. He possessed not only the *jus privatum,* or title to the sea bottom, in trust for the public use and benefit, but also the *jus publicum,* or the right of governing the waters over the same for the protection of public rights and the security and welfare of the realm.

As for British inland waters, "To the Sovereign also, and to the same extent, belonged the title and exclusive authority in and over the waters and bottom in all navigable rivers, bays, cove, inlets and other arms of the sea as far inland as the tide ebbs and flows."[9]

England has relatively few large fresh-water lakes and ponds, and apparently for this reason they were not covered by common law. According to Gould, "The early authorities lay down no definite rule respecting property in inland lakes and ponds otherwise than by limiting the property of the Crown to tide waters."[10] Gould, Farnham, and Whittlesey, however, are in agreement that English law evolved eventually to the fairly definite point that nontidal lakes are the subject of private ownership.[11] As late as 1878 Lord Cairns said, of the longest inland lake in the United Kingdom, which is also one of the largest in Europe, "It is, however, necessary to decide whether the Crown has of common right a *prima facie* title to the soil of a lake; I think it has not. I know of no authority for saying it has, and I see no reason why it should have it."[12] Gould's summary follows:

> It appears, therefore, that by the law of England the Crown and the public have no such rights in fresh-water lakes as they possess in tide waters; that the soil and fishings in them are private property; and that, while the rule which extends the riparian owners' title *usque ad filum aquae* does not appear to have been applied to lakes, as to unnavigable streams, and is an inconvenient rule for the determination of rights in large lakes, yet the public have no greater privileges in them than in fresh-water rivers. The public right of navigation in them doubtless depends upon prescription and proof of long-continued user.[13]

But the English law governing nontidal rivers developed much more precisely, because of the importance of water rights in an agricultural community and because of the need of power for mills.[14] The English law was that the ownership of land under a nonnavigable stream, provided that one owned the land flanking one side, was private. This was expounded in an opinion of the Honorable Lucilius A. Emery, formerly Chief Justice of the Supreme Judicial Court of Maine:[15]

> By the English law of the time a grant of land with a non-tidal river as a boundary included the land under the river to its middle line, *ad medium filum aquae*. And this was the rule in grants direct from the crown, which grants were always construed strictly against the grantee. *Lord v. The Sydney Commissioners*, 12 Moore P. C. 473. It followed, of course, that a grant of land through which a non-tidal river ran included

the whole bed of the river within the upper and lower limits of the grant. So complete was this ownership thus conferred, the grantee acquired (unless excepted from the grant) the exclusive right of fishing in the river adjoining his upland and could grant that right separately, retaining all his other rights (14 Lord Halsbury's Laws of England p. 50). Indeed, his ownership was esteemed so complete that he was regarded as having seizin of the river as well as of the land. Thus Sir Edward Coke in his Institutes at p. 200 (folio ed. temp. James I) states the rule as follows: "So if a man be seized of a river and by deed doth grant a separative piscatory in the same, and make the livery of seizin, the soil doth not pass, nor the water." In fine all such rights were presumably private. The public does not appear to have had any right of navigation on non-tidal rivers except such as it may have acquired by prescription or Act of Parliament.

The late Edward P. Ricker suggested that the colonial ordinance had its origin in Roman law, which held that rivers and lakes were common property, and only the natural right of flowing water, the air, the sea, and the shores of the sea remained for the public.[16] Thus in Louisiana, a state strongly influenced by the Napoleonic Code, the bed of a navigable lake cannot be privately owned.

It may well be asked why the Massachusetts Bay Colony, in spite of the sacred tradition of private property rights to which the people had been accustomed in England, should at a very early date have decreed free fishing and fowling in great ponds. Before they left England, the lives of these people had been minutely prescribed. The law of the land regulated church attendance and distribution of their property at death. Strict and sometimes severe laws controlling hunting and fishing were among the objectionable limitations on human freedom. After 1539 poaching was a felony in England,[17] and at times felony was punishable there by forfeiture of life or limb.[18] Even though the poaching laws were relaxed by 1552,[19] the reaction against them by the settlers in the Massachusetts Bay Colony is usually given as the reason for the colonial ordinance providing for free fishing and fowling in great ponds of ten or more acres.[20] In the case of *Commonwealth v. Alger* (7 Cushing 53, 68 [1851]), the court stated the purpose of the ordinance as follows: "To declare a great principle of public right, to abolish the forest laws, the game laws, and the laws designed to secure several and exclusive fisheries, and to make them all free."

The section of the ordinance giving special privileges in ponds and tidal rivers can, however, be attributed more appropriately to the rigors of the Massachusetts frontier.[21] The pioneer colonists were interested primarily in wresting the means of subsistence from the ground, forest, sea, and inland waters. Many were adventurers, occupied chiefly with hunting and fishing.[22] It was imperative that the colonists should have fish and game for sustenance; so access to them became a matter of public concern. Since most of the early settlements were made on the coast or on streams within the tide-water area, privileges were given upstream as far as the tide went.

As for great ponds, the common privileges idea was also entirely in accord with a fairly general colonial concept of the use of many town facilities in common. In this respect the great-pond ordinance is a carry-over from feudalism. Osgood has likened the early New England town to the manor.[23] The monarchial idea was exemplified by the proprietor. By far the greater part of the land in the New England colonies was granted to proprietors, who in turn allotted it to individuals for a consideration.

Settlement of townships was completed in part by the laying out of common fields. Some towns

> [had] many common fields, each of which, under the authority of the town, had its associated proprietors. These had common fences and were cultivated under a joint system. . . . Common fences and herds were characteristic accompaniments of the system of common fields and joint cultivation which were the basis of the town economy. They appear in all towns. . . . All grants of land were made subject to the right of the community to open highways through them.[24] . . . The town herd and herdsmen figure in the local annals of all parts of New England. They had their origin in the system of common fields.[25]

For some time there were common fields, common fences, and common herds, and occasionally common markets and mills. In Boston the common market was an elaborate affair, with regular officials to enforce the market rules, which had originated in medieval towns. There were some municipal mills. Private mills, fostered by the government, were usually limited monopolies, regulated in the public interest.[26] In 1633 the general court ordered that all swamps of more than one hundred acres lie in common for any free inhabitant to fetch wood at seasonable times.[27] Thus the atmosphere was appropriate for establishing the uses of common ponds as well.

Although by 1635 the undivided fields and meadowlands belonging to the Town of Cambridge had been separated into individual allotments, similar action was not taken in Newbury until 1686, and a common land system prevailed in part of Salem until after the Revolution.[28] Frederick J. Turner said that the tendency to parcel out the common lands did not become marked until the eighteenth century.[29]

The builders of the Massachusetts Bay Colony were in contact with the Indians, who lacked our concept of private property and wanted territory only for hunting and fishing. They often sold large tracts of land with all the formalities of English law, supposing that they were giving only the right of hunting and fishing on their grounds in common with themselves, and that they could therefore grant the same land to others at a later date.[30] While the colonial ordinance was, of course, not of Indian origin, there are, nevertheless, similarities in the two concepts of common grounds and ponds for hunting, fishing, and fowling. Professor Robert P. T. Coffin of Bowdoin College remarks on this point, "Like the old Abenakis, Maine farmers look on all lands as a common hunting and fishing ground."[31] Clive Day, using more modern language, concludes that the spirit of the Puritan colonies was in these regards more socialistic than capitalistic.[32]

Before 1641 Massachusetts had many common commercial, economic, and social undertakings. Besides this, the Puritans regulated business, fixed prices, taxed excess profits, and, since there was no separation of church and state, they controlled religion and the suffrage. The case of Robert Keayne in 1639 illustrates the economic control of the government over individuals. He was fined by the magistrates and also admonished by the church for taking a profit above sixpence on the shilling. At the same time John Cotton decreed that a vendor may not sell above the current price.[33] Hamilton Basso must have been right when he said that Franklin D. Roosevelt and his New Deal were influenced by this Puritan philosophy.[34] In the colonial period, tremendous discretionary authority was exercised by the government, which frequently restrained the manifestation of even a minimum of liberty by the individual. The occasional general courts held in 1640 and later dealt almost entirely with local legislation of a temporary character.[35]

According to Governor Winthrop, "The people had long desired a body of laws, and thought their condition very unsafe, while so much rested in the discretion of magistrates."[36] Despite opposition to the movement by most of the magistrates and some of the elders, who feared that the people lacked experience to act wisely, the body of "Common Liberties" was created in 1641, embodied in an act comprising one hundred sections.

Important amendments were made in 1647, but thereafter, although new editions and revisions of the colonial laws appeared in 1660, 1672, and 1814, the only changes in this particular ordinance consisted of slight alterations in spelling and punctuation.[37] The last version in its final and modernized form follows:[38]

Acts Respecting Liberties in Common, As To Flats, &c. To Pass Over Lands, And To Remove Out Of The Colony.

Sect. 1. It is ordered, by this court decread and declared; that every man, whether inhabitant or foreigner, free or not free, shall have liberty to come to any publick court, council, or town meeting, and either by speech or writing, to move any lawful, seasonable, or material question, or to present any necessary motion, complaint, petition, bill, or information, whereof that meeting hath proper cognizance, so it be done in convenient time, due order, and respective manner. [1641]

Sect. 2. Every inhabitant who is an householder shall have free fishing and fowling in any great ponds, bays, coves and rivers, so far as the sea ebbs and flows within the precincts of the town where they dwell, unless the freemen of the same town or the general court have otherwise appropriated them:

Provided, that no town shall appropriate to any particular person or persons, any great pond, containing more than ten acres of land, and that no man shall come upon another's property without their leave, otherwise than as hereafter expressed.

The which clearly to determine;

Sect. 3. It is declared, that in all creeks, coves, and other places about and upon salt water, where the sea ebbs and flows, the proprietor, of the land adjoining, shall have propriety to the low water mark, where the sea doth not ebb above a hundred rods, and not more wheresoever it ebbs further:

Provided, that such proprietor shall not by this liberty have power to stop or hinder the passage of boats or other vessels, in or through any sea, creeks or coves, to other men's houses or lands.

Sect. 4. And for great ponds lying in common, though within the bounds of some town, it shall be free for any man to fish and fowl there, and may pass and repass on foot through any man's propriety for that end, so they trespass not upon any man's corn or meadow. [1641, 47]

Sect. 5. Every man of, or within this jurisdiction, shall have free liberty (notwithstanding any civil power) to remove both himself and his family, at their pleasure, out of the same; provided there be no legal impediment to the contrary. [1641]

The content of all versions after 1648 was similar. They differed from the 1641 version in two respects: first, the privilege was extended to a greater number of people; and second, the additional right was given to pass and repass on private property (if not cultivated) in order to make use of the privilege. At first the privilege of free fishing and fowling was confined to householders within the limits of the town in which they resided; this was now greatly extended, and the former denial of the privilege if it involved trespass on private property was revoked and the right to trespass was conferred, provided the property was not cultivated.

Except for two brief periods, the Massachusetts Bay Colony claimed and exercised some jurisdiction over the Province of Maine from 1651 to 1692. When the great-pond ordinance was adopted, the Colony had no jurisdiction over Maine, and hence the ordinance did not apply to the Province.[39] Neither did it apply to the Plymouth Colony until it was incorporated with Massachusetts Bay by the charter of 1692.[40] Despite this, there is evidence that the same principles were valid in Maine before 1692. According to Mr. Justice Savage of Maine,[41]

But we think it does not admit of any reasonable doubt that the principles of the ordinance were recognized and practiced here prior to 1692. The same conditions which led the people of Massachusetts to declare "free fowling and fishing" as one of their "liberties" existed here. There was the same necessity for a resort to fishing and fowling for sustenance. In both cases, the colonists were in a comparatively uninhabited and not very fertile country. It was a wilderness. They gained only a scanty subsistence from the soil. Husbandry was attended with failure of crops and depredations from savage foes. The common law of England, which restricted the use of ponds and streams to private owners was not suited to their conditions and necessities. It is commonly said that the common law of England was brought over by the colonists, and, in a general sense became their law, but it is held that they adopted only so much of it as was suitable to their new conditions and needs, consistent with the new state of society, and conformable to the general course of policy which they intended to pursue. *Cottrill v. Myrick,* 12 Maine 222; *Concord Co. v. Robertson,* 66 N.H. 1; *Storer v. Freeman,* 6 Mass. 434 [a Cape Elizabeth, Maine, case]; *Commonwealth v. Alger,* supra. The picture of these struggling colonists, so familiar to every reader of history, clearly shows how very inapplicable to their conditions was that principle of the common law which gave the exclusive right of fishery in a pond to the owners of the soil underneath. Such undoubtedly was the origin of the "liberty" which was declared in Massachusetts in 1641.

The historical proof given by the court to show that fishing and fowling were free in Maine before 1692 was that the Council of Plymouth had granted lands on the Kennebec River "to the Plymouth adventurers." The Plymouth Colony conveyed these lands to William Bradford and associates, who, in 1654 at a meeting held at "Merry Meeting," where "the people generally assembled," ordered and agreed *"that fishing and fowling be free to all the inhabitants as formerly."* The conclusion of the court was that "under the common law of this State, based now in part upon the Colonial Ordinance, but beginning before the ordinance was extended here, all great ponds without exception are public."[42] This rule applies likewise to the portion of Maine which comprises former Acadian territory under the jurisdiction of France in 1641 and 1647.[43]

One may quote William Willis on the result:[44]

> The extension of the laws and jurisdiction of Massachusetts over this territory had an important influence upon its settlement and prosperity. Hitherto we may presume that no permanent code of laws had been established; the records furnish no indication of the kind, but temporary ordinances were framed, as they were called for by the wants of the people and the emergency of the occasion, and the execution of these must have been inefficient and fluctuating. But when the laws of Massachusetts were introduced, sanctioned by her example and power and enforced with rigor, security was afforded for the enjoyment of property and civil privileges.

The Supreme Judicial Court thus demonstrated that the Massachusetts ordinance, although it was in opposition to the English common law, was also the general practice in Maine. The English common law was not in its entirety transplanted to Massachusetts. "And except so far as they adopted and used the common law, it was not in force here. It is on this ground that the courts have many times declared that various laws of England have never been laws here." Settlers in Maine were close to Massachusetts and looked to Massachusetts definitely for leadership; many settlers in Maine had emigrated from Massachusetts. The court regarded these as other cogent reasons leading to the conclusion that fishing and fowling, at least on great ponds, were free in Maine from the beginning.

Since Maine was a part of Massachusetts from 1692 until 1820, the early acts of the Massachusetts general court concerning ownership of water for power and other purposes, riparian rights, and millsites are fundamental in Maine water-power law.[45] The citizens, town officials, and courts of Massachusetts have, from a very early date, sought to restrict the use of waters in great ponds to local public purposes, and have been reluctant to allow them to be used for commercial purposes or for the service of inhabitants of more remote localities. This shows an early precedent for the staunch localism in recent Maine policy. Thus, thirty-three inhabitants of Roxbury in 1739 complained to their selectmen that a local mill was erected to grind corn for local families, but that the millers had fallen into the habit of grinding large quantities of wheat from Boston. The selectmen were asked to stop the drawing from the great pond of more water than was required for family grinding. The selectmen thereupon ordered that no Boston wheat be ground in the mill unless it could be done without damage to Roxbury and Brookline. This report was discussed and approved at town meeting.[46] In 1783 the selectmen, in response to a petition, forbade the drawing of large amounts of water from the pond. On September 5, 1794, it was voted "that it is the unanimous Sense of the Inhabitants of the Town of Roxbury, that Drawing the waters from Jamaica Pond for any other purpose than for the use of a Grist Mill for the Inhabitants of Roxbury, and Brooklyn . . . will be injurious to the Inhabitants of the Town of Roxbury in General and more Particularly to the Abuttors of the Pond."[47]

That the great-pond ordinance of 1641 was a settled rule of property in Massachusetts was stated by its Supreme Judicial Court as early as 1832. Even to question it as a settled rule of property, said the court, would be extremely injurious to the stability of titles and the peace of the community. "It is founded upon a usage and practice so ancient, immemorial, and unvarying, that without tracing its precise origin, it must now be deemed a rule of common law proved by such usage."[48]

Massachusetts and Maine are the only New England states which have this unusual law, although it has influenced the custom of New Hampshire.[49] But the notion prevailing in New England that only two states in the Union have such a law is mistaken: Louisiana by statute and the state of Washington by its constitution retain the title to navigable lakes for the public.[50]

With one exception, when the Massachusetts legislature amended the ordinance in 1869 to make ponds of twenty or more acres instead of ten or more acres public,[51] neither state legislature has changed the fishing and fowling provision, but the judiciary has extended it to include much more than that. In the early agricultural economy, the rights of fishing and fowling and a means of access to exercise these rights was about the only use of much value existent in the ponds, but the courts of both Maine and Massachusetts have held that the first privileges were illustrative of a general principle which has been extended from time to time to include other privileges pursuant to public requirements and the changing conditions of society. They have extended the meaning to include bathing, the use of water for washing, for watering cattle, for preparation of flax and other domestic and agricultural uses, for boating, for skating and riding upon the ice, and for cutting ice.[52] Eventually the courts went so far as to say that this included public ownership of great ponds.

In 1863 the Massachusetts court declared that great ponds were by the colonial ordinance made public, to lie in common for public use.[53] This was repeated much more emphatically in 1872, when Mr. Justice Gray began his decision with the statement that great ponds are public property,[54] and it was very much in evidence as a doctrine in the Watuppa cases.[55]

In 1882, however, the Maine court suggested the desirability of curtailing the privileges, using language not entirely complimentary to hunters and fishermen. Mr. Justice Barrows wrote:[56]

It may be true that our ideas of "great ponds" are not precisely similar to those which our ancestors brought from England—that there no longer exists the same necessity for free fishing and fowling to enable men to get the means of sustenance, which existed in 1641—that the right is now chiefly exercised by pleasure seekers and idle tramps who might be more profitably employed, and who cause more loss and destruction in timber and wood-lands than their pursuits yield advantage in the way of pleasure or profit—that their outgoings and incomings are attended by constant trespasses upon the farms which lie in their way, and in short that it would be for the general good to restrict the privileges that they have heretofore enjoyed. But these are considerations to be addressed to the legislature rather than to the court.

In 1885 the Maine court said that great ponds are public,[57] and cited the Watuppa cases as precedent in the important decision rendered in *Auburn v. Union Water Power Company.*[58] Possibly because of the dissent of Mr. Justice Spear in the advisory opinions of 1919, the Maine court avoided a direct statement of public ownership on this occasion, when it said:[59] "Whatever doubt might otherwise arise from a critical study of the subject as a matter of legal history, it must now be accepted as the common-law doctrine in Maine that the State holds these ponds in trust for the use of the people of the State, together with the right to control and regulate the waters thereof."

In a dissenting advisory opinion, Mr. Albert M. Spear contended that the privilege of pursuing free fishing and fowling did not constitute public ownership of great ponds.[60] His historical and legal reasoning behind this view are of interest primarily to the specialist. The stand was courageous, challenging as it did a concept already accepted in theory and practice for more than half a century. Its significance under *stare decisis* is relatively small, however, because advisory opinions carry less weight than decisions, and a dissenting advisory opinion lags far behind that.[61] Mr. Justice Spear summarized his stand as follows:[62]

[The ordinance] was merely a declaration of public policy, and . . . it did not convey any title in fee to the public, nor obtain . . . its title to great ponds "by virtue of the ordinance," but by concession when it was separated from Massachusetts and became a State; that, having sold the lands, with great ponds thereon, without reservation, the ponds passed with the lands to the grantees; that the State thereby parted with its title, which vested in the grantees, subject to the common use created by the application of the ordinance; and that the dicta of the court, which would seem to hold, notwithstanding the State had thus conveyed its lands and ponds thereon, that the ordinance vested a title in the State which its deeds did not convey, are erroneous in giving to the ordinance the power of a "rule of property," which it never had, nor was intended to have.

Maintaining that the ordinance conveyed no property right in the great ponds to the state in its organic capacity nor to the people in their sovereign capacity, Mr. Justice Spear argued that the "decision" of the court that the ordinance gave the state the title to great ponds was based on a dictum. "But a dictum is not a judicial decision. It is binding upon no one, not even the Judge who utters it."[63] Yet, despite the fact that the Maine courts have *said* many times that the state owns the great ponds, the court actually took its major premise from the Watuppa decision:[64] "Under the ordinance, the State owns the great ponds as public property, held in trust for public uses. It has not only the *jus privatum,* the ownership of the soil, but also the *jus publicum,* and the right to control and regulate the public uses to which the ponds shall be applied."

But Mr. Justice Spear argued as follows: "The phrase, 'ownership of the soil' by itself, would clearly indicate a fee; but, when limited by the phrase 'held in trust for the public,' the interpretation of the ordinance is in harmony with the construction that the great ponds, by whomever held, are impressed with the trust of the ordinance, and that the State has such ownership in trust as will enable the court to enforce its provisions." But this Massachusetts dictum, he asserted,[65] was incorrectly applied in the Maine case *Auburn v. Union Water Power Company.*[66] Here it conferred a common right (fishing and fowling), residing in the individual only (free for any man to fish and fowl, pass and repass), upon a municipal corporation. (The court allowed the city of Auburn to take water from a great pond for domestic supply without paying damages.)

One fallacy in this opinion is Mr. Justice Spear's conception of a dictum and its effect. It is often difficult to differentiate between dictum and opinion. What is considered part of the logical reasoning process of one judge is superfluous to another. Mr. Justice Spear's charge that public ownership in this case is pure dictum is not convincing. Assuming for the moment that he has proved it, his narrow interpretation of the effect of a dictum may well be challenged. For example, the *obiter dictum* in the famous Dred Scott decision[67] was regarded as a judicial decision with tremendous consequences. According to Professor Frederick C. Hicks of the Yale University Law School, some courts, troubled by this problem, redefine the rule of precedent and apply it to constantly reiterated dicta.[68] Mr. Justice Spear says that our courts have many times repeated the dictum of the Massachusetts court. Actually, however, the public ownership interpretation was not grafted into the Massachusetts law in the dictum of the Watuppa decision, because thirty-six years earlier the Massachusetts court said that great ponds were public,[69] and twenty years later Judge Gray began a decision thus:[70] "By the law of Massachusetts, great ponds are public property . . ." Even the dissent in the Watuppa cases said great ponds were the property of the Colony.[71]

The answer to Mr. Justice Spear's contention that great ponds are private property by virtue of common-law sale of lands, which includes waters thereon, appears to be that when the legislature granted land titles they were acquired on the condition or presumption that nobody could acquire property in great ponds.[72] In brief, since public ownership of great ponds is the common law of Massachusetts and Maine, the common-law transfer of land would be made according to the principles of the law itself. Furthermore, in all land grants from the government to the subject, the terms of the grant are taken most strongly against the grantee and in favor of the grantor—reversing the common-law rule as between individuals—because the grant is supposed to be made at the solicitation of the grantee in a form prepared by him and submitted to the government for its allowance.[73]

The interpretation of the ordinance on the legislative right to dispose of waters of great ponds is of the utmost importance to Maine because of its extensive system of lakes. The state has 1,620 lakes (1,568 wholly within its borders) with an aggregate area of 2,300 square miles, or one-fourteenth of its total area.[74] These lakes are important for water power because they provide natural reservoirs or storage basins, lessen the frequency and violence of freshets, and are at high elevations at the heads of rivers in the state. According to Professor Felix Frankfurter and Professor James M. Landis, the key to the development of Maine water-power resources lies in the development of water storage.[75] The lakes have good rock bottoms which do not leak and thus provide naturally excellent storage. "The Kennebec River has more lakes feeding it than the giant Orinoco . . . which is 3,000 miles long; and the Penobscot has more lakes than the Amazon."[76]

The climax of the contest over the use of the waters of great ponds was reached in the famous battle to save the lakes, which was decided in March, 1907.[77] This controversy showed the development of two competing concepts of public welfare: first, the development of mill power from water to provide employment and a means of livelihood; and second, the use of water for direct consumption, recreation, and, eventually, a competing business use for recreation.

The Union Water Power Company of Lewiston asked the legislature, as guardian of Maine's great ponds, for permission to draw down the water of the Rangeley lakes six feet below the low water level from December 1 to April 1. They maintained that this was necessary to keep the mills on the Androscoggin River in constant operation during periods of low water, that the men were idle four weeks in 1903 and 1904, and that sometimes the mills were forced to close in the late afternoon because of lack of power. The company considered this a reasonable request, maintaining that the welfare of the mill cities depended upon a constant supply of power, and that the lakes usually fill up again. The proponents contended their purpose was a public one, since 15,000 operatives were directly affected, and their families were dependent upon their work.

Senator Mills summed up the issue in the legislature:

> It is simply an issue between the manufacturing interests of the State and the summer industry. Both of which are important. I believe there is room enough for both on the Rangeley lakes and the other lakes—to expand and get all that water that is required and needed, but if we are to discriminate in any respect, or in the slightest degree, I believe we should legislate in favor of that industry which keeps the people—the operatives busy all the year round.

Not only did the water-power and mill interests support the measure, but the Lewiston Board of Trade and the Merchants' Association organized campaigns to push the bill. They maintained that Lewiston attracted little summer trade, and that manufacturing twelve months in the year was more important. Some believed that it was selfish to keep the water from the mills for the pleasure of summer visitors and sportsmen.

The opposition was led by the late Edward P. Ricker, a pioneer in Maine's recreational development, in a press campaign and in the committee hearings, while Senator Hastings and Senator Staples voiced the same arguments in the legislative debate. They asserted that not only would this valuable summer business be damaged for all time, but the railroads and their allied interests would be hurt by the passage of the bill. Ricker produced a letter from the United States Bureau of Fisheries which stated that the lowering of the water level in the lakes for four months would seriously reduce the number of fish. A low level would cause the water to become polluted, and decaying vegetation along the shores, drying in the sun, would tend to cause disease. It was also argued that, according to the Maine law whereby littoral proprietors own to the natural low-level mark and the state owns the bed of the lake, a recession of the water would leave exposed unsightly and stenchy banks in the area between the natural and artificial water levels, an area actually created by the state itself. Cottage and hotel owners would have no remedy against the author of the nuisance.

Ricker wanted the Androscoggin mills to have all the water storage they could get, but felt that they should not receive irrevocable rights which jeopardized greater interests. His argument that the mills had been able to run for thirty to forty years without drawing down the water level of the lake failed to recognize the growth of the mills, their greater demand for power, and the recent power shortages. He suggested that steam plants would be sufficient to tide them over possible periods of water shortage. But the ideal solution would be the construction of the Aziscoos dam, which would give ample water storage for the Androscoggin River without affecting the lakes. To the Union Water Company's contention that this would be too expensive and that the damage caused by flowage would be excessive, the reply was that the money their lobby used against the bill could pay much of the cost of the dam. So far as expense was concerned, Ricker gave it as a conservative estimate that the amount of lake water requested by the Union Water Power Company was worth $1,500,000 annually. The company was asking the legislature to give away this valuable water, owned by the people of Maine, to a corporation to increase dividends for private profit, with the prospect as well of creating a dangerous precedent.

Ricker maintained that it would be unconstitutional for the legislature to pass this bill and succinctly summarized this view: "I do not believe that the Legislature has any authority to divert property held in trust by the State for public uses to the private use and advantage of any corporation, to the injury of citizens and property owners of the State." The validity of this view depended on three main assumptions: first, that the legislature can authorize the use of lake waters for public purposes only; second, that manufacturing is not a public purpose; third, that the rights of littoral proprietors can be superseded only by exercising the right of eminent domain. The first and third points differ in that the first involved legislative control over public property, whereas the third pertained to the whole question of the use (or inability to use) private property. And in the light of court decisions handed down before 1907, Ricker was right. The constitutional issue was, however, oversimplified at this time and there was virtually no analysis of cases available to throw further light on the subject.

The leading decision cited by the opponents of the bill, *Fernald v. Knox Woolen Company*,[78] indicated the need for legislative authority to control the use of lake waters. But it did not consider on what bases such waters could be drawn below their natural low water line. All that the decision showed was that a corporation has no right to lower the level of a great pond; such a right would be inconsistent with the existence of the pond as a pond, and might interfere with the rights of littoral proprietors.

If exercised to its fullest extent it would destroy the pond. All the water might be drawn out and its bed left dry, a mere stream of running water only remaining. And if exercised, to any extent, the necessary effect must be to widen the shores and deprive the adjoining land owners of their natural water frontage: for it is the settled law of this state that lands, bounded on a great pond or lake, extend only to the natural low-water line, and that all beyond is owned by the state. And this natural water frontage may be as valuable to the land owner as the right to draw water is to the mill-owner. But whether of equal value or not, it is of equal validity in law, and entitled to equal protection.[79]

As great ponds and lakes are public property, the state may undoubtedly control and regulate their use as it thinks proper. But in the absence of legislative authority, no individual or corporation can lawfully draw down the water of a great natural pond or lake below its natural low-water line.[80]

This decision comes under, but does not fully cover, point three as outlined above. And it did not say that a legislature could not, if it saw fit, authorize the drawing of lake water for manufacturing (point one). Yet an earlier Massachusetts decision, *Attorney General v. Revere Copper Company,*[81] declared that any attempt of a town to convey a great pond to a private individual would be *ultra vires* and invalid. The water had been used for mills, but, as the area of the surface and quantity of water were diminished, to that degree the public was abridged of its rights of bathing, boating, fishing, and cutting ice in the pond.

In the debate in the State Senate vague references were made to the second point, viz., that manufacturing was not a public matter, and that the use of the water would be conveyed to a private corporation for private profit.[82] Ricker cited *Kaukauna Water Power Company v. Green Bay and Mississippi Canal Company*[83] to prove that the Wisconsin legislature had been unable to authorize the lowering of the level of a lake for manufacturing purposes even if the riparian (littoral) proprietors received compensation. But the case was inapplicable to Maine because it involved the use of private property only.

We may now proceed to discuss three relevant questions corresponding to the three assumptions made by Ricker in declaring the proposed legislative action unconstitutional. First, May the legislature authorize the use of lake waters for public purposes only? Since Maine owns its great ponds, it follows that their control and disposition rest with the legislature, unless prohibited by the constitution. Numerous Massachusetts and Maine decisions show that lawmakers can dispose of lake waters for public purposes, but it is more difficult to show that the purpose thus involved is the only purpose.

The original purpose of the great-pond ordinance was to assign them to public uses, subject, however, to reasonable abridgment. Thus, in 1871, the Massachusetts Supreme Court upheld a statute which abridged public fishing rights in certain great ponds, giving the rights to littoral proprietors; but the object of the act was to encourage the cultivation of fish.[84] This is similar to the recognized right to limit the fishing season for public benefit. Again in 1872 the court sanctioned a legislative grant to an aqueduct corporation to take water from a great pond for the use of the inhabitants of neighboring towns, a public use.[85] And in the famous Watuppa cases it was asserted that "under the ordinance, the State owns the great ponds as public property, *held in trust for public uses.*"[86] Here the use of the water for domestic purposes, for the extinguishment of fires and for other municipal and public uses, was sanctioned. Although only a 4 to 3 decision, the majority included eminent jurists,[87] and the decision was followed by the Maine court in *Auburn v. Union Water Power Company,*[88] a leading case.

The Union Water Power Company was organized under the general laws of the state and drew water from a great pond, some of which was used for the operation of mills. The legislature subsequently gave the city of Auburn authority to draw water from the same pond for domestic purposes such as extinguishing fires; supplying hotels, livery stables, and laundries; and for sprinkling streets.[89] The power company's suit for compensation was denied by the court on the basis that the use of water for domestic purposes is of primary importance, while the right to use it for mechanical purposes is of secondary only. Holding that water for domestic use is a necessity without which man cannot exist, whereas its use for mills is merely a convenience, the court saw no reason why those who want it for domestic use should be compelled to buy it from those who want it for the use of mills. The court clearly indicated why water for mills is subordinate to its use for domestic purposes:[90]

> Health is of more importance than wealth, and cleanliness is next to godliness; and we hold that the right of the people to an abundant supply of pure water by which their health and cleanliness may be secured, is paramount to the right of millowners to have the water for propelling their machinery; and that, to the extent that the two rights conflict, the latter must yield. Of course private property can not be taken for public uses without making compensation for it. But the waters of great ponds and lakes are not private property. They are owned by the state; and the state may dispose of them as it thinks proper.

However, this decision did not go so far as to say that the waters could not be taken for manufacturing. It said, "the state may dispose of them as it thinks proper," and in this case it was proper to give preference to domestic purposes over mechanical. Actually, the power company had been using the water for manufacturing purposes for more than thirty years, and the controversy arose only when it tried to collect compensation for damages from the city of Auburn. Similarly in *American Woolen Company v. Kennebec Water District,*[91] the court upheld an 1899 statute allowing the corporation to take water from China Lake, a great pond, to supply four municipalities with water for domestic and municipal purposes without awarding compensation or requiring proceedings for condemnation.

The Maine legislature has also granted to private corporations the right to raise, store, maintain, and control the waters of great ponds for manufacturing purposes. For example, several corporations were allowed to deepen the channel of Canaan Pond four feet and to use the waters of this pond and its tributaries to that extent for running mills.[92] In 1893 the legislature gave the right to drain Kidder Pond to drought level.[93] In the Town of Bluehill a right was granted to lower a pond three feet for four months in summer.[94] No compensation was required in the first and second cases.

Judicial decisions through 1907 indicate that corporations could not lower great ponds without legislative authority and that the legislature could permit the use of the water for public purposes without requiring compensation; manufacturing was regarded as secondary. In answer to the charge that the Union Water Power Company's request for the use of Rangeley water was the first of its kind in the state, the three foregoing instances were cited by the company. However, these were without judicial review.

In the advisory opinions of 1919 the Maine justices had this to say of the use of the waters of great ponds for manufacturing:[95]

> Our Legislature has often granted to private corporations the right to raise, store, maintain, and control the waters of great ponds for manufacturing purposes; the corporations paying damages for all flowage caused thereby upon the land of littoral proprietors. By virtue of these grants many of these corporations have made large expenditures in the construction of dams, in the erection of industrial plants, and in the acquisition of flowage rights, which flowage rights have become part and parcel of their vested property rights. While the State may hold the waters of great ponds in trust for the people and may regulate them as it sees fit, while the littoral proprietors may use them for their private purposes as hereinafter stated, *while the Legislature may grant their use to*

> *water power companies to be controlled for manufacturing and industrial purposes,* or to municipalities for domestic and other uses regardless of damages to millowners on the outlet streams . . . it never has been suggested that the State has the rights to compel either the littoral proprietor to pay for the uses to which he may lawfully put the water . . . , nor that the millowner on the outlet stream could be compelled to pay for the use of the waters that constitute the natural flow of the stream.

This seems to indicate that the court justified the use of lake water for manufacturing solely because corporations had done it for some time, had invested money in good faith, and had acquired property rights by prescription. One of the most important phrases above (italicized) was merely asserted by the court without proof. The authority given was *American Woolen Company v. Kennebec Water District.*[96] This case referred to the right of the legislature to grant lake waters for domestic and municipal uses and not for manufacturing and industrial purposes. The facts that the quotation was part of a summary made by the court before the advisory opinions were given and that advisory opinions in Maine do not have the binding force of decisions in adjudicated cases indicate that this is most inconclusive. It is more pertinent to conclude that what is owned by the people may be transferred by the legislature unless it is prohibited by the constitution. It seems that, whereas private property can be taken only for public uses, to take public property for private uses to the injury of citizens is entirely arbitrary.

Although somewhat off exact center, the situation has many similarities to Governor Dewey's recently successful fight with the Niagara Falls Power Company on the taxability of water used by this company. Solicitor General Judd of New York said that the agreement "establishes for the first time in this State, or in any State, the proposition that where public waters of a State are used for private purposes, a charge may be made by the State since such gifts of nature belong to all the people and may not be used by any private interests without fair compensation to the people of the State."[97]

Second, Is manufacturing a public purpose for which private property may be taken in Maine? (For detailed discussion see pp. 165–169.) The answer was decidedly in the negative until 1926, when the Maine courts became somewhat more liberal, and, without stating in so many words that power for manufacturing was public, permitted private property to be taken for transmission lines where approximately one-third of the electricity would be used for lights and two-thirds for power. (See *Smith v. Power Company,* 125 Maine 238 [1926], explained on p. 178.) In 1907, however, without doubt manufacturing was considered a private purpose.

Third, Is eminent domain necessary to infringe upon the private property rights of littoral proprietors? The littoral proprietor is presumed to have bought his land knowing that he could acquire no property in the great pond. Nevertheless, his ownership to the low water mark and his frontage on the pond constitute part of his property rights. In Massachusetts an adjoining landowner who is deprived of his natural water frontage on a great pond can obtain redress by injunction.[98] The Fernald case, on which Ricker and associates relied, answered this question emphatically in the affirmative. The evidence indicated that, among other things, the lowering of the water in the pond for manufacturing purposes reduced the value of cottage lots. The court noted that the lowering of the water widened the shores and deprived the littoral proprietors of their natural water frontage. "And this natural water frontage may be as valuable to the land owner as the right to draw water is to the mill owner. But whether of equal value or not, it is of equal validity in law, and entitled to equal protection."[99]

The Maine advisory opinions of 1919 answered the question directly with this statement:[100] "He [the littoral proprietor] cannot be deprived of that full enjoyment, except it be taken from him for public uses under the exercise of the right of eminent domain, with the accompanying payment of just compensation." The conclusion is that the proposed act to lower the level of Rangeley Lake was inconsistent with Maine jurisprudence, at least in 1907. The decisions indicate that, on the basis of the rights of littoral proprietors, eminent domain was necessary to infringe upon their property, and in 1907 the use of electricity for manufacturing was not only regarded as secondary to domestic uses, but it was not held to be a public purpose. Although the Maine legislature has granted the use of waters of great ponds for private purposes, the weight of judicial decision, except for dicta in an advisory opinion, is cast heavily in the direction of public uses only.

The eventual solution of the controversy over the lakes was the incorporation of the Androscoggin Reservoir Company by the legislature of 1909 with authorization to build a dam near Aziscoos Falls to store water for use of the Androscoggin River and Valley.[101] The statute gave the corporation the right of eminent domain and the flowage rights included "any state or public lots." All property rights and franchises within Maine could be acquired by the state if it should legislate to acquire, maintain, and operate a system of water storage at the headwaters of the Androscoggin River. The state would be required to make just compensation, but no payment would be exactable for the value of the franchise. The act also forbade power generated at the dam to be transmitted outside Maine. Private enterprise was permitted to continue its operations. The lakes were saved, the mills obtained their power, and the Androscoggin River, except for recent pollution problems, is considered one of the best managed in the country.[102]

The evolution of the great-pond ordinance from its first limited extension of popular rights above those of private property in the way of provision for fowling and fishing to the widest possible view of the nature of public rights in great ponds, all achieved through many successive legislative but mostly judicial interpretations of a principle, illustrates the dynamics of one phase of Maine's public power policy. Since the law in itself provided for little administrative discretion, it remained for the courts to adjust it to the prevailing economic philosophy. But when that philosophy changed many years ago from collectivism, the great-pond ordinance changed too, but in exactly the opposite direction. Is this an exception to the rule that judges are supposed to be more conservative than legislators? Is this great-pond ordinance an exception to the general rule that *stare decisis* is the antithesis of liberalism?

To evaluate the importance of the law in relation to Maine life is difficult. Particularly in the early years, it must have contributed materially to the amenities of settlers in rural communities. Later it became involved in the spoils for which conflicting economic and pressure groups fought. Yet the law is of more than just historical importance. From the matter of public control of the waters of great ponds is emerging a new and entirely different issue—the control and distribution of hydroelectric power in a federal system.

In the present nation-versus-state controversy over the erection of multiple-purpose dams, some New England states are emphasizing that local water rights are still state prerogatives over which the national government lacks jurisdiction. By virtue of the great-pond ordinance, Massachusetts and more especially Maine have possession of huge quantities of water with the legislative right to dispose of them, also great and potentially greater storage reservoirs which are a key to the development of Maine's power resources. Thus the great-pond ordinance may become a bulwark of defense if Washington should attempt to assert authority to construct little T.V.A.'s in northern New England contrary to local desire. Or from an outlander and more liberal point of view, local legal rights may prohibit regional planning for the totality of New England's industrial resources.[103]

A middle course appears on the horizon. The question may well be raised whether national and state water-resource policies will not, in various programs such as the T.V.A. and the water-pollution control act of 1948, reflect participation of *both* national and state governments in future. Washington's superior financial resources for a national and regional power policy, together with decentralization for deciding vital questions of policy and administration at the grass roots, may be the way out for much of the nation-versus-state controversy on power policy and administration.

## CHAPTER II

# The Mill Act: Development of Settlement and Industry as Affected by Power

The importance of rivers in the location of pioneer New England settlements is shown in Edward Johnson's celebrated chapter on the manner of planting towns and churches.[1] The rivers afforded a means of transportation and communication, and fishing and trading communities grew up along their banks. William D. Williamson records early settlements along the Piscataqua, Penobscot, Kennebec, Saco, Pemaquid, Sagadahoc, Sheepscot, and Damariscotta rivers.[2] The grant of the Plymouth Company included fifteen miles on either side of the Kennebec River.

It is reported that Sir Ferdinando Gorges sent for craftsmen to build houses and sawmills in his attempt to make a settlement in southern Maine after 1623.[3] Sawmills were needed also to provide lumber for blockhouses and ships, and to establish the lumber industry.[4] Sawmills driven by water power were in successful operation in New England more than thirty years before an attempt was made to build such mills in England.[5] Captain John Mason (who divided his grant with Gorges, the former taking New Hampshire and the latter Maine) sent eight Danes to build mills, saw timber, and make potash. A sawmill was erected at his plantation at "Newichawanock" in 1631. This, according to Ridlon, was the first sawmill in New England.[6] A corn mill was erected a few years later.

Pioneer householders had to grind their corn by hand, aided by crude samp mills, or sweep and mortar,[7] which were often kept going from early morning until sundown. In 1632 the settlers at

Piscataqua dispatched to Boston a small vessel laden with corn to be ground by a windmill. The town sometimes established the mill as a public undertaking, but might encourage a private enterprise by granting a limited monopoly. The latter was regulated by law, and, like the grain elevators and railroads of later date, was often "private property affected to a public use."[8] As an example of the latter method, in 1643, at a meeting of the Boston selectmen, the monopoly of erecting public corn mills in the city was granted to four men and their partners upon condition that within three years they should erect and forever maintain one or more corn mills. As an encouragement they were granted three hundred acres of the town's land in Braintree, and the selectmen promised to help them obtain voluntary assistance in any emergency requiring a large force to dig trenches or build embankments.[9]

In 1650 the general court for the Province granted a privilege to operate a sawmill, "with unius animous [*sic*] and free consent," with the stipulation that the grantee pay twelvepence for every thousand feet of board sawn; in 1651, in connection with another privilege, the amount set was only sixpence.[10] In 1661 the selectmen of Strawberry Bank granted liberty to Captain Pendleton "to set up his windmill on Fort Point . . . , because the mill is of such use to the people."[11]

War with the Indians broke out in 1674 and continued, with short intervals of peace, for nearly a century. "No part of the entire colonial territory suffered so heavily at the hands of the French and Indians as did this region."[12] To maintain a garrison at Fort Loyal (Falmouth) in 1684, a tax was laid on all sawmills. In this way £93 sterling was collected.[13]

So great was the need for gristmills and sawmills, and also for settlement, that special inducements were offered by the general court and by landed proprietors. Land was usually granted on fixed conditions, including the provision that a specified number of settlers be settled thereon within a given period of time.[14] In 1680 the general court of Massachusetts granted a mill privilege of sixty acres of land each to two men for millsites at Falmouth, and referred the matter to the president of the Province with the request that he grant them accommodation of timber for their mill. The president thereupon granted them forever the liberty and privilege of the fresh-water stream for a new sawmill and gristmill, and also the liberty of cutting all the timber that might be brought down conveniently on that stream for the use of their mill, they paying to the lord proprietor £5 a year in good merchantable boards at the usual price.[15]

The general court sometimes referred petitions for mill privileges to special committees for investigation.[16] It would be interesting to speculate whether political spoils played any part in the granting of petitions. Naturally, no records can be expected to reveal much information on this point. However, the proprietors were sometimes able to get themselves paid for occupying the site rather than submit to the usual procedure of proprietors paying bounties to obtain the setting up and operating of mills.

The British authorities encouraged the construction of mills to supply the great demand for lumber, especially for shipbuilding. One interesting limitation was made: because of the scarcity of trees large enough for masts for the Royal Navy, the 1691 charter of Massachusetts Bay reserved all trees of the diameter of twenty-four or more inches for this purpose, much to the indignation of the inhabitants of Massachusetts and especially of Maine.[17]

Because of the importance of the miller in the community, it was enacted, in November, 1693, that one miller to each gristmill was exempted from military service, along with members of Harvard College, masters of arts, schoolmasters, deacons, and sheriffs.[18] A law passed in 1709 required that millers have scales and weights to weigh corn, and limited their fees to one-sixteenth part.[19] A law of 1728 upheld the same maximum rate, and required millers to grind all corn brought to them within three days.[20]

In 1729 a miller was given a grant with a privilege for thirty years on condition that the corn of the Indians should be ground toll free during that period and that the mill would not overflow meadows of settlers during the summer.[21] In 1730 the proprietors of North Yarmouth granted to two men "so much of the river at the lower falls as may be needful for a grist mill" and ten acres adjoining.[22] Territory at Gardiner was granted by the proprietors to three Massachusetts men as agents on condition that they introduce one hundred settlers (with the usual provision for clearing the land, building a church, and providing for a minister), but the proprietors reserved for themselves "the butts and brows necessary for erecting such mills as the proprietors shall think proper to erect."[23] These proprietors granted to James Bowdoin a mill privilege with the right to flow land free of any claim for damages.[24] In 1760 the general court approved payment of £20 to encourage a man to carry on the hulling of barley in his mill, the first operation of this kind in America.[25]

The importance attached to gristmills is indicated by the persistence with which the proprietors of Turner struggled to get one set up. The act granting the proprietors a township was passed in 1768 with the following conditions: "the grantees within six years to settle thirty families in said Town, build a house for public worship, and settle a learned protestant minister."[26] Up to 1771, repeated offers of money and land had attracted no settlers, but there were some by 1772, and efforts were concentrated on the erection of a sawmill and a gristmill. Two lots were offered to prospective millers, but without success. Four months later an additional bonus of £20 sterling was included, on condition that the mills be maintained for the proprietors and the settlers for twenty years. In 1774 this bounty was raised to £25 and the maintenance term was reduced to twelve years. A few months later, an offer of an additional £10 still failed to induce anyone to erect a mill. At last, on October 25, 1774, a miller took over the site, erected a mill, and agreed to maintain it for twelve years in return for the land and £33.6*s*.8*d*.

Despite the natural advantages of Maine, its administration by a political authority inferior to that of other colonies made settlement unattractive. "Our atmosphere was salubrious and healthful, . . . our water privileges, our conveniences for trade, our fisheries and navigation, were all superior; and enjoying the friendship of the natives among us, we had reason to repose equal confidence in public safety. Though the several governments possessed distinguishing characteristics, neither was attractive to emigrants."[27] Some unfavorable stories, however, had been in circulation about the Maine climate, soil, and general ecology—a cold and sterile region, "not inhabitable by our English nation."[28] After the erection of forts between 1750 and 1755, however, settlers began to move in, including many persecuted religious dissenters who came north from Massachusetts.[29]

Unlike the seventeenth-century resident proprietors of Plymouth, Massachusetts, and Connecticut, the absentee proprietors of the eighteenth century in Maine were not motivated by the religious factor.[30] The majority were land jobbers or speculators, courtiers, adventurers, broken-down gentlemen who aspired to wealth but were unable or unwilling to labor and economize to attain it. Some, it is true, were men of rank, fortune, and distinction who had lofty sentiments and spent large sums in attempts to place settlers on their extensive grants in the Province. But these proprietors knew nothing of the country they had acquired. The men they sent out as settlers were actuated by sordid motives, and had none of the virtues requisite for founding a great state.

More and more mills came into operation for mercenary reasons. Even some of the learned clergy became builders and owners of lumber mills. London merchants and other wealthy capitalists invested in timberlands and sawmills in New England. By 1785, eastern lands were in great demand, and, according to Williamson, "there was a passion for obtaining settlers' lots, millsites, and water privileges."[31]

Under the English common law a man is entitled to the use of his own property unless the sovereign takes it away from him for a public use. But on the American frontier, private property rights were not sacred. Water power was a necessity to propel mills. When population was sparse, and mills were far apart, there had apparently been no objection if the dam and mill of a riparian owner caused water to overflow the lands of riparian owners above him. However, as population increased and land values went up, objections were made to the flooding of land by other than the owner. A single riparian owner could insist on full observance of his private property rights and thereby prevent a millowner from utilizing all the power of the stream.[32]

Obviously, the time had arrived for sound legislation to deal with this increasingly serious source of ill feeling. Consequently, in derogation of the common law, the Massachusetts general court passed the famous Mill Act in 1713. "[It] was founded on necessity, based on the considerations of the watershed of Massachusetts and Maine, at a time when a twelve-foot head of water was a monstrous power, and what would now be tiny mills were necessities of domestic and industrial life."[33] According to this act, the owner of a dam site had the right to build a milldam, and to overflow even his neighbor's land. The neighbor had no legal means of preventing such flowage; he could only attempt to collect just compensation. The injured neighbor's rights as a riparian owner were private property rights, including possession of the river bed and every other right except that of public passage. The new law amounted in reality to the extension of the right of eminent domain to the property of private persons or of companies, and the only excuse for its passage was the great need of the settlers for mills. The object of the statute, as set forth in the preamble, was stated as follows:[34]

> Whereas it hath been found by experience that, when some persons in this province have been at great cost and expence, for building of mills serviceable for the publick good, and benefit of the town, or considerable neighbourhood, in or near to which they have been erected, that, in raising a suitable head of water for that service, it hath sometimes so hapned that some small quantity of lands or meadows have been thereby flowed and damnified, not belonging to the owner or owners of such mill or mills, whereby several controversies and lawsuits have arisen; for prevention whereof for the future,—Be it therefore enacted . . .

The substance of the original Mill Act is contained in the first two sections:

> Sec. 1. That where any person or persons have already, or shall hereafter, set up any water-mill or mills, upon his or their own lands, or with the consent of the proprietors of such lands, legally obtained, whereupon such mill or mills is or shall be erected or built, that then such owner or owners shall have free liberty to continue and improve such pond, for their best advantage, without molestation.
>
> Sec. 2. And if any person or persons find themselves agrieved and damnified in their propriety of lands, by its being flowed by the owner or occupant of such mill(s) stopping or raising the water, that, in every such case, the party so damnified in his propriety, (upon) (making) application for relief to the court of general sessions of the peace in the county where such mills or pond is, the said court be and hereby are impowered to issue out a warrant, directed to the sheriff of the same county, to summon and impanel a jury of good and lawful men, at the proper cost and charge of the owner or owners of such mill or mills; and the jury shall be sworn by a justice of (the) peace, to a faithful, indifferent apprisal of the yearly damage done to (the) (any) person complainant by flowing his or their land as aforesaid.

The Mill Act was a decidedly liberal piece of legislation for that era. The private property rights of certain riparian owners were subverted to more important needs in an agricultural economy—namely, a plan to encourage mills for the convenience of the people and also to promote settlement for the advantage of the proprietors. The law required a few people to give up their individual rights to obtain more important rights for all—to get their corn ground and lumber sawed. It is an excellent example of the idea of certain individuals yielding their old common-law rights, and in return receiving more important rights through government.

The regulation of millers and the Mill Act present something of a parallel to government aid and regulation of railroads many years later. After a long period of extending aid and eminent-domain privileges to railroads, the government stepped in and exacted duties or obligations in return. Similarly, for mills, Massachusetts gave public aid in the first instance and in the next century regulated their rates. With the passage of the Mill Act quasi privileges of eminent domain were given to the millowner. Yet in return for this substantial favor no additional requirements were placed upon him. He had, as a matter of fact, been bound to serve all customers at reasonable and nondiscriminatory rates or charges for several years before he was given vast water rights; to this existing obligation no further obligation was added by the Mill Act.

The original act mentioned only the necessity for overflowing *small quantities* of land, a natural circumstance at the time in view of the small size and local nature of the early mills, but no mention was made of reservoir or storage dams or of the effect of these as coming within the act. But on February 27, 1796, the general court of Massachusetts passed an amendatory act, the preamble and first section of which are as follows:[35]

Whereas the erection and support of Mills to accommodate the Inhabitants of the several parts of the State ought not to be discouraged by many doubts and disputes; and some special Provisions are found necessary relative to flowing adjacent lands and mills held by several proprietors: Therefore, be it enacted, etc., That where any person hath already erected, or shall erect any water Mill on his own land, or on the land of any other person by his consent legally obtained, and to the working of such mill, it shall be found necessary to raise a suitable head of water, and in so doing any lands shall be flowed not belonging to the owner of such mill, it shall be lawful for the owner or occupant of such mill to continue the same head of water to his best advantage in the manner and on the terms herein after mentioned.

Sections 8 and 9 of the new act reiterated principles established as early as 1709 that millers must keep seals and weights and take not more than one-sixteenth part of the grain for their services. Further, in 1809 Acting Governor Lincoln suggested that the general court extend "the principles of our laws, respecting the overflowing of lands by grist and saw mills, to certain factories and other labor saving machines."[36] Without specifically mentioning water rights, an act defining the general powers and duties of manufacturing corporations was passed.[37] This law referred to corporate organizations "for the purpose of carrying on any kind of manufacture."

Because of the increase in population and the setting up of more mills and consequent competition among them for flowage rights, with greater damage to private property through overflowage, the act adopted by the legislature of Maine in 1821 included certain restrictions: limits were placed on the height to which water could be raised, and no milldam was permitted to injure any previously constructed mill.

In 1841 its language was recast in these words: "Any man may erect and maintain a water mill, and a dam to raise water for working it, upon and across any stream that is not navigable . . ."[38] This for the first time expressly mentioned a dam, and inserted a new condition that the dam should be upon and across a nonnavigable stream; section 2 provided that no dam should be built to the injury of an existing mill or millsite.[39] Another very important change was that under this revision no longer could lands be overflowed only when such a process was found *necessary* to raise a suitable head of water to run the mill. Flowage rights were granted to any man to raise water for working his mill. Further, in the revision of 1857 the word "dam" became plural,[40] and has remained so ever since.

The evident purpose of both the omission of necessity and the addition protecting other mills on the same stream was the encouragement of manufacturing industries and the injury of none. In a later case the Maine court quoted an early Massachusetts decision to this effect:[41] "The encouragement of mills has always been a favorite object with the legislature, and though the reasons for it may have ceased, the favor of the legislature continues." State supervision of dams was required by the legislature in 1875, with the provision that a resident engineer, chosen by the governor and the council, should inspect dams "erected for the saving of water for manufacturing or other uses," and require that they be kept in a safe condition.[42]

In 1881 the Maine legislature made optional the assessment of damages in gross instead of yearly damages if the millowner so elected,[43] but this method is now used with comparative infrequency. In practice, rights are acquired usually by voluntary agreement. A corporation often purchases much larger areas than are likely to be affected, including farms where the damage would be substantial; tracts which are in excess of those needed are sold.

The main provisions of the present Mill Act are contained in the first four sections.[44]

> Sec. 1. Any man may on his own land, erect and maintain a water-mill and dams to raise water for working it, upon and across any stream, not navigable; or, for the purpose of propelling mills or machinery, may cut a canal and erect walls and embankments upon his own land, not exceeding one mile in length, and thereby divert from its natural channel the water of any stream not navigable, upon the terms and conditions, and subject to the regulations hereinafter expressed.
>
> Sec. 2. No such dam shall be erected or canal constructed to the injury of any mill or canal lawfully existing on the same stream; nor to the injury of any mill site, on which a mill or mill-dam has been lawfully erected and used, unless the right to maintain a mill thereon has been lost or defeated.
>
> Sec. 3. The height to which the water may be raised, and the length of time during which it may be kept up in each year, and the quantity of water that may be diverted by such canal, may be restricted and regulated by the verdict of a jury, or report of commissioners, as is hereinafter provided
>
> Sec. 4. Any person whose lands are damaged by being flowed by a mill-dam, or by the diversion of the water by such canal, may obtain compensation for the injury, by complaint to the superior court in the county where any part of the lands are; but no compensation shall be awarded for damages sustained more than three years before the institution of the complaint.

Although the Mill Act was passed to satisfy pressing needs and apparently gave satisfaction to the majority of the people, some opposition was to be expected. In Massachusetts complaints were made to the general court that the county courts had not called the juries as required by law. Once the general court ordered that the jury be appointed to assess the damages, and again the general court ordered that action on a petition be postponed.[45]

In Maine a petition declared that a dam and sawmill erected at Machias in 1774 had damaged another erected in 1765, and had also destroyed large quantities of grass growing above the mill over thousands of acres of choice meadowlands. The petitioners claimed that this grass was necessary to preserve the lives of their cattle, "their almost whole dependence for support these distressing times."[46] A committee was appointed to view the premises and report to the court, but immediately after this the Machias area was very much concerned with the war, and the records make no mention of the report of the committee or whether it ever reported at all.

But apparently the Mill Act was well received generally. Williamson says that in 1796 the law regulating mills "prescribed a cheap and expeditious mode of assessing and recovering damages, for the flowage occasioned by dams."[47]

Mill acts have been sustained by state and federal courts on various principles or a combination of principles: first, that mills are for a public purpose, and private property may therefore be taken under eminent domain; second, that the acts are statutory regulations of rights common to riparian owners, and the stream must, of course, be considered a unit in order to obtain full utilization of its power; third, because of a general-welfare clause in some state constitution; and fourth, because of long usage or prior decisions.

The right of eminent domain raises a fundamental question: To what degree can the legislature interfere in order to permit one man to make use of the entire power of a stream and utilize another man's property, even against his will, by paying him damages? Under its police power a state may exercise jurisdiction over the rights of private property to conserve the public peace, health, and safety, but it cannot transfer property right to another person or to the state itself except for public uses after just compensation has been made.[48] But eminent domain is a highly specialized branch of the law, and its interpretation varies with different courts and their personnel. Henry P. Farnham said that under eminent domain one landowner cannot be permitted to take water power of another to further his own ends unless he intends to use the power for the direct benefit of the public, as by the erection and operation of a public mill, where everyone will have a right for work to be done upon payment of a toll controlled by the legislature.[49] The flowing of lands for manufacturing, he said, must come under eminent domain, and any statute which permits the flowing of such land for a mill which is not to serve the public is unconstitutional.

Farnham claimed that the peculiar conditions in early Massachusetts which help to explain the Massachusetts doctrine have served to mislead other courts into holding that the creation of power for mills was a public use which justified the exercise of eminent domain.[50] The Maine court has said, also, that the doctrine was adopted in other states principally on the authority of Massachusetts precedent.[51] The Wisconsin court said that mills, although they are not indispensable, are so convenient and useful to the public that permission for lands to be overflowed is a constitutional exercise of eminent domain for a public use. (There was, however, a strong dissent.)[52] In Connecticut a mill for grinding flour and feed to supply the surrounding community is held to be a public use and comes under eminent domain.[53] In Kansas the utilization of an otherwise wasted power by the construction of mills is so advantageous to the general public that the enactment of a statute permitting overflows is within the constitutional power of the legislature.[54]

In *Head v. Amoskeag Manufacturing Company*,[55] the United States Supreme Court noted that in most states the validity of the mill acts was assumed without dispute; they were never considered invalid until 1870, and then in three states only because of incompatibility with their respective constitutions. John M. Gould said that the acts were invalidated in four states because they authorized the taking of private property for other than public uses.[56]

Michigan's Mill Act was invalidated because it was held that there was no public necessity for the taking of private property to justify the use of eminent domain.[57] A Wisconsin statute permitting the erection of a dam and providing for the award of compensation for land overflowed in an action of trespass was held illegal, as an action for trespass is not in itself just compensation, and the statute permitted the flowing of lands before the making of compensation.[58] This did not, however, invalidate the Mill Act of the state. Other courts have condemned similar acts because the mills were not for public purposes. In Tennessee the legislature allowed backflows for gristmills, but the court would not extend it to sawmills and paper mills.[59] Even though statutes provide for legislative regulation of mill rates, private property cannot be taken, because millers are not compelled to serve all comers.[60]

But the courts of Massachusetts and Maine have adopted an entirely different doctrine. The Massachusetts Mill Act was adopted for special reasons, long before the United States Constitution was adopted and long before many areas were settled. The Massachusetts Constitution does not expressly prevent the taking of private property for private uses. In the very early case of *Spring v. Lowell,* which did not question the validity of the Mill Act, Justice Sedgwick remarked:[61]

> It may be observed that the sacred rights of private property are never to be invaded but for obvious and important purposes of public utility. Such are all things necessary to the upholding of mills. Hence the legislature have authorized mill-owners to invade the property of their neighbors, even real property, which by our laws seems to be regarded as the most inviolable, so as to render it wholly useless, by overflowing it with water, whenever the same shall be *necessary* to the beneficial occupation of the mills. This invasion of private property is authorized only by statute, and in no case but from *necessity* for the attainment of the objects intended.

The court has upheld the validity of the act on the ground stated above, together with the principle given in *Darling v. Blackstone Manufacturing Company:*[62]

> The legislature has regarded the water power of the streams as *publici juris;* and it is for this reason that it subjects the interests of agriculture to it, and authorizes mill-owners to flow the meadows above them to such an extent as it deems advisable, for the purpose of obtaining power to carry on business that is in its nature strictly private . . . On any other principle it would be difficult to sustain the constitutionality of the mill acts. Undoubtedly this policy has done much to increase the population and wealth of the State.

In *Spring v. Lowell,* mills were considered a public purpose, whereas in the Darling case the law was justified because water power is *publici juris.* In the next case the court returned to the original doctrine "because [mill acts] lead incidentally to the promotion of 'one of the great public industrial pursuits of the Commonwealth,' that they have been heretofore sanctioned by the court, as well as by the legislature, as being a legitimate exercise of the right of eminent domain justifying the taking and appropriation of private property."[63]

As early as 1831, the Massachusetts court said that the Mill Act depended partly upon public interest "and partly upon the nature of the property, which is often so situated that it could not be beneficially used without the aid of this power."[64] Twenty years later this court said:[65] "It is a provision by law, for regulating the rights of proprietors, on one and the same stream, from its rise to its outlet, in a manner best calculated, on the whole, to promote and secure their common rights in it."

This doctrine was elaborated in the Head case by the United States Supreme Court.[66] Without expressly saying that the act could come under the doctrine of eminent domain, the Court held the act

> considered as regulating the manner in which the rights of proprietors of lands adjacent to a stream may be asserted and enjoyed, with due regard to the interests of all, and to the public good, is within the constitutional power of the legislature. When property, in which several persons have a common interest, cannot be fully and beneficially enjoyed in its existing condition, the law often provides a way in which they may compel one another to submit to measures necessary to secure its beneficial enjoyment, making equitable compensation to any whose control or interest in the property is thereby modified.

This doctrine was, however, flatly rejected by the Vermont Supreme Court in *Avery v. Vermont Electric Company.*

> The position seems to assume that the land goes with the stream instead of the stream with the land, and to give the riparian owners a joint interest in the land because of their peculiar rights to the water. But the owners of the various properties are the several and independent owners of their respective parcels of land, and their only right to the water is such as this ownership gives them. To say that one's holding of the land is subservient to such uses as the lower owner may desire to make of the water, is to reverse all our theories regarding the use of streams.[67]

New Hampshire and Massachusetts shied away from justification under eminent domain after 1867. In *Great Falls Manufacturing Company v. Fernald,*[68] the New Hampshire court cited Article 5 of its Constitution: "Full power and authority are hereby given to the General Court from time to time to make, ordain, and establish all manner of wholesome and reasonable orders, laws, statutes, ordinances, directions and instructions, so that the same be not repugnant or contrary to this Constitution, that they may judge for the benefit and welfare of the State." The court then said that the matter was of such general public advantage that it was for the welfare and benefit of the state. In *Lowell v. Boston,*[69] the Massachusetts court, in distinguishing the Mill Act from a statute then before it which was held to be unconstitutional, said:

> regulation of the rights of riparian owners, both in respect to the stream and to their adjacent lands, liable to be affected by its use, involves no other governmental power than that "to make, ordain and establish all manner of wholesome and reasonable orders, laws, statutes and ordinances," as the General Court "shall judge to be for the good and welfare of this Commonwealth, and for the government and ordering thereof, and of the subjects of the same."

This quotation cited Article 4, section 1, chapter 1, of the Massachusetts Constitution.

One of Maine's most recent cases involving the Mill Act rejected the law on the basis of eminent domain, "for our mills are not of public use, as the term is understood in law, and our constitution does not authorize taking for the benefit of the public as does that of Massachusetts . . . *Flowing of riparian lands is an adjustment and regulation to ensure development of reasonable use of such lands among riparian owners.*"[70] It should be noted in explanation of this that the Constitution of Maine does not contain a specific general-welfare clause comparable to that of the Massachusetts and New Hampshire constitutions.

The Massachusetts court hinted, in 1851, that the age of the acts and the precedents of early decisions might be bases for maintaining the statute. "Whether, if this were an original question, this legislation would be considered as trenching too closely upon the great principle which gives security to private rights, it seems now too late to inquire, such legislation having been in full operation in this state a century and a half; but we think the principle itself is manifest."[71]

In *Jordan v. Woodward*[72] the Maine court held, in essence, that although it was bad law, the act must be tolerated because of its great age and general acceptance, but it should not be extended. Because this decision has been important in deciding cases in other states and because it is the only valid basis for the mill acts today, it deserves consideration. By taking a narrow view of the term "public use" the court disposed of the eminent-domain basis for the act in Maine. The act "is derogation of the common law, and the natural right of the citizen, and should not therefore be extended by implication."

> The Mill Act, as it has existed in this State, pushes the power of eminent domain to the very verge of constitutional inhibition. If it were a new question, it might well be doubted whether it would not be deemed to be in conflict with . . . the constitution . . . But the reasons in which this policy originated have long ceased to exist. Private capital has largely accumulated, and now seeks investment in mills of various descriptions, or in other enterprises for private gain. . . . We do not intend to question the authority of the existing Mill Act of this State. From its great antiquity, and the long acquiescence of our citizens in its provisions, it must be deemed to be the settled law of the State. Nor are we inclined to extend its peculiar provisions by implication.[73]

Former Chief Justice Lucilius A. Emery of the Supreme Judicial Court of Maine, in summing up the place of the Mill Act in the state, said:[74] "the practice was begun so early and has continued so long, . . . it has become, not the rule, but an established, solitary exception proving the rule."

Despite the contention that the Mill Act violated the Fourteenth Amendment to the United States Constitution, the United States Supreme Court, in *Otis Company v. Ludlow Manufacturing Company*,[75] upheld the constitutionality of the Massachusetts act. The law was valid because of the public nature of the mills in early Massachusetts, because of local conditions in New England, because special consideration should be given to decisions of state legislature and courts, and because of the venerable age of the law. Mr. Justice Holmes gave several reasons for sustaining the law, but the importance of its age was the basis for accepting its constitutionality in the Maine court many years before the United States Supreme Court acted upon it:[76] "... the liability of streams to this kind of appropriation and use has become so familiar a conception in New England, where water power plays as large a part as mines in Utah, that it would not be very extravagant to say that it enters as an incident into the nature of property in streams, as there understood." In determining whether a statute of a state is constitutional, the court "cannot wholly neglect the long settled law and common understanding of a particular state ... We are bound to be very cautious in coming to the conclusion that the Fourteenth Amendment has upset what thus has been established and accepted for a long time. Even the incidents of ownership may be cut down by the peculiar laws and usages of a state."[77]

That the Mill Act is an early example of state particularism is shown by the decision of the Maine court that mills outside the territorial jurisdiction of Maine are not entitled to the benefits of the statute.[78] In fact, Mr. Justice Sidney Thaxter of Maine has said that the rights under the Mill Act would never have been given if the power was to be used for the benefit of another jurisdiction.[79] Gould claims that the principle described above is generally accepted under the mill acts of other states.[80]

In 1860 the Wisconsin Supreme Court sustained the state's Mill Act for precisely the same reason that the Maine court gave five years earlier. Here the judges said they would come to a different conclusion if it were a new question, and they gave consideration to the effect of a departure from established policy. It was observed that large amounts of capital were invested in mills since the court originally sanctioned the act, and important rights had been acquired in mills and water powers under the impression that all courts in the state would adhere to the original decision. "The rule *stare decisis* has great force in such a state of things, and emphatically applies."[81] And almost under protest, because the statute conflicted with the constitutional rights of the individual, the Minnesota court said:[82] "The decisions, however, are so numerous, and by courts of so great authority, that we are constrained to hold the law to be constitutional."

The Massachusetts Mill Act is almost national in importance, for it has been in effect in at least twenty-nine states, with local variations.[83] Thus it has resulted in a more nearly uniform national watershed policy than one might suspect, and its early economic and legal justification becomes of more than local interest. The Massachusetts courts have been extremely liberal in their interpretation of the act. Some states limited the rights to gristmills,[84] but in Massachusetts the principle was extended to mills for any manufacturing purposes.[85] Mr. Justice Gray noted that throughout the New England states, as in many other states, the statutes are equally comprehensive.

The Mill Act played an important part in the development of settlement and industry in Maine. A cardinal feature of the power policy of the state was that water power should be developed by private initiative. The Mill Act put a premium on the rights of those who erected the first mills on a stream. Water privileges were devoted to private use and were subject to little more regulation than under the law of contract; there were few assurances that maximum benefits would result from the use of water resources. With industrial expansion, both the courts and the legislature broadened such rights. Their interpretations made millsites extremely valuable and set the stage for private capital to develop the power. Thus vested property rights were established in early power development.

A later reaction against the Mill Act caused pressure groups to support limitations on its provisions. Occasionally legislatures whittled down its scope; another technique was to stress existing private property rights inherent in the flowing stream. Some of the opposition to construction of multiple-purpose dams today in northern New England probably stems from hostility to the Mill Act which served to make New England riparian owners highly conscious of their well-established private property rights in flowing streams.

As a corollary to the policy of public ownership of great ponds there has been deduced the fixed principle of the public ownership of the water of all nonnavigable rivers and streams, together with the equally vital and fundamental principle of private ownership of land, including the beds of nonnavigable rivers and streams. With private ownership goes the right to use the water flowing in such rivers and streams and to dispose of it under the law of contract. Much misunderstanding has been exhibited under this head in Maine water-power controversies, and confusion has apparently arisen between the conception of the public ownership of great ponds and that of the private ownership of the beds of nonnavigable rivers. From this has emerged the fairly popular but erroneous belief that the water powers of the state are owned by the people.

In England, nontidal streams, like great ponds, were held to be private, but the colonists, as we have seen (chap. i), modified this presumption to suit their needs, and early settlers were given special privileges in great ponds. Members of the propertied class, to whom the franchise was limited, had the power to shape the law in their own pecuniary self-interest. However, they had a mutual interest with other classes in developing the amenities of life. Thus, while the propertied lawmakers retained possession of the bed of a river and the flow of water, they developed the right of free passage on that river to all persons alike. English law was followed in Massachusetts to the degree that a grant of land embracing a nontidal river as boundary included the bed to the "thread" of the river.[86] But because of the need for edible fish to pass up and down the rivers and the need of settlers to enjoy cheap transportation, English law was modified so that nontidal, privately owned rivers became public ways for the movement of fish and for transportation.[87]

Thus in Maine a public easement exists: "those [nontidal streams] which are sufficiently large to bear boats or barges, or to be of public use in the transportation of property, are highways by water, over which the public have a common right."[88] This principle was of the greatest importance for the lumbering industry of Maine. Subject to this qualified right of public passage, nontidal rivers and streams in Maine are "wholly and absolutely private."[89] Notice the language of the decision:

> He does not own the water itself, but he has the right to the natural flow of the stream, and the right to the use and benefit of it, as it passes through his land, for all the domestic and agricultural purposes to which it can be reasonably applied, and no proprietor above or below can unreasonably divert, obstruct or pollute it.[90]

> The right to the use of a stream of water, is incident or appurtenant to the land, through which it passes. It is an ancient and well established principle, that it cannot lawfully be diverted, unless it is returned again

to its accustomed channel, before it passes the land of a proprietor below. Running water is not susceptible of an appropriation, which will justify the diversion or unreasonable detention of it. The proprietor of the water course has a right to avail himself of its momentum as a power, which may be turned to beneficial purposes. And he may make reasonable use of the water itself, for domestic purposes, for watering cattle, or even for irrigation; provided it is not unreasonably detained, or essentially diminished.[91]

This use of water is called a mill privilege, and is an integral part of the riparian owner's estate. In an advisory opinion on the whole subject of such riparian rights given to the state legislature by the Supreme Judicial Court of Maine, these words occur:[92]

The riparian proprietor may avail himself of the momentum of the stream as power for manufacturing and industrial purposes, provided, of course, the water is not thereby unreasonably detained or essentially diminished (*Blanchard v. Baker,* 8 Maine 253–266). He can build dams upon his own land to develop power for milling and manufacturing purposes, subject to the provisions of the Mill Act and to the payment of damages for all flowage caused thereby; but the flowage rights thus acquired become property rights in the nature of an easement appurtenant to the manufacturing plant. All these rights which the riparian proprietor has in the running streams are as certain, as absolute, and as inviolable as any other species of property . . . He can be deprived of them only through the powers of eminent domain constitutionally exercised.

Former Chief Justice Lucilius A. Emery of the Supreme Judicial Court of Maine, discussing the same subject, said:[93]

He [a riparian owner] can construct upon his own land, and upon the lands of others with their consent, dams and other structures and appliances for the utilization of the power for propelling machinery and other lawful purposes. And since to make the power economically efficient there must usually be some detention of the water to raise a sufficient head, he can detain it for that purpose for and at such times as may be reasonably necessary under all circumstances. *Gould v. Boston Duck Co.* 79 Mass. 442. *Springfield v. Harris* 86 Mass. 494.

This exclusive right of the riparian owner to erect and maintain dams, etc., and raise a head of water for the utilization of his water power was exercised by the Colonists, not as a statutory right, but as a common law right, and it is such a right today. As was said by the Court in *Corse v. Dexter* 202 Mass. pp. 32, 33, "The creation of a head and fall of water and the use of it for mill purposes necessarily interfere with the natural flow of the stream. The right thus to use the waters of a stream is inseparably connected with the ownership of the land through which the water-course flows. It does not depend upon the acquisition by deed or prescription of rights above or below the dam."

With respect to the Maine situation, Judge Charles Evans Hughes is reported to have "expressed himself as impressed with the strength of the position of the riparian proprietors as described by the Justices," in 118 Maine 503, 507 (1919).[94]

More recent decisions by the United States Supreme Court, however, indicate that the Mill Act will have less significance in future. The implications of these decisions are that the private citizen has no title of ownership or property rights in developing water power upon nontidal rivers if they be navigable in fact. Under the definition of Mr. Justice Reed in *United States v. Appalachian Electric Power Company,* 311 U.S. 377 (1940), national jurisdiction has been extended far into nonnavigable rivers previously controlled by the states. (See chap. vii.)

Since the benefits of the Mill Act were limited to riparian owners on nonnavigable streams, it early became necessary for the Maine courts to define a navigable river. In order to protect property rights and yet to accommodate the use of streams to the needs of a frontier society, the courts distinguished between technically navigable rivers and floatable or public-highway rivers. Thus, a privately owned stream suitable for floating boats, rafts, or logs became subject to the right of public passage. From an early date the Maine policy, as contrasted with the new national policy, was that the natural condition of streams determines their navigability. This idea was stressed as late as 1910,[95] but was explicitly stated in 1884:[96]

> It is the *natural condition* of a stream which determines its character for public use. And it must be its navigable properties in a *natural condition, unaided by artificial means or devices.* It is well settled in this state and elsewhere that, if a stream is not susceptible of valuable use to the public for floatable purposes, without erections for raising a head, it cannot legally be deemed a public stream, even though it might be easily converted into a floatable stream by artificial contrivances.

Although floatable rivers were in a limited sense navigable, the court would not limit the application of the Mill Act to nonfloatable rivers. Such an interpretation would have confined generous mill privileges to a few insignificant streams in the state and would have defeated the purpose of the act. The court recognized the importance of this decisive point in *Veazie v. Dwinel*:[97] "for were all our streams, which are capable of floating rafts or logs, to be deemed *navigable* within the meaning of the statute, it would at once place out of the protection of the law all the mills and dams now existing on the *floatable* streams in the state. The act contemplated no such destructive operation, and cannot receive such construction." The court here distinguished between *navigable* rivers technically so-called, where the tide ebbs and flows, and rivers which are *floatable* and subjected to the servitude of the public and which are therefore denominated public highways. A number of years later the court suggested that a floatable stream is the least important of the classes of streams called navigable.[98] Maine did not want floatable rivers to be considered navigable in the technical sense, because that would have given the national government control over many Maine rivers.

Except for narrow and rigid interpretations of the term "public use" under eminent domain,[99] the Maine courts have followed those of Massachusetts in broadening the original Mill Act so that reservoir dams should come under it as well as mill or working dams.[100] Although a reservoir dam was erected in the Province of Maine as early as 1817, this type of dam was not important in early mill history. Much later it became one of the numerous technological developments in power production.

In the Butterfield case[101] it was stated that the statute did not prescribe the manner in which the head of water should be raised; this was left to the millowner. The design of the reservoir dam was "to raise a suitable head of water and to control and use it in such a manner as to enable him to employ his mill to the best advantage during the whole year." (In 1875 the court narrowed the interpretation slightly by saying the mill and dam must both be upon the land of the millowner to bring a case under the statute.[102] In this case the millowner leased the reservoir dam, so the damages came under common law.)

In 1881 the doctrine in the Butterfield case was reaffirmed. "The reservoir dam is within the Mill Act. It has ever been so held. The statute authorizes the erection of dams. It does not restrict the millowner to one dam."[103] The Massachusetts court was quoted: "Reservoir dams for the benefit of mills upon the same stream have been held to come within the protection of the statute; and this although such a dam may not be immediately connected with or very near the mill."[104]

Another series of decisions gave preference to the prior owners of millsites on a stream and allowed them to increase the height of the dam and thereby overflow more land. The first proprietor of a dam on a stream has a better mill right than one coming later, and if his dam is temporarily destroyed he does not lose his prior right on the stream unless he has abandoned his site.[105] If a dam becomes dilapidated and lets water escape, the owner has the right to repair it, although this may raise the water higher and retain it longer than was the case when the mill was in poor repair. In 1874 the court stated that the owner could maintain the dam as it was when deeded to him.[106] Twenty-seven years later the court extended this principle to include the right to flow back the water virtually as high and far as he should deem necessary for the profitable working of the mill.[107] One important and absolute exception was made. When a second mill has been built above the flowage of the first and older mill and dam, the flowage of the first cannot be increased by raising the dam or by other appliances to lessen the original efficiency of the mill above. In short, the first millowner can flow back more and more land as long as it does not interfere with another mill, but at that point the right ceases. The purpose of this requirement, of course, was to increase the number of mills on a stream. Maine had, however, very few reservoir dams in the nineteenth century, and the issue did not become acute until 1924.[108]

In spite of the early decisions on the Mill Act, it was the custom to erect storage dams by legislative sanction. The Aziscoos dam for the Androscoggin River, the Ripogenus dam for the Penobscot, and others were organized by act of the legislature. Despite some opposition based on an improper use of the right of eminent domain, the right was consistently granted with one exception, the Kennebec storage controversy.[109] In 1924 the Supreme Judicial Court of Maine reaffirmed the doctrine that reservoir dams come within the Mill Act. Thereafter, reservoir dams, notably the Brassua dam and the reservoir behind the Gulf Island dam, were built under the authority of the Mill Act without special legislation.[110] The court held here that the Mill Act extended to a reservoir dam on a tributary of a tributary of the river on which the mill is located.

The facts in the case *Brown v. DeNormandie*[111] were: DeNormandie, representing the Pepperrell Mills, owned a mill and dam site on the Saco River at Biddeford, and proposed to raise a storage dam at the outlet of Kezar Lake, a tributary of a tributary of the Saco River, for the benefit of the dam some sixty miles away. Chief Justice Cornish ruled that the benefits of the Mill Act applied to one continuous flow of water, regardless of geographical names:[112]

> The test is not one of terminology but of hydraulic fact, namely, is the reservoir dam situated upon a non-navigable stream, whose stored water in its natural flow to the sea, regardless of intervening forms of water, whether stream or river or lake and of the names that may have been given to them, passes through and aids in propelling the wheels of mills belonging to the owners of the reservoir dam. If so, such a stream is within the contemplation of the Mill Act whether it requires an hour or a day or a week or longer for the water to reach its destination. Such a dam thus located and thus owned meets the purpose of the existing Act and complies with both its spirit and its terms.

Since Chief Justice Cornish indicated that the court had decided, in *Nelson v. Butterfield*,[113] that a reservoir dam came under the Mill Act,[114] William B. Skelton maintained that the only real question in the case was whether the Mill Act would justify a reservoir dam on the continuing part of a river bearing another name.[115] Although Senator Carter was unquestionably in error when he claimed that *Brown v. DeNormandie* was the first occasion for this ruling, his interpretation was correct, that Judge Cornish's decision so stated the law that the companies dared to go ahead under the Mill Act to build storage dams without legislative sanction.[116]

In the 1925 legislature Senator Carter, Representative Wing, and others opposed the broad interpretation of the Mill Act by the Supreme Judicial Court of Maine in *Brown v. DeNormandie*, because the court held that the act included storage dams.[117] This interpretation gave the power companies, and especially the Insull interests,[118] valuable rights in Maine—rights never intended when the act was first passed—and all at the expense of individual rights. Senator Carter explained that *Brown v. DeNormandie* originated when some people, who did not wish their homes flooded, asked the court to set a limit on the distance back from the water mill which owners of the dam could go, and the court had said:[119]

> The Mill Act speaks as of today and the individual who or the corporation which can meet its requirements, . . . can take advantage of its provisions and aid in building up the industries of the State as the State evidently wishes should be done. Moreover, to ask the Court to set an arbitrary limit to the location of a reservoir dam above the benefitted mill is to ask not judicial action on our part but legislative action, a request with which we cannot comply.

Senator Carter inferred from this that the court held it could not set a limit to which the owner of a dam can go, but that it was the privilege of the legislature to do so. Since the sovereign gave to the early settlers this right of eminent domain, the sovereign must take it back, because it now applied to all industries at all distances.

In 1927 Senator Carter introduced a bill to limit the Mill Act to milldams, and to require corporations to go to the legislature so that each case for the erection of storage dams could be decided upon its merits, as had been the practice before the decision in *Brown v. DeNormandie*. "I claim that my bill . . . carries out the request of the Court."[120]

William B. Skelton, past president of the Central Maine Power Company, opposed the Carter bill for two reasons:[121] first, the necessity of obtaining legislative permission for every storage development would delay development and make it a political issue; second, it would make power development by mills impossible. Under the Mill Act a public utility and (or) a mill may flow land not for public uses. But if storage were severed from the Mill Act, the legislature could no longer legally authorize mills to create dams, for they are not public utilities and the legislature could make such authorization only for public purposes. Attention was also directed to the need for reservoir dams to keep water enough for the mills to run continuously, and to the amount of money already invested and the number of people dependent upon these industries in the state.

The bill was reported out of committee "ought not to pass." Senator Carter was apparently preparing to seek passage of the minority report through the session, but he died suddenly and his measure was defeated.[122]

The province of New Brunswick, inspired by the example of Ontario, laid plans to develop power at Grand Falls on the St. John River, three miles beyond the Maine boundary. According to the plan, 73 per cent of the storage essential to the economical development of the project was within the state of Maine. This involved more than 4,500 square miles of Maine territory, with a drainage area supplying over 50,000,000,000 cubic feet of water capable of storage and appropriate release. With the storage available only on the Canadian side of the line, Grand Falls would develop less than 60,000 hp. for commercial use. With the storage available in Maine, more than twice the amount of power could be developed.[123] And in order that the New Brunswick project might utilize Maine land, some private individual could easily acquire a power site and erect a mill on the St. John River or one of its tributaries within the state, and, by virtue of the Maine Mill Act, over 4,500 square miles of Maine territory would be subservient to the New Brunswick development.

Governor Brewster felt that the legislature should not permit this region, which Maine had obtained only after sacrifice and struggle and long negotiations, to lose its chief resource. Therefore he advised that *"the Mill Act must be modified at least in its application to these streams and possibly this will be required for the entire state as well to prevent an unconstitutional discrimination."*

But some of the senators felt that no amendment was necessary, because the International Joint Commission, which has jurisdiction over boundary waters between the United States and Canada, would allocate to Maine and Aroostook County the proportional part of the power Maine would contribute to the Grand Falls power development. The interests of Maine were thought to be safe in the hands of the three men representing the United States on the commission.[124] It was also felt that the adoption of the amendment would be a precedent for a general change of the Mill Act.

Proponents of the measure, on the contrary, felt that the damage caused by the dam would be extensive, as it would flood valuable farm lands, several hamlets, and about ten miles of highway.[125] Senator Carter saw great cause for alarm.[126] "The northern border of our state and the whole of northern Aroostook, the whole St. John Valley, under our present Mill Act is open to the urge of Canada at Great Falls without any protection to ourselves and without any possibility of opening any negotiations whereby if Grand Falls takes our storage we shall have some of its power." Representative George C. Wing, Jr., of Auburn, favored the amending measure as a step in the right direction for the protection of individual rights. Here was an opportunity for the legislature to limit the broad interpretation of the Mill Act by the Supreme Judicial Court of Maine in *Brown v. DeNormandie.*[127] The amendment was passed, classifying rivers so that it applied to the St. John River and its tributaries, and requiring the approval of either the legislature or the Public Utilities Commission before a dam could be built.[128] Because of this amendment, the Grand Falls Development Company does not own and control the storage water of Aroostook County. Since part of the power of the Grand Falls development originates in Maine, and Maine land is flowed, the International Joint Commission, after a hearing, allocated to the state of Maine 2,000 hp. from this project.[129]

In 1927 the International Paper Company went before the legislature and attempted to do what the Aroostook amendment prevented it from doing under the Mill Act, namely, to create a development of at least 4,000 hp. on the Fish River. Objections to the bill were: (1) its provision for an interchange of power (transmission) with the Grand Falls plant in New Brunswick, although an equal amount would have to be imported as was exported per calendar year, and the contract must be approved by the Maine Public Utilities Commission and the governor and council; (2) the turning over of the best watershed remaining in New England to the International Paper Company of Maine, New York, and Canada; (3) the permission accorded the International Paper Company, a private corporation, for the purpose of delivering power to a foreign utility in Canada, with the right to come into Aroostook County and sell electricity in territory served by the Gould Electric Company, a public utility; (4) the destruction of some beautiful lakes and fine fishing.[130] The measure was defeated in the legislature.[131]

The International Paper Company returned to the 1929 legislature and overcame some of Maine's traditional anticorporation attitude by agreeing to a charter in which several important promises were included. The charter was limited to forty years. The company agreed to build a $3,000,000 paper mill on the St. John River in

Maine and to operate it for ten years or forfeit the charter, using at least half of the wood from Maine; to pay the state $5,000 a year for five years and, if necessary, the same amount for two more years to compensate for the destruction of fish, and to supply electricity to the state of Maine from the Grand Falls development.[132]

The need for these storage rights was great, as the company owned 550,000 acres of timberland on the St. John River above Van Buren. It was estimated that the construction of the reservoirs and the acquisition of flowage rights would amount to $2,600,000. The opposition spoke frankly of the "soulless corporations," suggested holding out for a $6,000,000 mill and postponing action on the measure, but the bill was passed by large majorities. Thus, after three legislative sessions, marked by suspicion and hostility and an attitude very discouraging to a large industrial enterprise in Aroostook County, a great development was finally sanctioned and built.

At the Wyman dam development at Bingham, areas bordering on the river which included undeveloped privileges were purchased by the Central Maine Power Company. It is difficult to distinguish between the value of a privilege, which is controlled by ownership of a site where a dam can be constructed, and the right to flow above the dam. In determining adequate compensation, the question arose, when the Central Maine Power Company built the Wyman dam, whether the company had to compensate the owner of an undeveloped water-power site for the destruction of that site for power purposes, or had only to recompense him for the damage to his land as such which he suffered. In a 3 to 2 decision, the court decided on the latter alternative.[133]

The power company's contention was thus upheld that the right of a man to build a dam and appropriate water power obtainable thereby was only a contingent right—that his right existed only if someone else had not already built a dam which interfered with his contingent right, or with which the building of a dam would interfere. The dissent of Chief Justice Pattangall assumed that the building of the Wyman dam destroyed the rights of the two land companies to make developments upon their own undeveloped dam sites. This dissent failed to see that their right was contingent and depended upon the fact that no lower proprietor had theretofore built a dam which flowed back upon their potential sites. Instead, dissent was based on the contention that a man's right to build a dam upon his own land is absolute, and concluded that flowing out is taking away his absolute property right.

The majority ruled, however, that the nature of his right is contingent upon the fact that someone else has not already appropriated the stream by building a dam and overflowing his land; hence the logical and necessary conclusion that he is entitled to compensation for land damage only. But if the premise and conclusion of Mr. Justice Pattangall were accepted, anyone who built a dam would be obliged to pay everyone above on the stream for every foot of head he occupied, for there are as many dam sites as one can build dams across the river to hold a head. The majority opinion was based on the so-called "law of prior appropriation," or "Massachusetts rule," which was enunciated by the Massachusetts court, but not until after the separation of Maine from Massachusetts. The case,[134] however, was in process of litigation at the time of separation and was therefore held declaratory of the Massachusetts law and was binding on the Maine court.

The role of the Mill Act for more than two hundred years in Maine raises many economic and social questions which cannot be answered. To what extent did this law and its application result, directly and indirectly, in the erection of sawmills and gristmills, the promotion of industry and settlement, the growth of cities, and the industrial evolution of the whole community? What other policies did it precipitate? Some of these questions will receive further treatment in subsequent chapters. So far it is apparent that the impact and ramifications of the policy extended far beyond New England. Except for its present significance in assessing damages for the few remaining power sites, perhaps it is correct to conclude that the importance of the Mill Act is largely historical. It is a landmark in the evolution of Maine's power policy, and has contributed much to life in the area.

## CHAPTER III

# The Increasing Complexity of the Economy: Manufactures and Tourists

Except for the Mill Act of 1713 (see chap. ii), the state had no real power policy until much later. Legislatures were concerned primarily with the growth of settlement and industry, and water power was merely one means of attaining these objectives. The land policy was liberal; it was, however, allied with mill privileges, and was aimed at settlement of the state. In 1824 Maine enacted a law to promote the sale and settlement of public lands which, among other things, reserved millsites for those persons who, within three years, "shall erect the first saw and gristmill thereon."[1] In 1828 the reservation of millsites was omitted.[2]

The years of the Embargo and Nonintercourse acts and the War of 1812 had destroyed the commerce of the smaller New England ports, and greatly stimulated domestic manufactures. Van Wyck Brooks asserts that the younger merchants in rural areas took advantage of the numerous waterfalls to set up textile mills, paper mills, shoe factories, and iron foundries.[3] E. W. Morehouse suggests that the abundance of water power in New England gave the Yankees an industrial head start when they turned from maritime merchandising to manufacturing.[4]

The two principal industries, lumbering and textile manufacture, are inextricably connected with the state's water resources and its power policy, without which neither could have reached its towering position in the state's economy. Both profited from benevolent legislatures.

Lumbering depended upon water resources for dual purposes, to propel sawmills and also as an inexpensive means of driving logs downstream to the mills. Primarily, however, the industry depends upon the availability of raw materials for its location. Although it was expedient to erect sawmills close to settled areas whenever possible, it was frequently necessary to erect them at some distance, where a satisfactory fall of water could be obtained.[5] Many satellite communities were thus established.

The Saco River and vicinity was the first center of lumbering in Maine, and by 1800 there were seventeen sawmills above the falls.[6] From here the industry advanced north with the frontier. By 1822 much lumbering went on in the Androscoggin Valley, where Brunswick was the center of the industry. "But the length and difficulty of the Androscoggin drive put that river behind the Kennebec in importance . . . From this central river large-scale operations were transferred to the Penobscot, which became the heart of the industry during the most prosperous days."[7] Bangor, with its favorable position with respect to lumber supply, abundant power to propel mills, rivers suitable for long log drives, and harbor for transportation of the finished product, was, until 1861, the greatest lumber center in the world.[8] By 1861 lumbering was on a rapid decline, as all regions except the Allegash district had been thinned.

While numerous attempts were being made to attract industry and call attention to the abundant supply of power, individuals and corporations were busy acquiring valuable sites,[9] especially from 1869 to 1909. Speculators took advantage of liberal timberland policies, and one of Maine's greatest natural resources was almost lost.[10] The lands were valuable because of their timber; that many lots contained potentially rich power sites was little appreciated. Thus the state of Maine surrendered not only its timberlands but also nearly all its power sites to private interests. The sale prices varied from twelve and a half cents to fifty cents an acre. According to Percival P. Baxter, a single undeveloped water-power location in Maine, given away with the timberlands, was sold in November, 1917, for $500,000.[11] The loss of the forests caused great resentment in Maine for many years. This resentment was carried over into the formation of a policy to conserve water power, in the determination that this resource, once owned largely by the state, should be used for the benefit of the people. It was an important reason for the study of the water power of Maine ordered by the legislature in 1867.

By the end of the nineteenth century the lumbering boom had given place to the more steady pulp and paper industry, which eventually became first in importance in Maine on the basis of amount of capital invested and value of the product. A relatively large amount of water power is basic for this industry. With the availability and abundance of spruce, and reasonable proximity to streams on which to float it to mills, Maine had the essentials right at home,[12] and sufficient industrial experience with which to improve its natural situation.

Power was, at first, of fundamental importance in determining the location of industry, and hence industry was attracted to Maine. The price of the commodity and labor costs were less than they are today, but power costs were high. Power could not be brought to industry. Factory sites were chosen, preferably, near a labor supply, but if labor was lacking or insufficient, workers were attracted to the mills. In this manner communities like Biddeford, Saco, Lewiston, Livermore, Rumford, Augusta, Fairfield, and Millinocket grew up along the riverbanks. The influence of the great factory city of Lowell, Massachusetts, spread to other textile towns north of Boston,[13] and was undoubtedly felt in Maine, though on a smaller scale. As manufacturing and industry developed, farseeing men realized that cheap power was essential for the operation of machinery massed in factories, which were requiring power in a degree hitherto undreamed of.

In the early nineteenth century, New England manufactured much of the nation's supply of wool. By 1820 there were nine cotton and woolen mills in Maine.[14] Woolen mills were usually on the smaller streams, whereas there were cotton plants in six or seven centers, deriving their power from the largest rivers of the state. Lewiston became the leading cotton city in Maine. Historically considered, cotton was Maine's most important industry, and it remained so until the turn of the century. Southern cotton had not yet become important.[15] By 1889 Maine had risen to fifth position in order of importance in the woolen-goods industry.

It is impossible to separate the industrialization of Maine and the consequent importance of mill privileges from the growth of railroads; each was a complement to the other and they emerged almost simultaneously. According to the late Senator Charles B. Carter, Maine was industrialized because of two factors: the development of low-cost power used by private enterprise at or near the dam sites, and the coöperation of the railroads through the establishment of differential, preferential commodity freight rates, which existed until they were abolished by the Interstate Commerce Commission.[16] In fact, when some of the biggest mills were first established in Maine, the railroads brought in their building materials free so that the railroads could help create new customers for themselves. And they transported cotton goods, shoes, and lumber at rates as nearly equal as was possible with those charged other manufacturers nearer the markets.[17]

This era in Maine came later than in Massachusetts. The explanation lies in the attitude of the people toward corporations and internal improvements and the reflection of this attitude in state institutions. According to Frederick J. Turner, the rugged eastern hinterland which skirted the Maine coast imparted a pioneer tone to the life and characteristics of the Maine people which still endures.[18] The consequent self-reliance, rugged individualism, distrust of the wicked city, and other characteristics usually associated with western settlement left numerous impressions on state institutions, including prohibition (1851), particularism, distrust of the executive (with the provision for a council chosen by the legislature to advise the governor), distrust of corporations, and opposition to a social-service state.

Farmers tended to be individualistic and conservative, and opposed internal improvements and other aids to industry which would mean higher taxes and higher wages. Manufacturers, on the contrary, favored government aid to their enterprises and government protection of them, and corporate activity. They were instrumental, eventually, in obtaining state aid for railroads in Maine, but not until Massachusetts had forged far ahead.

Maine showed an early hostility to corporations, or, as Governor Joshua L. Chamberlain expressed it, "an insane prejudice" against them.[19] In 1847 the power of the Maine legislature was restricted by an amendment to the constitution forbidding it to lend the credit of the state directly or indirectly or to increase the state debt beyond $300,000, except for war emergencies.[20] This amendment delayed the construction of several contemplated railroad projects, and it was only slowly that Maine's hostility to railroad corporations began to lessen. The legislature authorized several cities and towns to grant financial assistance to them,[21] and in 1867 substantial aid by municipalities was sanctioned by a permissive law.[22] Between 1860 and 1875 Maine's railroad mileage more than doubled.[23] Outright state aid and permissive statutes for Bangor to supplement this aid helped to make possible the opening of the European and North American Railway in 1871. The state likewise gave liberal assistance to the Bangor and Aroostook in the 'nineties. This line "breached the upper Penobscot Valley from the west to tap its potential water powers."[24]

Maine's rate of population growth increased steadily until about 1850. Up to that time each decade showed an average gain of 80,000 inhabitants.[25] The California gold rush of 1849 had much to do with the initial decline, but the trend of opinion in the 1850's was that the state's restricted policy in encouraging local enterprise gave young people no incentive to stay in Maine. The greatest loss by emigration consisted of males under twenty-one years of age. In 1851 Governor John Hubbard deplored the migration of young people from the state, and welcomed the multitude of French Canadians moving into Aroostook County.[26] In 1856 Governor Samuel Wells praised the policy of encouraging the introduction of foreign labor, and stated, quite incorrectly, that it soon amalgamated with the native population.[27]

The census of 1860 showed a 50 per cent falling off in the previous rate of increase. That of 1870 revealed a loss in the total population of 1,364, with more than 116,000 Maine-born people residing in other states.[28] New Hampshire was the only other state in the Union showing a decrease in this decade.[29]

Governor Selden Connor in 1878 saw in agriculture Maine's greatest future, since trade and manufactures would flourish in proportion to the increase in food products,[30] and reported the greatest immigration into the fertile Aroostook County in twenty years. In 1881 Governor Harris M. Plaisted reported population increases of between 3 and 4 per cent in the last decade, mostly to Androscoggin

County because of its manufacturing interests and to Aroostook County because of agricultural attractions.[31] By 1891 the exodus of Maine citizens had been stayed. A substantial gain in population was reported, notably in the last years of the 1880–1890 decade.[32] In his messages of 1893 and 1895 Governor Henry B. Cleaves reported that population was again increasing. Water power was being rapidly utilized,[33] and private capital was creating new and diversified industries in Maine. The significance of power and industrial development in providing, also, a means of livelihood for surplus farm population, which otherwise migrates, must be considered in accounting for the new trend in population statistics.

Yankee ingenuity and the innate qualities of Yankee workmen in industrial New England were of first importance.[34] All the water power in the world means nothing without skilled and inventive operatives. Much of the leadership, enterprise, and high intelligence which produced industrial New England is credited to descendants of the old native stock.[35]

Maine mills were usually worked by Yankees before the Civil War, but soon thereafter French Canadians began to appear in mill towns,[36] and after 1878 began a mass invasion of New England.[37] In cities such as Lewiston and Waterville the French outnumbered the Yankees. Despite the new social and cultural problems thus created, these workers were welcomed by mill operators, as they were hard-working, industrious, and, for a long time, docile in labor relations. European and Canadian immigrants have played a vital part in supplying power in industry. They are considered to be more amenable to change and to new ideas than the natives. Whatever the truth in these judgments, in 1893 and 1895 Maine was worried about indiscriminate immigration as a menace to legitimate labor.[38]

The original idea for a hydrographic survey of the state probably came from John Alfred Poor in 1845 or 1846. In one of the memorials in favor of a railroad in northern Maine, he observed that the mountainous regions of the state, with rivers that descend from high elevations by circuitous courses through rich forest and soil, "may in time rival any region of the globe in the extent of its manufactures and commerce. Its great and distinguishing natural feature is its water-power, surpassing that of any section of the globe of equal extent."[39]

In his inaugural address of 1851, Governor John Hubbard suggested a comprehensive survey of the natural resources of the state, and calm, judicious legislation to advance their development.[40] In memorials to the legislature in 1858 on behalf of the Maine Agricultural Society, and in 1861 for the European and North American Railway Company, both prepared by Poor, a public survey of the water power was strongly urged. In September, 1866, he wrote to the Governor upon the development of the state, and especially upon the advantages of a hydrographic survey.[41] An appropriation for this, to bring the natural resources of the state to the knowledge of the public and to encourage investment in its water powers and improvement of them, was recommended in 1867 by Governor Chamberlain. The survey was authorized subsequently by the legislature, and the Governor and council appointed John A. Poor, A. D. Lockwood, and Hannibal Hamlin commissioners. Poor, as chairman, wrote the report submitted to the Governor that year. In 1867 Poor attempted to set up a "statistical society" for the promotion of industry, but the response was poor.[42] Not until 1887 was the State Bureau of Industrial and Labor Statistics created.[43]

Walter Wells, superintendent of the hydrographic survey, foresaw the possibilities of Maine's water resources. His classic study of Maine power, in 1869, analyzed the geographic, topographic, and meteorologic conditions of the state. The conclusions indicated great potentialities for Maine as a manufacturing center, primarily because of its abundant power and high elevation, but also because of favorable location, lakes, climate, and winds.

The shore line slopes upward 140 miles into the interior of the state, and several important rivers flow through this into the sea. Many of the unused water-power sites in Maine, he reported, were fully equal to those at Lowell, Massachusetts, in improvability, and several exceeded them in natural power.[44]

Wells estimated that 1,229,200,000,000 cubic feet of water were discharged annually by the rivers of Maine. From a mean elevation of 600 feet their descent would yield 4,429 hp. for each foot of fall. Thus the total horsepower from this fall would be 2,657,400 annually, which is equal to the work of 34,000,000 men working without interruption for one year.[45] Chamberlain estimated that the rivers of Maine yielded 6,600,000 hp., which would equal the labor ten hours a day every working day in the year of more than 80,000,000 men.[46] The report of the Maine Water Power Commission in 1920 was more conservative, putting the total at 1,500,000 hp. for developed and undeveloped power.[47] Wells concluded that manufacturing by water power was the most promising of all resources for Maine, and that a great system of manufacturing was inevitable, "a question only of time and of proper exhibition of our resources."[48]

Wells attributed the failure to use this great resource to the disturbances connected with the northeastern boundary, which had discouraged immigration and improvements for many years; to the ignorant and bigoted early policy of the state in opposing combinations of capital necessary to improve power; and to the failure of the state to ascertain and advertise its resources. He supported the recent change in state policy with its liberal provisions for the encouragement of industry, including: (1) exemption of new manufacturing establishments from taxation (by statute, after 1864, a town could exempt from taxation for ten years manufacturing establishments within its bounds, including machinery and capital used for operation);[49] (2) highly favorable provisions relating to flowage (payment of damages under the Mill Act prevents an obstinate landowner from holding up water-power development); (3) permission to towns to subscribe to the stock of manufacturing enterprises (the legislature usually permitted this, allowing towns to coöperate with parties improving their water power by subscribing to the capital stock employed in the manufactures); and emphasized the anxiety of all classes of people to have the abundant water power developed and put to use.[50]

Of equal importance was the excellent opportunity for investment in these undeveloped powers. "Unquestionably privileges that in the older States would be held at thousands of dollars can be purchased for scores in this State; privileges of great capacity, well situated, improvable at small outlay, and which are thus in the market at merely a nominal rate simply because their *owners have not the means for their development.*" In fact, some proprietors were advertising their willingness to sell on very favorable terms, on condition of improvement of power, or even to *give* the power to responsible people.[51]

Governor Joshua L. Chamberlain, of Civil War fame, later president of Bowdoin College, warned that "in our way of doing business Maine has become an old and exhausted State, before her true wealth has begun to be developed."[52] The shortsighted policy of shipping out the raw materials of Maine to others who had harnessed the forces of nature (power) to their team had enabled other states to prosper. While they were getting rich by using their power, Maine folk were still sentenced to hard labor in its preindustrial age. The people of Maine were slow to realize that true labor must seek to work most advantageously "where mind can best win mastery over the utilities of nature."[53]

Chamberlain, however, foresaw a great future for manufactures because of the abundance of Maine's water power, which would likewise stimulate commerce and agriculture,[54] and in his message of 1870 recommended that this power be developed.[55] In an address at the Centennial Exhibition at Philadelphia in 1876, he prophesied a new public attitude toward industry. The people of Maine, he said, no longer opposed capital. They invited skill, diversification, and division of labor. Although Maine had lost golden opportunities to industrialize when foreign investments were available and industry had gained a better footing elsewhere, diversified industries, which would bring about a balance between industry and agriculture, meant future prosperity for the state. "It does not appear to me that the only manufactures we should long for are the great ones which bring in crowds of foreign operatives who do not understand our institutions, and who do not enter into our social life and well-being. My hope for Maine lies largely in those many minor industries . . . that are pressing into service natural motors and native skill all over the State."[56]

Thus Chamberlain had the imagination and perspective in the formulative stage of Maine's industrial growth to realize that the great water-power resources should be put to the best possible use, and that this best use was not entirely for mass production in huge mill cities. More important was to be the diversification of industry, the use of native skills in scattered areas. The total throughout the state would amount to a rather large income in an economy suited to Maine. The state is justly proud of its eminent general-statesman-scholar.

Governor Sidney Perham expressed a similar point of view in 1871,[57] and Governor Nelson Dingley, Jr., in 1874 considered that water-power resources, equal to the working energy of 13,000,000 men, constituted Maine's greatest chance for economic salvation if only the legislators encouraged development.[58]

In 1871 the House of Representatives asked the Supreme Judicial Court of Maine for advisory opinions on three questions relating to the right of the legislature to authorize municipalities to grant gifts or loans to encourage manufacturing; also a further question, whether the muncipalities could establish manufactories entirely on their own account, run by town officers.[59] All three questions were answered decisively in the negative. The court advised that such gifts or loans would not be for public purposes but to foster individual or corporate enterprise, and that the state must accord no special or exclusive preferences to any industry. Likewise, municipalities could not go into business themselves. This would coerce a partnership, despotically taking the control of capital from the owners, and pledging all the property of the inhabitants to the contingencies of business nongovernmental in nature.

Decisions upholding these opinions were soon made. In *Allen v. Jay* the court nullified the action taken at a town meeting to lend municipal money to a company as an inducement to bring a sawmill and a box factory into a community, because the removal of a mill from one town to another is a private matter for private gain. If a town lends money for a particular object, it is "favoritism"; if it lends to all, it is virtually a division of property under the name of a loan—"communism incipient if not perfected."[60] In *Brewer Brick Company v. Brewer,* the 1864 statute permitting towns to exempt new industries from taxation for ten years was held unconstitutional. To exempt one estate from taxation would proportionally raise the tax rate of others, and for a private purpose. The benefits which the town would obtain "are precisely those arising from the introduction of capital or labor, and none other."[61] The legislature cannot give this discretionary power to municipalities, because "if . . . each town has the right to tax part and exempt part of the property located therein, . . . uniformity in relation to the subject-matter, as well as to the ratio of taxation, is at an end."[62]

Various studies of power resources were given wide publicity. By the early twentieth century, Maine citizens had become "commodity-conscious" and were convinced that power was the magnet to attract industry, as it had been in the eighteenth and nineteenth centuries. Maine's power complex persists, in spite of economic and technological changes in both manufacturing and the power industry.

The agrarian-industrial economy of Maine has become more diversified with the addition of a third element, the tourist business. A threefold economy brought greater opportunities as well as many complications. Agriculture, industry, and recreation constituted competing pressure groups in the determination of Maine's public power policy. According to the late Charles Eliot, discovery of the picturesqueness and summertime healthfulness of the Maine coast was made about 1860.[63] The late Edward P. Ricker set 1870 as the approximate date when the state began to consider the possibilities of the summer-resort business.[64] It was soon realized that the interior with its beautiful lakes was as important as the coast; its longer season was an advantage to the tourist business.

In their messages to the legislature, Governor Nelson Dingley, Jr., in 1874, Governor Edwin C. Burleigh in 1891, and Governor Henry B. Cleaves in 1895 recommended various measures to promote the new industry.[65] Despite some opposition, progress was made. In 1902 Charles Eliot urged legislative action to encourage associations to preserve the scenic beauty of the summer colonies of coastal Maine.[66]

The modest beginnings of tourism had caused no conflict with industry or agriculture, but, as its proportions increased, clashes occurred between manufacturing and the tourist industry over the use of the waters of Maine's rivers and lakes. In 1907 the infant industry was seriously threatened by the lake controversy. Maine appeared to be at the crossroads; the alternatives in creating a new phase of the power policy were either to give the lake water to industry at the expense of the tourist business, or to save the lakes for the tourist trade at the expense of manufacturing. The outcome, that the lakes were saved and, at the same time, in a way that enabled the industries to use their power, undoubtedly did much to save the tourist trade and lay a firm foundation for its future. The solution of the controversy showed that as early as 1909 Maine recognized that the waters of its rivers and lakes did not belong exclusively to any one interest. The waters should be put to a multiple use, not only for earning profits by industry and by the tourist trade but also, as in the T.V.A. recreational programs of recent date, for adding to the amenities of life. The contest between the manufacturing interests and the resort owners also showed the need of a commission to investigate, regulate, and plan for the scientific use of Maine's great water-power resources. It was maintained that if Maine desired to assume active control of its water powers or storage reservoirs, it should take early and adequate steps to establish a state policy for two reasons:[67] to anticipate private power rights becoming more firmly entrenched, and to head off the denser settlement of the shores of its lakes, with risk of land damages being increased if ponds and lakes were to be used as reservoirs. The conflict eventually made necessary a more precise power policy.

Maine has done much recently to encourage the tourist trade. The influx of thousands of tourists and summer campers in the coastal, mountain, and inland lake regions produced a volume of business exceeding $100,000,000 annually before the war, and the indications are that this volume can be increased.[68] The degree to which the tourist economy has already developed, aided by a sensible power policy which included all the various uses of the waters of the state, is evidence of the shrewdness of the pioneers of this industry in Maine.

More recently, sportsmen objected to the flooding of wooded areas by dams for power because of obstructions to navigation of the area flooded. In response to these protests the legislature passed a statute in 1929 requiring that all land be cleared before it can be flooded.[69] This law was blamed by power interests for holding up development in Aroostook County. The proposal for a huge storage basin on the Fish River, opposed by sportsmen, was impaired by this law.[70] Sportsmen also opposed the erection of a large dam on Millinocket Lake which was to have held twenty feet of water, and construction was stopped at a height of ten feet. The additional ten feet would have flooded approximately 4,000 acres of land which would require the expenditure of $800,000 for clearing alone.[71]

Another phase of the tourist-industrial conflict has been the struggle over the use of river waters. Pollution caused by large mill cities and industrial uses generally makes the rivers less attractive for fishing and pleasure. At present this problem is acute only on the Androscoggin River, but it threatens to increase in magnitude.[72] Governor Horace A. Hildreth urged that Maine solve its own pollution problems to prevent the federal government from answering "with controls that we do not like any more than the other innumerable controls that have been enacted by the Government in the last decade."[73] The recent state law heads off new sources of pollution. Funds were given to the Sanitary Water Board to make a substantial survey of coastal and tidal waterways in Maine. More than 6,000 miles of rivers and streams have been surveyed, also coastal waters, where particular attention was paid to salt-water beaches.

The impact of the national water-pollution control act of 1948 has not yet been felt in Maine. In theory this interesting law requires participation of *both* national and state governments to solve pollution problems, but whether it works out that way in practice remains to be seen.

# CHAPTER IV

## New Technologies of Power Production and Distribution; of Finance

Many volumes have been written on technological improvements in the production and distribution of power. The attempt here will be to survey certain major developments which have had an impact on Maine's policy, and to consider the degree to which state policy is in tune with these developments. The changes include the controversy over steam versus water power, the consequences of the electrical age, mass production and distribution, interconnections, and regional integration. The central theme is that technology makes possible, even requires, stream control, the use of steam as an auxiliary to hydroelectricity, and a much wider geographical area for the production and distribution of electricity.

The great contest between coal and water as sources of power began more than a century ago. A technological improvement in water wheels in the decade after 1840 put water power at an advantage over steam. By utilizing more of the force of the water the water turbine outmoded the pitch-back water wheel, and at the great industrial centers it added one-fourth to the available power.[1] In 1840, at Lowell, Massachusetts, water power cost $12, and steam $90, per hp.

Steam penetrated New England industrial cities when water power became inadequate and the price of fuel was low, but it did not make much headway in Maine because of the greater distance from fuel supplies. However, a few sawmills were operated by steam in the 1820's, and the legislature incorporated more in the next decade.[2] Mills were established at the power site, and the machinery was connected to the power by means of short belts or shafts. As late as 1900 there was no transmission in the modern sense.[3]

When, in the 1880's, technology gave the world the incandescent light which made electric current available for residential lighting and the arc light for street lighting, the electric industry began. According to one authority, the first electric light and power was used in Maine on January 5, 1880, at the spool mill of the Willimantic Thread Company.[4] But Maine was slow to realize the inherent significance and great possibilities of water energy converted into electricity for heat and power. In early newspaper publicity, only lighting was mentioned as a motivation for the new enterprise.[5]

The advantage of electricity over water power is that it is flexible in application and accessibility for light, heat, and power. New uses stimulated efforts to increase and improve production and transmission. Mass production in centrally located power plants and increased efficiency lowered the cost of electricity, but other manufacturing costs began to increase—labor, machinery, taxes, capital charges. The advancement of technical knowledge and equipment, especially the development of alternating current and other transmission facilities, made electricity more accessible. Thus power as a magnet in attracting industries became less important than proximity to markets and raw materials. The site of power gradually ceased to control the location of industry, for power could be brought to industry. Indeed, distances of three hundred miles are now attainable. Even greater distances can be attained by displacement (a plant increasing its imports from one side of its area and its exports on the other side). The impact of T.V.A. power is sometimes felt as far away as Chicago.[6] The National Resources Committee has referred to an era when power can be transmitted economically several hundred or a thousand miles.[7]

Although some water-power projects do not require storage, others need a reservoir dam and an artificial lake produced by impounding water. Many large water volumes must have stream regulation because of the wide variation in natural stream flow. Movable gates in the sluice or spillways to aid in regulating the flow of water, and flashboards on top of the dam to increase its head, are legal under the Maine Mill Act if they are used with uniformity and regularity.[8] Under this act, huge dams, entirely beyond the comprehension of the legislators of 1713, can overflow acres of property with payment for damages only. In reply to the contention that damages from overflow at a dam were too remote from the mill to which electricity was transmitted for the Mill Act to have application, the court said:[9]

> It is immaterial how far distant the wheels are from the machines, provided the one propels the other. Power is transmitted from wheels to machinery at a distance as directly by electric currents through wires, as by belts, or shafts, or other appliances. When water wheels propel electric generators and the electricity thus generated flows over wires and propels machines even at a distance, the wheels directly propel the machines.

The contest of steam power versus water power has ebbed and flowed, depending on the fluctuations of cost, and technological and political developments. For a long time water seemed victorious, though a recent interlude favored steam again. The economics of the war and postwar periods, however, have again focused attention on water power. Government power promoters favor hydroelectricity, and principally as a result of their activities hydro capacity has increased. But this is not attributable to the economic superiority of water power, because the costs of public power often are not comparable to the costs of privately owned steam and water plants.

The fact that Maine was distant from fuel supplies affected competing costs of steam and hydro power, and probably still does. Engineers and economists should make a careful study to ascertain whether it is expedient to continue transporting fuel to Maine for the manufacture of electricity, or (a free flow of current assumed) whether greater economies could be obtained by creating that electricity in southern New England, where tidewater coal and oil can be used, and transmit electricity, rather than transport fuel, to Maine. Many of Maine's newer steam plants are thermally efficient but, except for the Central Maine's 100,000 kw. steam plant at Wiscasset, they are smaller and therefore less efficient economically than the larger units closer to coal and oil supplies in Boston and Providence.

Steam generation requires less investment than water power, and the installations can be made more quickly, but operating expenses for fuel and labor are greater. Coal and oil are the principal fuels used in Maine today to generate electricity by steam. A difference of one dollar a ton on coal amounts to about one-half mill per kw-h in the cost of power in a modern steam plant, though in a less efficient system it might be as high as one mill.[10] In 1929 Thomas A. Edison stated that, although the thermal efficiency of coal had been doubled within a very few years, coal was only about 20 per cent efficient in contrast with 90 per cent efficiency for hydroelectric power generation.[11] Since then, however, the increase in steam efficiency has been rapid. Only about 15 per cent as much coal per kw-h was required in modern plants in 1936 as in 1900.[12] Between 1936 and 1948 the number of pounds of coal per kw-h was reduced from 1.440 to 1.302.[13]

The Power Survey Committee of the New England Council cited figures to show the steady increase in fuel costs delivered at Boston during the last ten years.[14] The increase in price from 1938 to 1947 was more than 76 per cent. Costs for Maine are somewhat proportionate. Largely because of the transportation increment, coal per million Btu delivered at Wiscasset, Maine, cost, in 1947, $4.06 more than at Boston. According to figures of the Maine Public Utilities Commission, the costs of coal delivered to coastal points in Maine on September 1, 1940, and 1948, increased from $6.00 to $11.64 per net ton; for oil the change was from $0.0268 to $0.0723 per gallon.[15]

The Power Committee of the Twentieth Century Fund, quoting bulletins of the Federal Power Commission and the National Resources Committee, concluded:[16]

> The relative advantage of water and steam plants has changed from time to time. Between 1920 and 1938, fuel consumed per kilowatt-hour declined 60 per cent in steam plants; this and other economies have favored steam. The cost of converting water power into mechanical power has fallen relatively little since 1900, but technical improvements have made it possible to construct higher dams at lower cost. Materials are used more economically and new types of construction equipment save labor. Nevertheless, the cost of steam generation has declined more rapidly than hydro.

When and where hydroelectricity is cheaper than steam power, sometimes it is cheaper in the end to pay higher prices for steam power and establish mills nearer to markets and raw materials, thus saving on transportation costs. Then again, some textile industries needed steam at certain points in their industrial processes; so it was natural for those needing power and also steam for processing to choose steam rather than water power.

Steam plants are required to supplement or "firm up" water power during the seasons when it is less plentiful. The use of steam auxiliaries began in the Central Maine Power Company system in 1910 with the construction of a plant at Biddeford. The next year one was added at Farmingdale, and another in 1913 in Lewiston. The Cape plant was constructed at South Portland in 1922. More recently two modern plants were added, Bucksport no. 2 in 1940 and Wiscasset in 1942. Each of these steam plants has shown a greater production efficiency per unit than the plant previously constructed, and the most recent Wiscasset plant is somewhat more than twice as efficient as the early ones in the system.[17] The total rated capacity of the six steam plants in the Central Maine system in 1948 was 102,000 kw.[18] The capacity of the Mason plant at Wiscasset was doubled in 1947, and in September, 1950, the company announced that this plant alone will become a 100,000 kw. station.

In recent years the great demand for firm power in Maine has changed steam from an auxiliary to a basic status. New steam installations have made a more dependable generating capacity than hydro would provide. In the steam-versus-hydro controversy, some of the former is essential, even at the T.V.A., to stabilize water power. When both must exist side by side, the controversial question sometimes becomes: Which should be relegated to secondary status?

The recent rising prices of coal and oil and the uncertainty of delivery because of coal strikes now give water power certain advantages over steam. Furthermore, water power needs to be integrated in a conservation program. Conservation is no longer a static policy of saving; it is a broad and dynamic policy which requires the wise use of all energy resources. The necessity of saving coal and oil for more highly specialized war purposes may make water power more than a matter of cost. Mr. Justice Jackson, in the Hope natural gas decision,[19] stressed the need for obtaining the highest possible use from each category of the nation's energy resources.

The history of power company organization in Maine begins with small, independent plants, often the outgrowth of mills which had installed generating plants for their own use.[20] The situation at Skowhegan is typical of the organization of the independent power and light company in Maine. Uncertainties there about water-power rights encouraged litigation, and practical questions of allocating expenses of dam and flume maintenance came to the fore. The industrialists, realizing these handicaps, engaged a law firm to search water-power rights in 1886, and were advised that a corporation should be formed to which all owners could convey their rights. Thus the Skowhegan Water Power Company became the effective local agency which introduced unity of ownership and control.

At first power companies were chartered as public service corporations by special act of the Maine legislature, and their territory was assigned by the legislative act. In 1895 they were permitted to organize under the general laws, but they could not operate in territory where another company was serving or was authorized to serve unless they were specifically authorized to do so by the legislature or by the consent of the prior company.[21] In 1901 this law was modified and a special act was again required to enable a new company to enter the field of an existing company;[22] no longer was the consent of the prior company sufficient. In 1909 Maine made it illegal for corporations to transmit hydroelectric power outside the state. In 1913 the Public Utilities Commission was established in Maine, with general regulatory authority over these former legislative tasks.

According to Professor Orren C. Hormell of Bowdoin College, a large majority of the electric utilities in the state up to 1911

> were not only owned by Maine capitalists but were in most cases locally owned and operated. They were still largely in the ownership and control of the original local promoters whose thrift had accumulated capital sufficient to begin the development of local resources. . . . Local capitalists in such municipalities as Auburn and Lewiston, Wiscasset, Searsport, Belfast and in some fifty other communities still owned and operated the electric utilities serving the community.[23]

Although organized as private business and motivated by profit, these early companies were community undertakings, controlled by local interests, and they had a genuine desire to serve local needs.

Because of technological advances it soon became evident that the smaller companies were no longer adequate to satisfy local needs. Reserve power was necessary to supply new demands as they arose. The advantages of unified management, greater financial resources, interconnecting companies, and pooling of loads on large central stations sealed the fate of the community company.

Private power systems in the country generally have expanded without regard to state lines,[24] but those in Maine are an exception. New Hampshire and Vermont transmit hydroelectricity to Massachusetts and Rhode Island in wet periods, and when it is dry they sometimes receive steam power from Boston and Providence. The New England Council concludes that New England is one of the most highly interconnected areas in the country,[25] and asserts that this was a big factor in the war effort.[26] Maine, however, is outside the otherwise integrated power-supply area of New England; although power can now be imported in emergencies, Maine cannot reciprocate.[27] The power embargo of the state is obsolete from the standpoint of the efficient and economical regional power operations of modern technology.

Since Maine power cannot cross state lines, interconnections are essentially intrastate. The Central Maine Power Company is an example of mergers in which one company served two or more communities; also of the later necessity, technologically and economically, for interconnection with contiguous intrastate companies. Originating as a small electric lighting plant in Oakland, the Central Maine Power Company in 1899 served about one hundred customers and lighted the streets from dusk until ten o'clock in the evening. In 1901 the company secured a contract to light the streets of Waterville. In 1905 it was chartered by the Maine legislature as the Messalonskee Electric Company, and was authorized to provide electricity to Waterville, Oakland, Fairfield, Benton, and Winslow.[28] In 1910 it became the Central Maine Power Company, and within the next few years it purchased numerous smaller companies. The Central Maine and the Cumberland County Power and Light Company found interconnections mutually advantageous in 1924 and thereafter. The high and low water stages of the Saco River and those of the Androscoggin and Kennebec rivers occur at diffferent times; hence an interconnection forestalled the use of a higher cost steam plant.[29] In order to take advantage of the different precipitation on the Aroostook and Penobscot rivers, the Gould Electric Company and the Bangor Hydro-Electric Company made an interconnection in 1926 or 1927.[30] The Central Maine Power Company and the Bangor Hydro-Electric Company are interconnected; the former ties in with smaller companies of the northwest and the latter with those of the northeast.[31]

As early as 1908 the securities of the Central Maine Company had been sold to the people served, and the number of these shareholders grew rapidly after 1918. Professor Hormell has stated that probably the ownership of the voting stock in the company was held by Maine people down to 1925, at which time the holdings passed from the people of Maine when the Middle West Utilities Company of Chicago purchased the common stock.[32]

The Cumberland County Power and Light Company, serving southern Maine, was chartered in 1907. Up to 1920,

> [it] was probably controlled by capital foreign to the state of Maine. From 1920 to 1922, however, the policy was inaugurated of selling preferred stock with voting power to consumers and employees. Potential, if not actual control, was probably in the hands of Maine people from 1922 to 1924. The control, however, definitely passed to capital foreign to the state when in 1925 the National Electric Power Company, a holding company under the control of the Albert Emanuel Company of New York purchased 99 per cent of the common stock. Another chapter in consolidation was written in January, 1927, when the Emanuel interests sold their controlling stock to the Middle West Utilities Company which already controlled the Central Maine Power Company.[33]

In Aroostook County the Gould Electric Company, Inc., established by the late Senator Arthur R. Gould, was incorporated in 1917.[34] In 1929 the name was changed to the Maine Public Service Company. Its subsidiary, the Maine and New Brunswick Electrical Power Company, Limited, with a plant located in New Brunswick, is primarily a generating company selling the major portion of its power under Canadian license to the Maine Public Service Company. A number of small Aroostook companies were acquired in 1927 by the Central Public Utility Corporation, predecessor of Consolidated Electric and Gas Company, under the presidency of A. E. Pierce of Chicago. In 1929 Maine Public Service acquired twelve affiliated distributing companies which operated in fifty-four townships. Additional mergers were made in 1933, 1943, and 1945.[35] Forced, however, by the Public Utility Holding Company Act of 1935 to divest itself of the Maine Public Service Company, Consolidated, sold it, on April 8, 1947, to a syndicate for $3,042,000.[36] This group in turn put the stock up for public sale. The shares are held by residents of thirty-six states, with no large individual stockholder. The ten largest stockholders account for only 7,900 of 105,980 shares. Of these, 3,500 shares are held in the state of Maine.[37]

Another group of consolidations resulted in the incorporation of the Bangor Hydro-Electric Company in 1924, approved by the Public Utilities Commission on February 17, 1925. The E. W. Clark Company and the Clark family of Philadelphia were very influential in stock ownership and positions on the board of directors. This corporation was never controlled by the Insulls or any of the holding companies, and in March, 1948, between 60 and 65 per cent of the stock was owned and held by Maine people.[38]

This brief survey of power company expansion and mergers before 1925 indicates that Maine had several strong companies organized on an intrastate sectional basis. It required the advent of the Insull holding company, however, to further integrate and coordinate some areas. Even that failed to bring about interstate interconnections.

The Middle West Utilities Company, the top holding company of the Insulls, owned in 1925 the Twin State Gas and Electric Company, which did a public utility business in several towns and cities in New York, Vermont, New Hampshire, and Maine. Between May and August, 1925, the Middle West Utilities Company bought the common stock of the Central Maine Power Company. In that period it also bought a controlling interest in the Manchester, New Hampshire Company, the Rutland Railway and Light Company property, and several small utilities in Vermont.[39] The story of the sale of Central Maine was told by its president, Walter S. Wyman, at the Federal Trade Commission hearing in 1932. He and Guy P. Gannett did not control the Central Maine Power Company by their own ownership, but they did "with ours and other stock that my friends owned."[40] "We gave the Middle West Co. an option on our stock, which had added to it later other stocks that gave the Middle West control." It was also brought out that the price paid per share was $140, and that, before this consolidation, very little of the stock had been sold on the market. Small and spasmodic sales had been made at $50 to $60 a share.

About August, 1925, under the direction of the Middle West Utilities Company, the New England Public Service Company (NEPSCO), the major subholding company in the system for this area, was organized in the state of Maine.[41] Through common stock ownership, NEPSCO was controlled directly by the Middle West Utilities Company. The reason given for its organization was consolidation of the control of the Middle West Utilities Company's operating companies in the three northern New England states.[42] This arrangement continued until 1928, when the Middle West Utilities Company transferred NEPSCO's securities to another subholding company, the National Electric Power Company. Thus Middle West controlled the National Electric Power Company, which controlled NEPSCO. And the latter owned directly the equity stocks of the Central Maine Power Company, the Cumberland County Power and Light Company (now merged with the Central Maine), and the Central Vermont Public Service Corporation. It also owned about one-third of the securities of New England Industries, Inc., which was incorporated in 1929 and wedged into the Insull hierarchy to promote, supervise, and control the industrial investments.

Central Maine had investments in the Cushnoc Paper Corporation and two or three industrial companies before its sale to Middle West in 1925.[43] It had bought small amounts of the stock of the Edwards Manufacturing Company of Augusta largely because of its interest in the water power which the Edwards mill owned on the Kennebec River. In October, 1927, the Central Maine Power Company purchased control of the Edwards Manufacturing Company.[44]

Martin Insull, president of Middle West, discussed, on several occasions in 1925 and thereafter, this and similar ventures into textiles. His plan was to organize a company and provide it with capital for the purpose of assisting industrial development in territories served by subsidiaries of Middle West. The first real step in this direction was the acquisition of the Androscoggin mill in Lewiston in 1928. The evidence indicates that the purchase was a rather reckless one, resulting from a conversation between Insull and Wyman, who had some knowledge of the companies but had not thoroughly investigated them. The mill had lost money heavily and in June, 1928, its stockholders voted to liquidate. They were employing about a thousand workmen at that time. Several meetings were held in Lewiston-Auburn in an attempt to raise money to restore the mill to operation, but all such efforts failed.

Wyman was close to the local situation, but Insull's decision appears to have been impulsive. Wyman, after describing the failure of attempts to restore the mill to operation, testified revealingly on Insull's decision to make the purchase.[45]

> Mr. Insull was in town not long afterwards and I told him about the situation and he said, "Well, why don't you buy it?" I said, "I don't know anything about running a textile mill," and he said, "Well, you can hire somebody that does." As a result of that discussion, the New England Public Service Company, I think, bought the majority of the stock of the Androscoggin Mill, paying for it approximately $100.00 per share—bought it from the general public.

NEPSCO acquired a controlling interest in the Hill Manufacturing Company in Lewiston, and in July, 1929, the Bates Manufacturing Company was purchased. In July, 1930, the York Manfacturing Company of Saco was added to the group. Since all these mills were large users of power, it was typical of Insull methods to acquire them and put money into them to assure their continued operation and purchase of power. The argument was that prosperous mills meant prosperous communities which, in turn, made prosperous power companies possible. For instance, the timely purchase of the Androscoggin mill enabled it to continue operation and certainly proved to be a great boon to Lewiston and vicinity.

Of tremendous significance, yet difficult to evaluate, is the degree to which the purchase of these mills was motivated by their valuable power holdings which were acquired with the purchase. The Edwards Company owned jointly with a paper company a power dam on the Kennebec River at Augusta, a site that would become more valuable with the construction of the Bingham dam and the resultant improved water flow at Augusta. Wyman maintained that this purchase would prevent the waste of power at the Edwards Company dam and also benefit the company.

Stephen J. Kennedy summarized NEPSCO's control over the headwaters of the Androscoggin:[46]

Ownership of the Bates Manufacturing Company also gave the utility working control in the Union Water Power Company of Lewiston. In addition to the dam at Lewiston, this brought to the New England Public Service Company control of the dams at the Rangeley Lakes, about seventy-five miles to the north, which were entirely owned by the Union Water Power Company, and also substantial control of the Azicohos Dam on the Magalloway River, a tributary of the Androscoggin, in which the Union Water Power Company held a 25 per cent interest. Since the New England Public Service Company had just completed construction of a new dam at Gulf Island and had purchased the Barker Mill at Auburn which owned the Deer's Rip Dam, and at which a new automatic hydro-electric generating plant had just been completed, this control over the headwaters of the Androscoggin was highly important to the power company.

The industrial holdings of NEPSCO were segregated, however, under the control of New England Industries, Inc. Middle West organized the Mississippi Valley Utilities Investment Company with capital to assist industrial development in the territories served by Insull subsidiaries. This led to the organization of New England Industries, Inc., in 1929; the capital was subscribed about one-third by NEPSCO and about two-thirds by the Mississippi Company.[47]

An investigation by the Federal Trade Commission in 1931 summarized the Insull industrial interests in Maine as follows:[48]

In 1930, the New England Industries, Inc., was formed by the utility system, and all the industrial enterprises . . . owned by the Insulls were turned over to the new company. Some of the factories and industries had been acquired conditionally, on the purchase of power sites sought by the group. At the end of last year [1930] New England Industries, Inc., owned control of the Edwards Manufacturing Company, the Bates Manufacturing Company, Hill Manufacturing Company, Androscoggin Mills, and York Manufacturing Company. The operation of these mills provided steady employment for 4,200 persons with weekly payrolls aggregating $71,000.00, chiefly in textile and newsprint manufacture.

Besides its venture into textiles, New England Industries, Inc., began in November, 1929, the construction of a new pulp and newsprint plant, the Maine Seaboard Paper Company at Bucksport.[49] The Industries expended $11,977,196 on the plant,[50] which began operation in November, 1930. Besides these investments, New England Industries, Inc., according to Stephen J. Kennedy, by December, 1933, lent $5,379,000 to certain mills to finance the purchase of new machinery and to provide for general plant rehabilitation. A loan was also made to the Keyes Fibre Company during its bankruptcy proceedings, 1932–1934, and NEPSCO, the Industries, and the Central Maine Power Company together owned enough to bring this company into the fold also.[51] In contrast to the two previous years, the mill showed a slight profit for 1933. During this period $4,240,000 was borrowed.[52]

Two distinct points of view were advanced in 1945 on the results of the Insull holdings in Maine. The Honorable Sumner T. Pike, then commissioner of the Securities and Exchange Commission, in a commencement address at Bates College condemned the utilities:[53]

> It happens that in this part of the State of Maine one of the most fantastic examples of monopoly gone wild occurred when Samuel Insull of Chicago bought our power companies which sell electric current, then bought or built cotton and pulp mills to make sure that they would buy the current which he had to sell, and later bought banks to lend money to the mills so that they could pay their power bills, This all, incidentally, with other people's money, not Mr. Insull's. In our shop at the SEC we are now attempting to salvage the remains of this particular mess and to get back to the hornswoggled investors such portion of their original stake as was not wasted in this so-called empire building.

The veteran journalist Sam E. Conner immediately took exception, contending that the state benefited because Walter S. Wyman induced Insull to buy Maine mills which were in bad shape and were thereby kept from liquidation. When the Insull financial empire began to crumble, he wrote, the Maine companies, thanks to the leadership of Wyman and Skelton, were in the clear. Kennedy also maintained that because of the expenditures made upon new equipment under the Insull regime and further improvements under subsequent management, these mills obtained modern equipment and were in a position to compete effectively in the market in 1936.[54]

The statements of Pike and of Conner are, on closer analysis, not actually contradictory. Pike, as a federal official, was concerned with the activities in the high echelons of the Insull hierarchy and with the interests of investors. On the national level his view is correct.

Conner considered the situation on a state and local basis. The evidence indicates that the holding companies did pour money into local industry and kept it going. Insull money may have been tainted, but in a time of depression and crisis this shot-in-the-arm braced many communities for survival. The issue is not clear-cut between nationalism and particularism, for many local investors were losers. Although the Insull hierarchy was top-heavy, much discretionary authority rested with local line officials. These grass-roots agents were not merely yes-men for Middle West: their planning and decisions were highly particularistic.

The account of the Insull crash, the reorganization of Maine power and textile companies, applications of the Holding Company Act, and subsequent sales and court litigation has been given elsewhere.[55] Though important, it is extraneous to the study of Maine power policy.

# CHAPTER V

## The Fernald Law: Quantitative Analysis

Representatives of powerful out-of-state corporations saw opportunities, soon after the turn of the century, to make huge profits by developing Maine power and selling it in the large industrial centers in southern New England. These groups had profited by the several investigations of Maine's great power resources and understood their potential value even if the citizens of Maine were not yet aware of it. One plan contemplated by large Boston interests was to develop water powers on the St. John, Penobscot, Kennebec, Androscoggin, and other rivers, tie them together, and sell the electricity in Massachusetts. They tried to obtain from the legislature the right of eminent domain to take land on which to build transmission lines into Massachusetts. As regional power development this program would have been sound if the power and transmission plants did not cost too much. The plan tied together diverse river flows with sites for steam power stations where water-borne coal was cheaper, in order to serve concentrated power loads in southeastern New England, thus getting the advantages of larger producing units.

Certain home elements were determined, however, that Maine's power policy should be isolationist. They fought to save "Maine power for Maine people." Said Edward P. Ricker in this connection, "The scheme might have gone through had not one of these Boston gentlemen divulged it to a Maine man not in sympathy with such a gigantic wrong to the people of this state. Attorneys were employed to oppose the scheme and it was killed in committee."[1] Yet in 1907 the Maine legislature, according to Ricker, "without quibble or question" granted to the Twin State Gas and Electric Company, incorporated in Connecticut in 1906, enormous rights and privileges to acquire and control water powers. It could generate, manufacture, store, transmit, lease, or sell gas or electricity, and had the power to acquire water powers and water rights and to construct reservoirs, dams, and water towers. But when the nonresidents Chase and Harriman, who owned the Indian Pond power on the upper Kennebec River talked of developing it and taking it out of the state, the citizens of Maine awoke and kept the Indian Pond power in Maine.[2] Reports are that the law was passed to spite H. I. Harriman of the New England Power Company.

President Theodore Roosevelt's conference of governors in 1908 ushered in a conservation era throughout the country. In Maine, where there was considerable agitation to conserve water power, the legislature acted at its next session in 1909. Unless power could be developed it could not be conserved, and to let it run unharnessed was waste. So conservation meant development, and a few citizens were advocating state aid where private capital was lacking. In 1909, conservation, in Maine, meant also particularism—preventing corporations from transmitting power to other states.

The Fernald law was a partial outgrowth of the battle to save the lakes in the previous session of the legislature. That contest aroused greater interest in the water resources of the state, and the Fernald-Ricker interests continued the propaganda in the form of saving the power for the people of Maine.[3] It was a political issue which appealed to the masses. Governor Bert M. Fernald recommended, in his message to the legislature at the beginning of the 1909 session, that "no grant should be made of water power privileges without compensation, nor without restriction that will properly protect the rights of the public from whom the privileges are derived."[4]

An act to prohibit corporations from transmitting hydroelectric power beyond the confines of the state was introduced by Senator (later Governor) Percival P. Baxter. The bill was discussed at some length, and the sentiment of the Senate was revealed by a vote on the motion to postpone indefinitely. Twelve senators were in opposition and fifteen in favor of the bill, which passed the House with comparatively little opposition. Those who advocated it felt that by keeping power within the state new industries would be attracted. This was a major reason for the law. In the second place, with hostility to the motives of out-of-state capital and corporations recent and active, it was believed that the law would keep out trusts and speculators of other states, that Maine power should be preserved for Maine people. This tenet was later extended to preclude control by the national government or regional agencies. Finally, it was hoped that the policy would tend to extend rural electrification.

Senator William H. Looney summarized the arguments in favor of the bill as follows:[5]

> We felt that the great natural resources of the State, as crystallized and developed in electricity and motive power, should be preserved. We all know that heretofore our forests have gradually, little by little, disappeared and have gone into the hands of speculators, so that now I understand the entire domain of the State, so far as our great forests are concerned, is owned by practically 40 men. I understand also that certain speculators in other states are coming in and trying to secure possession of our water powers. Now it is an open secret that the Executive of the State, representing as I believe the best interests of the State and voicing the sentiment of the people of the State, desires that these great natural resources should be preserved and that they should not be taken up and possessed by the trusts, monopolies, and speculators from other states; so that this bill simply provides that electric power and water power shall not be transmitted to other states without the consent of the State. Now, can there be any objection to a reasonable bill of that kind. In the last analysis, that is all it means, that the State itself shall hold in reserve these great natural powers and resources and that they shall not be allowed to go beyond the limits of the State without the consent of the State. It seems to me if a measure of a policy like that had been followed in this State for the past years, the State would have been millions and millions of dollars richer than it is now; and so, for my part, I am one of those who believe that the policy of the Executive of the State is just and right, and that this bill, embodying as it does the idea of all those who believe in preserving and keeping intact the great natural powers and resources of the State, should pass.

Senator (later Governor) Carl E. Milliken's support of the Fernald law was based on the belief that several men behind the Standard Oil Company were trying in Maine and other states to obtain water resources for development and that they should be required to go before the legislature before being allowed to set up trunk lines into other states.[6] Ricker maintained that, by a policy of out-of-state transmission, "Maine would be merely a power station for Massachusetts or Connecticut, employing but few hands to tend dams and stations, instead of doing what Maine should do—develop great industries here to utilize the powers on the spot, the same as is being done in the few industrial water power centers that we now have and which are adding so greatly to the wealth and prestige of Maine."[7]

The Fernald law is brief and definite. It differs from other non-export laws in that the Public Utilities Commission has no discretion in regard to allowing power to be transmitted. Special permission must be granted by the legislature. The law was enacted four years before Maine had a Public Utilities Commission. It reads as follows:[8]

> No corporation, unless expressly authorized so to do by special act of legislation, shall transmit or convey beyond the confines of the state for the purpose of furnishing power, heat or light, any electric current generated directly or indirectly by any water power in this state; nor sell or furnish, directly or indirectly, to any person, firm, or corporation, any electric current so generated to be transmitted or conveyed beyond the confines of the state for any of such purposes. Nothing in this act, however, shall prevent any railroad corporation doing business in this state from transmitting electric current, however generated, beyond the confines of the state for the purpose of operating its road between some point in this state and any point or points beyond its confines.
>
> This act shall not apply to any corporation now engaged in conveying or transmitting electric current beyond the confines of the state or chartered or empowered so to do, nor affect or impair any existing contracts for the transmission of electric current beyond the confines of the state.
>
> Any corporation violating any of the provisions of this act may be dissolved and its franchises forfeited to the state upon proper proceedings to be instituted by the attorney general whenever directed by the governor.

The law is very clear. It applies to corporations only; there is no law against transmission by private individuals, partnerships, or trusts. Actually, a small amount of power is transmitted to New Hampshire by the Swans Falls Company, which is not a corporation but a voting trust.[9] The other exceptions to the law relate to electricity on railroads;[10] in order to make the law nonretroactive, a "grandfather" clause permitted those engaged or empowered to engage in such transmission before the act became effective, to continue to do so. Otherwise, a special act of the legislature is necessary to sell hydroelectric power outside the state. The law does not apply to electricity generated by steam. While Ricker expressed personal dislike for some of these exceptions, he explained the necessity for including them in order to meet the requirements of the interstate law and thereby make the act constitutional.[11] Through these loopholes Maine legally exports small quantities of power to New Hampshire and Canada, and, in reverse, imports some power. On the basis of 1926 statistics, Professor William E. Mosher indicated that Maine exported 2,803,706 kw-h and imported 823,946 kw-h.[12] A wide variation exists between those figures and the ones supplied by the Maine Public Utilities Commission.[13] According to the latter, Maine utilities imported more than five times as much power in 1945 as in 1926. With one exception, the amount imported has increased steadily each year. The amount imported in 1945, however, constituted an increase of almost 25 per cent over the 1944 importation.

To what waters does the Fernald law apply? Specifically, the law states that electric current generated "by any water power in this state" cannot be exported. In 1909 it was assumed that Congress had jurisdiction over navigable rivers and states had jurisdiction over nonnavigable rivers. But Maine did not want floatable rivers to be considered navigable in the technical sense, which would have given the national government control over many Maine rivers. The late Paul L. Bean, formerly chief engineer for the Maine Public Utilities Commission, was of the opinion that the head of tidewater marked the head of federal jurisdiction in Maine. He believed that the Saco River above the city of Saco, the Androscoggin above Brunswick, the Kennebec above Augusta, and the Penobscot above Bangor were considered nonnavigable.[14] Without doubt, these limits were in full accord with the federal interpretation at the time, and meant that the federal government had jurisdiction over a very small part of the Maine rivers. Thus the conclusion is that Maine has considered the Fernald law applicable to its nonnavigable rivers. Under the standard definition of a decade ago, this put all important water powers under the Fernald law. Federal jurisdiction was confined to the navigable portions of streams. However, Robert D. Baum suggests that national authority to regulate projects on nonnavigable waters affecting navigation dates from 1899.[15] The numerous tide mills on those navigable waters are small. To date, federal authority has not been asserted, because no power projects in Maine operate under Federal Power Commission license.[16]

This was Maine's interpretation of the application of the Fernald law, an interpretation which evolved for some thirty years after the passage of the law in 1909. However, a series of decisions by the United States courts in 1940 and thereafter have made the foregoing interpretation obsolete. Since these important decisions not only concern the application of the Fernald law to Maine's rivers but go to the very core of the validity of the nontransmission principle itself, consideration of these recent cases must be deferred. (See chap. vii.)

Whether the Fernald law would apply to tidal power at Passamaquoddy Bay is of academic interest only, because the Quoddy law specifically authorized the transmission of that power to other states.[17] The Roosevelt administration urged the legislature to create the State Quoddy Authority in 1935. Before the tidewater case, *United States v. California,*[18] in 1947, it was assumed that Maine would have jurisdiction over Quoddy power, and on this assumption the Maine legislature passed numerous acts to aid Quoddy.

Four months after the tidewater decision the Supreme Court ordered, adjudged, and decreed as follows:[19]

> The United States of America is now, and has been at all times pertinent hereto, possessed of paramount rights in, and full dominion and power over, the lands, minerals and other things underlying the Pacific Ocean lying seaward of the ordinary low-water mark on the coast of California, and outside of the inland waters, extending seaward three nautical miles . . . . The State of California has no title thereto or property interest therein.

In the decision the Court had said that whatever any nation does in the open sea is a question for consideration among nations themselves and not their separate governmental units. Whatever the national or state governments do in the ocean is subject to treaty obligations; even the oil about which the state and nation were contending might well become the subject of international dispute and settlement.[20]

On the basis of the foregoing, it may be that Quoddy is beyond the Fernald law and belongs under federal jurisdiction. The erection of dams under the ocean, the allocation of territorial waters between the United States and Canada, even the power itself generated by the building of such dams might involve the national government in international controversy. Certainly the tidewater decision paves the way for a gigantic federal power project in Passamaquoddy Bay if Congress ever wants to go that far. Furthermore, the tidewater decision may point to the unconstitutionality of that part of the ordinance of 1641 which gave littoral proprietors up to one hundred rods of tideland. Such an eventuality would have the effect of transferring payment for damages to fishing interests by the construction of Quoddy dam from the state to the national government.

The topography of Maine, with interior mountains, numerous lakes, and several rivers flowing into the Atlantic, provides a natural hydroelectric power setup. The rocks in the rivers are hard, and tend to rest at right angles to the current, with consequent rips, rapids, cascades, and cataracts—the stuff of power. The average rainfall is approximately three trillion cubic feet, of which the rivers carry off about one and a quarter trillion feet.[21] The descent of this huge volume of water, if it were completely utilized, would yield more than two and a half million horsepower, gross.

The importance to New England of Maine's vast hydroelectric resources of the 1920's was realized when the United States Geological Survey estimated that Maine surpassed all the states east of the Rocky Mountains except New York, North Carolina, Tennessee, Georgia, and South Carolina in potential water power available 90 per cent of the year. In power available 50 per cent of the year, Maine surpassed all states east of the Rockies except New York and North Carolina.[22] The average cost of commercial power purchased from public utility companies in Maine in 1922 was less than in any state in the East, except South Carolina, Georgia, and Alabama, and at the same average cost as the latter. Rates for lighting, however, were considerably higher.

In 1924 the power investigating committee of the Associated Industries of Massachusetts estimated that the amount of undeveloped water power available in New England, if developed for complete utilization of the flow available 60 per cent of the time, was more than four and three-fourths billion kilowatt-hours in an average year. It was estimated that 75 per cent of this undeveloped power was in Maine, and that nearly three billion kilowatt-hours, nearly all of which would be developed in Maine, could be delivered to industries taking large amounts, at a cost of from 0.7 to 1.5 cents per kw-h, if it were not for the Fernald law.[23]

That the power companies were correct in asserting that a big demand for Maine power existed in New England is indicated by the fact that although in the three southern New England states, with their more convenient and cheaper access to coal imports, more than four-fifths of their electricity was produced from coal,[24] yet, even so, Massachusetts in 1926 imported 20 per cent of its power, and Rhode Island 38 per cent.[25] On the basis of 1943 figures from the Massachusetts Department of Public Utilities, the ratio of kilowatt-hours of steam generated to kilowatt-hours consumed for that year was 69.7 per cent, and the ratio of kilowatt-hours imported to kilowatt-hours consumed in Massachusetts was 22.8 per cent.[26] It was once suggested that the other New England states might find it necessary to obtain power from Canada because of Maine's embargo, though the import of such power would have to be in large quantities to be economically sound.[27]

At the time of the agitation for transmission of surplus power in the late 1920's, it was estimated that in an average year 678,080,000 kw-h more than was generated by water power in 1927 could be generated by existing water-power installations.[28] Much of this would have been secondary power for which Maine had relatively light demand but for which a market existed in eastern Massachusetts, where steam was the principal source of energy.

The United States Geological Survey estimated, in 1933, that Maine had more than 50 per cent of New England's potential power within its boundaries. For power that could be available 90 per cent of the time, Maine possessed 53.7 per cent of New England's potentiality, and for power potentially available 50 per cent of the time, Maine had 54.3 per cent.[29]

Conservative estimates of Maine's undeveloped water power by the Maine Public Utilities Commission in 1939 are that for flow 50 per cent of the time Maine could develop 702,453 hp.; for flow 90 per cent of the time, 339,468 hp.[30] In these estimates economic feasibility was not taken into account. Some sites are reported to be highly desirable and already in the blueprint stage, but others would flood out valuable property above the dams. A few are too remote for profitable development; they are in uninhabited areas and the cost of highways to make construction work possible would be excessive.

The Maine figures are based on stream-flow records averaged over a great many years, and are more precise than those of the Federal Power Commission in that they stipulate the time the potential power could be available. The Public Utilities Commission would no doubt agree that Maine's power potentiality would be increased tremendously by including in the totals power which could be available for shorter periods of time, say 15 or 20 per cent. Whether the expense of additional generators and dams to obtain this marginal power two or three months in the year is justified depends upon the cost and availability of alternative sources of power, a condition of war or peace, depression or prosperity, need for multiple-purpose dams, technological progress, conservation programs, and general economic planning.

One of the most specific Federal Power Commission estimates of the Maine power situation was announced in 1941 during an investigation of the Passamaquoddy tidal power project. The report was unfavorable to Quoddy, because the potential water powers of the Maine rivers might be developed considerably cheaper than either steam or tidal power from the all-American Quoddy project.[31]

As a result of this last-mentioned investigation, the Federal Power Commission suggested a tentative plan for the coördinated development of seventeen power sites in Maine. The sites contemplated for development were tabulated in a time sequence of three stages in accordance with the increase in demand for power. The first stage contemplated the development of hydroelectric plants on the west branch of the Penobscot River. The second stage provided for eight power plants in the Penobscot River basin, four on the east branch, one on the Mattawamkeag River, and three on the main stem of the

Penobscot. In stage three there would be four water-power plants in the upper part of the Kennebec River basin, between Bingham and Moosehead Lake.

The estimate of the unit cost of this energy per kilowatt-hour, on the basis of federal or state financing, is given in the accompanying table. On the basis of private financing with interest at 5 per cent and the payment of taxes, the estimate was as follows: the

| Stage | No. of plants | Annual energy output in kw-h | Annual charges | Unit cost of energy, mills per kw-h |
|---|---|---|---|---|
| Stage 1........... | 5 | 530,000,000 | $ 794,000 | 1.50 |
| Stage 2........... | 8 | 870,000,000 | 1,741,000 | 2.00 |
| Stage 3........... | 4 | 1,044,000,000 | 2,028,000 | 1.94 |
| Stages 1–3 combined........ | 17 | 2,444,000,000 | $4,563,000 | 1.87 |

annual charges for the five plants in stage 1 would be $1,363,000, and the unit cost of energy 2.57 mills per kw-h; for stage 2 the annual charges for the eight plants would be $2,988,000, and the unit cost 3.43 mills per kw-h; the annual charges for the four plants in stage 3 would be $3,616,000, and the unit cost 3.46 mills per kw-h. The annual charges for the three stages combined, seventeen plants, would be $7,967,000, and the unit cost 3.26 mills per kw-h.

In January, 1947, the Federal Power Commission estimated that Maine had 2,448,000 kw. of undeveloped power. Estimates for the other New England states totaled 900,000 kw.[32] Or, to put it in a more spectacular manner, Maine had, according to these estimates, more than 70 per cent of the undeveloped power in New England. In August, 1948, the commission gave a revised estimate of Maine's undeveloped power—1,807,000 kw., about 26 per cent below the 1947 figures.[33] The factor of additional development in the interim does not help to explain the most recent estimate, because Maine has had virtually no new developments between 1941 and 1948 which would require to be subtracted from the earlier figures publicized.

In response to questions about the bases for these estimates, the commission answered as follows:[34]

> The amounts of available undeveloped water power shown in the above-mentioned tabulation, by states and regions, are based on estimates made by river basins in accordance with the presently conceived plans for the best over-all development of the rivers. They are based on the best information available to the Commission and are derived from studies made by the Commission's staff either independently or in conjunction with studies by the Army Engineers, from studies made by the Army Engineers, the Bureau of Reclamation and other agencies, and from various reports. They are subject to revision either by increase or decrease as additional information becomes available concerning stream flow, reservoir sites and other pertinent matters. The figures represent the estimated rated capacities of generators which would normally be installed at hydroelectric developments, assuming reasonable regulation of flow by storage, depletion of flow due to consumptive use in different sections of the country and other factors which are pertinent to the best over-all development of the river for power and multiple-purpose use.

Unfortunately, this explanation ignores the vital factor of availability of the power in question, that is, whether it would be available 90, 50, or 15 per cent of the time. Without this information the estimate is of relatively little value. Also, it should be noted that these estimates are for the best over-all development of the river for power and *multiple-purpose use.* Multiple purposes usually mean a large share of federal participation in flood control, irrigation, and power; economic feasibility is not always a prime factor.

A highly significant study of the power resources of Maine and New England was completed late in 1948 by the Power Survey Committee of the New England Council. Power capacity was estimated on the basis of flow available 20 per cent of the time. Exclusive of international sites located on the St. Croix and St. John rivers and exclusive of the Quoddy project, this report estimated that Maine has new power sites economically feasible for construction, totaling 263,000 kw.[35] The estimate for New England is 420,000 kw. Dual-purpose projects would bring it close to 500,000 kw. Thus more than half of the potential power is in Maine. Whereas the three southern New England states have already developed 82 per cent of their worth-while power projects, Maine's proportion is only 65 per cent.

After estimating the growth of power load in the next ten years, the committee concluded that if all the feasible undeveloped water power in New England exclusive of Maine were developed within ten years, it would provide only one-fourth of the estimated amount required. The difference would have to be made up through the use of steam.

In Maine it is possible that all the estimated increase in load could be carried by constructing new feasible hydro plants. Making allowance for dependability there is still more than enough feasible hydro power to carry the increase in load, and there will be some left over to apply to later years. . . . The total development of the feasible water power in Maine must wait for a corresponding load growth within the state.[36]

The report of the Federal Power Commission to Senator Leverett Saltonstall of Massachusetts challenging some of the conclusions of the New England Council was made public by him in July, 1949. The commission estimated that 3,119,000 kw. of water power is practical for development in New England under suitable load conditions, as contrasted with the New England Council estimate of 500,000 kw. Of this amount, 1,807,000 kw., or about 65 per cent, is in Maine. This includes Quoddy, certain international streams, and redevelopment of existing power plants with more regulatory storage.

The Federal Power Commission indicated three fundamental differences in approach in the two estimates of undeveloped power potentialities. The N.E.C. considered, first, independent power development at individual projects, instead of the entire river as the unit of development; second, single-purpose instead of multiple-purpose development; and third, projects which would be economically feasible with private financing, about twice the annual charges that would be incurred under federal financing. The commission also labeled "arbitrary" the N.E.C. approach in computing on the basis of stream flow available 20 per cent of the time. This "approach does not consider the needs for peaking power in the area from the standpoint of electric loads and the best use of hydro resource in conjunction with steam-electric plants."[37]

If one accepts the estimate of Maine's undeveloped power by the Federal Power Commission, the statement of the Public Utilities Commission may well be questioned that, although Maine has "numerous small water power sites that could be used, they are not economically possible of development in competition with steam generation."[38] But the most recent study of the latent power of Maine and New England, by George H. Arris, financial editor of the Providence *Journal-Bulletin,* supports the contention of the Maine commissioners.[39] Arris says that Maine needs more steam and not hydro plants in order to get more of its generating capacity into the "dependable capacity" category. His survey estimated that 358,975 kw. were feasible of development in Maine from an engineering standpoint, disregarding economics. Application of F.P.C. plans in certain parts of Maine would, he asserts, necessitate abandoning some big installations already in existence in exchange for all-inclusive installations; flood out a dam, two paper mills, and up-river property near Augusta; interfere with the Little Androscoggin River, which empties into the main stream almost in the heart of the Lewiston-Auburn urban area; cause heavy flowage on the lower Androscoggin, which is thickly dotted with industries depending on the river for power and processing water; and finally, create power at remote sites, some three hundred miles from the southwestern corner of the state, which Maine would not want because line losses and other expenses would make it cheaper to build steam-electric stations at the load centers.

The shortage of hydroelectric power in Maine within the past few years and the large amounts generated by steam are not due entirely to a lack of potential water power. The situation at first arose because many of the contemplated developments of the middle 'twenties were not undertaken after the defeat of the surplus power export bill. Subsequently, some of these large projects were put into operation and one is now under construction. Maine's more recent needs have been for firm power. These needs have been met by steam installations, which are not only dependable but also were quicker and cheaper to put in operation at the time. The status of numerous power sites which would have been too expensive to consider for development a few years ago has now changed. The disproportionate rise in cost of alternative sources of power—coal and oil—often makes formerly marginal water-power potentialities now very much worth while.

It would be grossly unfair to accuse national or state engineering staffs of exaggerating or underestimating the amount of power that may be made available at some future date. Genuine differences of opinion are recognized, and higher estimates are explained by such variables as the use of dissimilar load factors, different potential sites, the effect of storage reservoirs, redevelopment of existing plants, and engineering and (or) economic feasibility. More important is the difference in approach: single-purpose versus multiple-purpose projects, and independent power projects versus river-basin development. Furthermore, some estimates may have been mostly desk jobs, others perhaps only partly so. In the final analysis the great discrepancies in estimates show that many people are semantically confused. Although the agencies surveying the Maine and other New England power potentialities disagree on amounts, each (except the Public Utilities Commission, which confined its estimates to Maine) has applied its own formula consistently to all six states. All agree that Maine has between 50 and 65 per cent of the latent hydroelectric power of the region, except the Arris report, which gives Maine slightly more than 30 per cent. Obviously, then, the Fernald law does keep an undetermined quantity of undeveloped Maine power out of the other New England states.

# CHAPTER VI

## The Fernald Law: Opposition, Evaluation

Economists often assert that the most important reasons for determining the location of industry are accessibility of raw materials, proximity to market for the finished product, adequate supply of labor, cheap power, and financial assistance.[1] When the Fernald law was passed in 1909 and transmission lines were in their infancy, power was important in the location of industry. But the situation changed with the development of longer and more efficient transmission lines, decrease in power costs through mass production, availability of cheap steam power, and increase in other costs in the manufacturing process. Unless power is of major importance in production, as it is in a few industries, notably in aluminum production,[2] where it is dominant, new industries must now give greater consideration to proximity to markets and raw materials.

It would be difficult to name many industries that came to Maine solely because of cheap power. According to Edward E. Chase, the cotton textile and the woolen industries were the only ones in Maine which clearly owed their creation to water power, and there had been no important new development in these industries in Maine for forty years, except the natural growth of the best companies.[3] He excluded lumber and the pulp and paper industries because he considered that they depended as much upon the availability of raw materials and water transportation as upon power. Harold J. Boyle, financial editor of the Portland *Press Herald* and former member of the Maine Public Utilities Commission, observed that Maine's big mills and plants date from the last century.[4]

According to George D. Bearce, general manager of the Maine Seaboard Paper Company, the power supply was of secondary importance in selecting the location of the paper mill in Bucksport.[5] The availability of shipping facilities was the major reason in this instance. The location on tidewater affords shipment by boat, and there is also a rail connection for the shipment and receipt of raw materials, largely pulpwood, sulfur, and fuel. Next in importance was an available supply of fresh water, since the plant requires approximately 12,000,000 gallons a day. The power supply was secondary, because of modern transmission techniques.

The importance of the cost of power in attracting new industries depends on the extent to which it is the controlling element in cost of manufacture and distribution. Fifteen years ago, when the transmission issue was acute, the pulp and paper industry, the greatest industry in Maine, counted its power costs as representing from 2 to 4 per cent of the manufacturing cost. The textile industry counted power costs at 1.3 per cent.[6] For all manufacturing industries in 1939 the figure was about 3 per cent of all costs if one assumes that expenditure for fuel, as for electrical energy, is to be placed in this category.[7]

The iron and steel industry, although requiring greater power than others, and to a lesser extent the metal products industry will not enter the state of Maine because these three manufacturing operations are conducted almost invariably within easy access of raw materials.[8] That leaves the following industries with an installed capacity in horsepower for each $1,000 value of manufacturing cost: stone, clay, glass products, 2.264; lumber and allied products, 1.769; food and kindred products, 1.454; chemicals and allied products, 1.325; rubber products, 1.224; paper, printing, and so on, 1.210; textiles, 1.056. It should be noted that paper and textiles, Maine's greatest industries, require less power than the others, an indication that power did not bring them to Maine.[9]

The Power Survey Committee of the New England Council concluded that "except in a few industries the cost of power averages less than two per cent of the total value of manufactured products in New England industries. It is, therefore, obvious that the question of cheap power is not a determining factor in management decisions regarding location of business.[10]

Professor Lincoln Gordon neatly summarized the status of power in industrial location:[11]

> It is evident that low-cost power alone does not suffice to create an industrial area with any wide degree of diversification. The specifically power-oriented industries are few in number and limited in character. But where low-cost power and electro process raw materials occur in conjunction, the groundwork exists for industrialization on a substantial scale. This combination is the key to policy in industrial development around the public power projects of the Northwest and the Tennessee Valley.

These are huge multiple-purpose projects involving appreciably more than power, and some are closer to markets and materials than if they were at Bingham or Eastport, Maine.

At the hearing on the power bills, Walter S. Wyman, president of the Central Maine Power Company, stated that manufacturers regard Maine as an unfavorable place for industrial establishment.[12] A New Jersey plush manufacturer considered the area north of Boston rather wild country, and did not want to inspect a proposed site in Maine without a guide. Said Wyman, "The impression prevails to an astonishing extent among the manufacturers with whom we have to deal that the Eskimos, Polar Bears, and reindeer are giving the people of Maine a very hard fight to keep from being pushed off into the Atlantic Ocean." Wyman referred to a large power-consuming concern which the industrial department of the Central Maine Power Company had signed up for settlement in Maine, "but for that one concern that we have actually landed, we have negotiated with more than fifty. They have all been going somewhere, but that is the only one out of fifty that we have landed into the State of Maine."

The fact that Maine is in the extreme northeast, far from the big markets in New York, Philadelphia, Chicago, and other large cities tends to overcome the advantage of cheap power within the state. It was maintained that power companies could not develop additional power in Maine because markets for it were lacking. This prevented one large industry from coming to Maine. The company wanted power within eighteen months, but the Central Maine Power Company could not promise to have it on tap by that time. Colonel Francis H. Farnum asserted that this was one of the biggest electro-chemical companies in the world, and it wanted 18,000 primary hp. of cheap hydroelectric power. The finished plant would have cost $10,000,000 and the industry would have employed from 800 to 1,000 persons. Colonel Farnum said that to have supplied power as cheaply as this industry required would have necessitated the development of a plant generating 100,000 hp. But Maine had no market for the surplus 82,000 hp., and three years would be required to build the plant. Had the law permitted companies to develop a surplus and sell it in other states, arrangements probably could have been made for the manufacturing company to be supplied.[13] In short, if promises of power will attract industries, developed power will attract them much more readily. Mills go into a state after, but not before, rivers are developed.

Various attempts to prove the success of the Fernald law by listing the increased taxable property of utilities and industry in Maine since 1909 have been futile because they failed to show any connection between them. Maine's conservative interpretation of the terms "public purpose" and "public use" virtually precludes local financial assistance to new industry. Although communities sometimes agree by a majority vote to exempt prospective industries from local taxes, the practice is, strictly speaking, illegal. Chambers of commerce can, of course, make private grants to attract industry, and extralegal, low evaluation of property is another means of circumventing the rule. However, in some southern communities the combination of outright legal exemption for a period of years, a wage differential, and a public power system do attract new industries.

Harold F. Schnurle, legislative agent for the Central Maine Power Company, attributed Maine's industrial growth to six basic reasons, the first of which is the industry and character of the people.[14] Labor turnover, even during boom periods, has been a negligible factor. When a Maine man takes a job, he sticks to it for life. Other factors Schnurle listed were: second, a supply of basic raw materials; third, an unlimited supply of processing water of unusual quality; fourth, extensive water-power sources; fifth, a great transportation system; sixth, Maine's proximity to the richest markets in the world. He stated that within a radius of 450 miles live 26.68 per cent of the population of the United States, who purchase 31.70 per cent of all goods retailed in the country, and pay 35.06 per cent of the federal income tax. Schnurle said that approximately sixty new manufacturers had come to Maine in 1946. Although many of these plants were small, others were of substantial size and some were nationally known producers.

Maine's industrial growth, however, in terms of manufacturing employment between 1939 and 1947 was only 21 per cent, an increase well below the national and New England averages. For manufacturing purposes Maine rates below the New England average in climate, access to domestic and foreign raw materials, proximity to markets, and adequacy and cost of transportation facilities; but it rates better than the New England average in water supply and adequacy and cost of electric power.[15] Thus Maine's power magnet becomes somewhat demagnetized in competition with other principles of industrial location.

In continuing an evaluation of the success of the Fernald law in achieving its objectives, one must observe that the law did not prevent out-of-state interests from controlling all important power companies in the state, with a single and notable exception, in addition to some textile mills, two decades ago. Control was regained not because of the Fernald law but because the Insull empire crashed during the depression and Maine management had manipulated itself into strategic positions of control in the local hierarchy.

Despite the overwhelming popularity of the Fernald law when it was passed in 1909, a dissenting minority voiced disapproval. Not only did this group reflect the attitude of the corporate interests, but also the view that localism of this sort is unfortunate for the country itself. Senator John E. Warren, one of the chief opponents of the bill, was the only senator to question its constitutionality in the debate.[16]

> It is restrictive legislation. I believe that it is inexpedient and will do us harm. We have fortunately vast resources in our water power, but water power is good only as it can be used. It has indeed a potential value, but you must find a use for it. The only reason for confining it here to the State of Maine is the thought that if we do not wire it out of the State, manufacturers will come to the State of Maine and use it. It would be equally true that if we objected to the shipment of lumber beyond our State, that people might come here to build their houses, and, if we did not ship our potatoes, they might come here to eat them,

and, if we did not ship our Poland Spring Water, . . . they might come here to drink it. It is the potential power that is in it just as it is in a man's own person to do a day's work, and his day's work goes to waste unless he can find a place to put it. We might equally well enact a law that none of our citizens should go out of the State to work on the principle that we would like to have them put their work in here. It restricts the liberality of the State, or open principle that exists.

We hear a good deal about the Constitution. I am not an advocate of constitutionality, but I doubt very much whether we could put up a barrier of this kind.

The legislature of 1911 saw the Democrats in power for the first time in more than thirty years, controlling both houses and the governorship. In spite of hints later that this Democratic landslide was a result of the Fernald law passed in the previous session, the law proved popular with legislators as well as with the public. Governor Frederick W. Plaisted (D.) supported it.[17] The House in the 1911 session supported the Fernald law, and passed a resolution that no corporation engaged in the transmission of power should be granted unrestricted rights of eminent domain.[18] The results of the 1910 elections may more appropriately be attributed to charges of extravagance of the Fernald administration, the fact that the Governor had alienated the more radical prohibitionists by vetoing a bill which made imprisonment the sole punishment for certain violations of the liquor laws,[19] and the nation-wide swing of the pendulum at that time.

In 1911 Representative Howard Davies of Yarmouth introduced a bill that would have prohibited foreign corporations from engaging in the business of generating electricity by water power within the state of Maine. Reported out of committee "ought not to pass," the bill was held over for the next session of the legislature because it was introduced late in the 1911 session.[20] The report of the judiciary committee that it "ought not to pass" killed the proposal in 1913.[21] This extreme measure was occasioned by an attempt of New England power interests to obtain a special charter making an exception to the Fernald law and enabling them to raid the territory of the Maine power companies, presumably with the idea of buying them up at their own price for a fine business opportunity in Maine.[22] In this same (1913) session the attempt to permit interstate transmission of power made little progress. Likewise an attempt to abolish the exception to the Fernald law permitting transmission of power by electric railways failed. The first change was felt to be too drastic, and the amendment would have made it possible for street railways to carry any amount of power to other states for any purpose.[23]

In 1915 an attempt was made to amend the Fernald law by giving the Public Utilities Commission discretionary power to permit out-of-state transmisison with the right to terminate this grant upon two years' notice.[24] Passage of this amendment would have made the Maine law similar to other nontransmission laws. Senator Cole and Senator Garcelon supported the bill, maintaining that the state was fully protected by the provision for the recall of power if it were needed locally, that the disadvantage of an extreme location and excess freight rates hampered Maine industrially, and that comparatively little power could be developed under a nontransmission policy. The opposition contended that this would be only the entering wedge for unlimited transmission which would make Maine merely a power station for other states. The proposal was indefinitely postponed.[25]

The contest was resumed in the 1917 session with a new proposal, the Cole bill, designed to permit out-of-state transmission on approval of the Public Utilities Commission when rates within the territory served by the corporation were reduced to a schedule not exceeding five cents per kilowatt-hour for lighting and one cent for heating and power. Little interest was displayed in this bill, and the argument that power problems should be consolidated under the jurisdiction of the Public Utilities Commission did not carry much weight. More important was the belief that once surplus power got across state lines and into interstate commerce the state would have no authority to recall it.[26]

In 1923, Clarence C. Stetson of Bangor, formerly with the United States Department of Commerce, bitterly attacked Maine's nontransmission policy as provincial and selfish. He also took the unique position that Maine should not try to become an industrial state.[27] Because of the lack of a large supply of raw materials other than timber, he judged it unsound to attempt to force the growth of new industries. Maine's immediate future, he asserted, rested not in industrial development but on the fulfillment of a four-point program: the development and conservation of natural resources; the protection and enlargement of fisheries; the expansion of the summer trade; and, most important of all, the encouragement of farmers, the restoration of abandoned farms, and the improvement of social and economic conditions in rural districts. The majority of voters undoubtedly accept this program, but they reject his main premise. In like fashion, George Otis Smith of Skowhegan, director of the United States Geological Survey and later chairman of the Federal Power Commission, attacked Maine's power embargo in a series of open letters in 1924,[28] but the issue did not become acute until 1927 and 1929.

Before the Insull interests penetrated the state, Governor Brewster referred to "the very definite assurance of the one in control of the chief corporation concerned that under no circumstances would an attack be permitted upon the Constitutionality of this [Fernald] law."[29] This promise was kept. The strategy was to effect the transmission of surplus power not by judicial decree but through the legislature and popular referendum. In 1925 the legislature agreed to permit the sale outside the state of any power generated from the tides at Passamaquoddy Bay, and this was supported in a referendum. When, in spite of the Fernald law, the Insulls secured control and established themselves in Maine, the power companies began to agitate for the right to transmit surplus power to other states. Realizing the strong sentiment for the Fernald law, they sought permission, in 1927, to transmit surplus power only, with a guaranty that the Maine market would be served first. Six power bills, four for the transmission of surplus, were introduced in this session, most important of which were the Smith bill (divorce system) and the Oakes bill (compact system).

The divorce system, planned by five of Maine's ablest corporation lawyers, was an example of shrewd Yankee ingenuity which attempted to separate the generation from the transmission of hydroelectric power so that, although Maine's surplus could be sold outside, this surplus would still be controlled by the state. The Smith bill aimed at creating a transmission company to do an interstate business which would be regulated by the national government just as railroads were. It would, however, be prohibited from generating any power and could obtain power from generating companies only as approved by the Maine Public Utilities Commission. The commission could allow the sale of nothing but surplus power not needed in Maine to the transmission company. The national government could regulate interstate rates and interstate contracts, but it could not regulate the companies manufacturing the power any more than it could regulate the manufacture of boots and shoes about to be shipped out of the state. It was thought that as long as the state kept control of the *source* of its power by exercising its exclusive right to control and amend the charters of the generating corporations, it would have the entire situation in hand.

In answer to the rural opposition to the Smith bill, Walter S. Wyman, president of the Central Maine Power Company, offered an amendment whereby every public utility licensed to sell surplus power to the transmission company would spend, for ten years only, one-half of its gross receipts from such sale in building rural lines within the state, with a limit of $250,000 a year to be spent by any one company.[30] The Smith bill as amended passed both houses of the legislature, subject to a popular referendum. But it was vetoed by Governor Brewster,[31] and his veto was sustained. The Governor said that the largest electrical interests in the country had entered Maine within the past two years with full knowledge of the restrictive law. Primarily because the Attorney General advised that the act was likely to mean loss of state control, it was rejected.

At the Republican state convention in 1928 no recommendation was made on the transmission issue, but the platform called for a study of the water resources to permit the legislature to "promptly legislate in accordance with the facts thus obtained . . . and the State should in no wise surrender its control over the Water Power resources within its borders."[32] The Governor and council ordered such a study on November 27, 1928, but the result was a meager and unsatisfactory pamphlet authorized by the power committee of the Maine Development Commission.[33]

In 1929 the power companies came back to the legislature with the Smith-Carlton bill, precisely the same as that of the previous session and with the same legal doubts attaching. An order was introduced calling for $10,000, to enable the state to obtain an opinion on the legal aspects of the divorce system from former Justice Charles Evans Hughes. It was learned that the Central Maine Power

Company had received an opinion from Judge Hughes, and that the latter had told former Governor Owen Brewster, who consulted him, that he could not advise the state until the power companies would say that they would not request any further information of him. Since the companies did not know what opinions might be desired later, no such release was forthcoming. A subsequent order stipulated the names of former Attorney General George W. Wickersham or John W. Davis, but it was rejected because of the expense in time and money and the feeling that the opinion would settle nothing. The legislature's attempted face-saving device was the adoption of an entirely inadequate amendment to the effect that if one section of the act should be declared unconstitutional, the entire act would be null and void. During the course of its progress in the legislature, the power companies accepted an amendment which provided for an excise tax of 4 per cent on the gross operating revenues of the companies receiving permission to sell surplus power. This bill was passed, subject to a popular referendum.[34]

With a few exceptions, most of the legislative debates on the proposition were particularistic and superficial, relying upon prejudice, emotion, and sometimes minor issues. Of interest, but fortunately not typical, is the following:[35]

> God Almighty placed no coal or no oil in the State of Maine, so far as we know. He did place three rivers or four rivers or perhaps five or more, and if he had wanted them in Massachusetts, Connecticut, or Rhode Island, He would have put them there. He placed them up here for the benefit of the citizenship of the State of Maine, I believe, and unless we see fit to thwart His intention, we will leave them there and use them there up to the amount that the citizenship of Maine will need them, not only today but in future generations.

Former Governor Percival P. Baxter, who in 1927 had opposed the Smith bill and pleaded for caution and deliberation, in 1929 came out in support of the Smith-Carlton bill.[36] He did not favor burdening the Public Utilities Commission with the task of determining and controlling the contracts for surplus power because he felt that the commissioners were not informed and had been absorbed in other problems. He preferred a special board on power export to supervise this function. He asserted that the power companies had changed their attitude. He asserted that the Honorable

Harvey D. Eaton of Waterville, then president of the Central Maine Power Company, once told him that when they were ready to take power out of Maine nobody could stop them.[37] During that period the companies were interested in unrecallable and unlimited export, but now they were willing both to export only surplus and to make its recall certain. Further, the state had two ways of controlling the amount of surplus to be exported. The Smith-Carlton bill was an adaptation of the Baxter amendment to charters. The greater right of total exclusion under the Baxter amendment included the lesser right of limiting the amount of power exported. Furthermore, the state could control the exportation of electricity by its taxing power. The Smith-Carlton bill provided for a tax on exported power. This tax could be made so heavy that export would be unprofitable, and could be used as a last resort in controlling power companies. Therefore, the former Governor maintained that his position was unchanged, that he had never opposed surplus export, provided it could be recalled. Although he asserted that it was the power companies that had changed, one must conclude that his attitude toward corporations had undergone change likewise.

The power companies, in agitating for permission to transmit surplus power, claimed that the Fernald law restricted power development because no new industries were attracted to provide market for further development; that if power would attract industry, developed power would attract them more readily; that mass production would lower the cost per unit; and that taxable wealth would be increased. Walter S. Wyman estimated that fifteen years after passage of the Smith-Carlton bill Maine would receive $2,000,000 a year in taxes on property not existing in the state at that time. It was estimated that the Central Maine Power Company had over 125,000,000 kw-h of surplus power running to waste in 1929, and that Maine was capable of generating much more, with the owners ready and willing to make immediate development if a market could be found.[38] This power is not comparable with firm power, which must be ready on demand. Consequently, it is less valuable and is sold at a much cheaper rate when available. It is often difficult to find a market for dump power, and none existed in Maine. But power companies in Massachusetts would welcome the opportunity to use Maine's part-time power, thereby enabling them to shut down some of their more expensive steam equipment as long as dump power could be supplied. Maine power companies pleaded that if they were allowed to transmit surplus power, this delivery would be maintained only until there should be a local demand, for they still preferred to sell near the source.

An investigation by the Federal Trade Commission in 1932 of public utility corporations included testimony relative to the campaign for the Smith-Carlton bill in Maine in 1929.[39] Walter S. Wyman stated that he consulted the Middle West Company and Martin Insull before the campaign was undertaken, and that no limit was set on the total amount to be spent. Campaign expenses were borne by the New England Public Service Company (NEPSCO).[40] Expenditures were transferred to NEPSCO to avoid the charge that power companies were including the cost in their expense accounts. Expenditures of NEPSCO would not be part of the operating costs. The power officials considered this a fair arrangement, since NEPSCO owned all but four shares of the voting stock of the Central Maine Power Company.

The state campaign was in the hands of three men: Edward F. Merrill, Carroll N. Perkins, and (in a private capacity) State Senator John W. Leland. After canvassing the entire state together, they separated, and each concentrated on a section of the state. They selected for each county a campaign chairman, and often assistants, who were told to ask for more money whenever they needed it. No county chairman or payee was required to make any report of expenditures, although some did so.

Dempster MacMurphy of the publicity department of Middle West Utilities of Chicago was sent to Maine to assist in publicity work at a cost of $4,498.87. Among the items of expense charged to the campaign were fliers printed in English and French, meals supplied on election day (presumably to keep election workers present during the entire day), 1,000 tire covers containing a legend about the referendum, and a donation of $2,000 to the Franklin Memorial Hospital. Between August 26 and September 9, 1929, Gannett newspapers were purchased as follows: $10,025.46 for 106,291 copies of the *Press Herald,* 81,554 copies of the *Evening Express,* and 33,316 of the *Sunday Telegram.* Advertising expenses were incurred in various papers, which included higher rates for guaranteed space. Free copies of these papers were distributed to nonsubscribers, and it was reported that newsboys received as high as two cents a copy.[41]

In a general statement of expenses incurred, expenditures were classified as follows: newspaper advertising, $20,842.66; circulars, posters, electrotypes, $33,424.10; services and expenses, company representatives, $131,966.54; clerks (not regular), $1,111.65; services and expenses, New England Public Service Company employees, $415.76; auto hire, $593.16; D. MacMurphy, $4,498.87; meetings and miscellaneous, $1,247.15; services and expenses, intercompany, $2,028.77; total $196,139.66. This was later amended to the final total of $199,815.66.

Company officials made radio broadcasts and supplied speakers at various meetings and at some of the county fairs. Since NEPSCO owned the stock of a number of manufacturing establishments in Maine, efforts were made to get prominent industrialists in these factories to support the surplus export bill and even to use their influence with employees.

The Central Maine Power Company claimed that it was well known throughout the state that they were anxious for the vote to be favorable on the measure, and insisted that the campaign was undertaken because they believed the passage of the act would benefit the state and country as well as themselves. But the strong sentiment of the people of Maine for the Fernald law, in spite of open attempts of the power companies to get it repudiated, is shown by the testimony of President Walter S. Wyman in response to a question whether it was known that campaigners were paid for their services.

*Answer:* "I should think so; I think that the knowledge that the company was active in trying to get this law passed was so general and so thoroughly known to everybody that probably no man who exerted himself at all for the passage of it was regarded as an independent person who was working just on his own judgment."

*Question:* "Now, were there not some independent people up there working on their own judgment who were not paid?"

*Answer:* "That I do not know, sir."

*Question:* "You do not mean to imply that all of the people who acted for this act were paid, do you?"

*Answer:* "Well, there was quite a lot of them paid, I guess."

Wyman also stated that the company had plans for the development of the Kennebec and other Maine rivers of around 500,000 hp. at a cost of about $100,000,000 over a period of fifteen to twenty years. By 1925 they felt that unless surplus could be exported the development program would have to be stopped. Each time an additional development was put into service a large amount of surplus power came on the market immediately and this had to be sold and absorbed until the Maine customers could use it, as otherwise it became too great a burden on the company to carry. When the act was defeated, most of the development program was abandoned.

According to further testimony, the company considered that its profit from selling waste power every year would have been substantially greater than the cost of the referendum campaign, and that an intensive campaign was necessary because no general election came at the time and no candidates were interested in their own election. It attributed the defeat of the bill to "the fear that if it went out that Maine would become a power station, that industries would not come in, that if a company could sell it outside, that they would sell it rather than develop the State of Maine."

This omits, however, the strong rural sentiment which opposed the sale of power to other states when many farmers at home lacked it, and also the staunch anticorporation attitude. The opposition was spearheaded by the Portland *Evening News,* edited by Dr. Ernest Gruening. Feature articles and editorials during the summer of 1929 were intensified for three weeks before the vote. In a tone similar to that of the editor's *The Public Pays,*[42] antiutility propaganda was masterfully displayed with slogans: "For lower rates vote No"; "Shall the voters of Maine become Yes-men for Samuel Insull?"; "Insull against the state of Maine"; "A vote of No is a conservative vote—a safe vote"; "If you are in doubt you had better retain the power. You always can give the power away if you want to do so."[43]

On June 8, 1929, about two hundred citizens (business and professional men and women, Grangers, and representatives of women's clubs) met at Augusta and formed the Consumers' Protective League to retain power as a means of furthering rural electrification and reducing rates. The political basis of this league is not entirely clear. There were rumors, subsequently denied, that its actual objectives were to elect a United States senator and a governor, and to build up an organization of liberals favoring public ownership. The league maintained that it had no party workers and had collected less than $1,000, which was spent for gathering data for printing.

A large number of Maine farmers opposed the transmission of power to other states, arguing that all Maine interests should first be supplied and that it would then be found that no surplus was available for outside consumption.[44] Because of the marvelous electrical age in which we live, the state of Maine, within twenty-five years, would need all its power.[45] The Grange adopted a resolution at Augusta, in December, 1928, opposing exportation of power, and petitions with approximately 6,000 signatures of voters were sent to the legislature.

Many leaders campaigned actively against the surplus export law, including Owen Brewster, Mayor John Wilson of Bangor, and State Senator Paul Frederick Slocum of Standish. The arguments were that Maine power should not be sold in other states when large areas in rural Maine lacked it, that exported power would be sold for five mills or less when domestic lighting in Maine was nine cents, a ratio of 18 to 1, and that much money was being spent to obtain an affirmative vote which would be a sellout to the Insulls. These arguments were dramatic.

The replies were more difficult to comprehend: that firm power required for domestic and rural lighting and dump power for transmission are not comparable; that rural electrification depends on distribution costs and not on the availability of power;[46] and that transmission of surplus power might benefit Maine as well as Insull. Likewise, the opposition paper overemphasized the fact that the Cumberland County Power and Light Company used a steam auxiliary that summer from the Knightsville plant, again confusing firm and dump power with the idea that Maine had a power deficit instead of a surplus.

In reporting their victory after the referendum the Portland *Evening News* attributed it to the Consumers' Protective League, with a skeleton organization and a pittance of friends, supported by that paper. "Apparently these forces furnished the stimulation which brought the voters to the polls on their own initiative." It would have been more accurate, however, to have stated that the Maine people voted against it not because of any newspaper or league, but because the ordinary voter feared that the exportation of dump power would prejudice local interests and detract from the historic policy of keeping Maine power within the state as a means of stimulating home industry. Actually, the vote was close in nearly all counties, but in spite of the expensive campaign of the power companies they lost the referendum approximately 64,000 to 54,000. Heavy rain in eastern Maine and showers in other parts of the state undoubtedly helped to keep down the vote.[47]

The results of the congressional investigation of power and holding companies reacted very unfavorably on corporations throughout the country. This and the charge that the corporations controlled the Republican leaders in the 1932 elections probably did more to aid the victory of the Democrats in the Maine elections of September, 1932, than any other single issue.

It is somewhat surprising that the power companies spent almost $200,000 to try to amend the Fernald law, when it is probably unconstitutional and might have been tested in the courts for much less money. But it has not been so tested, and nothing indicates that it will be, at least on the initiative of the power companies. They appealed to the voters, but will not challenge them in the courts. They accepted the result of the 1929 referendum; in fact, eighteen years later they had representatives appear before a legislative committee to support the power embargo. Apparently the power companies preferred to forego extra profit and seek the good will of the voters of the state, who, after all, control corporation charters.

In the opinion of John T. Gould, before the 1929 referendum the power companies had operated "on a policy so public-be-damned that they appeared somewhat silly when they shifted around and began trying to be good fellows. Nobody who knows the setup in Maine credits the power companies with pure hearts and clean hands, but since that referendum an effort has been made to shake as many hands as possible and smile heartily at the right times."[48] Not only was a change in attitude good "public relations," but also the corporations, once again under Maine control, were soon to become staunch supporters of the embargo law. An accelerated demand for power soon took up the slack in power supply. Subsequently the companies have at times experienced stringent regulation of their corporate structure by the Securities and Exchange Commission; likewise, it is noted that the Federal Power Commission has become more active, and its jurisdiction has been enlarged. Now, thanks to the Fernald law, the Maine power companies are among the few large utilities in the country not participating in interstate commerce. Hence they remain outside the jurisdiction of the Federal Power Commission. The power companies like it that way. Thus the interests of the power companies and the voters coincide to the extent that the power embargo law precludes the former from additional national regulation and at the same time keeps power at home as the voters wish.

Three power measures were introduced in the legislature in 1947. One would have authorized the governor and council to enter into interstate compacts with the other New England states for the development and improvement of rivers flowing through two or more states. Another proposed to give the governor and council authority to accept money made available by the federal government for the construction or expansion of hydroelectric power reservoirs, dams, or generation plants on Maine rivers. The third would have authorized interstate transmission of hydroelectric power.[49]

Reputedly put forward by the Hearst newspapers, George Brady, a Boston editorial writer, appeared before the legislative public utilities committee and declared that the Fernald law had retarded Maine's growth. He read a statement from Henry J. Kaiser, who predicted a race to build industry in New England if Maine would export hydroelectric power. The statement read in part:[50]

> The people of Maine, Massachusetts and the other New England states can be the richest people in the nation or the poorest.
>
> If you develop your woefully neglected water power you can expand your industries tremendously and create thousands of new ones.
>
> But if you continue to waste power—your most valuable natural asset—you will lose factory after factory until your famous manufacturing centers will decline in production and prosperity.

Brady told of a bill pending in Congress to survey the full potentialities of Maine rivers for power development. He said that the bill was an attempt to obtain $50,000,000 for Maine, and argued that if the Maine legislature refused to sanction export the state would not get federal aid. He also predicted lower residential rates within the state if the bill were passed.

President William B. Skelton of the Central Maine Power Company contended that the three bills "aim directly at public ownership and control. We are opposed to the repeal of the Fernald Act because it will destroy control by the State over a natural resource that is a magnet to draw industry to the state." According to Harold F. Schnurle, legislative agent for the company, the legislation stemmed from "a source which has neither a direct nor an indirect interest in the welfare of the people of Maine." He said that the proponents were unaware of the fact that the price of electric energy is only one of the factors involved in the total cost of production of most manufactured goods. Furthermore, in a New England compact, Maine, "which is reputed to have at least 50 per cent of all the undeveloped water power in New England, would have one-sixth of the voting power in any tribunal created for such a purpose."

Albert C. Blanchard of the Bangor Hydro-Electric Company maintained that there was no demand in Maine for a T.V.A. or a Hoover Dam, and added that he believed in private enterprise instead of governmental operation. Senator Brooks Savage of Skowhegan said that Maine was in no desperate need of outside help to develop its power. Senate President George D. Varney of Kittery opposed the legislation "because it takes away the power of the legislature and turns it over to the governor and council. It is the duty of the legislature to decide whether or not we want to go into a compact with other states for development of hydroelectric power."

Needless to say, the public power and export power bills did not get far in the legislature. The House accepted without debate an adverse committee report on the acts.[51] The public power issue overshadowed the transmission proposal in 1947. It would now be difficult to poll the opinion of voters or legislators solely on the transmission issue because it is inextricably connected with federal aid and public power.

As we have seen, the original purposes of the Fernald law were, first, to attract new industries to Maine; second, to keep the power away from the trusts; and third, to extend rural electrification. But it is logical to conclude, from the evidence presented, that the

Fernald law has not made Maine an industrial state and cannot do so; and that it delayed but did not keep out the trusts. That a restrictive policy cannot solve the distribution problem for rural electrification will be shown in chapter ix. Thus, the law has not accomplished its original purposes. Its one achievement to date has been to prevent, or at least stall off, federal regulation of Maine power, a corollary to the preclusion of heterogeneous trusts.

# CHAPTER VII

## The Constitutional Issue

With the sentiment of the people of Maine strongly favorable to the embargo of hydroelectric power, Maine's future place in any regional or national power setup will depend primarily upon the constitutionality of the Fernald law. This is the key question: Has a state the right to enact a law prohibiting corporations from transmitting to other states electric power generated from water power? The controversy is largely one of state rights versus national rights, of the reserved power of the state versus the commerce clause of the national constitution. The constitutional pegs upon which Maine apparently hangs the Fernald law are the right to legislate for the general welfare (conservation) under the reserved powers of the state[1] and the rule that "Corporations shall . . . forever be subject to the general laws of the State."[2] The fact that the Fernald law refers only to corporations suggests regulation of corporations. Here we have an explicit state law; the celebrated *Gibbons v. Ogden* decision, however, gave Congress plenary control over interstate commerce, but later decisions gave the states limited concurrent authority, usually for quarantine and health laws, safety, and morality, if the regulation was reasonable and Congress had not acted.[3]

Although a number of decisions may be cited on both sides, unfortunately none deals with a set of circumstances that parallel the Maine situation. This may be partially explained by the fact that Maine is the only state having a policy of virtually complete restriction, so no case including the same points has yet arisen.[4]

It is interesting to observe that the utility commissioners themselves admit uncertainty. The Special Committee on Water Power of the

National Association of Railroad and Utilities Commissioners made a survey of nonexport laws and concluded that "such provisions may become of prime importance in the future in preserving to the people of the state the first call on its natural resources, but the fact should also be noted in connection with this provision that its constitutionality is by no means free from doubt."[5]

One must approach a discussion of the constitutionality of the Fernald law with caution. Representative Hale of Maine quoted Professor Felix Frankfurter to the effect that no good lawyer would express a positive opinion on its validity.[6] The timing factor is vital to the answer. Was the law constitutional during the controversies of the late 'twenties with the Court of "nine old men," or under the "Roosevelt Court" of the late 'thirties, or under the Court of 1950, which seems more sympathetic toward decentralization? Can Maine continue to stall off a decision four more decades to a Court of 1990? How far may one rely on *stare decisis,* in the manner of 1930 or 1950? To what extent are minority opinions, particularly of the 5 to 4 or 6 to 3 variety, valid for precedent? The political factor also is important. The action of Congress under the Constitution, particularly its definition of navigable rivers, and the law revitalizing the Federal Power Commission in 1930 are relevant.

The argument for the Fernald law rests on three main tenets: first, Maine is not regulating interstate commerce because virtually no Maine power crosses state lines; and (or) second, the law is a conservation measure for Maine people and is valid under reserved powers; and (or) third, Congress can delegate, actively or passively, authority for the states to work out some of their own power problems. The opposite view denies the validity of these tenets, and extends the reverse of the third with the contention that Congress has already established a license policy which the Federal Power Commission has not yet put into effect in the state of Maine.

The contention that the Fernald law regulated hydroelectric power before it entered interstate commerce was made forty years ago, when the law was passed. Proponents admitted that when power once became part of interstate commerce, the state's right to regulate it ceased. The argument is still advanced in some quarters. And the noted lumbering case *Coe v. Errol,*[7] decided by the United States Supreme Court in 1886, established a precedent for the validity of the Fernald law. It declared that products do not become subjects of interstate commerce until they are committed to the common carrier for transportation to the state of their destination or have started on their passage to that state. Until then, products are subject to the jurisdiction of the first state. From this decision it appears that Maine might control its hydroelectric power from the time it leaves the generator until its journey outside the state begins. Also, in the E. C. Knight case, the Supreme Court said that manufacture was not commerce: "an article which is manufactured for export to another state does not of itself make it an article of interstate commerce, and the intent of the manufacture does not determine the time when the article or product passes from the control of the state and belongs to commerce."[8]

Two child labor cases also distinguished between manufacture and commerce. In *Hammer v. Dagenhart*[9] the Court said that a federal statute attempting to keep products made by child labor out of interstate commerce was invalid because the law did not regulate commerce but manufacture. The child labor tax law of Congress was nullified by the Court in *Bailey v. Drexel Furniture Company.*[10] This involved the taxing power and not interstate commerce; nevertheless, the same principle was applied—that the law regulated hours of labor in factories and mines, which was a state right. More recently the Court again took this conservative view in *Railroad Retirement Board v. Alton Railroad,*[11] a case involving a compulsory retirement pension act, and in *Carter v. Carter Coal Company*[12] the Court refused to allow Congress to control wages, hours, and working conditions in coal mines because they are matters anterior to the beginning of an interstate transaction. This view was somewhat strengthened also by a decision in *Utah Power and Light Company v. Pfost,*[13] which recognized state control of electricity for a tax purpose. An Idaho statute taxed the generation of all electric current in that state. Some of this energy was transmitted to Utah, and the Utah Power Company, a Maine corporation, maintained that the Idaho tax law was a burden on interstate commerce. But the United States Supreme Court recognized the distinction between manufacture and transmission, ruling that a state tax on generating was not a tax on interstate commerce and citing the E. C. Knight case as a precedent.

The only difference in analogy is whether the Court would make any distinction between taxing power and the prohibition of interstate commerce, or of controlling the manufacture in order to prevent such interstate commerce from being carried on. Granted that a difference exists between a tax entirely for revenue purposes and a tax as a regulative measure, the Court used some rather strong language in stating that generation is local, "and hence the commerce clause of the Constitution does not prevent the state from exercising exclusive control over manufacture." Producing electricity within a state is purely intrastate business, "subject to state taxation and control." And a quotation from *The Daniel Ball*[14]—"whenever a commodity has *begun to move* as an article of trade from one State to another, commerce in that commodity between the States has commenced"—shows that possibly the Fernald law may not interfere with interstate commerce, as hydroelectric power has not "begun to move" as an article of commerce. Thus, too, in the dissent of Mr. Justice Holmes in *Pennsylvania v. West Virginia,*[15] he supported the state law restricting the transmission of natural gas because the statute reached the natural gas before it began to move in commerce of any kind. "I think that the products of a State until they are actually started to a point outside it may be regulated by the State notwithstanding the commerce clause."

In defending the power embargo on the basis of reserved powers, *Geer v. Connecticut* is one of the earliest cases exhibiting circumstances somewhat analogous to the Maine situation. The point at issue was whether Connecticut had the right to regulate the killing of wild game within its borders and forbid transmission outside. Since wild game belong to nobody in particular until reduced to possession, it was held that they are common to all, and police regulations may direct the manner in which they may be enjoyed, and the Court said in part:

> The preservation of such animals . . . is a matter of public interest, and it is within the police power of the state, as representative of the people in their united sovereignty, to make such laws as will best preserve such game, and secure its beneficial use in the future to the citizens, and to that end it may adopt any reasonable regulations, not only as to time and manner in which such game may be taken and killed, but also imposing limitations upon the right of property in such game after it has

been reduced to possession.[16] . . . The right to preserve game flows from the undoubted existence in the state of a police power to that end, which may be none the less efficiently called into play because by doing so interstate commerce may be remotely or indirectly affected.[17]

But in a vigorous dissenting opinion Mr. Justice Field said, "When any animal . . . is lawfully killed for the purpose of food or other uses of man, it becomes an article of commerce, and its use cannot be limited to the citizens of one state to the exclusion of citizens of another state."[18]

The principle of the Geer case was applied later in *Lacoste v. Department of Conservation,*[19] when a Louisiana law placing a severance tax on wild fur-bearing animals and alligators was upheld. The Court ruled that the wild life belonged to the state, and it could make the payment of the tax a condition precedent to the divesture of the state's title. This did not constitute an interference with interstate commerce, even though many of the skins were to be shipped to other states. And in the McCarter case the Court ruled that the state of New Jersey was justified under its police power in passing a law preventing riparian owners from diverting the fresh waters of a stream into another state. In rendering the decision Mr. Justice Holmes said:[20]

We are of the opinion, further, that the constitutional power of a state to insist that its natural advantages shall remain unimpaired by its citizens is not dependent upon any nice estimate of the extent of present use or speculation as to future needs. . . . It [the state] finds itself in possession of what all admit to be a great public good, and what it has it may keep and give no one a reason for its will. . . . A man cannot acquire a right to property by his desire to use it in commerce among the states. Neither can he enlarge his otherwise limited and qualified right to the same end.

The statement of Mr. Justice Holmes, that "what it [the state] has it may keep and give no one a reason for its will," implies that the Maine legislature can retain hydroelectric power without giving a reason for so doing. This statement was characteristic of Justice Holmes, who hesitated to rule that state regulations interfered with or burdened interstate commerce. While he was with a majority of the justices in 1908, his famous dissents after that date show that the precedents were then established against his view.[21] More recently, however, Holmes's views are being revived. *Sligh v. Kirkwood*[22] is additional evidence that Maine's restrictive policy is valid. Here the Court upheld a Florida statute forbidding the sale or shipment of immature citrus fruits because the matter was primarily local and affected interstate commerce indirectly; therefore it was within the range of the state's police power until Congress acted.

One of the cases supporting a retention policy is less significant because it was decided by a state court and was never challenged in the federal courts. This was *Kirk v. State Board of Irrigation.* Kirk secured a state permit to use the waters of a river to generate power on condition that none be sent to other states. He appealed to the Nebraska courts against this limitation, but the right to prevent the transmission was upheld. The court said in part:[23]

> This State then has such a proprietary interest in the running water of its streams and in the beneficial use thereof that it may transfer a qualified ownership or right of use thereof. When it grants such ownership or right of use it may impose such limitations and conditions as its public policy demands. Under such circumstances the State may reserve such a right of ownership and control of the beneficial use of running waters of the streams as will enable it to prohibit the transmission thereof beyond the confines of the State.

The Geer and Lacoste cases dealt with wild game, and the McCarter case with water, natural resources. The natural resources were owned by the state, which had absolute right to make such qualifications as it saw fit in allowing them to be reduced to the possession of individuals. From these cases the rule may be deduced that the state may regulate natural resources for conservation purposes until they are actually reduced to possession. The truth of this was shown in *Ohio Oil Company v. Indiana,*[24] when the Court held that a statute intended to prevent the *waste* of natural gas was valid, but that after the gas was reduced to possession the state's power to regulate it ceased. The Geer, Lacoste, and McCarter cases regulated natural resources *before* the reduction to possession had been completed.

The decision most nearly approaching an opinion on Maine's power embargo was rendered in *Pennsylvania v. West Virginia.* Although the majority of the Court opposed confirming the idea of a local preference for the use of natural gas, it should be noted that the case was argued, reargued twice after that, and finally decided by a vote of 6 to 3. Such a close case decided little beyond the particular issue submitted at the time. The dissent of Mr. Justice Holmes has also influenced other justices recently:[25] "I see nothing in the commerce clause to prevent a State from giving a preference to its inhabitants in the enjoyment of its natural advantages; . . . the Constitution does not prohibit a State from securing a reasonable preference for its own inhabitants in the enjoyment of its products even when the effect of its law is to keep property within its boundaries that otherwise would have passed outside."

In much the same vein of thought, Mr. Justice McReynolds dissented in the Louisiana shrimp embargo case, suggesting that a state may regulate the transportation of wild things in ways not permitted when wheat is the subject matter.[26] In 1949 Mr. Justice Frankfurter dissented on the issue of a state withholding from interstate commerce a product derived from local raw materials to satisfy a local need: "For me it has not been put to rest by *Pennsylvania v. West Virginia.*"[27] Four justices dissented in *Hood v. Du Mond.* They felt that the commerce clause should not be stretched to forbid New York's attempt to protect the healthful supply of milk, even though some of the consumers happened to live in Troy, New York. Mr. Justice Frankfurter opined that a state is not barred from licensing an activity merely because it is interstate commerce. Two opposing philosophies were outlined by Mr. Justice Black. Whereas state trade barriers to interstate commerce bring about "Balkanization" of commerce in the United States, others prefer this to governmental regulation of free enterprise. "To them the spectre of Bureaucracy is more frightening than Balkanization."[28]

Professor Arthur W. Macmahon of Columbia University recently raised the question whether federalism could be revitalized by liberating the frozen energies of the states. With respect to the Fernald law this would mean a relaxation of the restraints of the commerce clause as a restriction on state action. Such devolution could be achieved in either of two ways. First, Congress could legislate for state regulation, with the Court not listening too closely to congressional legislation which might be judged not entirely relevant. Second, the Supreme Court could take the initiative; the silence of Congress would mean consent.

If Congress does not desire uniformity in regulation under an overburdened Federal Power Commission, it might step out of the picture on its own initiative and delegate jurisdiction to the states, either with or without national standards. But this raises a constitutional question: Can Congress delegate its power to the states? The courts are unwilling to make any blanket formula. They have been anxious to answer no more than the actual points in question, and have been careful to make no dictum indicative of precedents for this type of case.[29] On the other hand, by passing the Webb-Kenyon Act and the Ashurst-Summers Act, which, respectively, forbade interstate shipments of liquor and prison-made goods into states regulating or prohibiting the sale of such products, Congress specifically sanctioned state regulation. The Court ruled that the exceptional nature of the subject regulated (liquor) was the basis for the exceptional regulatory power exerted; many times the Court upheld liquor regulation which would have been repugnant to the Bill of Rights had its like been applied in other matters.[30] The Court sustained the restrictions on prison-made goods on the basis of police regulations, mentioning precedents such as diseased livestock, lottery tickets, food and drugs, liquor, immoral women, and kidnapped persons.[31] Thus the scope of federal police power was widened.

Could Congress likewise permit state regulation of hydroelectric power? But it is difficult to classify electricity under police power. A somewhat better analogy is the judicial decision upholding the McCarran Act, which permitted some state regulation of insurance. The Court said that state regulation discriminating against interstate commerce which would be invalid under the commerce clause in the absence of congressional action may be validated by the affirmative consent of Congress.[32]

Without specific action, a "silence of Congress" doctrine might be indicative of toleration of state regulation. In general, however, if uniform regulation is required, state action in the absence of congressional action is void. For example, a state law regulating the use of ship cabins on the Mississippi River,[33] state regulation of railroad rates,[34] and a state workmen's compensation act affecting a stevedore[35] were declared invalid, in spite of the absence of congressional action, because the matters required a uniform policy. But state regulation of pilots[36] and state regulation of ferry rates[37] were permitted by the Court because they were of local and not national concern. In 1932 Professor Edward F. Dow summarized this as follows:[38] "The doctrine, once admitted by the courts, that a state might regulate commerce in the absence of congressional action even though such regulation affected interstate business, is no longer tenable in the light of a series of Supreme Court rulings. Hence it is no defense for the Fernald Law to claim it is regulating a field left vacant by Congress."

A more recent decision which interpreted the "silence of Congress" doctrine against the states placed the Court as final arbiter in such controversies:[39] "For a hundred years it has been accepted constitutional doctrine that the commerce clause, without the aid of Congressional legislation, thus affords some protection from state legislation inimical to the national commerce, and that in such cases, where Congress has not acted, this Court, and not the State legislature, is under the commerce clause the final arbiter of the competing demands of state and national interests."

Even if Congress should delegate regulatory power to the states and the courts should allow this delegation, the fact remains that Congress could later reassume jurisdiction. Proof of this is found in *Port Richmond and Bergen Point Ferry Company v. Board of Freeholders of Hudson County,*[40] where the Court, after upholding state regulation of ferry rates, said, "If Congress at any time undertakes to regulate such rates, its action will, of course, control." So, even if its legality is assumed, this doctrine offers Maine no real guaranty against federal control.

One may postulate that the "silence of Congress" doctrine to date has been the most effective means of maintaining the Fernald law. For forty-one years the Maine power embargo has been unchallenged by Congress, the courts, or the Federal Power Commission. It may be argued, on the contrary, that the "silence of Congress" doctrine is now of merely academic interest, because the Flood Control Act and amendments to the Federal Water Power Act have already determined national power policy, but the regulatory commission has not yet applied its mandate in Maine.

It may be argued that the Fernald law could be upheld by the Supreme Court's interpretation of the Fourteenth Amendment in *Barbier v. Conolly*. The Court said that the amendment was not "designed to interfere with the power of the State, sometimes termed its police power, to prescribe regulations to promote the health, peace, morals, education, and good order of the people, and to legislate so as to increase the industries of the State, develop its resources, and add to its wealth and prosperity."[41] This case dealt, however, with equal protection of the law. Interstate commerce was not involved, and the opinion did not sanction state legislation to increase its industries and develop its resources by preventing interstate commerce.

Arguing on the basis of authority, Senator Owen Brewster has referred to an unnamed justice of the Supreme Judicial Court of Maine, who, as a member of the legislature, recorded his opinion as favorable at that time to the constitutionality of the power embargo.[42] In a series of articles on the power question in 1928, Franklin Fisher, a Lewiston attorney and former Deputy Attorney General, concluded that the law is constitutional. The late Roy L. Fernald, prominent in state politics and holder of several public offices, came to the same conclusion in his study of the question. Fisher also suggested that the power companies failed to challenge the law because they feared an unfavorable decision.[43]

Much more evidence can be presented against the validity of the Fernald law than for it. The argument that the power embargo regulated hydroelectric power before interstate commerce began, as in the E. C. Knight case (1895), requires consideration. The era of the late 'nineties, dubbed "the Dark Ages of the Supreme Court," required, according to Professor Edward S. Corwin, decisions after 1905 to correct a "century of error."[44] The extremely narrow view expressed in the Knight decision was temporary. The Addyston case greatly weakened or limited it. The Court said that the contracts under consideration were for the *sale and delivery* of pipe in another state, and that this was interstate commerce, although the vendor might have agreed to manufacture in order to fulfill the contract of sale.[45] In 1905 Mr. Justice Holmes announced for the Court the doctrine of a flow or current of commerce so that national jurisdiction over interstate commerce would extend back to what otherwise had been intrastate commerce.[46] Here it was the purchase of cattle destined for interstate commerce.

The Shreveport decision and that of *Wisconsin v. Chicago, Bur-*

*lington and Quincy Railway Company* went still further in determining federal power to regulate intrastate commerce. In the former the Court said that the authority of the federal government to regulate interstate commerce carried with it the right to regulate incidentally intrastate commerce also, whenever intrastate regulation is necessary for the protection of interstate commerce.[47] Chief Justice Taft succinctly stated the opinion of the Court in the Wisconsin case:[48]

> Commerce is a unit and does not regard state lines, and while, under the Constitution, interstate and intrastate commerce are ordinarily subject to regulation by different sovereignties, yet when they are so mingled together that the supreme authority, the Nation, cannot exercise complete effective control over interstate commerce without incidental regulation of intrastate commerce, such incidental regulation is not an invasion of state authority.

Two brief quotations from *Lemke v. Farmers' Grain Company*[49] hit at the heart of the Fernald law. The first is: "Nor will it do to say that the state law [regulating the buying of grain] acts before interstate commerce begins. It seizes upon the grain and controls its purchase at the beginning of interstate commerce." The second was quoted from the Minnesota rate cases: "The principle which determines this classification [between federal and state power] underlies the doctrine that the states cannot, under *any guise,* impose direct burdens upon interstate commerce."

After President Franklin Roosevelt's attack on the Supreme Court, a reaction began in 1937 against the railroad retirement and poultry cases. The Court took a broad view on the beginning of interstate commerce in *National Labor Relations Board v. Jones and Laughlin Steel Company,*[50] involving the National Labor Relations Act, and in *Mulford v. Smith,*[51] where the new Agricultural Adjustment Act was upheld because "it purports to be solely a regulation of interstate commerce, which it reaches and affects at the throat where tobacco enters the stream of commerce—the marketing warehouse." *Hammer v. Dagenhart* was expressly overruled in *United States v. Darby Lumber Company,*[52] a case involving the Fair Labor Standards Act. Mr. Justice Stone declared: "The power of Congress over interstate commerce is not confined to the regulation of commerce among the states. It extends to those activities intrastate which so affect interstate commerce or the exercise of the power of Congress over it as to make regulation of them appropriate means to the attainment of a legitimate end, the exercise of the granted power of Congress to regulate interstate commerce." Even insurance was brought within the scope of the commerce clause.[53] In 1942 the Court supported national authority to regulate the marketing of intrastate milk when its sale and competition with interstate milk affected its price structure.[54] The Supreme Court sanctioned national jurisdiction over utilities supplying power wholly within a state preponderantly for intrastate uses, but where a small part of the service was for railroads, steamships, and telephones engaged in interstate or foreign commerce. The *effect* upon interstate or foreign commerce, not the *source* of the injury, is the criterion for determining the limits of authority.[55]

The Federal Power Commission likewise has not favored local utility company barriers to interstate transmission. In 1940 the commission refused to recognize a subterfuge whereby the Hartford Electric Company tried to avoid federal regulation by selling power within the state to another company which sold part of it in Massachusetts.[56] The commission ruled that some of the Connecticut power was consumed in Massachusetts. The fact that the transmission was by facilities owned in part by another company which was interposed as an intermediary in the sale, or the fact that title to the energy changed at a point of delivery within the state, did not rob either the transmission or the sale of its interstate character. Dr. Robert D. Baum has cited another case showing no clear-cut distinction between interstate and intrastate transmission.[57] An intrastate company in New Jersey sold power to a second company, which had a direct connection with a New York company at the state border. The F.P.C. asserted jurisdiction over the local company because it was part of an interstate power-pool system. One cannot be impressed with the contention that the Fernald law is state regulation of intrastate commerce and therefore constitutional as a state prerogative.

Several decisions hold that a state cannot regulate the transmission of natural gas beyond its borders. The Indiana court decided that such a law constituted state interference with interstate commerce:[58]

It is no doubt true that there is a point at which a natural or manufactured product is not an article of interstate commerce; but when it assumes such a form as fits it for transportation from state to state, it is, so far as the law of interstate commerce is concerned, transformed into a commercial commodity. For the purpose of taxation, an article of property may not be regarded as a commercial commodity until it has started on its way from one state to another; but property that may become an article of commerce cannot be kept in the state where it was produced, by a state law forbidding its transportation.

Although this is a decision by a state court, it was cited and used as a precedent in two decisions of the United States Supreme Court, *Ohio Oil Company v. Indiana*[59] and *West v. Kansas Natural Gas Company.*[60] In the latter case, Mr. Justice McKenna referred to the Indiana case as a "valuable" one.[61]

In *Ohio Oil Company v. Indiana*[62] the statute in question was designed to prevent waste of gas and oil, and the interstate commerce clause was not actually concerned. The point at issue was whether the regulation to prevent waste took property without due process. Mr. Justice White limited the doctrine established in *Geer v. Connecticut;* wild game is public property which *all* people may attempt to reduce to possession, but natural gas is not public property because it can be reduced to possession only by surface owners. Hence there are two broad types of natural resources, one over which the state government has complete jurisdiction, and one over which it has partial control. This control may be exercised, however, only until the gas is reduced to possession. After that it is private property, and the state cannot prohibit the owner from shipping it outside. This is of extreme importance as a precedent for the Fernald law. It shows that the Geer, Lacoste, and McCarter cases referred to resources which are common to all inhabitants, and about which the state had the right to make such regulations as it saw fit before resources could become private property (reduced to possession). Natural gas is not common to all inhabitants, only to the surface proprietors. Hence the state's control is not plenary, and is lost after gas is reduced to possession.

The next case was *Kansas Natural Gas Company v. Haskell.*[63] A 1907 Oklahoma statute forbade any corporation in the state to transmit natural gas to other states. The natural-gas wells of Oklahoma produced a great surplus for Oklahoma, but this excess was required to meet the wants of neighboring states, where it could be sold at a profit. The United States Circuit Court for Oklahoma answered in the negative a key question similar to the one which would be involved if the Fernald law had been before the courts: Can the state prohibit the exportation of natural gas beyond its borders and thus conserve it solely for the use, benefit, and enjoyment of its own people? This court ruled that when gas is reduced to possession it becomes a product for interstate commerce and that, while the state may regulate it under its police power for health and safety, it cannot prohibit its exportation. The decision was affirmed by the United States Supreme Court in *West v. Kansas Natural Gas Company*. Mr. Justice McKenna showed that the purpose of the statute was not to conserve the supply of natural gas, but to keep it out of interstate commerce.

It is interesting to note that in one of the most significant sections, part of which is quoted below, the Court used the same argument that the opponents of the Fernald law had used during the debate in the Maine Senate two years before.[64]

> Gas, when reduced to possession, is a commodity; it belongs to the owner of the land; and, when reduced to possession, is his individual property, subject to sale by him, and may be a subject of intrastate commerce and interstate commerce. The statute of Oklahoma recognizes it to be a subject of intrastate commerce, but seeks to prohibit it from being the subject of interstate commerce, and this is the purpose of its conservation. In other words, the purpose of its conservation is in a sense commercial,—the business welfare of the state, as coal might be, or timber. Both of those products may be limited in amount, and the same considerations of the public welfare which would confine gas to the use of the inhabitants of a state would confine them to the inhabitants of the state. If the states have such power, a singular situation might result. Pennsylvania might keep its coal, the Northwest its timber, the mining states their minerals . . . embargo may be retaliated by embargo and commerce will be halted at state lines. And yet we have said that in matters of foreign and interstate commerce there are no state lines. In such commerce, instead of the States, a new power appears and a new welfare, a welfare which transcends that of any State.

By substituting the words "electric current" for "gas" in the quotation, one may infer by analogy what the Court might well say if it were deciding on the validity of the Fernald law. Perhaps of equal importance are two paragraphs which the Court quoted from *Haskell v. Cowham*[65] in the United States Circuit Court of Appeals, Eighth Circuit:

> No state... may prevent or unreasonably burden interstate commerce within its borders in any sound article thereof.
>
> No state... may substantially discriminate against or directly regulate interstate commerce or the right to carry it on.

Still closer to the Maine problem is the case of *Pennsylvania v. West Virginia.* When gas began to get scarce in West Virginia, the legislature attempted to prohibit its exportation to other states in order to continue to give an adequate supply to local consumers. The Court ruled that this was imposing a burden on interstate commerce and that the state could not regulate interstate transmission for the advantage of local consumers, and stressed the importance of this issue, hinting at the embargo argument and its consequences. What may be done in one state may be done in another, and what may be done with one natural product may be done with others. Ten states exported natural gas, and those exporting other natural resources would, if added to these, make a large number of states which might desire to place embargoes on their natural resources. The Court then went on to show that in spite of the importance of the question its solution was not difficult:[66]

> The purpose in this [commerce clause] is to protect commercial intercourse from invidious restraints, to prevent interference through conflicting or hostile state laws, and to insure uniformity in regulation. It means that in the matter of interstate commerce we are a single nation—one and the same people. All the states have assented to it, all are alike bound by it, and all are equally protected by it. Even their power to lay and collect taxes, comprehensive and necessary as that power is, cannot be exerted in a way which involves a discrimination against such commerce...
>
> Natural gas is a lawful article of commerce, and its transmission from one state to another for sale and consumption in the latter is interstate commerce. A state law, whether of the state where the gas is produced or that where it is to be sold, which by its necessary operation prevents, obstructs, or burdens such transmission, is a regulation of interstate commerce,—a prohibited interference... The West Virginia Act is such a law. Its provisions and the conditions which must surround its operation are such that it necessarily and directly will compel the diversion to local

consumers of a large and increasing part of the gas heretofore and now going to consumers in the complainant states, and therefore will work a serious interference with that commerce.

The implications of an article by Professor Felix Frankfurter and Professor James M. Landis on interstate compacts dealing with hydroelectric power in 1925 are against the Fernald law. "Congress alone can regulate interstate commerce; the flow of energy from State to State is interstate commerce; therefore, its control is beyond the authority of the States."[67]

Although the Attleboro case was concerned with the regulation of rates, some of the language used has more inclusive implications.[68] The Rhode Island Public Utilities Commission attempted to regulate the rates on electric current supplied by a state corporation to the Attleboro Steam and Electric Company. The contract between the two companies provided that the Rhode Island corporation should supply electricity to the Massachusetts corporation at a basic rate for twenty years. In the Rhode Island Supreme Court it was held that the rule of the Public Utilities Commission imposed a direct burden on interstate commerce and was invalid because of conflict with the commerce clause of the Constitution.[69] Of fundamental importance is the statement that *"the transmission of electric current from one State to another, like that of gas, is interstate commerce."*

Quoting from the Kansas Natural Gas Company case, the Court stated:[70] " 'the commerce clause of the Constitution, of its own force, restrains the States from imposing direct burdens upon interstate commerce,' and a state enactment imposing such a *'direct burden'* must fall, being a direct restraint of that which in the absence of Federal regulation should be free." The Court said that the measuring stick to test the legality of state regulation was whether or not the business was of local or national interest. In this case the regulation was deemed to be of national importance, and the fact that only 3 per cent of the electricity generated was in interstate commerce made no difference. The Court also hinted again at the embargo argument, saying that if Rhode Island could regulate the interstate rates and indirectly benefit its own consumers, Massachusetts could do likewise. One important passage in the decision follows:[71]

> Plainly, however, the paramount interest in the interstate business carried on between the two companies is not local to either State, but is essentially national in character. The rate is therefore not subject to regulation by either of the two States in the guise of protection to their respective local interests; but, if such regulation is required it can only be attained by the exercise of the power vested in Congress.

Mr. Justice Brandeis dissented on the ground that, only 3 per cent of the business being interstate, the case was of local and not of national importance. He also said that rate regulation is not a direct burden on interstate commerce.

The importance of the Attleboro decision to a discussion of the constitutionality of the Fernald law depends upon the degree of similarity held to exist as between a law preventing interstate commerce and a law regulating interstate rates. In the Attleboro case the Court ruled that the regulation of interstate rates of a company whose business was only 3 per cent interstate constituted a regulation of interstate commerce. If this is a burden on interstate commerce, certainly a law which *prevents* interstate commerce *in toto* constitutes an even greater regulation. This was the view taken by Professor Orren C. Hormell of Bowdoin College:[79]

> From a governmental and constitutional point of view it seems to the writer that much of the controversy over the transmission of water power out of the state is largely a futile expenditure of effort. The supreme court in the case of *The Public Utilities Commission of Rhode Island v. The Attleboro Steam and Electric Co.*, January, 1927, declared that "the transmission of electric current from one state to another is interstate commerce." When we consider that from the days of John Marshall the supreme court has frequently denied the right of the state not only to regulate interstate commerce but also to interfere with interstate commerce, we must realize that our attempt to retain the electric power may become a futile expenditure of effort whenever the supreme court is called upon to interfere.

A Louisiana statute preventing the exportation of shrimp resulted in a case of importance to the problem in Maine. The Supreme Court held the Louisiana act void, and in so doing limited its decision in the case of *Geer v. Connecticut.* For many years Louisiana shrimp were exported to a canning factory in Mississippi; approximately 95 per cent of the shrimp taken in Louisiana were for this purpose. The law declared that shrimp were the property of the state, and forbade interstate transportation unless the heads and hulls had been removed, showing that the purpose of the act was to induce canning plants to settle within the state so that they could utilize the shrimp. The shrimp and hydroelectric acts were passed for the same main purpose—to induce new industries to settle within the respective states, thereby adding to their general welfare and prosperity.

Mr. Justice Butler said that the purpose of the law was not conservation but[73]

> to prevent the interstate movement of raw shrimp from the Louisiana marshes to the plants at Biloxi (Miss.) in order through commercial necessity to bring about the removal of the packing and canning industries from Mississippi to Louisiana . . . A state is without power to prevent privately owned articles of trade from being shipped and sold in interstate commerce on the ground that they are required to satisfy local demands or because they are needed by the people of a state.

The Court recognized that the state owns and can control animals *ferae naturae* within its borders, not as proprietor but in its sovereign capacity as representative of the people. While the state could retain shrimp for consumption, the case clearly showed that the act was not to give the inhabitants the privilege of eating shrimp, but to compel the canning of them within its borders. The act did not apply to shrimp canned within the state. Since the state authorized the interstate shipment of the food, it released its control, and those taking the shrimp (reducing to possession) became entitled to the rights of private ownership and the protection of the commerce clause.

These decisions qualified and limited the state's control over wild game. This has best been summarized as follows:[74]

> From the statement in *Geer v. Connecticut* that the state is proprietor in behalf of the people the Court deduces the principle that the control of the state is limited to conservation. The reason for this deduction is not clearly apparent. Even though the state is proprietor only as representative of the people, why has it not the authority to exercise its control over wild game for the industrial as well as for the alimentary welfare of those for whom it stands? Granting that there may be a distinction, it is hard to believe that the Court is not paring down *Geer v. Connecticut* in order to prevent as far as possible interference with interstate commerce. Whatever the motive for the decision, the case seems to

have an important bearing on water power legislation. Restrictions on the exportation of water power may be designed to attract industries and manufacturing plants as well as to conserve a natural resource. The Court might draw a distinction between absolute prohibition and the according of preference to local consumers.

In the West Virginia natural-gas case,[75] the Court hinted at the suggested distinction between absolute prohibition of export and the according of preference to local consumers. Before the non-export statute was passed, and gas had merely begun to get scarce in West Virginia, the pipe-line companies adopted a policy of giving preference to local consumers during six months, November to May, the colder months of the year, and long-time contracts contained provision for this preference. The Court mentioned this policy in a statement of the facts and, without saying it was permissible, went on to show that such a policy could no longer (1922) be tolerated simply because the increasing population and demand for natural gas in West Virginia left no surplus for outside consumption. Consequently the law was prohibitive and preferential.

But Dr. Elsbree's prediction of a distinction (note 74 *supra*) has just been announced. Although apparently in the realm of dicta, the Court, in sustaining state conservation and regulatory rates, said that "the only requirements consistently recognized have been that the regulation not discriminate against, or *place an embargo on* interstate commerce, that it safeguard an obvious state interest and that the local interest at stake outweigh whatever national interest there might be in the prevention of state restrictions." *Cities Service Gas Company v. Peerless Oil and Gas Company,* 340 U.S. 179, 186–187 (1950). (Italics mine.)

The language of the Court in *Baldwin v. Seelig*[76] was strongly in favor of free trade among the states when it said, "What is ultimate is the principle that one state in its dealings with another may not place itself in a position of economic isolation." This statement, although it was made with reference to attempted regulation of interstate commerce by the receiving rather than by the sending state, implies opposition to the extreme particularism of the Fernald law. This case also emphasized that none of the state statutes pronounced valid relative to inspection laws, game laws, and laws intended to curb fraud or exterminate disease were nearly as drastic as the milk law in question, "which would neutralize the economic consequences of free trade among states." This doctrine was extended more recently by a 5 to 4 decision which outlawed New York's attempt to deny additional milk distributing facilities which would curtail the volume of interstate business and protect and advance local economic interests. The majority of the Court said,[77] "*This Court consistently has rebuffed attempts of states to advance their own commercial interests by curtailing the movement of articles of commerce*, either into or out of the state, while generally supporting their right to impose even burdensome regulations in the interest of local health and safety." The Court continued that the economic unit is the nation, which alone has power to control the economy; the corollary to this is that the states are not separable economic units.

The short quotation recorded above hit at a crucial point in state and national regulatory administration. The reserved or residual powers under the Tenth Amendment cannot be lumped together as a basis for state regulation. They require segregation. The traditional police-power categories, such as public health, safety, morals, and fraud, are still presumably state prerogatives, in spite of the emergence of a national "police power," under the commerce clause. Education and newer categories such as conservation are generally reserved to the states also. But when "general welfare" and "public convenience" are invoked, these more general terms are focal points at which national-state relations defy formulae. A power embargo cannot qualify under state police power. It could be a state right for the conservation of natural resources if hydroelectricity is a natural resource and its regulation does not unduly interfere with interstate commerce. But if a law withholds a commercial commodity from interstate commerce for the economic interests of a state, the validity of that law is extremely doubtful. Five justices said that New York could not do so.

The foregoing cases, although they are not strictly analogous to the case which would arise if the constitutionality of the Fernald law were being decided, contain several relevant Court decisions: first, that states may not keep natural gas out of, and withdraw it from, interstate commerce; second, that states may not prevent the exportation of raw shrimp to other states; third, that the transmission of hydroelectric power falls under interstate commerce; fourth, that a state cannot regulate interstate wholesale electric rates; fifth, that states cannot advance their own commercial interests by interfering with interstate commerce. The differences between these cases and the hypothetical Fernald law must now be considered.

Point 1. In the natural gas cases no property rights existed until gas was *reduced to possession*. After that the courts claimed that the states could not keep it out of interstate commerce. In the shrimp case the statute allowed them to be reduced to possession, after which they could not be kept out of interstate commerce. So reduction to possession is important. Hydroelectric power is not a tangible product. Can it then be reduced to possession? If not, the natural gas cases might not be applicable, because the gas was held not to be a subject of interstate commerce until reduced to possession.

However, reduction to possession may be of little or no significance if electricity is not a natural resource. (See point 4.) The Court held that natural resources are products of commerce when ownership is established. Before that time they are subject to state control. But, since artificial products do not exist until they are made, it is difficult to establish a dual relationship or ownership of them.

Point 2. The West Virginia case dealt with actual transmission of a commodity already in interstate commerce, whereas the Maine case does not attempt to *withdraw* a commodity from interstate commerce, but to *prevent it from getting* into interstate commerce. The question is whether the same set of principles would apply to a statute which *prevents* interstate commerce as to a statute which attempts to *withdraw* commodities from interstate commerce.

Point 3. In the West Virginia case the people outside the state had become dependent upon the gas obtained by interstate commerce, and as a result the law worked a hardship on those people by depriving them of a customary product. Considerable attention was paid by the Court to the fact that several out-of-state municipal waterworks, charitable and penal institutions, schools, and private homes had become dependent upon the supply of natural gas from West Virginia. The Louisiana statute, likewise, attempted to withdraw shrimp from interstate commerce where another state had become dependent upon the supply for canning factories. People outside Maine, however, are not accustomed to use Maine power, so the law in question does not do so much harm as did the West Virginia and Louisiana laws.

Point 4. The gas cases dealt with natural resources, and the Fernald law deals with electric current (hydroelectric power) generated from water power. Whether natural gas and hydroelectric power fall into the same category as a product of interstate commerce is a moot question. Although cases prove that the states can act to conserve their natural resources, is hydroelectric power a natural resource? This has been called a metaphysical question, but it may be very pertinent if the states can regulate their natural resources but not products manufactured from natural resources.

While no cases can be cited to prove that hydroelectric power can be reduced to possession, the Supreme Judicial Court of Maine has ruled that, although measured differently, it is a commodity just as much as kerosene.[78] The Attleboro decision held it to be a commodity subject to the commerce clause of the Constitution. From this there is a strong implication that hydroelectric power can, like any other commodity, be reduced to possession. Mr. Justice Edward F. Merrill of the Supreme Judicial Court of Maine, and former legislative agent for the Central Maine Power Company, believes that hydroelectric power can be reduced to possession.[79] Although it cannot be seen, electricity can be measured and controlled. The fact that it is a product which is sold by measure is evidence that ownership is definitely established in the company generating or selling it. It is contrary to both law and practice to claim that a commodity which is owned and sold cannot be possessed by a company or individual. Therefore it is logical to conclude that electricity can be reduced to possession.

The second difference is more incisive. It is argued that the Fernald law does not regulate interstate commerce because it hits at the very source and prevents interstate commerce in hydroelectric power. Commerce among states means commerce that begins in one state and ends in another, but there is actually no such thing as commerce in power that begins in Maine and ends in another state.[80]

But is it not true that prohibition of interstate commerce constitutes a more drastic regulation than partial restriction? "It [interstate commerce] cannot be regulated or restrained by a state"[81] is a significant quotation from *West v. Kansas Natural Gas Company*. In this case there had been no interstate commerce in natural gas. Some individuals and corporations had acquired wells or rights and were preparing to begin shipment, but not one of them had shipped a foot of gas. Had this fact been regarded as significant, it would surely have been urged in the case, but counsel did not stress it, nor did the Court even mention it.[82]

Other quotations show that prohibition of commerce is a regulation of it:[83] "The privilege of engaging in such commerce [interstate] is one which a state cannot deny." "No state by action (or inaction) may prevent, . . . discriminate against, or directly regulate interstate commerce or the right to carry it on." The last few words are of paramount importance in this case. The prime purpose of the Fernald law is to prevent corporations from carrying on interstate commerce in hydroelectric power. So it is apparent that the state of Maine, by action of the Fernald law, not only prevents and restrains interstate commerce, but also regulates the right to carry it on.

Too much emphasis should not be placed on the *movement* as a test of the power to regulate. Robert L. Stern's thesis in 1934 was that the courts tied up commerce with interstate movement at the start, but in later cases this element was very slight and incidental; the effect of the practices upon business in other states, upon price, supply, and competitors, were the important factors.[84] Although it is not the generally accepted view, it is sometimes contended that the Founding Fathers intended the phrase "among the states" to mean not *between* but *throughout* the United States.[85]

The third difference between the Maine situation and the West Virginia case concerns the effect upon other states. In some of the examples cited, citizens of one state built up cities and great communities about a commercial situation, but, with the Fernald law in existence, very little electricity has been shipped out of Maine and no out-of-state communities are dependent upon Maine power. Nevertheless, a small stream of hydroelectric power flows from Maine in interstate commerce channels, because the law permits corporations engaged in such interstate transmission before its passage in 1909 to continue to do so. Likewise, a small amount is exported by a trust. In 1920 the Maine Water Power Commission investigated these cases and found that the small stream of interstate transmission in operation at that time was not in violation of the law.[86] So in this respect the present case is not entirely dissimilar to the West Virginia case. It is also important to note that in the West Virginia case the attention paid by the Court to the effect upon outside users was not in connection with the question whether the statute burdened interstate commerce. Four questions were answered by the Court in deciding the case: (1) whether the suits involved a justifiable controversy between states; (2) whether the suits were brought prematurely; (3) whether the right parties (the states and not the pipe-line companies) were brought into the suit; and (4) whether the statute was a burden upon interstate commerce. The effect of the statute upon outsiders was not considered in answering the fourth question, but only in the general statement of the facts and the first question, whether a real controversy existed.[87]

The fourth difference between the natural gas cases and the Fernald law concerns the nature of the two commodities withdrawn or kept out of interstate commerce, natural gas and hydroelectric power. It is doubtful whether hydroelectric power can be considered a natural resource. Water power is recognized as a natural resource, and as such it is usually measured in terms of horsepower. Even hydroelectric sites are recognized as natural resources.[88] But hydroelectric power, measured off the generator in terms of kilowatt-hours, is a commodity manufactured from a natural resource. Its status is well stated by Dr. Elsbree:[89]

> One refers to the "generation," "production," or even "manufacture" of electric power. With respect to hydro-electric energy we say that it is "generated" by falling waters. In order to obtain the final utilizable product water must be impounded, dams constructed or natural sites harnessed, and generating apparatus installed. The energy secured is an artificial product whose generation from the basic natural resource requires large financial investment and great technical skill. Steam power is not called a natural resource, although its generation requires the consumption of natural resources—coal or oil.

Again, in the opinion of Edward F. Merrill, hydroelectric power is not a natural resource.[90] It differs from natural gas in that the latter is consumed, whereas the power generated by falling water does not use up the resource, but simply makes use of it for the manufacture of power. Evidence from the law and custom of the state of Maine also indicates that electric power is not a natural resource. This is summed up by Professor Edward F. Dow of the University of Maine as follows:[91]

According to the law of Maine as laid down by the courts, the riparian land owners not only own the banks, but the stream bed and the right to the use of the water flowing over their lands. Thus while the water itself belongs to the state, the use is wholly private except on state owned power sites. When utilized to create power, the running water creates private property rights, unlike the water or game conservation cases, where ownership remained in the public until consent should be given to reduce the public property to possession. It may be seriously questioned, therefore, whether hydro-electric power is in the category of a natural resource.

Although refraining from using the term "natural resource," the Supreme Court strongly inferred in *Utah Power and Light Company v. Pfost* that hydroelectric power is an artificial product. Extracts from the decision make this contention clear.[92]

Appellant here, by means of what are called generators, converts the mechanical energy of falling waters into electrical energy. Thus by the application of human skill, a distinct product is brought into being and transmitted to the places of use. . . .

The process by which the mechanical energy of falling water is converted into electrical energy, despite its hidden character, is no less real than the conversion of wheat into flour at the mill.

In this case the Court was not deciding whether electricity is a natural resource, but whether its generation and transmission are one process or two. In deciding that they were two processes, however, the Court distinctly made the point that electricity is a manufactured product, created by the application of human skill, and not a natural resource. There is also a New Hampshire decision throwing additional light on the question. Although the issue was one of eminent domain, a doctrine which was repudiated by the Maine court, the following language is significant:[93] "Like water, electricity exists in nature, in some form or state, and becomes useful as an agency of man's industry only when collected and controlled. It requires a large capital to collect, store, and distribute it for general use." While conceived in nature, human skill develops the product.

This evidence that hydroelectric power is an artificial product and not a natural resource is a strong indication that the Fernald law is unconstitutional. If it is not a natural resource, then the argument that a restrictive policy is within the state's power of conservation is weakened.

Yet any study of the conservation of natural resources which did not include hydroelectric power would be incomplete. Research looking to the best use of power either before or after it is transformed into electricity is a contribution to the conservation of a natural resource. The recent tendency is to use a more inclusive term, "our energy resources," in dealing with forms of power.[94] Thus, while evading the precise category in which hydroelectric power falls, this classification stresses "the growing concern for the conservation of the sources of power." Although there is some justification for this new emphasis on the conservation of energy resources instead of natural resources, it leaves unsolved the fundamental question whether the courts would permit the state conservation measures to apply also to manufactured energy.

The conclusion regarding the four differences between the natural gas, electric rate, and shrimp cases, on the one hand, and the hypothetical power embargo case, on the other, is that the first three differences form strong precedents against the constitutionality of the Fernald law. The fourth difference (natural resource or manufactured product), however, is even greater evidence for the illegality of the Fernald law, because in this case, unlike the others, the argument cannot be supported that Maine legislated to conserve a natural resource.[95]

A good summary of the situation was given by Professor Orren C. Hormell in 1933, but it was less decisive than his summary drawn up six years earlier:[96]

> In considering all the cases concerning exportation of natural resources, the two cases, one having to do with wild game and the other with water, are generally regarded as exceptions to the rule that a state cannot prohibit or restrict the exportation of its natural resources. The final decision with regard to the validity of the Fernald law probably will depend upon whether the majority of the court will follow Justice Holmes's liberal views on the police power of the state or the more conservative views of the majority of the court as expressed in the West Virginia and Kansas cases.

During the sixteen years since that was written, the tendency has been toward centralization, although one might argue that it is from a liberal and not a conservative point of view. Professor Henry Rottschaeffer, discussing in 1948 the expansion of federal powers since 1933, stated that "if Congress believes the nation's economic welfare to require the adoption and execution of a particular policy, it may use its commerce power to effectuate that policy on a national scale even though the immediate incidence of the regulation is outside the field of interstate commerce itself."[97]

Grounds for controversy still exist and the decision will depend mainly upon the political and economic philosophies of the personnel of the court at the precise time the judgment is handed down; but the natural resources and electric cases indicate that the Fernald law is invalid.

Several events in the late 'twenties and early 'thirties combined to bring about more stringent federal regulation of interstate power and holding companies. The great depression and holding-company failures focused attention on the towering vastness of many economic enterprises. Scarcity of money helped to cause consumer dissatisfaction with rates; and losses by investors increased the agitation for more effective regulation of the electric power industry. Corporation "public relations" campaigns in Maine and throughout the country and pressure on legislatures and regulatory commissions were exposed.

Technological advances, too, accelerated the amount of power crossing state lines, and the Kansas Gas Company and Attleboro decisions prevented state regulation of this transmission. According to Professor Merle Fainsod and Professor Lincoln Gordon: "The result of these decisions was to create a no man's land where states could not act and where the federal government had not yet acted. Efforts were made to close this gap during the 'twenties by invoking federal power; but these efforts were strenuously and successfully opposed by the utilities. The gap remained open until the passage of the Federal Power Act of 1935."[98]

In 1934 about 17 to 18 per cent of all electricity generated crossed state borders and nearly 100 per cent of the electricity used within several states was imported, whereas in other states a major part of the power was exported.[99] Nelson Lee Smith, until recently chairman of the Federal Power Commission, estimated in 1946 that the interstate movement of electricity was about 20 per cent of the total consumption.[100]

Along with the reorganization of the Federal Power Commission in 1930 and changes in its leading personnel with the coming of the New Deal,

> a new conception of the Commission's powers and responsibilities began to emerge. This new spirit was soon evident in a tendency to subject licensees to much more rigorous supervision, particularly in controlling accounting practices and in the determination of the actual legitimate costs of license projects . . . As a result of a number of clarifying amendments to the Act of 1920, embodied in the Federal Power Act of 1935, the control of the Commission over water-power resources was reinforced and the supervision of licensees effectively buttressed.[101]

The argument of the late 'twenties was that the Fernald law did not conflict with the jurisdiction of the Federal Power Commission so long as interstate transmission was not prevalent. The validity of that contention is doubtful. It now remains for Maine's non-transmission policy to be examined with reference to the subsequent power act and resulting interpretations by the courts and Federal Power Commission.

Federal Power Commission jurisdiction over Maine power might be asserted on one or more of the following bases: its function of planning an interconnected and coördinated power system, with broad power to compel interconnection in time of war or emergency; its license authority on navigable rivers and their tributaries, and its consequent right to investigate and assume control over unauthorized power projects; its power over navigation through flood control and multiple-purpose dams. The Federal Power Act authorizes the commission to plan an interconnected and coördinated system. These interconnections are to be voluntary, and the function of the commission is to encourage rather than compel them. It is required to consult with state commissions in arranging regional districts. In time of war or other emergency, however, the commission's power to compel interconnections is much broader. Thus, in the period immediately preceding the war, the commission found a tight power situation in the southeastern states and ordered several utility companies to interconnect their systems to supply energy over the interconnected network to defense industries and communities requiring power beyond the capacity of the local generating plants.[102] Although without judicial review, it appears that this authority is clearly within both the statutory authority of the Federal Power Act and the constitutional authority of Congress. In the event of war or emergency, the same situation might well prevail in Maine and some of the other New England states. An administrative order in a national defense area would surely insist upon a free flow of surplus power from a "have" state into a "have-not" state, Maine's Fernald law to the contrary notwithstanding.

Strong evidence indicating disapproval of the Fernald law by the Supreme Court, on grounds different from those of the conservation cases cited, has more recently been derived from *United States v. Appalachian Electric Power Company*.[103] This momentous decision of the United States Supreme Court in 1940 and its subsequent corollaries constitute what appears to be a departure from the doctrine of *stare decisis* with respect to control over nonnavigable streams. They are decisions by which the Fernald law may be obliterated, which may erase the distinction between navigable and nonnavigable rivers, obliterate the private property rights of riparian owners on the hitherto nonnavigable streams in Maine, and extend the scope of the commerce clause indefinitely. They indicate a positive means for the national government to expand its control over state power projects located on what is now considered a navigable stream. Furthermore, these cases indicate that tributaries of navigable streams and upstream dams on nonnavigable portions of a navigable river, because of their effects on navigable portions, are also under the jurisdiction of the Federal Water Power Act and amendments.

Early in the Appalachian decision the Court reiterated its adherence to the generally accepted definition in *The Daniel Ball* of the basic concept of navigability. But the concept cannot be determined by a formula which fits every type of stream under all circumstances at all times. The Court then said that in the Federal Power Act of 1935 Congress had defined navigable waters as those "which either in their natural or improved condition" are used or are suitable for use. Contrary to the Maine interpretation that navigable rivers are those which are such in their natural condition, the federal interpretation includes in this category those which, aided by reasonable improvements, will create an interstate highway available for traffic.

The Court explained further that in determining what constitutes reasonable improvements a balance between cost and need must be reached at a time when the improvement would be useful. "Improvements that may be entirely reasonable in a thickly populated, highly developed, industrial region may have been entirely too costly for the same region in the days of the pioneers." Changes in engineering practices or the coming of new industries with varying classes of freight may affect the type of improvement. This interpretation, the Court contended, did not enlarge the federal power over navigation; it merely holds that "improvements make applicable to certain waterways the existing power over commerce."

The Court stated that the federal government's jurisdiction over navigable streams is no longer confined to the regulation of commerce on these waters. Navigability is but part of the whole. "Flood protection, watershed development, recovery of the cost of improvements through utilization of power are likewise parts of commerce control." Of more vital importance is this key sentence:[104] "The point is that navigable waters are subject to national planning and control in the broad regulation of commerce granted the Federal Government."

The dissent of Justice Roberts and Justice McReynolds was that according to the new doctrine almost every stream in the United States could be considered navigable with improvement. One could have added that anything that runs into anything else which runs into the sea had now become subject to national control. But that the tendency is to enlarge rather than limit the Court's interpretation was shown when it declared that Congress may exercise its control over the nonnavigable stretches of a river in order to promote commerce on the navigable portions, and that the tributaries of navigable rivers are subject to its jurisdiction for flood control purposes.[105]

In the New River case the power company objected to the Federal Power Commission license, especially in regard to rates, accounts, and eventual acquisition—matters unrelated to navigation.

But the Court declared that the federal government has domination over the water power inherent in the flowing stream which is navigable, that this flow is in no sense private property, and that the exclusion of riparian owners from its benefits without compensation is entirely within the government's discretion.

The federal government also has plenary power to exclude completely structures from navigable waters and to exercise dominion over flowage and its product, energy. Therefore, the United States may make the erection or maintenance of a structure in a navigable stream dependent upon a license. Since Congress could completely deny the privilege of erecting a dam on waters within its jurisdiction, it could likewise grant the privilege on terms. This "is the price which [respondents] must pay to secure the right to maintain their dam." This quotation was from the judgment in the Fox River case,[106] in which a state was allowed to grant a license for a dam on a navigable stream. By using that language the Supreme Court intended to show that neither the state nor national government violated the due process clause in granting conditional licenses for the erection of dams on navigable streams. Since Congress may regulate flood control under the commerce clause on navigable streams as now broadly interpreted, plus their tributaries, it follows that it can likewise regulate multiple-purpose projects on these streams, including power developments, even though flood control is of lesser importance than the other purposes of a project.[107]

In the Atkinson case, Oklahoma objected to the construction of a dam on what had hitherto been considered a nonnavigable river, and contended that the dam was preponderantly for water power and not for flood control. The evidence showed that for the purpose of flood control the dam would have a maximum height of 165 feet, whereas the reservoir for flood control and power development would necessitate a maximum height of 185 feet. The state objected to this additional 20 feet in height, which would result in the flooding of a very much greater acreage of Oklahoma domain than would a project for flood control only. To this the Court answered that the dam was intended basically for flood control, though it was hoped that power would pay the cost of building and that the extra height of 20 feet would increase some of the flood-control benefits, including river flow: "the fact that ends other than flood control will also be served, or that flood control may be relatively of lesser importance, does not invalidate the exercise of the authority conferred on Congress."[108]

A more recent decision by the United States Court of Appeals for the Fifth Circuit, that of *Georgia Power Company v. Federal Power Commission,*[109] has significant implications on the uncertain future of Maine's power embargo. It was not based on flood-control arguments, but held that the Federal Power Commission has *jurisdiction* over a contemplated power dam located four miles beyond the navigable part of the Oconee River in Georgia.

A splendid analogy may be drawn between the ecological and geographical setting of the latter case and that in Maine. The Oconee River is intrastate, partly navigable, partly nonnavigable, and joins the Ocmulgee River to form the Altamaha, which flows into the Atlantic Ocean. For many years it has been used for the transportation of timber and other products by pole boat, raft, and steamboat to Darien, the outlet for coastal and foreign ports. Much of its commerce was intrastate or foreign. With few exceptions, Maine rivers are intrastate, partly navigable and partly nonnavigable, flowing into the Atlantic Ocean, and were once in general use in the transportation of Maine's fish, lumber, and other products.[110]

The Georgia Power Company, as required by the Federal Power Act, filed with the Federal Power Commission a declaration of its intention to construct the dam in question. The commission, after hearings, ordered the power company to apply for and accept a federal license, because the proposed reservoir would reduce the navigable depths of the water below the dam and thus affect navigation. The power company contended that the Federal Power Act did not apply to a project on the nonnavigable part of a stream, or if so, to that extent the act was unconstitutional. But, supporting the finding of the Federal Power Commission that the proposed dam would affect navigation adversely, the Court ruled that one of the purposes of section 23(*b*) of the Federal Power Act[111] was to give the commission jurisdiction over a proposed structure in a nonnavigable tributary of an intrastate navigable stream.

The Court interpreted the Federal Power Act as an instrument evidencing a congressional intent to develop and utilize the navigation and water-power resources of the country. Licensed projects, therefore, must conform to a comprehensive waterway plan for the benefit of interstate or foreign commerce.[112]

> That Congress has the power to legislate where commerce between the states or with foreign countries may be affected is no longer an open question. And such power is not restricted to "an adverse effect upon the present and existing navigable capacity of federal waters"; it extends to navigable capacity after reasonable improvements which might be made, and whether the effect is beneficial or injurious. The Federal Power Act was intended to develop, conserve, and utilize the navigation and water power resources of the country, and to that end requires that projects licensed shall "be best adapted to a comprehensive plan for improving or developing a waterway or waterways for the use or benefit of interstate or foreign commerce," hence, "if upon investigation [the commission] shall find that the interests of interstate or foreign commerce would be affected," it may require a license.

This decision clearly indicates that any future dams on the nonnavigable portions of Maine rivers which will affect the flow of water on the navigable portions of those rivers will come under Federal Power Commission license. Whether the decision could be interpreted to authorize federal jurisdiction over the multitude of Maine dams already in use on the nonnavigable portions of these rivers, or whether an attempt by the Federal Power Commission to require such a license now would be retroactive calls for further analysis.[113]

The Central Maine Power Company and two paper companies plan to construct the huge Dead River storage dam on the nonnavigable part of the Kennebec River near Flagstaff. The development will create an artificial lake twenty-six miles long by means of a dam five hundred feet long and fifty feet high, impounding eleven billion cubic feet of water.[114] Costing between $8,000,000 and $10,000,000, it will create one of the largest storage basins in the East. It is said that the completion of this project will regulate the power flow of the Kennebec River and obviate the danger of spring floods in central Maine.

Now, in the light of the decision in the Georgia case, it is evident that the Dead River storage dam would come under the jurisdiction of the Federal Power Commission. The development would affect the navigable portions of the Kennebec River—for the better, to be sure, with the probability of eliminating spring floods; but the

Court has said that it is immaterial "whether the effect is beneficial or injurious." In granting and requiring adherence to a federal license, the big question is whether the Federal Power Commission would be willing to recognize the particularism of the Fernald law. There is no reason to predict that it would, because state barriers to interstate intercourse have always been unpopular with federal agencies and still are. If a federal license should require interstate transmission, it is difficult to think of a "liberal" court sustaining the Fernald law.

It was not expected that the Federal Power Commission would attempt to assume control of dams already constructed and in operation on the nonnavigable parts of Maine rivers. Not long ago, however, the commission did, as a matter of fact, assert control over somewhat similar projects in Vermont. For example: the Bellows Falls Hydroelectric Corporation, chartered in Vermont in 1792 as a canal company to make the Connecticut River navigable by Bellows Falls, took some water from the canal as early as 1802 to develop power.[115] Between 1857 and 1868 its navigation activities were discontinued, and its efforts were concentrated on power development. At various times the power project was reconstructed, in 1927 on a much larger scale. All these constructions were without any authority from Congress and without a license under the Federal Water Power Act of 1920. But in 1939 the Federal Power Commission began an investigation to determine the legal status of the project (no. 1855). The commission determined that the river was navigable and that, therefore the project was being maintained and operated in violation of the act.[116] In reply to the contention that the project was constructed under a state permit, the commission said:[117]

> Had the project been constructed, maintained and operated "under and in accordance with the terms of" a permit granted by the State prior to June 10, 1920, the contention would still be without avail. Even though a state has granted permission to the full extent of its authority, nevertheless a construction of the character here involved on navigable waters of the United States requires a permit by competent Federal authority.

Consequently, the corporation was required to apply for and obtain a license under the Federal Power Act.

The constitutional implications of this opinion may be of considerable magnitude for Maine, in view of recent Supreme Court decisions. If the Federal Power Commission should desire to initiate investigations to determine the legal status of the numerous hydroelectric dams in Maine, the evidence suggests that the courts would put them under the Federal Power Act, even though the dams are already constructed, because they are located on rivers capable of being made navigable, or on their tributaries, or on nonnavigable parts which affect navigability. But the Federal Power Commission has not yet attempted to assert jurisdiction over the Maine dams. Whether the commission will become more aggressive is a pure matter of conjecture; equally conjectural is the nature of the licenses that Maine corporations would be required to accept.

The commission found that the Vermont project was "best adapted to a comprehensive plan for improving and developing the Connecticut River for the use and benefit of interstate commerce, for the improvement and utilization of water power development and other beneficial uses, including recreational purposes."[118] The license was granted until 1970, and the operation by the licensee corporation of the project, so far as this involves "the use, storage, and discharge from storage of waters affected by this license, shall . . . be controlled . . . as the Federal Power Commission may prescribe for the protection of life, health, and property and in the interest of the fullest practicable conservation and utilization of such waters for power purposes and for other beneficial public uses."

The Vernon project (no. 1904), placed in operation on the Connecticut River in 1909 and 1910 and improved at intervals thereafter, was found by the Federal Power Commission in 1944 to be best adapted for navigation and the improvement and benefit of interstate water-power development. The commission ordered that a federal license be granted until 1970, the commission having rights similar to those retained in the Bellows Falls project.[119]

The supremacy of the Federal Power Act over state law was illustrated by Mr. Justice Burton in *First Iowa Hydro-Electric Cooperative v. Federal Power Commission.*[120] Although the analogy in Maine is again not precise, the decision has implications which may have a bearing on the Fernald law. In Iowa a state permit is required by statute for the construction of dams on navigable and nonnavigable streams and before water can be taken from them for industrial purposes. Section 9(*b*) of the Federal Power Act requires only that applicants for licenses must have complied with state laws on the development, transmission, and distribution of power. The state of Iowa opposed the granting of a license on those terms, contending that under the Federal Power Act applicants for license must meet *all* requirements, both state and federal, for the proposed project. But the Court ruled that were this contention valid, states would possess a virtual power of veto to destroy the act. "It would subordinate to the control of the State the 'comprehensive' planning which the Act provides shall depend upon the judgment of the Federal Power Commission or other representatives of the Federal Government."[121]

Analysis of the Iowa statute indicated a policy of state opposition to diversion of water from one stream to another. In considering the effect of the Federal Power Act upon the Iowa code and related statutes, the Court stated, "We find that when that Act is read in the light of its long and colorful legislative history, it discloses both a vigorous determination of Congress to make progress with the development of the long-idle water-power resources of the nation and a determination to avoid unconstitutional invasion of the jurisdiction of the states."[122] The decision indicates that the Iowa law relating to navigable waters is not recognized under the Federal Power Act. By inference it follows that the Maine law prohibiting corporations from transmitting hydroelectric power out of the state may conflict with a Federal Power Commission license which would insist that the power be distributed for the *summum bonum,* regardless of state lines.

Other cases show the success of the Federal Power Commission in extending its jurisdiction. *In the Matter of Pennsylvania Water and Power Company,*[123] the commission found that the Holtwood project on the Susquehanna River was being operated without federal license. The Court of Appeals for the District of Columbia affirmed the commission's order requiring the company to apply for a license, and rejected the company's contention that the act was not to be applied retroactively: "It cannot be considered, we think, that Congress meant to allow existing obstructions to continue unregulated in the navigable streams of the United States." The Supreme Court of the United States denied the company's request for certiorari,[124] and similar rulings have put the following projects under federal license: the Tomahawk project of the Wisconsin Public Service Corporation on the Wisconsin River; three projects of the Wisconsin-Michigan Power Company on the Michigamme and Menominee rivers; and, by a tentative decision of the Federal Power Commission,[125] three projects in Tennessee and North Carolina owned by the Aluminum Company of America and its subsidiaries. The commission has also set hearings which direct various companies to show cause why they should not obtain federal authorization for their projects.[126]

Investigations by the Federal Power Commission, as in Vermont, have brought to light a number of unauthorized power plants which appear to require federal authority but which are operating without specific approval. To date, little progress has been made in bringing these plants under license. The power companies have been unwilling to apply for licenses until the necessity for doing so is unmistakable. A mere assertion by the commission that federal jurisdiction exists is not sufficient. The failure of the commission in recent years to obtain appropriations commensurate with its accelerated functions has without doubt slowed its assertion of authority. The commission has issued no orders directed against Maine owners of power plants requiring them to show cause why a license application should not be filed under the Federal Power Act. No one is in a position to predict what the commission will do when hydroelectric plants in Maine are brought to its attention, nor, if jurisdiction should be asserted, what the Maine power companies would do at that time. The uncertainty with which the companies view their position was expressed in 1947, when the Maine Public Service Company indicated its inability to state whether any of its developments could be subjected to federal license.[127]

The decisions and orders mentioned here cast deep shadows on the constitutionality of the Fernald law. Congress can regulate navigable streams, their tributaries, and nonnavigable parts which aid or hinder navigation. If the Federal Power Commission should desire to extend the interpretation within Maine, private property rights of riparian owners on nonnavigable streams would be controlled by the national government because the latter streams now come under the provisions of the Federal Power Act.[128] The commission could then grant licenses for power developments on such streams and their tributaries. Since these streams have been declared subject to national planning, it seems likely that state particularism in a power policy may be superseded by a regional or national policy. This very point was implied recently: "And the suggestion that this project interferes with the state's own program for water development and conservation is likewise of no avail. That program must bow before the 'superior power' of Congress."[129]

If the national government should desire to institute a program of flood control in Maine under the Flood Control acts of 1936 and 1938, even though flood control should be of relatively less importance than power or other multiple purposes of the project, the Fernald law would have to fall. Although Maine's flood-control situation is not serious, there were severe floods in 1936. It is not inconceivable that a postwar flood-control project for work relief would cause much of Maine's hydroelectric power to be developed under federal license.

If the national government should decide to develop power under the guise of flood-control projects in Maine, it could easily dispose of that power by contracts to out-of-state users. By virtue of *Ashwander v. Tennessee Valley Authority*,[130] the government could generate the power as an incidental part of a flood-control program and an aid to navigation on the Maine rivers. Such a program might also be recognized for national defense. The resulting electric current, as property of the United States, could be disposed of by contract wherever a market exists, regardless of the Fernald law. More important, however, the Georgia decision shows that all dams constructed in future on the vast nonnavigable stretches of Maine's rivers which will affect navigation, adversely or even beneficially, will be subject to federal license. The Vermont orders indicate that Maine's dams already constructed may be brought under the orbit of Federal Power Commission license.

The cases cited might not provide a basis for declaring the Fernald law unconstitutional, but, what is just as important, they might well eliminate the *policy* of the Fernald law by a totally different process. By the broad concept of what now constitutes a navigable river, national jurisdiction could easily be extended far up into

Maine. It could even destroy power plants already erected by private corporations on a river if necessary to erect its own dam to improve navigation, flood control, or national defense. Then, with the vast rivers of Maine under the jurisdiction of the federal government, the power derived from them might become the property of the national government, and as such would be disposed of by out-of-state contracts. Or if the Federal Power Commission undertook to grant licenses for the power on these rivers under its jurisdiction and near-by states clamored for a supply of cheap power, it is probable that these licenses would not respect the particularism of the Fernald law.

The future policy of the Federal Power Commission in granting licenses in Maine is a moot question. It is conceivable that these licenses will give control of the dam to the commission in order that there be no interference with navigation, prescribing accounting methods and reserving the right to take over the dams later (as it did in Virginia), but not interfering with power induction itself. The commission would probably be less tempted to interfere with a private power project than to proceed with federal flood control and power development. On the other hand, if the commission used its discretionary authority to interfere with the sale of power, ample precedents indicate that the courts would sustain it. Such a policy would be most unpopular among the advocates of home rule in Maine and elsewhere. However, sixteen years ago Congress defined broadly the jurisdiction of, and delegated rather wide latitude to, the Federal Power Commission. Immediate responsibility for the assumption of this jurisdiction would rest with the commission, and ultimate responsibility with Congress, the judiciary, again, remaining in a stand-by position, as American federalism continues to fluctuate.

On the basis of the information available from Supreme Court decisions in 1929, the logical conclusion is that the Fernald law constituted regulation of interstate commerce by the state of Maine. From a survey of precedents for the increasing powers of the national government over interstate commerce and the decreasing rights of states to interfere with it, the Fernald law would undoubtedly be invalid. The Fernald law virtually prevents electric current from getting into interstate commerce. The evidence shows that this is a much more drastic regulation of commerce than other policies that the Court has refused to allow. In the Attleboro case, for example, state regulation of rates was prohibited, even though only 3 per cent of the company's business was interstate. The natural gas cases also have established strong precedents against the validity of the Fernald law. The fact that hydroelectric power is an artificial and not a natural product shows that the state cannot claim that the law is a conservation measure, which has been the basis for other restrictive policies. On the basis of the more recent decisions extending the jurisdiction of the national government over rivers for commerce, including flood control and power projects, the Fernald law policy would unquestionably fall whenever the national government asserts jurisdiction over the rivers of Maine.

In spite of the possible, even probable, illegality of the Fernald law, it still shapes the power policy of Maine and to some degree the policy of New England. How much longer this can continue is a matter of conjecture. The statement by the Supreme Court in 1940 in regard to the Federal Power Act (see p. 142) may be a warning to Maine.

# CHAPTER VIII

## Planning, Public Ownership, and State Development

At the turn of the century, important contributions were made to the knowledge of Maine water-power resources and their potentialities. Such research and fact-finding under national and state auspices were vital prerequisites to the development of wise legislation. Professor George F. Swain described with much detail these water powers in 1880, and Professor Dwight Porter in 1899 brought the report down to that year, adding much that was new.[1] In 1899 the Maine legislature created the Topographic Commission.[2] The three commissioners coöperated with the United States Geological Survey, and in 1902 the first truly scientific work on Maine water power appeared.[3] The previous studies had been based primarily on data gathered from widely scattered sources, supplemented by estimates, not actual measurements, of the fall or flow of streams, but this last-named work was the result of data obtained from stations established on several large rivers.

The power-embargo law represented what could not be done with Maine's power, but its proponents favored a constructive and positive policy also. The Maine Water Storage Commission was created in 1909 as an advisory body or planning agency to prepare recommendations for the legislature. Despite opposition by the power interests, the measure was passed in both houses without much protest.[4] Among its leading supporters were Carl E. Milliken, Percival P. Baxter, Edward P. Ricker, and John E. Warren. The statute provided for a committee of five: the governor, the state land agent,[5] and three men appointed by the governor and the council. They served without pay, but were allowed expenses. Among the most important duties of the commission were:

1. To collect information relating to the water powers, the flow of rivers and their drainage areas, methods for the improvement of natural storage basins, and plan for the improvement and creation of new storage reservoirs.

2. Before erecting a dam to develop water power or to create or improve a water storage basin, copies of plans for the construction of such dams and storage basins had to be filed with the Commission.

3. The Commission was instructed to ascertain what townships or parts of townships could be purchased by the State as a forest reserve or for conserving the water powers of the State.

The statute was based on a similar act of the New York state legislature, but the $5,000 appropriation a year for two years was wholly insufficient. With Governor Bert M. Fernald as chairman, and Land Agent Edgar E. Ring members ex officio, the other members who held office during the four years that the commission existed were Edward P. Ricker, J. M. McNulty, and E. C. Jordan. The belief that the purpose of this commission was to put the state into the power business undoubtedly hampered its prestige. Actually, the creation of this agency four years before the state began to regulate its public utility corporations showed that at least a small group of people were interested in state planning to obtain the greatest possible use of its water powers. But it is difficult to discover how much popular support the organization had.

The first report recommended to the legislature that the Maine Water Storage Commission be given authority as follows:[6]

First—To require every person, firm, or corporation, contemplating the construction of a dam for the storage of water or the development of water power in the State, to submit their plans to the Commission and obtain the approval of the Commission before beginning construction.

Second—To require every person, firm, or corporation applying for a charter for the development of storage or water power, to submit their plans to the Commission for approval before beginning construction; to provide for practically the same requirements in the case of agreements for the merger or consolidation of two or more corporations for the same purpose; to require the approval of the Commission in all cases of sale, assignment, disposition or transfer of any franchise of a company formed for the development of storage or water power.

Third—To assess and collect fees annually for all franchises of water power which may be granted hereafter by the State, the amount of the assessment being on a sliding scale and based either on the gross receipts of the company, or on the horsepower proposed to be developed.

Fourth—To assume control and regulation of all reservoirs now built or that will be built by private parties on lands in part or in whole controlled by the State, known as public lots or State lands, and on all great ponds and lakes of the State, taking care in such legislation not to injuriously affect vested rights. The suggested plan, briefly stated, contemplated the formation of river districts with district superintendents in charge of the regulation of reservoirs; said district superintendents to be appointed by the water users, approved by the Water Storage Commission, and reporting to the engineer of the Commission.

The commission suggested also that, since the state had not yet reached the stage for building storage reservoirs, it should insist upon full publicity for plans of proposed water-power developments by requiring the approval of the commission before allowing construction. Moreover, the state should charge an annual franchise fee for all new franchises of water powers or reservoirs granted. These franchises should be limited to fifty years, and possibly the state could place rentals on developed water powers on sites owned by the public. In 1911, by act of the legislature, the Water Storage and State Survey commissions were consolidated.[7]

The second annual report of the commission, in 1911, called attention to mergers of various water-power companies during the previous year in Maine, and suggested public regulation. Cyrus C. Babb, chief engineer, prepared a bill providing for extensive state control of the construction of dams, the taxation of water powers, and the regulation of storage reservoirs on the great ponds of the state.[8] The legislature of 1911 referred the bill to the following one in 1913. The bill was extensively modified, but was rejected in 1913.[9]

During Governor Haines's term of office, from 1913 to 1915, he did not call the commission together; he was hostile to its work and was instrumental in abolishing it.[10] Many had inferred from the reports of the Water Storage Commission that it was primarily an anticorporation agency, seeking to increase its own powers and put Maine into the electric power business by state development of power. But the cost of such a scheme (estimated by the chairman of the Public Utilities Commission several years later as

$150,000,000)[11] would have been prohibitive, and any meager experiments the state might have tried in this era could not have hurt corporate interests.

In the 1913 session of the legislature the big contest was over the creation of a Public Utilities Commission. When this was done the Water Storage Commission was abolished, and its functions were assigned to the newly created Public Utilities Commission.[12] The feeble effort to continue the staff agency gave way to the arguments that the functions of the two commissions were overlapping, and that money would be saved by having the engineers do the work of both commissions and use the same maps and materials. Assurances were given that the Water Storage Commission law was not abolished, but that the boards were merely consolidated. In theory this setup seemed plausible, with the Public Utilities Commission as an over-all water-resources body containing its own staff agency within the organization. But in practice it may well have been a misdirected policy for a regulatory commission charged with revaluation of property and investigation of accidents, complaints, and rates to be assigned also the duties of a water-power staff agency. With its tasks increasing each year, the commissioners had little time to take on the additional burdens of investigating water-power resources and of recommending a constructive and permanent plan for conservation.

According to Percival P. Baxter, the work done on water power by the Public Utilities Commission in its early history was clerical only.[13] Subordinate officials in the department were assigned the water-power work,[14] and from 1913 to 1918 only two small reports were issued, dealing with stream flow and other statistics.[15] The Public Utilities Commission explained that its inactivity was due to the inaction of the legislature in 1911, 1913, and 1915 with reference to the recommendations of the Water Storage Commission.[16] Because of the rejection of these bills, the Public Utilities Commission inferred that the state was not interested in the plans of the Water Storage Commission and appropriations for a comprehensive study to work out a new and larger plan. The Public Utilities Commission spent slightly over half of the money available for topographical mapping in 1917 and 1918. Of the $5,000 to be spent on water-power investigation in 1917, the Public Utilities Commission used only $219.41, and the balance lapsed into the state treasury. For the first six months of 1918 the commission spent only $10 for this purpose. But soon the commission requested that the unexpended balance of the previous year be restored to it, which was done. The result was a report in December, 1918, costing $9,363.36. Despite Baxter's contention that the report was hurriedly prepared and that most of the material was supplied by the corporations,[17] it was a valuable contribution to Maine water-power history, even though it made no recommendations for a policy. But one important water-power report in six years was not an enviable record.

In the legislative session of 1917, Baxter attempted to legislate for the creation of a Maine Water Power Commission with greater powers than its predecessor of 1909.[18] The vital part of the proposed measure called for

> a plan for the improvement and creation of such water storage reservoirs and basins as will tend to develop and conserve the water powers of the State, and [the Water Power Commission] shall report on what rights remain to the State in the natural storage reservoirs and basins, and in the developed and undeveloped water powers of the State, and the best method of developing them in the interests of the people of the State, and whether the same are in any respect being curtailed or otherwise being adversely affected by any person, firm or corporation.

In response to the argument that the act would discourage the investment of private capital and consequently retard the full development of water resources, Baxter contended that the proposed commission could suggest a constructive plan for a state policy which, if adopted by the legislature, would encourage outside capital to seek investment in a state with an established policy.

Although it was passed in the House, the measure was rejected in the Senate. Senator Davies summarized the opposition to the act:[19]

> 1. The act must create hostile feeling between the proposed commission and the Public Utilities Commission.
> 2. The expenditure required to carry out its provisions is unwarranted, at least until a campaign of education can be conducted.
> 3. The power given under the bill is altogether too sweeping.
> 4. The machinery of the bill is cumbersome and complicated.
> 5. The matter of investigation and report can be made in a better and more effective way by a legislative committee.

Other bills were introduced in this session to handle the investigation differently. One was by Representative Dutton to create the Maine Power Commission and provide for state ownership and development of water-power systems. This bill was endorsed by Gifford Pinchot, but he advised that a hearing on the pending water-power bills be put off until the next legislature, "with war so near us."

Senator Davies offered a resolution in the Senate which called for a water-power investigation by a legislative committee. Representative Barnes favored an investigation by the Public Utilities Commission. Baxter felt that these proposals were attempts by the lobby to sidetrack his bill for a permanent commission. Since the Public Utilities Commission was charged with the duties of the old Water Storage Commission, it had authority to investigate without further legislative enactment. The Davies resolution was defeated in the House.[20] Some hostility between House and Senate was shown on this issue. The House stood out for a permanent water-power commission, while the Senate defeated that measure, but voted for an investigation by a legislative committee. It was alleged that the Senate would have accepted an investigation by the Public Utilities Commission, but the House rejected the two other measures. This was a factor in a later contention that the Senate was favorable to corporate interests, while the House fought for the "people's rights."

The idea that the Fernald law might be unconstitutional was being sensed generally and hostility to corporations was growing in Maine; hence, in 1917, the practice was started of attaching a rider, the so-called "Baxter amendment" in all dam and power-company charters, prohibiting these corporations from engaging in interstate commerce. Hence, if the Fernald law should be nullified, it was argued that the same result would be attained because the corporations controlled by the state would be limited to intrastate business by their charters. The Gould Electric Company, the Clark Power Company, and the Fort Kent Electric Company had such riders inserted in their charters in 1917. Governor Baxter included this as a main tenet of Maine's public power policy, and he was instrumental in securing its adoption in the Republican platform of 1918. The Baxter amendment for the Gould Electric Company is typical:[21]

Electric current not to be transmitted beyond confines of state.

It shall be unlawful for said corporation to transmit electric current, generated within this state, for sale or use beyond the limits of this state, or to contract with any person, firm or corporation for the transmission or sale of electric current generated within this state beyond the limits of this state and said corporation shall not be permitted to acquire in any manner the franchises of or consolidate with or transfer or lease its property, rights and franchises to any other corporation, firm or person now transmitting or having the right to transmit electric power beyond the confines of the state, without express authority of the legislature.

The groundwork was well prepared in advance of the 1919 session of the legislature for the creation of a water-power commission. The platforms of the Republican, Democratic, and Labor parties urged thorough investigation of the state's water-power resources. The recent war transportation difficulties and consequent shortage of coal had made people throughout the country more conscious of the importance of hydroelectric power. It was felt that it was now time to study Maine's power potentialities. The only speech on behalf of the new commission was made by Representative Baxter, who showed conclusively the ineffectiveness of the Public Utilities Commission as a staff agency to supervise water-power resources.

The Maine Water Power Commission, as established by statute, consisted of ten members, the number regularly serving on joint legislative committees in Maine. The members were appointed by the governor, and were nominated as follows: three by the executive council; one a member of the Seventy-ninth Legislature to be named by the president of the Senate; two members of the House named by the speaker; a member of the Maine State Board of Trade to be named by the board; a Granger to be named by the Grange; a member to represent and be named by the State Federation of Labor; and a representative from the Savings Bank Association of Maine.[23]

By law the Water Power Commission was required to investigate and report on the water-power resources of the state (primarily a technical matter) and a water-power development policy for the state. The act appropriated $15,000 for 1919, plus $5,000 for the usual hydrographic and geological surveys, and a like amount for the next year. The provisions of the statute gave opportunity for its opponents once again to charge that the commission's purpose was to put the state in the power business. The commission was instructed to investigate and report on what rights remained to the state in storage reservoirs and basins and in developed and undeveloped water powers. It was given discretionary power to investigate the present ownership of water-power resources and describe each water power, whether developed or undeveloped, owned or partly owned by the state. A study was to be made of the corporations and individuals transmitting power outside the state under the exceptions to the Fernald law, and in this way discover whether any violations of this law were taking place. The commission was also asked to investigate and determine the advisability of storage reservoirs and basins and the undeveloped water powers being acquired and developed by the state or by private enterprise. If by the latter, the commission was asked to report a plan whereby the private owners could be encouraged to develop them immediately. Or if the commission favored state ownership and development, a plan for this project was requested.

Edward P. Ricker, chairman of the commission, transmitted the 1920 report to the governor and the council. It was reported that the state rights in storage reservoirs consisted of the limited right of control of the waters in great ponds, and certain public lots and lands held in trust.[23] Not recommending public development except inferentially, the commission deemed it unwise to recommend a definite plan which could not be put into practical operation without constitutional amendment. However, if and when the amendment should be made, the commission recommended the creation of river-regulating districts, each to include at least the whole or a definitely constituent part of the drainage area of one of the principal rivers of the state. Although a plan was prepared, it was not submitted to the legislature.

The committee on water conservation of the engineering council, representing the four great national engineering societies, expressed preference for private development of water power, although without so advising the Maine Water Power Commission. They suggested that the commission might be given quasi-judicial powers to deal with complaints of users of water power, subject to judicial review.

In the legislative session of 1921 the Maine Water Power Commission was continued, and was directed to report the water powers located on the public lots and on the possibilities of their development.[24] In the same session the legislature sent a memorial to Congress urging the amendment of the Federal Water Power Act of 1920 so that Maine's water powers might be saved for the benefit of Maine people.[25] Whether it be labeled particularism or states' rights, it shows the fear felt by the legislators that they might lose the power. The memorial read in part:[26]

> Believing that the future health and prosperity of the citizens of this State depends in a large measure upon the proper development and use within the State of the water powers which nature has placed within our boundaries; and
>
> Believing that the Federal Water Power Act recently passed by the United States Congress may result in the transmission beyond the borders of the State of the Hydro-electric energy generated therein, thereby causing serious and irreparable loss and injury to the health and prosperity of the State, and to the future growth of industries therein;
>
> Respectfully urge upon the Congress now in session the necessity of amending the said Federal Water Power Act in order that there shall be no Federal interference with and control of the water powers lying within the borders of the State of Maine....

In the second report of the Maine Water Power Commission, 1921–1922, the belief was expressed that the disinclination to develop power in Maine was due primarily to lack of a definite state attitude toward such development.[27] Since little development could be expected beyond the demands of the existing markets until the state formulated a definite policy which the business world considered relatively stable and permanent, the commission suggested that the tendency would be toward development by outside capital under federal license, a scheme inadvisable for Maine because the control of such developments would pass to the federal government. Consequently, the commission unanimously recommended the passage of the following amendment to the Constitution of Maine to bring the Maine definition of "public use" more into accord with that laid down by other states and by the United States Supreme Court:

> Sec. 20. Conservation, storage and control of the waters within the State. The conservation, storage and control by the State, or by a duly authorized public district or districts thereof, of the waters within the

state are paramount public uses and for the benefit of the people of the state; and the Legislature may provide for the same and the apportionment to and assessment upon the lands and property which shall or may be benefited thereby, the whole or any part of the cost including maintenance and control of said waters.

Although some opposition was voiced to the continuance of the Maine Water Power Commission in 1923 because of the expense, the bill was passed on the last day of the session.[28] Governor Baxter, however, took no action on it, and consequently the life of the commission expired. He vetoed the measure on the first day of the session of the next legislature,[29] and the Senate unanimously sustained the veto. The Governor saw no need for a separate commission to study Maine's water powers, and felt that the results accomplished by the commission did not justify its existence or warrant its cost. During the previous two years the Public Utilities Commission had taken over the work of measuring the flow of rivers, and, with the advisory functions omitted, a saving of $15,000 a year resulted, at a time when economy was being stressed. One cannot accuse Governor Baxter of inconsistency here as compared with his view in 1917 and 1919 that the Public Utilities Commission was an improper agency to advise the state on water-power problems. In 1925 it was felt that a staff agency was no longer advisable, and consequently the regulatory commission could satisfactorily supervise the routine mapping and statistical functions, as it still does.

The failure of the Maine Water Power Commission as a staff agency may well be attributed to the fact that it was not properly integrated within the framework of the state government, especially with reference to a conservative legislature and the state budget.

But other forces were at work simultaneously to assert public ownership of water power and make a start in the direction of public power. The movement flared up for a few years, and its leaders attracted attention disproportionate to their political strength. A precursor to modern public power policies, both sides three decades ago agreed on one basic postulate—that the power, whether public or private, should be kept at home. In this way the contest differed from that of today, for present advocates of public power are not always in agreement as to which level of government should control.

Arthur G. Staples assigns 1904 as the inception date for power under state auspices.[30] The proposal was based on the arguments that new industries would not be attracted to Maine without an abundance of developed power, that more private capital would be required than was available, and that private capital would not be willing to develop large quantities of power until a market was ready for it.

Since power had to be kept at home, perhaps Maine should encourage, participate in, or even undertake, its development. In his message of 1909 Governor Fernald had recommended that the water power be developed "under ultimate State ownership and control, so far as is practicable."[31] After the victory of the Democrats in 1911, Governor Frederick W. Plaisted in his inaugural address encouraged the development of water power by private enterprise and capital, and insisted upon the policy of retaining the power in the state. But, "the State will never, as a State, develop a single water power, build a single storage dam, or erect a single power station."[32] Republican Governor Carl E. Milliken also opposed state ownership in 1919 for the present because of "financial obstacles."[33]

N. B. ("Uncle") Tracey, a kindly old man, used to attend every session of the legislature armed with a copy of the charter of the Massachusetts Bay Colony given by William and Mary in 1691, from which he drew the inference that all water powers were common property and should be taken from the supposed owners and appropriated to the use of the state.[34] In 1915 the so-called "Tracey bill" was introduced to provide for a people's water rights and power commission of the state of Maine, but it was reported "ought not to pass" by the committee on interior waters. Nobody took Uncle Tracey himself seriously, but he undoubtedly reflected the attitude and the thinking of a number of people in Maine and elsewhere.[35]

What was happening in the state was not exactly a move for public ownership; it was an attempt to assert that the public already did own the water power. There was, of course, no legal foundation for such a claim and, after several years of agitation and discussion, it was abandoned. All power companies and millowners operating on water power continued to exercise their rights under the Mill Act. The promulgation of this theory was a manifestation of fear that power companies would become too powerful, and represented an attempt to curb them by disputing their long-established rights.

Attention was focused on state development of power in Maine, an issue which transcended party lines. The Republican Party was divided, the Ricker wing, or the "Reformers" advocating it, while the opposition came from the "machine" in the state. The latter group opposed any interference by the state in the control, management, or ownership of water powers.[36] The election of Governor Fernald in 1908 was a victory for the Ricker wing of the party. The controversy between the two groups for a period of twenty years (1904–1924) had, in the opinion of the late Arthur G. Staples, a deterrent effect on the development of power in Maine by outside capital, which remained quiescent through a feeling that a faction of the Maine legislature was "socialistic and confiscatory," and that only when Maine had a fixed and established policy would it be safe to develop the unused water powers.

At the 1913 convention of the State Grange a resolution demanded that water powers be developed "at the expense of the State, as wanted, and rented for the benefit of the State Treasury in order to relieve the pressure of taxation." At the 1915 convention of the same organization, hostility to the tendency of the corporations to monopolize power sites for private profit was the reason for the passage of a resolution favoring state ownership and development of unused power sites to give the people low rates for electric light and power.[37]

In 1917 a bill was introduced into the legislature to create a Maine power commission and provide for the purchase or taking of water powers for the development of electricity. Although the bill was favored by some outsiders, the Solons of Maine showed little interest in it.[38]

It was apparently the intention of the advocates of public ownership for Maine to acquire possession of power sites by purchase. Percival P. Baxter claimed that his resolution for an addition to the Republican platform of 1918 advocated a principle only, that Maine had *the authority and the right* to reacquire these wasted powers. The details were to be worked out after thorough discussion and investigation. Baxter stated that power sites had been given away when the land was sold for as little as twelve and a half cents an acre, "and now we must repurchase them at perhaps a hundred times the selling price. Whatever the price today, in ten or twenty years they will be worth double or treble the price."[39] Although he scored the shortsighted policy of corrupt men in these land deals, Baxter advocated due compensation:[40]

> The Water Powers of the State are, or were, before they were given away, a PUBLIC INHERITANCE. They were placed within our Borders by our Creator: they are the natural heritage of our people. Had it not been for selfish, short-sighted and corrupt men, the present and future generations of Maine people would now have this glorious, this invaluable inheritance, the equal of which cannot be found in any State of the Union. When the State once regains ownership of these Water Powers they should be held as a sacred trust for the benefit of future generations of Maine people....
>
> Some cry out: This is Socialism! Is it Socialism for the State of Maine to take back its great Inheritance and pay the present owners a fair price for it? If it is, the more such Socialism we have, the better for the State of Maine. Nobody will be wronged, nobody will be deprived of property without due compensation, but the State of Maine will regain a portion of her lost Inheritance squandered by our forefathers.

Standing on shaky ground, however, were those who wanted to reacquire the power sites on the basis of previous public ownership, unwise sale, or even fraud. On the analogy of what happened in the Yazoo land scandals in Georgia, Maine could not have made out a case. The sale by the Georgia legislature was upheld despite the charge of fraud, since this legislature represented the state, and an attempted repeal of the fraudulent acts by a subsequent legislature impaired the obligation of contracts for innocent third parties.[41] Senator Brewster took the sound view on this point when he declared that the Maine grants were made under due process of law. "If the disposition were improvident, it is the fault of our ancestors, and not that of the beneficiaries of their policy."[42]

The Maine Public Utilities Commission in 1918 made a lengthy and informative report on the special water-power investigation conducted by it, which included a study of legal phases and of changes which might be necessary in the law in order to achieve state ownership or control if that should be desired. The report on the legal aspects, made by the Honorable Lucilius A. Emery, former Chief Justice of the Supreme Judicial Court of Maine, concluded that an amendment to the Constitution of Maine would be necessary before the state could develop its power resources.[43]

That the state could not develop its power under the existing law was also the conclusion of the Supreme Judicial Court of Maine in an advisory opinion delivered in 1919 in response to five questions asked by the legislature, on the initiative of Percival P. Baxter, who championed the cause of state development. (The opposition attempted to sidetrack the questions of the Supreme Judicial Court with a plan to have them answered by a legislative committee consisting of lawyers.)

The main question, anticipated by former Chief Justice Emery and asked of the Supreme Court, was: May the legislature authorize the construction and development by the state of water-storage reservoirs and basins for the purpose of controlling and conserving the waters of the public lakes and great ponds, of increasing and regulating the flow of the rivers flowing therefrom, and of increasing the value and capacity of the water powers of said rivers? The Court replied that the answer might have been in the affirmative were it not for the last clause, as the state could improve public highways and waterways for transportation and navigation. But the last clause stated the dominant purpose, and the answer was therefore in the negative because the state has no power to tax for this undertaking, and such an undertaking would not be for a public purpose under eminent domain.

In regard to the limitations on the taxing power in Maine to encourage manufacturing the Court said, "A state is simply a political unit, and not a business corporation, except incidentally to further its political purposes. In its organization and machinery it is not adapted to acquire, own, manage, or make a profit out of lands or other property except for public uses."[44] Former Chief Justice Lucilius A. Emery reported that even if the state legally could acquire and develop its water powers, Article IX, section 14, of the Constitution, limiting the borrowing power of the legislature to $300,000, would have to be amended, unless the funds were raised by current taxation, to pay "just compensation" for property acquired.[45]

The second obstacle to the proposed plan was that private property could not be taken under eminent domain for this purpose.

"Private property shall not be taken for public uses without just compensation; nor unless the public exigencies require it." Whether the public exigencies require the taking of private property is a legislative question, but whether such taking is "for public uses" is a judicial question.[46] The crux of the entire situation is, of course, the interpretation of the term "public use," which is subject to either the broad or the limited meaning.

In the former category, public use is virtually synonymous with public benefit, public welfare, with anything that tends to enlarge the resources, increase the industrial energies, and promote the productive power of a large number of inhabitants of a state; leads to the growth of towns; and creates new resources for the employment of capital and labor.[47] In the limited meaning it is "use by the public" or by such numbers of the public as have occasion for such use. Public service corporations are familiar examples.

Former Chief Justice Emery maintained that the weight of opinion favored the latter interpretation,[48] and this is most certainly the construction put on it by the Maine courts. In *Jordan v. Woodward* the court stated:[49]

> That the existence of water-mills is a matter of public convenience at this day, is undeniable; so too is the existence of the shop of the smith, the store of the grocer, the house of the inn-holder, and a great variety of business enterprises in which our citizens employ their labor and capital. In fact there is no branch of lawful business which may not contribute to the public good, and for which there may not, to a certain extent, exist a public necessity. Yet to authorize the appropriation of private property for all these purposes, would be destructive of private rights, and unsettle the tenure by which property is holden. . . . Strictly speaking, private property can only be said to have been taken for public uses when it has been so appropriated that the public have certain and well defined rights to that use secured, as the right to use the public highway, the turnpike, the public ferry, the railroad and the like.

A nice distinction was drawn in another decision when the court said:[50]

> A distinction must be made between a public use and a use in which the public has an interest. In the former case, the public may control, because it is a use within the function of government to establish and maintain. In the latter case, it is a private enterprise that serves the public and in which it is interested to the extent of its necessities and

convenience. The former is clearly within the control of the legislature, while the latter may not be.

The more rigid and narrow interpretation of the term "public use" was adopted by the Maine court in 1905: "It is held, and we think properly, that the term public use cannot be construed to be the equivalent of general welfare or public good. It must receive a more restricted definition."[51] And the court adhered to the restricted definition when it ruled that manufacturing, generating, selling, distributing, and supplying electricity for power, for manufacturing or mechanical purposes, is not a public use for which private property may be taken against the will of the owners. The Maine justices based their advisory opinion on eminent domain and not on police power, but they quoted a Louisiana court on the latter: [The police power] "is a power to regulate the business of others, and not a power to go into business."[52]

Another question asked by the legislature was this: If the state constructed water-storage reservoirs, could riparian owners below be charged a proportional part of the costs of construction, or a rental or tax based on the increased power thereby made available? Since the answer to the first question was in the negative, this one was academic, but the United States Supreme Court said that no such charge or tax could be imposed, because it would violate the constitutional provision requiring all taxes assessed by authority of the state to be "apportioned and assessed equally according to the just value thereof." Nor could it be done in equity. If an upper proprietor desires to improve a storage system, he cannot charge part of the cost to a lower proprietor, since a person cannot be made a debtor against his will.[53]

Other questions concerned the right of the legislature to tax a corporation which has been allowed to erect a dam to control the waters of a great pond, both with and without the privilege of raising the natural level of the waters. These were apparently to pave the way for the Baxter proposals to lease power sites to corporations and to tax them. The answer was that as a property tax this could not be done, because water power as a separate entity is not taxable; but that as a franchise tax it could be done by putting into one class all corporations having express grants from the legislature to control the waters of great ponds.[54]

Since the acceptance of the proposal for state development of water power would require a change in the sacred Declaration of Rights, former Chief Justice Emery showed the need for an amendment to the state constitution to counteract the rigid interpretation of eminent domain. He stressed the need for providing in the amendment a specific designation of the particular purposes for which private property could be taken. If stated only in general terms—public welfare or benefit—the tenure of private property would be simply at the will of the legislature.[55] Then the courts could afford no protection to any owner.

Acting on the recommendations of the Maine Water Power Commission, Governor Percival P. Baxter led the movement for limited state development of water power, which was endorsed by a number of leading men in the state, including the Honorable John A. Peters and Edward P. Ricker, and by the Maine Federation of Women's Clubs. Opposition came from the power companies, the Maine press, the Associated Industries of Maine, the Master of the State Grange (but in the early stages, at least, not the entire organization), and many members of the Maine Bar.

Governor Baxter said that a true conservation policy called for the immediate development of Maine's great water resources. Unharnessed, this potential power is lost. Much of the power running to waste was formerly owned by the state, but was lost when the state sold or gave away its vast timberlands. Since the corporations claimed that Maine offered no market for more electric power, and they were interested in the right to transmit to other states, Governor Baxter felt that it was useless to expect further development on private initiative for the people of Maine. The only possibilities were a stagnant "do-nothing" policy or a constitutional amendment to enable the state to condemn and take over the undeveloped powers for the benefit of its inhabitants. His language in 1918 was much more inclusive than his later attitude:[56] "I do not fear public ownership of great natural resources which by every inherent right belong to the people of a state and should never have been alienated from them." His proposal stipulated that the state should, in general, refrain from disturbing the existing developed powers. But if Maine did acquire the right to take over undeveloped powers, it must also be given authority to acquire any developed powers that might be in that district; otherwise, a single sawmill might block a great water-power system.

One great difficulty which immediately arises when the latter part of the proposal is considered is this: Where would the state stop in taking over small existing developed powers? Once this right is acquired, its limits would be vague; too much discretionary power vested in the state might threaten corporation and individual developments. Probably with this in view, Governor Frederic H. Parkhurst was more cautious when he recommended, in his inaugural address, on January 6, 1921, the development by private capital under state *regulation* of hydroelectric power on the Maine rivers.[57] But he died in less than four weeks, and this paved the way for Governor Baxter to bring the issue to a head in that very legislative session.

Governor Baxter emphasized that he was not advocating public ownership of power resources. He wanted the state to make a beginning in the development of storage reservoirs, to have a storage reservoir system tried out in some suitable location. The decision whether the state should take over the developed powers or develop those undeveloped should be postponed for a time. His proposal was a little T.V.A. for Maine: the state should be allowed to develop power at the storage dam only as an incidental matter. The state should not distribute this power, but should sell it on favorable terms to public utility companies so that inexpensive power would not run to waste.

In his communication to the legislature embodying the proposed constitutional amendment, the Governor recommended, furthermore, that Maine "should have the right to connect the various electrical systems throughout the State, so that a surplus of power in one section can be used in another when there is a scarcity."[58] Realizing that owners of water power on the rivers are entitled to the natural flow of the river, he suggested that storage reservoirs be constructed on a business scale, the state deriving an income from them by selling or leasing the stored waters to lower riparian owners so that they would pay only for the increased flow occasioned by the construction of reservoirs.

The Baxter plan also called for a clause in the amendment prohibiting the transmission of power to other states. Many people in the state feared a federal superpower line under the Federal Water Power Act of 1920, and it was believed that freezing the nontransmission policy in the Constitution would strengthen the state's position. It was also believed that actual construction work on dams by the state might prove to be a bulwark against federal interference, because states and municipalities were accorded certain prior rights under the Federal Water Power Act.[59]

Governor Baxter deplored the fact that under Maine law water power was not taxable as property. With about 400,000 hp. developed, valued at $100 per hp. at least, and 1,000,000 hp. undeveloped, the state was losing a great source of revenue. Consequently, he recommended that the proposed constitutional amendment should also provide for including these valuable rights in property subject to taxation. Furthermore, again apprehensive that federal control might force transmission to other states, he pointed out that this part of the amendment would, in the event of federal control, permit a tax on hydroelectric energy generated in Maine and shipped outside. The tax feature was Governor Baxter's own contribution to the plan, as this was not included in the proposal of the Maine Water Power Commission.[60]

The proposed amendment, defeated partly because of its very size, would have given the state the right to develop storage; to own, control, and sell water power; to tax the energy of falling water in terms of power; and with rights of eminent domain even to enter on present properties and take them for public uses by giving just compensation. Following is the amendment as proposed:[61]

> The conservation, storage, control and use of waters, and the development, improvement, transmission, utilization, electrical interconnection, control and sale of water powers, by the State of Maine, either directly or through such public district or districts, as the Legislature may authorize and not otherwise are declared to constitute paramount public uses, for the accomplishment of which the right of eminent domain may be exercised, and in furtherance of which the right of taxation may be employed; and the Legislature may also provide therefor and for the apportionment to, and assessment upon, the lands and property which shall, or may be benefited thereby, and according to the extent of such benefits, the whole or any part of the cost of such conservation, storage, development, improvement, transmission, control, electrical interconnection, and utilization of said waters and water powers, including the cost of maintenance and operation thereof.

> For the purposes of taxation water powers and water privileges within the State, and hydro-electric energy generated therefrom, may be treated by the Legislature as property distinct from the land or structure to which they may be appurtenant, or from which they may be derived, and such powers, privileges and energy may be assessed for taxation in such manner as the Legislature may determine, at rates differing from the rate imposed upon real and personal property within the State: and such powers and privileges may be classified as developed, partially developed, and undeveloped, and a different rate of taxation may be imposed upon each class: provided, however, that all such taxes shall be apportioned and assessed equally at uniform rates of taxation throughout the State upon the same class of property.

Ricker, lamenting the loss of the timberlands, urged the acceptance of Governor Baxter's program in order to facilitate progress for the people of Maine as a whole instead of the financial advancement of a few special interests. The Baxter program merely represented a declaration of public rights which paved the way to state aid in the development of water power. After acceptance of the amendment, legislation would be necessary for state encouragement of water-power development.[62]

The opposition to the Baxter plan relied on the standard but usually valid arguments—public ownership, socialism, lack of money to engage in commercial enterprises, confiscation of property rights, and interference with private rights and initiative. Some inferred that under the amendment the state could enter fully into the ownership, management, operation, and control of every phase of water power.[63] But Ricker said that the question of commercial venture by the state was not involved, that it was a matter of establishing the right of regulation and control of public utilities as a commercial venture. Furthermore, no proposal was made to retard or take away the rights of private enterprise. On the contrary, it was a scheme to assist development, stabilize private endeavor, and protect investments.[64] Congressman John A. Peters likewise denied the charge that the Baxter plan went so far as to advocate "the ownership, management, operation and control of every phase of water power in the state." The plan was simply that of state development of storage reservoirs on a business basis, and if any potential power sites in a proposed storage basin were condemned it would be incidental to the development of a reservoir, or if power was incidentally developed at a storage dam and sold as a by-product so that it would not run to waste, that too would be incidental to the storage business.[65] However, the proposed amendment was rejected 84 to 44 in the House of Representatives, and 18 to 10 in the Senate.[66]

In his inaugural address of 1923, Governor Baxter said that if the financial condition of the state warranted he would advocate legislation supplementing the amendment to provide for state construction of reservoirs. Since that was impossible for the time being, the legislature should not go beyond submitting the amendment which would make it possible for future legislatures to take the next step forward if conditions should warrant.[67] A proposed amendment for storage by the state or private interests and assessment upon lands benefited thereby attracted little attention in the legislature of 1923. Senator Brewster spoke for it, and Senator Hinckley opposed it. The measure was defeated 24 to 4.[68]

After the defeat of the Baxter constitutional amendment, the Governor modified his policies and pushed a plan for lease of power sites to private corporations, with the possibility of the state taking over the site if public opinion ever came around to the Baxter way of thinking. Of course this referred only to lands owned by the state which were suitable for power sites. The fact that there were only sixteen of these, with one or two exceptions small ones,[69] suggests that the great issue made of it may have had political implications as well as the desire to keep these power sites from the corporations. The principle of lease was expressed by Governor Baxter as follows: "Maine should not *deed* away for all time the few water resources that the people now own; these either should be developed by the State, or leased so that the State will derive an income from them, and all the public waters in the State should yield a revenue to the people."[70] He likened his policy to that of Theodore Roosevelt, who vetoed a bill allegedly comparable to the Kennebec charter. In so doing the President had expressed disapproval of granting water-power rights on navigable streams to a corporation in perpetuity, and favored a policy of leases for fifty years.

The corporation lawyers argued that the state could lease "public," or "school," or "ministerial" lots on which the Kennebec dam was to be located. To this Governor Baxter gave the logical reply that if it can sell them it can lease them, and the proceeds can be applied by the legislature to public uses. State Senator Brewster explained that under the Articles of Separation Maine holds title to some of these lots for the benefit of schools which may be created later in these districts.[71] This limitation on their use may be altered or abolished by joint action of the legislature of Maine and the general court of Massachusetts, as was actually done with so-called "ministerial" lots.

To a limited degree this phase of the Baxter program has been recognized as part of the state's power policy. From about 1917 the policy was adopted that if the state should later acquire the property of water-resource companies, it is not obliged to pay for the franchise given to the companies. This was affixed to every new charter after 1920, and to many previous ones, with the added provision that the state may acquire the property of these companies by paying fair prices for all improvements and developments and for all money invested in the property, but not for the franchise itself.[72]

With only a few state-owned sites remaining, it was believed that they should be kept by the state. Since the state could not legally develop them, the corporations might do so under lease; otherwise they could not be developed at all. The plan was to grant the lease for a period sufficiently long to enable the corporation to obtain a fair return upon the original investment and to amortize it. But the state's interests should be protected (as they were not in the case of the timberlands) against a small group of private interests trying to obtain valuable state sites for little or nothing.

Both houses of the legislature passed in 1923 by overwhelming majorities an act giving the Kennebec Reservoir Company a valuable franchise and the right to acquire state-owned land at the proposed dam site on the Dead River. This was vetoed by Governor Baxter because the franchise granted in perpetuity to a private corporation was worth at least $1,000,000 and would eliminate the possibility of state development at a later date. In the message he contended that the passage of the charter was a betrayal of the trust imposed on the legislature by the people.[73] But both houses passed the act over the veto by overwhelming majorities.[74]

Governor Baxter immediately issued an official proclamation calling on the people to support a referendum on the charter to be acted upon at the regular election in September, 1924. Under his leadership, referendum petitions were sent to every city, town, and plantation, and an impassioned appeal brought "signatures pouring into my office daily."[75] The legislature began to take up the challenge by passing a resolution against the Governor's attack on the integrity of its members, and by starting a second referendum on the charter at a special election to be held in September, 1923, maintaining that the Governor's referendum would delay power development.[76] To this Governor Baxter replied that it was the corporations that were actually behind the second referendum, and that they had adopted the strategy of attempting to save their valuable franchise at a special election where the voting is usually light and a few thousand votes would ensure control.[77]

Since the controversy was preventing water-power development in the area, Governor Baxter offered a compromise measure, a plan to lease the land and water resources at the site to the corporation for forty years.[78] He presented a charter entitled "An Act to Create the Dead River Reservoir Company," under which the corporation would pay an annual rental of $25,000 a year for forty years. With the termination of the lease the state could take over the property at not more than one-half of the net costs of improvements. The state also would have the right to take over the property at any time during the lease by paying compensation. All profits over 6 per cent made by the company were to be credited to the state to reduce the purchase price if the state should buy it. No exemptions from taxation were granted, and Governor Baxter saw another source of revenue in taxing a $1,500,000 project. Out-of-state transmission was prohibited.

The proposed referendum never took place because both houses of the legislature, again by overwhelming majorities, suddenly repealed their own bill.[79] Some opposition to the Governor's compromise measure arose because the executive allegedly infringed upon the prerogatives of the legislature in working out a compromise with the power interests. Claims were made that he and State Senator Brewster, who was a party to the compromise, were motivated by aims of political advancement.

Governor Baxter was apparently determined to go before the people on the issue of establishing the principle of leases for a part of Maine's water-power policy if the legislature had remained adamant.[80] But the legislature did not accept the challenge; neither did the power companies or Governor Baxter.

The section of the Governor's message which provided the reason or excuse for the repudiation of this charter by the corporation follows:[81]

> In my opinion this will inaugurate a policy of leasing rather than deeding away the State's natural resources. If you adopt it, you will have placed upon our Statute books legislation that will be hailed as both wise and constructive, and you will have established a precedent and a policy that well may guide those who follow.
>
> . . . In my opinion this marks a new era in the water power history of the State of Maine. If this legislature in its wisdom enacts this [compromise] bill into law, it means that never again will a private corporation obtain storage rights from the State under a deed or transfer, but that all such rights, in all probability, hereafter will be granted on a lease with a rental accruing to the State and with proper safeguards to protect the interests of the people.

According to Governor Baxter, the terms of this charter were "unconditionally agreed upon as acceptable to all the incorporators." But it was embarrassing to the legislators, who had voted twice to deed away the property and give the franchise, to have to approve a bill whereby the state would receive $1,000,000 under a lease of privileges.[82]

However, before this charter could be acted upon, it was repudiated by the corporation. In a letter from Walter S. Wyman, president of the Central Maine Power Company, to Governor Baxter, April 6, 1923, the incorporators withdrew their support because of the interpretation put upon the transaction in Governor Baxter's message to the legislature.[83] Wyman claimed that at the conference, when an attempt was made at compromising with the opponents of the measure, the reason advanced for imposing the rental was that the state owned the land involved, including the banks and bed of the stream. But the Governor's message

> conveys to the Legislature and to the public the idea that the Central Maine Power Company and myself assent to the doctrine that there is some right belonging to the State in every storage reservoir which any

developing company should pay for, even though the State owns no land affected thereby . . . With this construction upon the Dead River charter, now before the people, its acceptance by me would be considered assent to all this doctrine. Although I believe the charter does not warrant such a conclusion, I cannot allow myself and the company which I represent to be placed in the position of apparently subscribing to the views expressed in and the impression conveyed by your message.

In another letter under the same date to Representative (later Governor) William Tudor Gardiner, William B. Skelton explained that the incorporators felt that the terms and conditions of the Dead River reservoir bill were "too burdensome and otherwise unsatisfactory" to warrant the great initial investment and maintenance charges which would be required. Governor Baxter then explained Wyman's "excuses": "I since have learned that his out-of-State associates pressed him hard and refused to abide by the agreement that he and Mr. Skelton made with me."[84]

Once again, in an effort to stimulate power production, Governor Baxter extended the olive branch to Wyman, asking for a conference to arrange a compromise and offering to call a special session of the legislature to effect its passage. Said the Governor: "On my part I should approach this subject without bearing in mind any of the controversies that have been indulged in in the past. I should endeavor to effect a settlement of a situation that ought not to continue." But on January 15, 1924, Wyman wrote the Governor that his company was not interested in the Dead River reservoir, as they had plans to construct one elsewhere (Brassua Lake and Moose River) which would suffice for the needs of the area.[85]

The attempt to put the state into the power business in the legislature of 1925 created little interest, and the bill was postponed indefinitely.[86] The measure was compared with the Ontario development, in which the government supplies the power and builds the transmission lines, and the towns form companies for distribution and price-fixing. But that is public power despite a degree of local control.

When Senator Owen Brewster was governor of Maine in 1925, he recommended the development of water resources by private capital under state control, advocating the "American traditions of private initiative as against public ownership." His panacea was somewhat similar to the revised Baxter program of long-term leases of state-owned sites.[87]

Development of power projects under state auspices depends in part upon the definition of the term "public use" under eminent domain. Liberal interpretation would aid condemnation of property for power lines; conservative interpretation would hinder or perhaps prevent the same. The narrow interpretation of "public use" as expressed in *Brown v. Gerald*[88] was slightly broadened by the Supreme Judicial Court of Maine in 1926, in *Smith v. Power Company*.[89] In 1905 the generation of electricity had been limited, but in the interval of twenty years its use had become more general, and it was apparent that its generation for manufacturing and other purposes might well be regarded as a public use for which private property could be taken to secure its transmission. Consequently, the court in 1926 allowed a taking of land for just such purposes as were denied in 1905.

However, Judge Deasy did not go so far as to say that a power transmission line carrying current, the use of which all are legally entitled to share on equal terms, was a public use. He said that it need not be answered in this case. But the decision allowed private property to be taken for transmission lines where one-third of the current would be used for lights and two-thirds for power. The court pointed out that the transmission of current for power was one of the company's primary purposes, but also said, "The public is concerned. It would be unreasonable to compel light users to abide in darkness or to submit to inferior and inefficient service."[90] In short, Judge Deasy limited *Brown v. Gerald* to its own particular facts and allowed the condemnation of land for the transmission of electricity for both light and power purposes.

After the heat of the controversy over the charters for the Kennebec and Dead River storage reservoirs had subsided and Governor Baxter was out of office, the legislature in 1927 approved without debate a favorable committee report on an amended act to create the Kennebec Reservoir Company.[91] By this act the same lots in question in 1923 were leased for the term of fifty years at an annual rental of $25,000. At the termination of the lease the state was empowered to take over the property and rights, paying the net investment not including compensation for the value of the franchise.[92]

The original bill introduced in 1927 asked for a perpetual grant. Former Governor Baxter, in a series of radio addresses, strongly opposed a lease in 1927 because of the agitation to repeal the Fernald law. He had favored leases in 1923 because the nonexport law was not in danger. But he wanted no rights whatever to be granted until the Wyman-Insull people ceased their political activities, dropped their campaign to repeal the Fernald law, and entered into a binding agreement never to export power.[93]

The charter was amended and extended every two years from 1929 to 1939 inclusive.[94] The 1937 amendment authorized the Kennebec Reservoir Company to sell to the Central Maine Power Company and authorized the latter to acquire the property and franchise. The sale took place, and the annual rental is now paid by the Central Maine Power Company. The site was being developed in the autumn of 1949.

With this exception, Maine has no general policy of leasing lands for power sites. While the state forest commissioner has authority to lease some state-owned lots and it is probable that some of these are flowed in power-storage development, so far as is known no site of any importance has been leased for the purpose.

The suggestion for state aid for power development was resurrected in February, 1950, by Seth May, an Auburn attorney.[95] Lest the "planners" use the national power shortage to usher in government ownership and operation of the hydroelectric industry, the thesis is that state development would forestall federal power invasion of Maine. If the state should aid the private companies (assuming their desire to participate), Maine's power would be developed without the interference of the national government in power projects. May suggested that taxpayers must bear the burden whether it be national or state development. If the state should stimulate private hydroelectric companies to develop this power, federal extravagance would be eliminated. "Indeed, what an encouragement it would be throughout the nation," wrote May, "for a sovereign State to meet the crusade for public absorption of private business and unbelievable Federal extravagance by deliberate assistance toward private development of this great resource!"

Somewhat reminiscent of the Baxter proposals of thirty years ago, this proposition shows how far some people are willing to go to adhere to Maine's power particularism.

Municipal ownership of electrical utilities has not made much headway in Maine. In 1927, Professor Orren C. Hormell listed only four municipal plants, at Calais, Van Buren, Lubec, and Kennebunk.[96] In July, 1949, Maine had six plants owned by towns, village

| | Operating property | Number of customers |
|---|---|---|
| Houlton Electric Department..... | $659,675.01 | 3,555 |
| Kennebunk Electric Light Department...................... | 247,390.64 | 1,421 |
| Lubec Electric Department....... | 262,791.92 | 1,069 |
| Madison Electric Works.......... | 260,639.94 | 1,424 |
| Squirrel Island Village Corporation | 28,151.33 | 107 |
| Van Buren Light and Power District....................... | 130,212.01 | 1,204 |

corporations, or districts.[97] (See the accompanying table.) The situation at Houlton is rather unusual in that the company was organized as a private company but is operated by the town through ownership of the company stock acquired by authority of a private and special act of the legislature. Since Maine has no general law that would authorize any municipality to go into the electric business, special legislation is required for each case. The policy of granting corporations immunity from competition makes it extremely difficult for municipalities to take over private power plants. Advocates of municipal ownership argue that this conservative policy aids "vested interests." Maine's municipally operated electric plants have enjoyed a moderate degree of success, although some have not been without difficulties. In general, rates are slightly lower than those of private utilities.[98]

Public ownership is not a live issue in Maine. A bill was proposed in 1947 to create an Aroostook Power Authority, advocating public ownership of electrical facilities in the county. It gathered little momentum. Existing conditions have not caused dissatisfaction or agitation for public enterprise, municipal rates are not sufficiently lower to arouse much sentiment for public ownership, and small independent plants do not fit well into the configuration of coördinated and integrated power systems. Furthermore, the traditional independence, individualism, and conservatism of Maine people are not conducive to public ownership of electric utilities. This is offered as an explanation, not necessarily as a justification.

## CHAPTER IX

### Rural Electrification; War Problems

Since light and power companies are public utilities for the public interest, it became a practice in Maine to grant them monopolistic privileges. Each corporation is assigned a territory to serve; before another corporation can operate in that territory the consent of the Public Utilities Commission is necessary. Consent is given only after determination by public hearing that public convenience and necessity require a second utility.[1]

In 1915 the legislature passed an Act to Aid Rural Electrification. It provided that ten or more individuals, contemplating in good faith the organization of a corporation, could obtain a hearing to seek a certificate of public convenience and necessity for the creation of a corporation to distribute electricity. The act required the existing utility to supply electricity to the new company "to the extent of its reasonable capacity and at reasonable rates," under the direction and control of the Public Utilities Commission.[2] No attempt was made to invoke this provision until 1929, when at Durham it was sought to form a corporation under the statute. At the hearing on July 6, opposition was presented by the Central Maine Power Company. The petition was denied because it was not drawn up in an accurate and precise manner.[3]

The argument of the power companies is that, as a business proposition, it is a slow process to extend rural lines because of the great expense and the small returns from the amount of power sold. Distribution and not production costs retard rural electrification. The cost of erecting poles and electric lines ranges from $800 to $2,000 a mile, the average being about $1,500.[4] Besides the initial or capital cost, the expense of doing business—interest, repairs, depreciation, and maintenance—would cost about $55 per customer per year exclusive of the cost of power. A number of power engineers are convinced, however, that the rural construction technique of many private utilities is unnecessarily costly.[5]

The rural argument is that power companies have been given a monopoly over all territory because they are public utilities. As public utilities they are supposed to serve the public, part of which lives in the country. Therefore it is unjust to consider each extension as a unit, and to maintain that it costs more to deliver in the country. Only after the company had served every home in the area would it be proper to strike an average cost of delivering a kilowatt in the territory served. An analogy is sometimes made with the rural deliveries of the Post Office Department.

On the other hand, undoubtedly some outlying farms could not afford to purchase electric service even if it were brought to the door, and others are in areas so remote and sparsely settled that it is not feasible to extend lines to them.[6] The controversy is a phase of the urban-rural conflict: Should urban customers pay higher rates so that the rural areas can be more adequately supplied with electricity, or should power companies be encouraged to keep out of territory which would raise the average rate? Many recent attempts of power companies and the Rural Electrification Administration to stimulate the use of electricity in rural areas offer hope for a partial solution of the problem. A greater demand for service in outlying districts would make it more profitable to extend rural lines and would tend to equalize urban-rural costs. The Public Utilities Commission has favored the financing by utility companies of line extensions so that the farmer's capital may be available for wiring buildings and purchasing equipment with which he can make a more profitable use of electricity.[7]

Maine's rural electric situation is complicated by geographic obstacles. In such a large and sparsely populated state it is more difficult to extend long rural lines to remote sections than in the small and more densely populated states of Rhode Island, Massachusetts, and Connecticut, which exceed Maine in percentage of total farms served. Although the population of Rhode Island almost equals that of Maine, it is crowded into a territory about one-sixth the size of Aroostook County; thus it is obvious that Maine's rural electric problems are greater. Vermont, however, has 80 per cent rural electrification and New Hampshire has slightly more than 90 per cent.[8] Although the physical conditions in these states are more nearly similar to those in Maine than in the other New England states, the analogy is only relative because Maine's geographical size is unique in New England.

The availability of current is not a factor in the rural electric problems of Maine; but geography is. In the ordinary village, according to an estimate of 1929, distribution of energy to residences averaged from 80 to 85 per cent of the total expense, while the generation of the power and its delivery to the switchboard made up 15 to 20 per cent of the cost.[9] Distribution costs in rural areas with long lines and fewer customers were said to be much greater. It was claimed that the Wyman dam at Bingham was capable of generating in one week enough electricity to supply all the unsupplied farmers of Maine for one year.[10] Thus, the position that the retention of hydroelectricity under the Fernald law can aid rural electrification is untenable.

In the middle 'twenties, power companies in Maine required guaranties of annual gross revenue during a five-year period amounting to one-third of the cost of rural extensions. Numerous appeals were made to the Public Utilities Commission for lower terms. The commission's surveys of each extension indicated that the annual cost to the electric company was somewhat less than 20 per cent.[11] Gradually, reductions in the requirements of the companies to guaranties of 20–25 per cent of the extension costs resulted in a relatively small number of cases which came to formal hearing before the commission in 1929–1930.

In 1931 Representative Louis A. Jack sponsored a bill to provide adequate rural electric service at just and reasonable rates. Three persons could organize a corporation to distribute electricity if the Public Utilities Commission approved. The controversy between the power companies and the rural interests at the committee hearing centered around a clause in the original bill which would have required utility companies to supply current to the new corporations at one-half cent a kilowatt-hour. Representative Jack asserted that in 1929 President Wyman of the Central Maine Power Company had said he would be willing to supply the power at that rate. Later, he and his attorneys modified the statement. It was also brought out that even if Wyman had made the offer, in view of the fact that this bill covered the entire state, other companies were not parties to the promise. Jack suggested an amendment that the price be fixed by the Public Utilities Commission. Senator Southard reported that the amended bill was favored by "various parties in interest,"[12] and it was passed without much opposition.

The only important change in policy resulting from this new law was that the number of incorporators was brought down from ten to three. Its essential provisions were:[13]

> Whenever, any electric light and power company does not supply reasonable adequate electric service in any portion of the territory in which it is authorized to furnish service, any three or more persons not receiving and unable to receive service, in the said territory, at reasonable rates, may themselves, form a corporation for the transmission, use and sale of electricity in such portion of said territory as may be designated by the public utilities commission and the electric light and power company authorized to furnish service throughout all such territory shall furnish the newly organized corporation with electric current sufficient for their needs, at reasonable rates to be prescribed by said public utilities commission. Said current to be furnished from the transmission lines of the said public utility most conveniently located for the purposes of the new corporation.

This statute was considered a stopgap by R.E.A. supporters ten years later. They maintained that it was inadequate in defining the powers of corporations, failed to permit the generation of power, made no provision for a membership coöperative setup, and left many questions of both substantive right and procedure unanswered.[14]

By 1925 the Central Maine Power Company employed the first full-time executive in New England for rural electrification.[15] In 1931 this company established a policy of extending rural lines when those desiring service guaranteed a minimum gross revenue, during a five-year period, amounting to $20 a month per mile of line extension.[16] This provision eliminated separate consideration for each individual line, and was based on average construction costs. According to the statistics of the Central Maine Power Company, rural extensions continued during the depression. From 1932 through 1936 the company built 256.24 miles "of strictly rural lines at a total cost of $323,389.51."[17]

In June, 1937, after a conference of representatives of the Public Utilities Commission and the Central Maine Power Company, the policy of line extension was amended to allow for farmers who did not desire service on a new line when built. The minimum monthly guaranty of $20 a month was reduced by $1.50 a month for each permanently occupied premise of an annual user, and by $9.00 a year for one occupied by a seasonal resident.[18]

In 1939 the Central Maine made plans for a group of customers to be served by ten or more miles of line, to arrange collectively for service in their area under guaranties and revenue status separate from the remainder of the system. Increase in consumption by the original customers and the addition of new customers was expected to allow the area eventually to obtain service at the company's general rates.[19] From 1937 through 1940, when the business upswing and the activities of the R.E.A. stimulated the demand for rural service, the Central Maine built 873.07 miles of rural lines at a cost of $1,156,352.99. In the calendar year 1941 this company and the Cumberland County Power and Light Company spent a total of $561,627 on 389.02 miles for 1,353 customers. The number of customers per mile, 3.5, was, however, the lowest for twenty years.[20] From 1927 to 1940 inclusive, the Cumberland Company, which had simpler rural problems because of shorter distances and greater density of population, had constructed 391 miles of rural lines at a cost of $427,891.95.

The Second World War directed power policy away from rural electrification and focused it on war production. Extension of rural lines was virtually suspended during the war in order to curtail the use of critical materials. At the end of 1941, rural extensions were limited to 1,000 feet; in March, 1942, this was reduced to 250 feet. Then, in July, 1942, they were eliminated entirely unless the premises had been completely wired before that time, or were new buildings ready for superstructure on July 1, 1942. With these two exceptions, the company was required to obtain the approval of the War Production Board before connecting a customer to a line.[21]

In 1931 approximately one-third of the Maine farms were supplied with electricity. This put Maine in sixteenth position in the country in the number of farms served; on the basis of percentage of total farms served, Maine occupied ninth position in the United States.[22] This was a good record in view of the difficult economic and geographical conditions under which it was achieved. On the basis of annual gross revenue received for farm service per farm served, Maine was reported as occupying forty-seventh position in the United States. This would indicate that either the rates in Maine were so low that the power companies received little income from the rural customers, or so high (or nonpromotional in form of schedule) that farmers used little current. Every Maine farmer would testify that the former alternative was absurd.

In 1935 Maine had 41,907 farms; 13,959, or 33.3 per cent, were receiving electric service.[23] At that time Maine was in eighth position in the country in percentage of farms served. During the next ten years the number of Maine farms served was almost doubled—26,775 out of a total of 42,184, averaging 63.5 per cent. But other states had advanced much more rapidly, and Maine's position dropped to nineteenth in 1945. On June 30, 1946, the R.E.A. estimated that 29,072, or 68.9 per cent, of Maine farms received electric service, and Maine was in twentieth place in the nation.

From 1934 until June, 1947, the increase in electrified farms in Maine was 125.6 per cent. Thirty-eight states, however, made more rapid progress during this period. According to the most recent available R.E.A. figures, of July 1, 1947, 31,493 Maine farms were served, and 10,691 were without service. The percentage was 74.7, and Maine was in twenty-third position. The Power Survey Committee of the New England Council gave Maine a slightly better record—76.6 per cent of farms electrified in 1947. The Public Utilities Commission now estimates that between 85 and 90 per cent of all farms in Maine have electric service.[24]

Urban electric rates in Maine have been high compared with those of other states. On the basis of 1947 figures of the Federal Power Commission, Maine was the ninth highest state in the Union for average monthly bills for 100 kw-h residential electric service in cities of 2,500 population and above. On the same basis, for 250 kw. Maine's average was seventeenth from the top.[25] Federal figures for 217 cities with a population of 50,000 and more indicated that Portland (Maine's only city with more than 50,000 inhabitants) had the one hundred ninety-sixth lowest monthly residential bill for 25 kw-h.[26] For 100 kw-h it was in one hundred eighty-fifth place; for 250 kw-h, one hundred forty-first place; and for 500 kw-h, eighty-fourth place. Whether these costs are necessarily higher, however, is another question. As for farms, the great majority served used electricity in small amounts for lighting, with very little for power and appliances. The fact that Maine occupied ninth position on the basis of percentage of farms served, in spite of holding only forty-seventh position on the basis of revenue per farm, indicated rapid progress in rural electrification in view of the adverse physical and economic conditions.[27]

The R.E.A. alleges that the commercial companies "skim the cream"; hence, consumption on R.E.A. lines is low—59 kw-h in December, 1946. The R.E.A. bases its estimates of feasibility in Maine on an average farm consumption of 90 kw-h or less per month; in other states it is planning on 250 to 350 kw-h. According to the R.E.A., "such expansion of rural electrification as has taken place has been due substantially to the organization of rural electric coöperatives. The sections of the state where the commercial companies made the greatest liberalization of their requirements are those in which coöperatives have organized or started to organize."[28] However, an objective appraisal cannot attribute progress in Maine's complicated rural electric problems substantially to any one factor.

The crucial point of disagreement between the Maine utility corporations and the R.E.A. has been over the interpretation of competition in territory assigned to the former. The power companies contend that they have monopolistic privileges in the territory they are serving or will serve when lines are extended. This territory, they say, belongs to them, and they want protection from competition in the territory of their potential customers. The R.E.A. says that if an area is not being served, it does not belong to the company. R.E.A. loans cannot be used to finance lines to take away a power-company consumer, but are available only to provide service to those who do not have it. Whenever a utility agrees to serve every consumer within reach, that company obtains a clear field. Until then, coöperatives say, they are not competing with utility company territory. In some states, notably Mississippi, Pennsylvania, and Wisconsin, the new electric coöperatives are protected by the use of injunctions to halt attempted invasions of territory preëmpted by them. In Wisconsin, friendly coöperation by the commission has restrained private companies from building rural lines adverse to public interest.[29]

The United States Supreme Court has declared that whether competition between utilities shall be prohibited, regulated, or forbidden is a matter of state policy, and that the state may alter this policy at will.[30] In Maine the legislature has insisted that public utilities are natural monopolies to be regulated by the Public Utilities Commission. Twice in recent years the legislature has refused to allow the R.E.A. to preëmpt unserved territory which would tend to establish competing electric systems unregulated by the commission. Both the Maine legislature and the commission have adopted the view expressed in the dissent of Mr. Justice Butler in the Tennessee Electric Power decision, namely, that competition will destroy the established companies.

According to the R.E.A., the "purpose of regulation is to protect the buyer of an essential service provided under monopoly conditions from exploitation by the seller. In the case of the coöp, the buyer and seller are identical. The public interest is protected because the coöp provides the service to all its members at cost."[31] Although this view is accepted in some quarters, Maine has adopted a more conservative philosophy. In Maine not only must regulation protect rates and service for the consumer, but—equally important—the regulatory commission must defend the rights of the utility corporation itself, its rate of return, and, because it is regulated, its monopoly. Thus, regulation and protection become bilateral.

Yet it would be erroneous to conclude that the conservative nature of the state accounts for the failure of the coöperative movement to flourish in Maine, because, in the conservative states of Vermont, South Carolina, Mississippi, and Texas, coöperatives are a powerful economic factor.

With the R.E.A. in Maine it sometimes became a question of *who* should supply the farmers with electricity more than *how* they should be supplied. For example, when the power companies were extending their lines into territory sought by the Sandy River cooperative, the important matter with Representative Mills was not that these farmers were being supplied, but that the electric coöperative was not supplying them.[32] Despite the R.E.A. contention that private enterprise cannot supply some rural areas with electricity, it is apparent that in a large and sparsely settled state there are areas inaccessible to coöperatives. Furthermore, the coöperatives are dependent upon the private company for their source of energy.

There are in Maine, as elsewhere, two distinct points of view and a middle ground on the matter of rural electrification. Professor James C. Bonbright of Columbia University considers this one of the most critical problems that our country will be called upon to face. "It concerns the whole economics of subsidies, as contrasted with the philosophy of individualism which calls upon individuals to assume the full costs of services performed for their benefit . . . Household and farm electrification, along with other utility services, is still generally ranked among those services for which the direct beneficiaries should pay in full."[33]

The philosophy of individualism predominates in Maine. One view is that the true success of the R.E.A. is measured not by the number of miles of lines it builds or the number of farms it serves, but by the number of persons it serves who otherwise would be unable to obtain electricity. Edward F. Merrill said on this point, "If the R.E.A. produces a demand for electric service which is met by a private utility, they have accomplished their true purpose, and that without the expenditure of public funds for the building of lines and other allied purposes."[34]

The R.E.A. states that its activities in Maine are far from typical because of the strong influence and aggressiveness of the commercial utilities, and rulings by state agencies. Threats by coöperatives to enter certain rural areas have doubtless stimulated the power companies to enter those areas, and it is difficult to accept the contention of the companies that they could serve some of these areas, but did not realize service was wanted until coöperatives had been organized.[35] The R.E.A. feels that the utility companies constructed "lines which hem in the coöps and which were built under construction programs which seemed to us more vigorously prosecuted than in similar areas where coöps had not started. This hemming in will prevent development of the coöperatives to the ultimate optimum size and scope which coöps have attained in other States."[36]

Some of these contentions of the R.E.A. again indicate its desire to supply electricity, to compete, and to expand its own activities. This policy does not fit into the present configuration in Maine. Hostility to the R.E.A. in Maine does not stem entirely from the power companies. It was emphatically stated by a rural representative that his constituents wanted electric service, preferably from the power companies instead of through a coöperative.[37] Many Maine farmers do not like the idea of borrowing money from the national government or anybody else.

The Kingman Electric Company was the first rural electric line in New England to be organized under the Rural Electrification Administration Act of 1936. The Maine Public Utilities Commission, in December, 1937, gave permission to the company to serve an area including the villages of Macwahoc, Kingman, Prentiss, Springfield, and Carroll. About 200 customers were served over 65 miles of line with energy purchased from the Bangor Hydro-Electric Company.

Friction arose, however, with the Danforth Electric Company. The Kingman coöperative planned to extend its lines across Washington County to a point very near the Town of Danforth, which is already served by a small local company with about 200 customers. An attempt was made on the open market to purchase the Danforth company as a physical and economic bridge to unserved farms. When the parties could not agree upon the price, Merrill maintained that the coöperative sought permission to build into Danforth and enter into competition with the local company. The Public Utilities Commission refused to consent to this.[38] At present the Kingman organization is serving 520 rural consumers with 136 miles of line in Penobscot, Aroostook, and Washington counties.[39]

A second project, Farm-Home Electric Coöperative, Inc., was organized in December, 1938, and was given permission by the commission to serve an area north of Patten and Island Falls, parts of Sherman, and the area south of Sherman. The line was constructed and energized in July, 1940, and the energy was purchased from the Maine Public Service Company at Patten. Two requests for extensions were subsequently granted. It now operates 158 miles of line, serving 349 rural consumers in Penobscot and Aroostook counties.[40] The Bangor Hydro-Electric Company assisted these coöperatives, lending them engineers, making blueprints, and aiding in their organization.[41] These two R.E.A. coöperatives were organized in Maine under the general corporation laws as stock companies, but their public utility status was not determined.

Four more such projects were organized; they petitioned for recognition in September and October, 1940. The Sandy River Electric Coöperative, Inc., proposed to serve the area east of Farmington and New Sharon, but this area included no sizable village. The Union River Electric Coöperative, Inc., of Aurora proposed to serve the area north of Ellsworth, starting at the lower end of Graham Lake and including the villages of Clifton, Amherst, and Aurora. It serves 230 members over 79 miles of line in Hancock and Penobscot counties. The Waldo County Electric Coöperative, Inc., covering about 150 miles to serve 450 members, proposed to serve an area in Waldo County north of Belfast. The Denny's River Electric Coöperative, Inc., of Meddybemps proposed to serve a section between Pembroke and Alexander in the vicinity of Meddybemps and Cathance lakes. It serves 30 members over 12 miles of line in Washington County, and is completing 75 miles of additional lines to serve 184 new rural consumers. A few months later a project was organized in the St. John's Valley under the leadership of Father Wilfred Soucy, comprising about 150 miles and serving 450 members. Recognition by the Public Utilities Commission was desired.

The Sandy River project originally had 236 members, and requested a line of 77 miles. In October, 1940, the Central Maine Power Company and Maine Consolidated Power Company made a new offer of $5.50 a month per mile plus taxes, about $1.00, with a one-year guaranty, instead of the usual $20 a month per mile for five years. The Public Utilities Commission ruled that these R.E.A. coöperatives were not public utilities, and therefore could not be organized under the general corporation laws under which the two earlier projects had been approved.[42] The new coöperatives subsequently made applications under the 1931 statute.

The Public Utilities Commission allotted the Sandy River coöperative 2.5 miles and 9 members, and some of the 9 had already been supplied with electricity by the Central Maine.[43] Supporters of the R.E.A. charged that during the delay of five months while the Sandy River applications were pending, the power company erected poles, strung lines, and invested a few thousand dollars when the commission was in process of determining whether the area belonged to the Sandy River Coöperative or to the Central Maine Power Company. This charge suggests, however, that not only did R.E.A. supporters desire to extend rural electrification, but also that they wanted it to be done by means of coöperatives.

Meanwhile, the Consolidated Power Company was authorized by the commission to sell to the Central Maine a part of its franchise covering the disputed area. Although Representative Mills implied that the sale indicated "some rather close connection between the Central Maine and the Public Utilities Commission," it may have been that the small private company could not compete with a coöperative financed by federal funds, and that the commission favors profit enterprises and opposes nonprofit business forms, or, more likely, that the commission usually authorizes bona fide sales such as this.

Although the power companies felt that the Sandy River coöperative was attempting to raid private territory, and its aspirations were curtailed to the extent that it did not give service, the Public Utilities Commission granted the petitions of the Union River Electric Coöperative, Inc., and the Denny's River Coöperative, Inc., and also granted extensions to the Kingman Electric Company and the Farm-Home Electric Coöperative, Inc. The commission authorized sale of the Princeton Electric Light District to the Denny's River Coöperative. The case of the Waldo County Electric Coöperative, Inc., was closed, as the petitioners supplied no further information.[44]

In the legislative session of 1941 there was introduced an Act to Aid Agriculture by Providing for the Organization of Rural Electrification Coöperatives. The bill was based on a model law drawn up by the R.E.A.; a very similar bill was presented to the Vermont legislature at the same time.[45] In its original form the bill provided for powerful coöperative organizations which the utilities claimed would have permitted unrestricted and unregulated competition with existing companies. Various rural groups, working together under the leadership of the State Grange, sponsored the act. Their spokesman was Representative F. Ardine Richardson, who maintained that farmers, in order to obtain service, had to contribute labor and poles and to pay a differential rate, and yet they received no equity in the lines they had paid for and had contracted to make profitable to the power company, because the lines became the property of the electrical corporation.[46]

The major public utility companies, spearheaded by the Central Maine Power Company, attacked the Coöperative Enabling Act. The steady increase in rural extensions by the power companies has been one of their chief arguments why the state should not permit rural electric coöperatives to "raid" the territory of existing companies and to establish competing systems in Maine under general corporation law, which is noted for easy procedure in this state.

At the hearing before the legislative public utilities committee, Edward F. Merrill presented specific objections to the original bill. By its definition of the word "person," cities and towns could form coöperatives to enter the utility field no matter how well or how reasonably they were being served by an existing utility company. Such a provision would have been pleasing to proponents of municipal ownership, but that was an entirely different issue. Also, the bill granted the corporation the right to perpetual existence. Since a charter is a contract which cannot be impaired by the state, this provision meant that the state could not revoke a franchise once it was granted. Further, the coöperatives were empowered to mortgage property and franchises, to consolidate, and to build dams and generating plants. Merrill saw in this a threat to Maine's Fernald law. Since loans would be made by a federal agency and the mortgage assumed by it, if one or several coöperatives failed and the R.E.A. acquired the properties and franchises by foreclosure it could consolidate these coöperatives and, as a federally operated utility business located in Maine under an irrevocable franchise, could generate power on Maine dams and send it out over federal wires to other states. This was undoubtedly an alarmist point of view. The R.E.A. promotes, but does not exactly operate, the power business. The 1936 law provides that the R.E.A. must dispose of foreclosed properties within five years.

By the provisions of the bill the coöperatives were specifically exempted from the jurisdiction of the Public Utilities Commission. Whereas one utility cannot operate in the territory of another without a certificate of convenience and necessity, coöperatives could operate in any area regardless of how well the existing utility served and regardless of the reasonableness of the rates. Furthermore, there was no supervision of their organization or financial structure. The coöperative could sell electricity not only to its own members but also to governmental agencies, political subdivisions, and other persons not exceeding 10 per cent of the number of its members.

Merrill contended that coöperatives were also empowered to place their lines along urban and rural highways without liability for damage and without the consent of town officials, whereas utility companies are required to comply with certain prescribed rules, to obtain permits from municipal officials after public hearing, and to pay for damages caused by the construction of their lines. Merrill said of this specific bill:[47]

> These coöperatives seek to do a public utility business in the state of Maine. Hiding behind the subterfuge of coöperative membership, they seek in fact all of the rights and benefits of public utility corporations, without assuming any of their responsibilities or burdens. From start to finish, this bill discloses that their desire is unrestricted territory, unrestricted rights, and uncontrolled operation.

While objecting to the bill, he stated the position of the power companies with respect to the R.E.A. as follows:

> I have no quarrel with the fundamental purpose of the R.E.A. which I understand to be that of enabling those in Rural Areas who, otherwise, cannot obain electric service, to obtain the necessary financial aid and technical advice to enable them to serve themselves.
>
> As long as they confine their efforts to that field they may well justify the expenditure of public funds in their enterprises.
>
> There is no justification, however, for an attempt upon their part to foster a law and advocate a law that will enable them to enter the territory of our local companies and attempt to serve those potential customers of ours which we are willing and able to serve.

By a unanimous vote the public utilities committee reported that the bill "ought not to pass," but, after a series of important amendments which brought the bill in line with the public policy of the state, it became law after a lengthy debate. The most important changes were that the coöperatives should not have perpetual existence, could serve their members only, should not have the power of eminent domain, and would comply with other laws and regulations applicable to electric companies; finally, that the Public Utilities Commission would have jurisdiction over the territory served, except in the matter of rates and regulation of securities.[48]

Section 24 of the act, which came up for radical change in the 1945 session of the legislature, now reads as follows:[49]

> Sec. 24. Coöperatives not public utilities. 1941, c. 281, g24. Coöperatives shall not be deemed to be public utilities; except with the consent of the public utilities commission, no premises shall receive service from any coöperative, if such premises were on the date of the organization of such coöperative receiving or prior thereto had been receiving electric service from a public utility, or which are situated on those portions of roads or ways along which the distribution lines of an existing utility are located, nor if such service from the coöperative is to be rendered in the territory in which an existing utility is authorized to render such service, unless and until such service has been requested of the existing utility by various persons whose premises are so located as to be fairly representative of the route or routes of the proposed distribution line or lines of the coöperative to be built in such territory and the utility has either refused or neglected for an unreasonable length of time to furnish such service; any existing utility may give its consent to a coöperative to serve any portion of the territory which said utility is authorized to serve. Any person who has been refused membership in or service by a coöperative may complain of such refusal to the public utilities commission which may, after hearing, upon finding that such service may reasonably be rendered, order such person to be served.

The act requires that Maine farmers who have been unable to get electricity apply again. Then, if the power companies once more fail to provide service, the coöperatives must obtain the consent of the Public Utilities Commission to build and operate their lines.

William J. Neal, acting administrator of the R.E.A., attributed the shortcomings of rural electrification in Maine to the unnecessary barriers set up by the Maine statutes which hindered rather than helped farmers in securing electrical service.[50] Because of these statutes, he asserted, Maine let go by default more than $500,000 of loan funds that Congress required the R.E.A. to allocate for rural electrification in Maine, and because of these legal barriers the R.E.A. could plan extension of electric service to only 1,300 Maine farms in its postwar program. "In the consideration of Maine we necessarily had to make our estimates on the basis of existing conditions. Therefore, we had to give due consideration to the existence of the barriers to rural electrification."

Acting Administrator Neal said that the R.E.A. could do nothing about the legal barriers, but he suggested that the State Grange and the farmers of Maine could. As a result, Representative R. Leon Williams of Clifton, in the 1945 session of the legislature, introduced a bill attempting to remove the coöperatives from the jurisdiction of the Public Utilities Commission.

The Williams bill attempted to repeal section 24, quoted above, and make it read as follows:

> Sec. 24. Coöperatives not public utilities. Coöperatives shall not be deemed to be public utilities; and they shall be exempt from the jurisdiction and control of the public utilities commission. A coöperative shall not furnish electric energy to any person who, on the date of the organization of the coöperative, was using central station electric service, except with the consent of the person supplying such central station electric service.

After a spirited public hearing before the legislative public utilities committee on March 1, 1945, this committee rendered a unanimous report that it "ought not to pass," and this report was accepted in each House without controversy.

As of March, 1945, the R.E.A. had self-liquidating lines which served about 1,200 Maine farms, and received loans of $635,000 from the federal government.[51] As of December 31, 1947, the R.E.A. had approved $1,198,500 in loans in Maine to its four coöperatives.[52] The loans will enable the borrowers to finance 746 miles of lines and other rural electric facilities to serve 2,990 rural consumers. Additional lines are to be built as fast as materials become available. Up to December 31, 1947, the R.E.A. had advanced $1,011,219 as loans in Maine, and the state's R.E.A. borrowers operated 490 miles of lines serving 2,469 farms and other rural establishments.

The R.E.A.'s latest debt-service summary, to the end of 1947, showed that Maine borrowers had paid $94,495 in principal and interest on their government loans. This included $3,474 paid on principal in advance of the time it was due. One borrower was ahead on payments, but three were behind. A total of $35,641 was more than thirty days overdue. These three borrowers are in process of refunding their notes in a thirty-five-year amortization, compared to the present twenty-five-year period. One of these borrowers, the Denny's River Electric Coöperative, started during the war with a unit of 12 miles of line serving about 30 customers—far too small to support the costs of necessary overhead. During the war this coöperative had some 90 miles of line consisting of poles, hardware, and transformers, but no wire. The interest on that investment and the depreciation charge continued, despite the fact that there was no revenue. The R.E.A. maintains that wartime dislocations account for a large share of the troubles of the other two coöperatives. There is, however, so little of the R.E.A. in Maine that its effectiveness is difficult to evaluate.

Maine utility law and its administration to date have favored private and not public enterprise. For this the R.E.A. blames powerful power lobbies and administrative rulings which generally have not favored coöperatives. It is, however, part of the democratic process of government for all interested groups to state their case legitimately before the voters and legislative and administrative bodies. The most extravagant power lobby for transmission of surplus power in 1929 was repulsed by the voters. The Maine voters still prefer to decide important issues for themselves; outside advice is not welcomed. No scientific evaluation of the influence of Maine lobbyists on administrative agencies can yet be made; outside lobbyists have one or two strikes against them at the outset. Perhaps this should not be so, but one must deal with realities. The administrators are experts, with their own philosophies and prejudices. Their appointment by the governor and the council in a strong Republican state is expected to produce regulatory agencies which reflect conservative policies, yet without being "yes men" for power companies, consumers, or federal agencies. The Maine statutes assume that there is an identity of interests up to a certain point; beyond that, conflicts are resolved within the discretionary authority of the Public Utilities Commission. It is true, though, and perhaps inevitable that national and state regulating agencies often play along with, and get the support of, their clientele; the danger is that those regulated may become the quasi regulators.

Maine's embargo on hydroelectric power and the resulting limitation of development to supply only the demands of the home market showed little flexibility under stress of war. When Maine needed more power during emergencies, lack of interstate interconnections prohibited outside assistance. The trouble started in the fall of 1941, when drought caused a shortage of electric energy. The storage reservoirs on the principal rivers were very low, and that on the Penobscot was empty.[53] Some industries which normally generated at least a part of their power from their own hydroelectric plants had to turn to the power companies to make up their deficiencies.[54] Since the power companies were short also, they were forced to develop more than 50 per cent of their power from their steam auxiliaries at that time. One of the advantages of steam plants is that they can be constructed, and therefore put into operation, more quickly than hydroelectric plants. The Central Maine had a large modern steam plant at Bucksport, providing 12,500 kw. of capacity; when the Wiscasset steam plant was ready in January, 1942, this brought an added capacity of 20,000 kw. In February the difficulty of delivering fuel oil by water reached a critical stage. Supplies of fuel oil at the steam stations were almost exhausted, and the Public Utilities Commission hastily considered ways and means of curtailing the use of power. In the first week in March, deliveries of fuel oil were made, and rather heavy rains averted a crisis.

During this critical period, information on plant generation, stream flow, water-storage conditions, coal and fuel-oil supplies, and auxiliary sources of power for use in time of need was accumulated each week for the Bangor Hydro-Electric Company, the Cumberland County Power and Light Company, and the Central Maine Power Company. In view of the fact that curtailment of power might become necessary, an exchange of information was created, with the coöperation of the War Production Board, in the office of the Public Utilities Commission. Complete information was assembled on a monthly basis for all users of 10,000 kw-h or more per month.

The pooling of information made possible reports to the Office of War Utilities, and it was used in arranging for fuel oil and coal among the several plants when critical conditions developed.[55]

The original difficulties centered in the industrial section of southern and central Maine, the location of several accelerated shipbuilding programs. The most critical power situation, however, developed in the fall of 1942 in northern Maine, where power developments by corporate enterprise had been strongly opposed twenty-five years earlier. By December, 1942, extreme drought was affecting Aroostook County. The construction of two large air bases in the area, together with the normal demands for power, required more power than could be produced by the Aroostook River. Power was purchased from the Fraser Paper Company at Madawaska, fifty miles away, and arrangements were made to obtain an additional amount at Medway, seventy miles south of Houlton. Early in January, 1943, it was apparent that even this supplementary power was inadequate to carry through the remainder of the winter.

The Public Utilities Commission, on the basis of data it had collected on customers, load, and available power, ordered the companies to discontinue most of their street lighting and all sign and display lighting. Customers, with the exception of airports and small industries, were asked to save 10 per cent of the energy they used ordinarily. Arrangements were made with two water companies to use their oil auxiliary engines, and the Aroostook Valley Railroad substituted a steam locomotive to ease its load. It was necessary to concentrate on restricting domestic and commercial lighting, since 43 per cent of the energy used was for the former, and 25 per cent for the latter; 30 per cent was used for power and 2 per cent for street lighting. A "Wattless Wednesday" was introduced to relieve the load in the middle of the week as well as on week ends. The Women's Citizens' Service Corps, a civilian defense organization, made a house-to-house appeal to domestic customers to save energy.

The extreme measures were lifted with the February thaw, and by the middle of March normal service was resumed. A new dam at Millinockett Lake created additional storage to aid the system. During the winter of 1943–1944 the demand was supplied regularly. Elaborate preparations had been made by the Office of War Utilities in Washington to deal with power shortages, but the curtailment in Maine was, as a matter of fact, handled almost entirely by the Public Utilities Commission and the power companies. Had Maine failed to solve the problem of shortages, the alternative would have been federal control during the emergencies. The Federal Power Commission has authority to compel interconnection in the event of war or emergency, and it set up an agency for the purpose of "assuring an adequate and dependable power supply in case of emergency."[56]

Extreme drought prevailed again in the summer of 1944, when the steam auxiliaries proved very helpful. In February and March, 1945, the War Production Board ordered a brownout in Maine as a fuel-saving measure, but with the opening of the rivers the order was rescinded.[57]

The Maine Public Utilities Commission, in its 1945–1946 report, expressed the belief that the companies were doing everything they could to bring service to all areas of the state where it was economically reasonable, and as rapidly as the supply of labor and material would permit.[58] Early in 1947 the Central Maine Power Company announced that it had completed 168 miles of rural lines since the war. In April, 1947, the company made plans for the installation of rural lines which had been delayed because of war restrictions.[59]

The power situation in Aroostook Country became serious once again in the autumn of 1947.[60] For several months power was rationed. In the emergency the Navy sent two destroyer escorts to Portland, whence, by relay to the Central Maine Power Company and the Bangor Hydro-Electric Company, power was fed into Aroostook. On appeal of the governor, Canadian mills arranged a complicated system of transferring power to allow the Fraser Paper Company at Madawaska to make power available to Aroostook. Also, hastily improvised Diesel plants were installed in the county. The Public Utilities Commission granted the Maine Public Service Company a temporary increase in rate of one cent a kilowatt-hour.

The Maine Potato Growers and Shippers Committee, Inc., the Aroostook Chamber of Commerce, and the Potato Starch Manufacturers, Inc., charged the company with mismanagement, failure to make provision for emergencies, and dividend payments of 8.5 per cent. But the Maine Public Service Company maintained that its generating equipment was sufficient before the war and that the drought was an act of God. Meanwhile, the War Production Board refused to give the company priorities for additional equipment, despite the fact that it was servicing large military installations at

Houlton and Presque Isle. When a water shortage developed in the winter of 1943–1944, the board then made some relief possible. Plans of the Maine Public Service Company to avoid further emergencies call for the installation of a 7,000 kw. steam plant at Caribou. This plant will require new transmission lines costing an estimated $106,143.[61]

The fact that the larger power companies in Maine are contemplating additional steam installations instead of hydro development is significant. The Public Utilities Commission has indicated that water power still provides about 80 per cent of the power generated in the state, but that steam generation is becoming of increasing importance each year. The situation was stated as follows:[62]

> Now the demand for firm power has brought steam plants from an auxiliary status to a firm position. Power is generally required from steam stations all of the year except a few weeks in the spring and at times up to half of the total energy is produced by these plants. Many factors have developed causing the former cheap hydro energy to increase in cost compared to lowered steam costs and the new load requirements in Maine will be met mostly by the addition of new steam capacity.

A more recent development is that Maine has gone into a Fernald law "reverse," through interconnection with New Hampshire companies for importation of power in emergencies. In April, 1950, only enough power had been imported to test the lines.

# CHAPTER X

## Charter Control

The great majority of the people of Maine believe that the only safe way to prevent hydroelectric power from becoming subject to national jurisdiction is to keep it entirely within the state. But in the late 'twenties another group of voters indicated that they believed that a retention policy keeps the power from being further developed and that consequently Maine's power will never be fully utilized. This group was willing to vote for transmission of the surplus to other states because of economic gains to Maine, but only so long as they were assured that Maine could still completely control the power. This minority group divided into two factions on the best method of transmitting the surplus, subject to recall as the power demands of Maine increased. One faction favored a compact among several New England states for the sale of surplus power; the other wanted to divorce the generation of power from its transmission and, by strictly regulating the generating corporations and forbidding them to engage in interstate transmission, to control the amount of power sold to the interstate transmission corporation.

A main tenet of the divorce system, the distinction between the manufacture and transmission of hydroelectricity, was recognized by the Supreme Court three years after the Smith-Carlton bill had emerged. An Idaho statute taxed the generation of all electric current in that state. Because some of this electricity was transmitted to Utah, the Utah Power Company claimed that the tax law was a burden on interstate commerce. The Court ruled that a tax on generating was not a tax on interstate commerce, and cited the E. C. Knight decision as precedent. Said the Court:[1]

The process of generation is as essentially local as though electric energy were a physical thing; and to that situation we must apply, as

> controlling, the general rule that commerce does not begin until manufacture is finished, and hence the commerce clause of the Constitution does not prevent the state from exercising exclusive control over the manufacture....
>
> Without regard to the apparent continuity of the movement, appellant, in effect, is engaged in two activities, not in one only. So far as it produces electrical energy in Idaho, its business is purely intrastate, subject to state taxation and control. In transmitting the product acrosss the state line into Utah, appellant is engaged in interstate commerce, and state legislation in respect thereof is subject to the paramount authority of the commerce clause of the federal Constitution.

Although the Court used some rather strong language in stating that generation is local and subject to state control, the tax was for revenue and not regulatory purposes. In contrast, the Smith-Carlton bill had for its objective not taxation but control of manufacture in order to regulate or even prohibit interstate commerce.

It must be admitted that the divorce system was nothing more than a guise or subterfuge attempting to guarantee Maine power for Maine people. The two companies, generating and transmitting, would be interdependent in that neither could function without the other. Hence a close and unusual relationship would exist between them. The nearest actual case was that of *United Fuel Gas Company v. Kentucky Railroad Commission.*[2] In an attempt to control gas rates, the West Virginia Company stopped its business in Kentucky and organized a subsidiary company in that state. The parent company sold gas to its offspring at the state line, and the young corporation, having paid a high rate for the gas, asked the Public Utilities Commission to approve a schedule of rates based on the cost of the power and operating expenses. The Court treated the companies as a unit, however, and refused to recognize the ruse. This refusal to recognize the obvious attempt to evade the law is significant.

For the divorce system, designed to afford state control of hydroelectric power, two principles were basic: it would be a regulation of intrastate commerce, and the state could control the charters of its corporations. The argument for state control of hydroelectric power through regulation of corporation charters is that corporations, since they owe their existence and powers to the state legislature, are subject to more stringent and perhaps more arbitrary control than private individuals.[3] Because the state is not compelled to grant charters and does so at its pleasure, it can insert whatever condition it pleases, even that of requiring corporations to consent in advance to exactions which could not be required of them under ordinary legislative powers, as, for example, an undertaking not to engage in interstate commerce.

The Maine Constitution stipulates that corporations shall forever be subject to the general laws of the state. The legislature in 1831 passed a declaratory act that it could amend, alter, or repeal acts of incorporation granted after that date. The Supreme Judicial Court of Maine ruled that a general law restricting the activities of a corporation amounts to a modification of, or an amendment to, its charter.[4] So the Fernald law is, and the Smith-Carlton bill would have been, in charters granted after 1831.

That a charter is a contract and that corporations cannot exceed the provisions of their charters was decided in the case of *Dartmouth College v. Woodward.*[5] In *Bank of Augusta v. Earle,*[6] the Court declared that a corporation can make no contracts and do no acts whether within or without the state which creates it, except such as are authorized by its charter. In *Perrine v. Chesapeake and Delaware Canal Company,*[7] the Court said, "The corporation has no rights of property except those derived from the provisions of the charter, nor can it exercise any powers over the property it holds except those with which the charter has clothed it."

Another precedent for control by charter is that of *Paul v. Virginia.*[8] The Court declared that a corporation is not a citizen in the sense that citizens of each state are entitled to all the privileges and immunities of citizens of the several states. The right of the state to exclude foreign corporations and to restrict their business was also upheld. To mention a specific example, Maryland granted the charter of the Baltimore and Ohio Railroad and the right to construct an interstate line on condition that the corporation pay every six months a bonus of one-fifth of the amount received for hauling passengers between the points. When the railroad maintained that the charter burdened interstate commerce, the Court ruled, in *Railroad Company v. Maryland,*[9] that this was incidental and that the state was justified in demanding the bonus as a condition to the granting of the privilege to the corporation.

A corporation is a mere creature of the legislature, and its rights, privileges, and powers are dependent solely upon the terms of its charter, according to *Oregon Railway and Navigation Company v. Oregonian Railway Company.*[10] In *Horn Silver Mining Company v. New York,*[11] the Court said that the granting of a corporate franchise rests entirely in the discretion of the state, and may be accompanied with such conditions as its legislature may judge most befitting to its interests and policy. In *Ashley v. Ryan*[12] the right of a state to impose such conditions as it deemed proper in granting charters to corporations was upheld, and the acceptance by the corporations of these conditions implied a submission to them.

Advocates of the Smith-Carlton bill leaned heavily on *Berea College v. Kentucky* as a precedent. The case originated from a state statute which forbade persons and corporations to maintain schools for unsegregated white persons and Negroes. Despite the weakness of an analogy between statutes involving social and racial questions in southern states and those preventing hydroelectric power from getting into interstate commerce, the language of the Court concerning the right of states to limit the powers of their corporations is significant. Said Mr. Justice Brewer:[13]

> Again, the decision by a state court of the extent and limitation of the powers conferred by the State upon one of its own corporations is of a purely local nature. In creating a corporation a State may withhold powers which may be exercised by and cannot be denied to an individual. It is under no obligation to treat both alike. In granting corporate powers the legislature may deem that the best interests of the State would be subserved by some restriction, and the corporation may not plead that in spite of the restriction it has more or greater powers because the citizen has. The granting of such right or privilege (the right or privilege to be a corporation) rests entirely in the discretion of the State, and, of course, when granted, may be accompanied with such conditions as its legislature may judge most benefiting to its interests and policy.

Admitting that the statute was contrary to the United States Constitution as applied to individuals and firms, the Court held the statute to be separable. "Such a statute may conflict with the Federal Constitution in denying to individuals powers which they may rightfully exercise, and yet, at the same time, be valid as to a corporation created by the State."

From these decisions Edward F. Merrill drew the following conclusions:[14]

1. Corporations are the mere creatures of the state which creates them.
2. They have only such powers or rights as their creator, the state, may at its discretion, confer upon them.
3. They have no right to exercise any power which the state withholds from them in the act creating them.
4. In creating corporations the state may withhold from them rights and powers which even the Constitution of the United States guarantees to individuals.
5. The construction of the charter of a corporation and the determination of the extent of its corporate powers is of a purely local nature, and is for the state court to decide.

In 1927 Senator Charles B. Carter, an ardent supporter of the Fernald law, introduced two bills into the legislature to strengthen charter control. The plan was to amend the charters of all corporations created in Maine since 1831 to generate, transmit, and distribute power. These bills would have been more stringent than the Fernald law. They would have prohibited transmission for out-of-state railroad electrification and would have stopped the small amount of Maine hydroelectric power used in interstate commerce before 1909, which under the Fernald law was permitted to continue in order to avoid retroactive legislation. But both bills were defeated; some supporters of Maine's embargo policy opposed the Carter bills because of the extremes to which they went to "out-Fernald the Fernald law." Granted for argument's sake that the retroactive features would be legal, that the state could alter all corporation charters since 1831, it was felt that this was unfair. Another objection was that, whereas corporations hesitated to attack the Fernald law, Maine's settled policy since 1909, they might feel justified in attacking these acts, and thus the Fernald law would come up indirectly for judicial review.[15] Despite the defeat of the Carter bills, the Baxter amendment principle remains, and this was believed to be the surest way for Maine to control its hydroelectric power. This opinion may have had merit fifty to seventy-five years ago, but charter control is discredited by more recent commerce decisions.

Although a state can control its corporations, it is equally recognized that no state can regulate interstate commerce. Consequently, with the Constitution as the supreme law of the land, no act of a state legislature attempting or pretending to control corporations can prohibit, restrain, regulate, burden, or otherwise interfere with interstate commerce.[16] In *Crutcher v. Kentucky* the Court said:[17]

> To carry on interstate commerce is not a franchise or a privilege granted by the State; it is a right which every citizen of the United States is entitled to exercise under the Constitution and laws of the United States; and the accession of mere corporate facilities, as a matter of convenience in carrying on their business, cannot have the effect of depriving them of such right, unless Congress should see fit to interpose some contrary regulation on the subject.

In the Addyston decision[18] the Court claimed that private contracts which burdened interstate commerce were void, and that the power of Congress was paramount to the constitutional guaranty of liberty to the individual to enter into private contracts. Since charters are contracts, as early as 1899 the Court was assuming this attitude in the interpretation of the commerce clause.

Control of corporations by the state was a principal issue in the Kansas Natural Gas Company case; the Oklahoma statute involved was expressly directed to the control of corporations. But the statute was held invalid. "At this late day it is not necessary to cite cases to show that the right to engage in interstate commerce is not the gift of a State, and that it cannot be regulated or restrained by a State, or that a State cannot exclude from its limits a corporation engaged in such commerce. To attain these unauthorized ends is the purpose of the Oklahoma statute."[19]

John W. Davis, Democratic candidate for president in 1924, was attorney for the states of Ohio and Pennsylvania in *Pennsylvania v. West Virginia.*[20] In the brief he discussed the possibility of West Virginia having done what the Smith-Carlton bill contemplated for Maine:

> The question whether West Virginia might originally have imposed upon corporations of her creation or upon corporations which she permitted to do business within the State the condition that they could supply fully the requirements of West Virginia consumers before taking any gas out of the State, is not involved. On principle the validity of such a statute may well be doubted.

*Terral v. Burke Construction Company*[21] is also very pertinent. The previous sharp distinction between a citizen and a corporation was whittled down. One significant part of the decision reads: "The sovereign power of a state in excluding foreign corporations, as in the exercise of all others of its sovereign powers, is subject to the limitations of the supreme fundamental law." In this case the Court nullified a state law which forbade a corporation to bring suit in a federal court, on penalty of losing its charter. The Court said that a state could not, in imposing conditions upon the privilege of a foreign corporation to do business in the state, exact from it a waiver of the exercise of its constitutional right to resort to the federal courts. How about a state preventing a corporation from exercising other constitutional and legal rights, such as engaging in interstate commerce?

Another strong precedent was established in *Frost v. Railroad Commission.*[22] A California statute attempted to force private carriers to submit to regulation by the State Railroad Commission in the same way as common carriers before they could have the use of the public highways. The case did not involve interstate commerce, but the question was whether a state could make an unconstitutional requirement of the corporations and force them to accept it in return for the charter and privilege of doing business. The power of the state to deny privileges and to grant them on condition was recognized.

> But the power of the state in that respect is not unlimited; and one of the limitations is that it may not impose conditions which require the relinquishment of constitutional rights. If the state may compel the surrender of one constitutional right as a condition of its favor, it may, in like manner, compel a surrender of all. It is inconceivable that guarantees embedded in the Constitution of the United States may thus be manipulated out of existence.

In rendering this decision, Mr. Justice Sutherland referred to *Western Union Telegraph Company v. Foster.* One sentence is particularly pertinent to this situation: "Acts generally lawful may become unlawful when done to accomplish an unlawful end."[23] If this principle is applied to the Fernald law and the Smith-Carlton bill, we can see that, although it is generally lawful for states to control corporations which are of their own making, yet when this control is exercised to accomplish an end in itself unlawful, the courts would almost certainly refuse to recognize it in this phase of its activity.

Local law and custom are important in determining the rights of corporations, on the basis of *Kirk v. State Board of Irrigation,*[24] and *Fox River Paper Company v. Railroad Commission.*[25] Nebraska was permitted to transfer qualified use of its streams on its own limits and conditions, one of which was that no power therefrom could be transmitted to other states. The Wisconsin statute contained a recapture clause, allowing the state to take over the power on its own conditions. These decisions were that in Nebraska and Wisconsin riparian owners could have no property rights in water power until the state gave its consent. In so doing the state could establish its own conditions, and these did not take property without due process, since riparian owners had no property rights in power except those granted by the state. The Court did not recognize that these cases referred to unconstitutional conditions and made no reference to them, apparently because property rights did not exist until after the state acted.[26]

Does the Fernald law in charters interfere with interstate commerce? The Fox River case was not concerned with interstate commerce and therefore does not answer the question. The Kirk case is more pertinent. But it was a decision of a state court upholding a state law, and therefore it is not strong enough to support a conclusion that Maine can likewise make power grants conditional upon the promise not to engage in interstate commerce. In short, while states can control their corporations, whenever this control is exercised to accomplish an unlawful end the right of the state ceases to exist. The regulation of interstate commerce is a national prerogative, and no such subterfuge as state control of corporation charters is a safe device for securing state control of hydroelectric power.

O. C. Merrill, as executive secretary of the Federal Power Commission in 1927, expressed doubts of the constitutionality of the Fernald law and the Smith-Carlton bill.[27] With reference to the Smith-Carlton bill he said:

> It would make the export of power subject not to a definite limitation applicable alike to interstate and intrastate commerce, but to a limitation indefinite with respect both to extent and to time and applicable

only to interstate commerce. I am inclined to the opinion that such proposals might be deemed discriminations against interstate commerce and not sustainable if suit should be brought in the Federal courts. Furthermore, such a proposal would seem to leave the transmission companies themselves in an unenviable situation. They are obligated to have a capital of not less than $100,000. They may purchase power only from corporations having a permit from the State. They cannot know when contract for either purchase or sale is made, how long such contract may be effective, how soon they may be deprived in whole or in part of their power, which they cannot use for the purpose for which they were built. I think that a transmission company would hesitate to purchase power on such limitations, and that prospective foreign purchasers of power from such a corporation would hesitate to depend upon a contract with such limitations.

Congressman Owen Brewster opined that the Smith-Carlton bill rested upon much thinner constitutional ice than the Fernald law.[28] The Honorable Harvey D. Eaton called the act a barefaced attempt by the Maine legislature to regulate interstate commerce, saying:[29] "Governor Brewster was absolutely right when he vetoed this bill two years ago on the ground that it was unconstitutional. And the Constitution has not been changed since." Eaton suggested on July 11, 1929, that Governor William Tudor Gardiner ask the Supreme Judicial Court of Maine for an advisory opinion on the validity of the proposed law, but the Governor felt that "the time is now past for submitting to the Supreme Court the question you suggest." Editorially, the Portland *Evening News* contended that the utilities knew the bill was unconstitutional, but wanted the referendum "to strengthen their stocks in the speculative markets." With a touch of grim humor, Representative Ellis L. Aldrich of Topsham brought out the point that the same company which owned and directed the generating companies would likewise own and direct the transmission company, with the result that Mr. Insull would be making contracts with himself, for himself, and by himself.[30]

A document by Charles Evans Hughes, former Justice and later Chief Justice of the United States Supreme Court, helps to support the conclusion reached in the present chapter of this study, namely, that the export of surplus power would weaken the Fernald law and that the recall of surplus power would be uncertain if a local demand for it should arise. This suggestive but inconclusive document was sent by Judge Hughes to the Central Maine Power Company on March 8, 1927, in response to three questions submitted to him by its president, Walter S. Wyman.[31]

You ask: *"First,* Would the enactment of the Smith bill weaken the present control of the State of Maine over the water power generated electricity needed now or in the future by its citizens?"

If it were assumed that the Smith bill is unconstitutional, it may be said that its enactment would not weaken the present control of the state of Maine over the water power in question, as in that case it would be ineffective. If, on the other hand, the Smith bill is constitutional, it would be effective according to its terms and the state would continue to have the power which it reserves.

I do not think, however, that these hypotheses exhaust the possibilities. The argument in opposition to the constitutionality of the Fernald Act, and to the invalidity of the attempt by the state to control for its own citizens the disposition of water power generated electricity, might be rendered more difficult if the state by the Smith bill adopted the policy of permitting electric current to be transmitted in interstate commerce subject to the permit of the Public Utilities Commission of the state. I am not attempting to give an opinion upon the constitutionality of the Fernald Act, but I think that the chance of sustaining such an Act, and such legislation as the Carter bills, would be to some extent diminished by such legislation as the Smith bill.

*"Second,* If the Smith bill is enacted and electricity is shipped out of the State under its provisions, would the Federal Government have power to regulate the rates of local generating companies for electricity used in the State of Maine?"

The federal government would have no power to regulate the internal commerce of the state as such. If it had power over the rates of local generating companies for electricity used in the state of Maine, it would be upon the ground that intrastate and interstate operations had become so commingled that the power to regulate and control interstate commerce in electric current, including interstate rates and practices, could not be effectively exercised without some measure of control over intrastate rates and practices. That is, in order to permit the federal government to deal with the rates of local generating companies for electricity used in the state of Maine, the situation must be analogous to that which obtains in the case of railroads in their interstate and intrastate operations. I do not know whether such a commingling of operations would result. I suppose that it is conceivable. The principle of law which is applicable is that above stated.

*"Third,* If the Smith bill is enacted and electricity is shipped out of the State under its provisions and a demand for electricity arose in Maine

which would necessitate a curtailment of the amount purchased and transmitted outside the State under its terms, would the transmission corporations organized under the Act be limited in their supply for outside the State to what electricity they could obtain in the nature of surplus as defined in the Act?"

The decisions are not sufficiently clear to make possible a definite answer to this inquiry, but I think that it would be unsafe to assume that the transmission corporations would be limited in their supply as stated in the question.

Despite contrary rumors, no evidence indicates that Judge Hughes in a private capacity ever gave a written opinion on the constitutionality of the Fernald law. Walter S. Wyman, as president of the Central Maine Power Company, testified at the hearing on the power measure in the 1929 session of the Maine legislature that he asked former Justice Hughes to give the company an opinion on the Fernald law:

I think perhaps we did ask him first what about the Carlton bill, and I think his reply to that was not an opinion on the Carlton bill, or Smith bill as it was then, but to the effect that it depended on the constitutionality of the Fernald law to a large extent. That is the impression he gave me. Then I asked him to give me an opinion on the constitutionality of the Fernald law, and that was in the summer of 1927, I guess, and in the winter of 1928 Mr. Hughes gave me a verbal talk on the constitutionality of the Fernald law.[32]

Then followed a very pertinent question from Senator Oakes: "Did he [Hughes] give you any statement that you could quote as to the legal effect of the export of electricity under the Carlton bill and the retention of control by the State of Maine?" To this Wyman replied: "I got nothing out of it that I could quote as being his opinion one way or the other. I have recently written him again reminding him that I have not yet received his opinion, and hoping that before he sails for Europe he would give it to us. I would be glad to show it to you if I ever get it."[33]

Unfortunately, Senator Oakes and Mr. Wyman were talking about two different matters; Wyman's testimony was on the Fernald law, Senator Oakes's question did not refer to an opinion on the Fernald law, but to one on the surplus power export bill. Although Judge Hughes had written to Wyman about the latter bill almost two years before the testimony, Wyman apparently misunderstood the Senator's question, for his reply followed the trend of his previous thought, namely, that Judge Hughes had not given him a written opinion on the constitutionality of the Fernald law. Wyman had recently referred, however, to the inability of Judge Hughes to give a definite answer, two years earlier, to the pertinent question of Oakes.

Likewise, the records of Judge Hughes do not indicate that he ever rendered a written opinion on the constitutionality of the Fernald law. On this point, after searching the files and his father's office diaries for that period, the Honorable Charles Evans Hughes, Jr., said:[34]

> The story, as revealed by our files and records is as follows: Late in February of 1927 my father was consulted by Mr. Walter S. Wyman, President of the Central Maine Power Company with respect to three specific questions relating to the so-called Smith bill which was then pending in the Maine Legislature. Under date of March 8, 1927, my father rendered a brief opinion of a couple of pages on these questions, the only one of which that related in any way to the Fernald Law, which had been earlier enacted, was whether the enactment of the Smith bill would weaken the present control of the State of Maine over the water power generated electricity needed now or in the future by its citizens. . . . [This opinion] expressly disclaims any attempt to give an opinion on the constitutionality of the Fernald Act and Mr. Wyman did not then ask for an opinion on that subject. Later, on September 9, 1927, Mr. Wyman addressed a letter to our firm in which he did request my father's opinion on the constitutionality of the Fernald law. My father was then, and for some time thereafter, under extreme pressure in meeting a heavy schedule of other professional engagements and was unable to take the matter up until April of 1928. On April 21, 1928, Mr. Wyman had a consultation with my father, the subject matter of which apparently included the question of the constitutionality of the Fernald Law, but we have no record of what advice my father gave orally on that occasion. A memorandum in the file by my then partner, Augustus L. Richards, who assisted my father in this matter, indicates that no arrangement was made for my father to send a written opinion unless the Central Maine Power Company called for it. Under date of February 8, 1929, Mr. Wyman wrote to Mr. Richards, saying that he had forgotten whether my father was to send any written opinion confirming the interview of April, 1928, concerning the constitutionality of the Fernald Act, and that he would like to have an opinion in writing. Mr. Richards replied that my father was then about to take a vacation in Bermuda and that shortly after his return would leave for Europe to take up his duties as a

judge of the World Court, to which Mr. Wyman replied under date of February 26, 1929, that there was no particular hurry about the opinion and if the company could have it any time that year it would answer the purpose. Apparently after my father's return from Europe in the fall he was again under heavy pressure of court and other professional engagements and, as you know, early in the next year, 1930, he was appointed Chief Justice of the United States, with the result that he was evidently unable to render the written opinion.

It is indeed unfortunate that no record is available of the conversation between Judge Hughes and Mr. Wyman on April 21, 1928. Business associates of Wyman have recently stated that, as they recall it, he reported to them that Judge Hughes said the Fernald law as it stood was probably unconstitutional but that another law could be or might be valid. Indirect information, based on the memory of a conversation which took place more than twenty years earlier, unsubstantiated by documentary evidence, is, of course, of little value for this study. However, some light may be thrown on the matter by a letter written on May 22, 1928, by Augustus L. Richards,[35] who assisted Judge Hughes. The letter was addressed to E. H. Maxcy, of Augusta, Maine, director and general counsel for the Central Maine Power Company, in response to the request for an opinion on riparian rights in Maine.

Judge Hughes did not, of course, undertake to advise Mr. Wyman as to the rights, under the Maine law, of riparian owners to erect dams upon streams passing through their property. The question before him was solely as to the constitutionality of the Fernald Act. His suggestion as to the possibility of more effective legislation was based upon the uncertainties inherent in the case of *Pennsylvania v. West Virginia*, 262 U.S. 363, as well as upon the question of what rights of control over the obstruction of streams might be vested in the State of Maine under the Maine law, as declared by the courts of Maine.

From this it seems apparent that Judge Hughes suggested the possibility of legislation more effective than the Fernald law. But the reason for such possible legislation and the content of it must remain entirely in the realm of speculation.[36]

What is the local law and custom in Maine in regard to the rights of riparian owners? Navigable and nonnavigable waters must be separated, and this study has indicated that water power on nonnavigable streams constitutes private property. Consequently, in this category there is no analogy between the situation in Maine and the Nebraska and Wisconsin cases. This conclusion is strengthened by an opinion of Augustus L. Richards, who assisted Judge Charles Evans Hughes at the time. After the Fox River decision the Central Maine Power Company consulted the Hughes law firm in regard to the right of the state to restrict the use of a milldam erected on a nonnavigable Maine river. Richards replied as follows:[37]

> My personal opinion is that if the law of Maine is as stated in the opinion of the Justices, the right of the state to restrict the use of such a mill dam, *in so far as such right is based upon the power of the state to protect and enforce the jus publicum with respect to the river,* would be limited in scope to the imposition of restrictions designed to preserve the freedom of passage for fish, boats, and logs. I do not think that the State could, *solely by virtue of such power,* impose restrictions upon the use or disposition by a riparian proprietor of any product, including electric current, manufactured by the use of the mill dam. You will understand, however, that this is merely my personal opinion. I do not know whether Judge Hughes would agree with me.

On navigable waters the riparian owner has no property rights beyond the low water mark.[38] In Maine, by virtue of the Colonial Ordinance of 1641, the riparian owner's jurisdiction is limited to the low water mark where the sea does not ebb above one hundred rods. In other words, if the tide ebbs more than one hundred rods, the title to the soil of the flats beyond the one hundred rods belongs to the state.[39] This principle has been recognized in the Maine courts on several occasions. The owner of flats may erect wharves and piers on them so long as navigation is not impaired, but until he builds upon them the public has a right to use them for navigation while they are covered by the sea.[40]

On navigable waters, then, the situation in Maine is essentially the same as that in Nebraska and Wisconsin, except that in Maine these water powers are not yet particularly valuable. Riparian owners have no property rights in the use of navigable streams until the state gives those rights, and if the states of Nebraska and Wisconsin could give qualified permission for the use of navigable streams, then it follows that Maine should be able to do likewise. But no state in granting qualified rights to power companies could thereby exclude ultimate federal control.

This analysis shows that the Fernald law, as a part of corporation charters, does not bring about unconstitutional conditions as interpreted by the United States Supreme Court so far as property rights in navigable rivers and great ponds are concerned. Within federal law, the state of Maine could undoubtedly make conditional grants to power companies on all but nonnavigable streams and the state could take over these developments as it saw fit, or at least until Congress desired to control the navigable streams. But, according to Maine law, the state is unable to take over developments on great ponds and navigable streams without judicial or constitutional change of the concept of public purpose. Furthermore, the constitutional provision limiting the indebtedness of the state prevents public ownership of expensive projects.

Former Governor Percival P. Baxter injected a novel argument into the divorce system by claiming that the water powers of Maine are valuable only because they draw their water from the great ponds which are owned by the public. Therefore an inalienable public interest is attached to this water, and thus the state controls its use by corporations and limits the export of power derived therefrom.[41] Although some justification existed for this argument so far as it concerned the use of waters of great ponds, its chief fallacy is that the great power sites are on streams and the fundamental principle governing them, at least until recently, is that the riparian proprietor owns the bed and the flow of the river, and that power is private property in Maine.

But more important is the question: Who owns the flow of water and the power on navigable streams in Maine? In the opinion of the Honorable Harvey D. Eaton, this question has never arisen in Maine. At one time he considered it almost academic because none of the numerous tide mills in Maine was worth fighting over in the courts.[42] The fact that the several official water-power investigations ignored this matter and were confined to power on nonnavigable streams indicates that heretofore it has been considered unimportant. Yet, with the national government and courts now enlarging their conception of navigable streams, the question may become of extreme importance.

In contrast with Maine's nonnavigable streams, where the riparian proprietor owns the bed and flow of the river (but not the right of public passage), the state owns the bed of the navigable streams, and, by decisions of the United States Supreme Court, riparian proprietors do not own the flow of these rivers. In *United States v. Chandler-Dunbar Company*[43] the Court ruled that the flow of the stream of a navigable river is in no sense private property, and that there is no room for judicial review, at the instance of a private owner of the banks of a stream, of a determination of Congress that such flow is needed for the improvement of navigation. In this case and also in that of *United States v. Appalachian Electric Power Company*[44] the Court stipulated, "that the running water in a great navigable stream is capable of private ownership is inconceivable."

From this it is implied that since private ownership in the flow of a navigable stream and consequently of its water power is lacking, either the federal or state government must be proprietor. In the Fox River case, without answering the question directly, the Court declared that in Wisconsin the state's consent is necessary for the construction of a bridge or dam in a navigable river, subject to the superior power of the United States over navigation. In the New River case, likewise, a clash of sovereignty arose: acts of both the federal government and the state of Virginia granted fifty-year power licenses. The Court replied that both the state and the power company held the waters and lands under them subject to the power of Congress to control the waters for the purpose of commerce, and that the "Federal Government has domination over the water power inherent in the flowing stream." Thus the conclusion must be that while the federal government may tolerate jurisdiction by the state of Maine over the water power on its navigable streams temporarily, the ultimate control of this power rests with Congress whenever it desires to assert its authority.

The excise tax on the gross operating revenues of the companies receiving permission to export surplus power was assailed as an unconstitutional state tax on interstate commerce.

> For said permission to sell the whole or such part of surplus power as the public utilities commission may determine, said person, firm, or corporation shall pay an excise tax to the state of Maine . . . of four per cent of the gross operating revenue receipts of said person, firm, or corporation received for selling the whole or such part of its surplus as is in this act defined and permitted during each calendar year.[45]

Since the proposed bill contained a clause that if one section should be declared unconstitutional the entire act would be declared null and void, it appears that the act would have been invalid on the basis of the tax provision alone. While it is a well-established principle that a state may levy severance taxes and production taxes,[46] this tax would have been on revenue received for selling surplus power authorized by the Public Utilities Commission in interstate commerce. The decisions are sufficiently clear to make possible a definite conclusion on this point, that such a state tax would conflict with the Constitution.

The *properties* of a company engaged in interstate commerce may be taxed by the state,[47] and the property tax may likewise be estimated *prima facie* by gross income.[48] On this basis a statute taxing gross revenue on the intrastate business of palace-car companies was upheld as it was in lieu of a property tax. The tax on gross receipts was considered merely as a means of getting at the full value of the property and it did not discriminate against interstate commerce.[49] A case in point was a decision of the United States Supreme Court upholding a Maine statute, passed in 1881, providing for an annual excise tax on railroads for the privilege of exercising their franchises, based on the gross transportation receipts.[50] By a 5 to 4 decision the Court held that resort to gross receipts "was simply to ascertain the value of the business done by the corporation, and thus obtain a guide to a reasonable conclusion as to the amount of the excise tax which should be levied; and we are unable to perceive in that resort any interference with transportation, domestic or foreign . . ."

But a state cannot tax interstate business. In *Galveston, Harrisburg and San Antonio Railway Company v. Texas,*[51] a statute taxing gross receipts of the intrastate business of an interstate railroad was declared invalid. It was considered a supplement to the regular property tax and an attempt to regulate interstate commerce. The Court reconciled this decision with that of the Grand Trunk by indicating that the Maine statute taxing gross receipts was a measure of the value of the property.

Furthermore, a state cannot tax for granting permission to engage in commerce among the states. In *Robbins v. Shelby County Taxing District,*[52] the Court ruled that a state could not tax traveling salesmen coming in to take orders to be filled subsequently from other states because the tax interfered with the federal power to regulate. In *McCall v. California*[53] a state tax on railway agents for the privilege of soliciting interstate passenger business was rejected, and in *California v. Central Pacific Railway Company*[54] a tax on several railway companies for the privilege of engaging in interstate commerce was declared unconstitutional. So too in *Leloup v. Mobile*[55] a license fee for the privilege of opening an interstate telegraph office was rejected. Said the Court, "No State has the right to lay a tax on interstate commerce in any form, whether by way of duties laid on the transportation of the subjects of that commerce, or on the receipts derived from that transportation, or on the occupation or business of carrying it on, and the reason is that such taxation is a burden on that commerce, and amounts to a regulation of it, which belongs solely to Congress." The tax provision of the proposed Maine law clearly proposed to levy a tax on the gross receipts of a corporation's property destined solely for interstate commerce, and intended its payment to be made a condition to continuance in the business of interstate transmission. It was a supplement to the property taxed.

Edward F. Merrill, one of the authors of the bill, was reported to have expressed his positive opinion that the bill as drawn up and presented to the legislature was constitutional, but added that he would not give any opinion on the constitutionality of the measure with the excise tax amendment included.[56] He had suggested, however, that the constitutionality of the excise tax provision could be tested only by the firms involved, namely, the generating companies selling to the transmitting company distributing power. Since these would be the persons benefited by the act, he thought it inconceivable that they would wish to destroy the instrument under which they did business. He is also reported to have added that the Maine consumer might be affected in such a way as to make him an interested party. Probably, however, this interest would not have been sufficiently direct to support a test case.[57]

With the power companies anxious to transmit but prevented by a law applying to corporations, why did they not reorganize as trusts and thus secure permission to transmit within the Fernald law? This question is of more than academic interest. Walter S. Wyman testified before the Securities and Exchange Commission that he had been advised by legal counsel that a trust could export power, and that thought was given to the possibility of organizing the Central Maine Power Company properties or at least some of its generating properties in the form of a trust.[58] In 1926 the New England Public Service Company purchased the Swans Falls Company in Maine, a small power company near the New Hampshire line. It had been owned and operated by Charles G. Moulton as an individual, but he made out a deed to trustees. Thus it legally sold power in New Hampshire. So close were its New Hampshire connections that in 1937 it was acquired by the Public Service Company of New Hampshire.[59] After the Insull failure, the rumors were that the New England Power Association, a voting trust, was interested in obtaining the power properties in Maine.[60] Had this occurred, there might have been occasion for further experiments with transmission by trusts. The practical obstacles to such a plan, however, were so great that no serious consideration was given to it. Wyman said it was difficult to conceive of having the property of Maine power companies owned by individuals; it would involve a cumbersome setup. It would be virtually impossible to establish and finance such an organization with capitalization of perhaps $100,000,000.

Besides the financial difficulties, other serious obstacles can be suggested. In the first place, it would be almost inconceivable to stretch the right to transmit the trivial amount of Swans Falls power into that of transmitting thousands of horsepower from entirely new sites not then in the possession of the company. In the second place, a trust or holding company converted into a trust was the owner of stock, but not of generating and transmission properties. Such organization would also require liquidation of power companies, or at least part of their properties. The greatest difficulty of all, however, is that such reorganization would have been extremely unpopular in Maine. The only reason for reorganizing as trusts would be to try to defeat the Fernald law, and this subterfuge again would have found the trustees in the same position as the corporations if they had elected to test the Fernald law in court. Although lacking control over trusts to the same degree as they can control corporation charters, a legislature and voters hostile to Insull-dominated trustees could easily have found ways and means to make their lives miserable.

# CHAPTER XI

## The Compact Plan

The New England Council has been active for many years in attempting to avoid federal regulation by working out regional problems. At its meeting in December, 1926, Secretary of Commerce Herbert Hoover said that from 8 to 10 per cent of New England's electric power participated in interstate movement, and this fraction gave the basis for some agitation for federal regulation.[1] Consequently, if New England could solve its problems, the states would be saved from further encroachment on the part of the national government. He suggested the compact as a solution—"to take the lead, in New England, in introducing a new idea in the decentralization of government by setting up an interstate compact."[2]

The Harvard Bureau of Business Research found in 1926 that interstate transmission of electricity was only about 9 per cent of the total power generated in the United States, and concluded that the problem was sectional rather than national.[3] The New England editor of the *Electrical World* advised Maine to export surplus power under either voluntary joint regulation of state commissions along the channel of the New England Council plan, or under congressional legislation delegating to state commissions regulative authority under interstate compacts.[4]

Governor Owen Brewster, in his special message to the legislature in 1927, spoke of a compact as the best means of solving the problem, though he admitted that an uncertainty remained regarding the degree of state control preserved under the compact plan.[5] The faction of those favoring the export of surplus power, led by Governor Brewster, supported regulation by interstate compact. In 1927 the Oakes bill[6] was introduced into the Maine legislature to provide for a "Commission to Negotiate a Treaty Regarding the Water Power and Electricity of New England." The bill was based on the idea that New England is a natural power division of the United States, and that regional development should be encouraged. The control, however, they felt should be by the state of Maine. The United States Constitution provides that states may enter into compacts or agreements among themselves if Congress gives its consent. The Oakes bill provided for Maine, Massachusetts, and New Hampshire (later the first two only) to appoint three commissioners each to investigate the power problem, to draw up a compact and to submit it to their respective legislatures. The other New England states were invited to join also. Thus, if two states and Congress agreed on a proposition, Maine could transmit power and have joint authority with the other state in the compact in regard to rates, length of contracts, amount sold, recapture provisions, and general regulation. The approval of Congress would be an indication of its willingness to abstain temporarily from direct regulation.

Professor Felix Frankfurter and Professor James M. Landis saw in the compact method a great possibility for regional control of hydroelectric problems, thereby avoiding federal regulation. Frankfurter visited Maine to advise the state how to solve its power problem easily, but the eminent professor did not have the answer the people wanted. He assumed that Maine's settled power policy was threefold:[7] first, Maine power for the people and industries of Maine; second, the surplus, after the needs of the state were satisfied, to be allowed to go outside only under conditions giving assurance that Maine did not lose control in future; third, fear of the assumption of national authority—legislative or judicial—over water power. It is now obvious, as it was not then, that Frankfurter was incorrect in his second assumption. But with these three hypotheses granted, he logically reasoned that, since Maine had a predominant interest in its water-power resources, the interest of the state was not only in local consumption but also in sale outside so far as the latter was consistent with local needs. He saw a situation which transcended state lines and yet ought not to be regulated from Washington because it was a regional and not a national problem. According to Frankfurter, the compact clause should be invoked.

> Resort to the Compact Clause is the effective way by which Maine can achieve the ends she had in mind in regard to her water power. By an arrangement with the other New England states, to which Congress undoubtedly would give its consent, Maine can work out the details for continuing to exercise effective control over her locally generated water power, while at the same time making a flexible provision for allowing under appropriate safeguards the export of any of her surplus water power, if and when a proper commission, on which Maine's interest is effectively represented, should find that there is an exportable surplus.... The road to wise water power development and the ample protection of the interests of Maine lies toward an interstate compact and not otherwise.

Frankfurter was not, however, advocating this plan to aid Maine in preserving its traditional particularism in hydroelectric energy, because, two years earlier, his important article in the *Yale Law Journal*[8] stated, "If and when circumstances which now call for solution through compact change, Congress is wholly free to assume control."

Protests were made in the press, especially on Frankfurter's second point.[9] One phase of the Maine attitude to the "easy Harvard plan" was expressed as follows: "Of course we do not perceive any difference between power leaving the state under compact between states and power so transmitted under Federal laws. We had as soon be run by Uncle Sam as by a five-to-one vote of the New England states." Representative Ellis L. Aldrich opposed the Oakes bill because Professor Frankfurter's reference to it as "an interesting experiment which he hoped Maine would undertake" meant that Maine would be experimenting—giving much to states having nothing to offer in return.[10] The proponents replied that the other states had markets to offer for the Maine surplus. Senator Charles B. Carter argued that, whereas the other New England states had developed virtually all their power and Maine was the only state having much undeveloped potential, Maine should not participate equally in a regional plan when it is the only state capable of selling power, and the other five are power-buying states.[11]

Although the Maine Senate showed considerable interest in the Oakes bill, it was defeated in 1927. Governor Brewster kept the idea alive, however, by naming Franklin Fisher of Lewiston to represent him at meetings under the auspices of the New England Council to discuss the possibilities of agreeing upon a power compact that summer. Fisher estimated that it would cost $20,000,000 to erect a transmission line from Bingham, a great source of power, to Boston, two hundred miles away; that the cost of developing this power, running expenses, interest, and taxes, would be so great that the power sold over this line would not much more than pay the annual charges. It was also believed that with $20,000,000 invested in an interstate transmission line the recall of power would be difficult if local demand should increase. If the power should be recalled and the expensive line become superfluous, Maine consumers would have to pay for it.[12] Governor Brewster's negotiations with the power interests indicated that no suitable compact agreement could be reached. When, in 1929, another bill to negotiate power compacts was introduced, it was defeated.[13]

The Honorable Harvey D. Eaton of Waterville, originator of the water-district legislation adopted throughout the country, considered electricity an unsuitable commodity for regulation by compact.[14] A compact is a contract, and one of the first requisites of a valid and enforceable contract is that one of the contracting parties shall have legal interest in, control over, or ownership of the subject of the contract to enable him to act in regard thereto. Measured by this standard concerning electricity of private companies, Maine simply fails to qualify.

A weakness of the compact, if made, would be its administration. This presumably would be carried out by its own administrative agency, which might be the respective public utilities commissions sitting in joint session. Maine commissioners would be prone to insist upon transmission of power under short-term contracts so that it could be recalled on short notice for home consumption. Yet the uncertainty of the source of power sold for short periods and the expense of erecting and maintaining extended transmission lines make long-time contracts imperative. Thus a compact would not give Maine much protection. A provision to recapture power would mean little if only long-term contracts promised the sale of that power.

The limitations of the compact system in a practical sense were clearly summarized by the late Professor William E. Mosher: "This [compact] solution is nearly ideal, but state jealousies are still too dominant to hope that it could be made effective on a large scale."[15] And according to Walter S. Wyman, "The minute you ask Massachusetts to enter into a compact they will begin to trade with you and trade the life right out of the proposition or else they won't play."[16] Representatives of some states could combine and discriminate against others. Interstate jealousies and the lack of a unifying force and a supreme authority might dissolve not only the board but the compact itself.

The technical committee on regional planning of the National Resources Committee concluded that compacts sometimes encourage particularism, selfishness, and jealousy on the part of individual states instead of the broad regional coöperation which is desired. The customary approach to a prospective compact is that, since every state is sovereign and equal, each should get as much out of what is to be settled or divided as any other state involved. Thus the making of compacts becomes a matter of horse trading, each state trying to derive the maximum benefit for itself.[17]

> These assumptions may be good jurisprudence and the proper bases of comity, but considerable question arises concerning their realism and social desirability. The unequal distribution of natural resources, of climate, of economic advantage, or of transportation facilities, with their resulting effects upon population concentration, wealth, and cultural opportunity, challenges these juristic and artificial hypotheses. In short, the assumptions of planning, chief of which is that resources, physical and human, should be used to the best social advantage irrespective of artificially established interests or boundaries—these assumptions quite naturally come into conflict with certain governmental theories. . . . However, there is eloquent evidence to the effect that the planner's analyses are difficult to achieve, particularly when related to natural resources, within the limits and the assumptions of the compact method.

A great objection to the Oakes bill was that a long time would be required for the states and Congress to come to an agreement; even the possibility of reaching an agreement was doubtful. The final agreement would have to be passed in identical form by the states becoming parties to the compact and by Congress. The proposals, counterproposals, deliberations, and compromises which would inevitably go into achieving the final compact would be very difficult, if not impossible. Several years might easily elapse during the deliberations. Referring to the "giant power" commission in 1931, Governor Gifford Pinchot of Pennsylvania concluded that "discussion of interstate compacts seems to be merely a way to prolong debate and keep us from doing anything."[18] Dr. H. L. Elsbree said, "This particular example, however, indicates that there are almost insuperable obstacles in the way of negotiating such compacts."[19]

O. C. Merrill, then executive secretary of the Federal Power Commission, had the following to say about the compact method:[20]

> I have little confidence in being able to settle such complicated matters as are here involved by means of interstate compacts . . . While Congress might assent to some definite proposals with respect to limitations on power export, assuming they would be agreed to by New Hampshire, Vermont, and Massachusetts, it is hardly to be expected that Congress would accede to a proposal for surrendering its general control over interstate commerce in electric energy except possibly for a temporary period and subject to resumption of that authority whenever it might desire to do so.

The crucial point is that a compact cannot operate as a restriction on the constitutional power of Congress. As decisions of the United States Court indicate, an interstate compact is no guaranty against federal control in spite of an original consent of Congress. If a federal statute should conflict with the compact, the former would be given preference. In *Green v. Biddle* the Supreme Court said that a compact is a contract and that no state can pass a law in contravention of that contract.[21] In this case Kentucky attempted to modify by statute its compact with Virginia. Its constitutional significance for Maine is that a compact, when made, is binding, except by mutual consent of the contracting parties. Maine could not, by unilateral action, alter a compact in order to recall power for local needs. When once negotiated, unless the compact vests wide discretionary powers in the states involved, the only provision for change would be for Congress to grant blanket authority to the states to alter the compact. It is extremely doubtful that Congress would ever do this; it is also probable that Congress would have no right to do so.[22]

Another important constitutional point is that an agreement by one Congress to assent to a compact does not bind another Congress from withdrawing that consent. At the most, permission of Congress for the states to make a compact precludes federal intervention for the time being only, and is merely an indication that one Congress is willing to agree to the provisions. What another Congress might say is unpredictable. This was clearly illustrated in *Pennsylvania v. Wheeling and Belmont Bridge Company,* growing out of a compact between Kentucky and Virginia for use of the Ohio River. A later Congress modified the compact by passing an act to erect a bridge across the river for the transportation of mails and other purposes. The point at issue was whether the compact was a limitation on the power of Congress to regulate commerce among the states. The Court ruled that a compact cannot be used to restrict the power of Congress; the compact was valid so long as it did not interfere with the constitutional powers of the national government. The Court showed the necessity for this principle: a different interpretation would give Congress and two states power to alter the Constitution in spite of the regular amendment procedure.[23]

In one key sentence Dr. Elsbree shows the legal limitations of the compact system. "Compacts among the states can provide for the regulation only in those matters over which the states have jurisdiction."[24] This again raises the fundamental questions: Is the Fernald law legal? Have states the right to control the interstate commerce in hydroelectric power? If so, the compact is unnecessary to avoid national control; it is important for regional administration. But if the states have no right to control transmission, the compact may be *ultra vires.* Then the courts might conclude that a compact is an illegal delegation of the power of the national government.

The Springfield *Republican* editorially commented on the limitations of compacts:[25]

> The interstate-compact clause of the present Constitution is obviously a vestigial relic of the first constitution, which was adopted in 1777 and endured about a dozen years. Under the Articles of Confederation the States were overshadowing in power, while the Central Government was so weak as to be treated with contempt. Our second Constitution was adopted in order to strengthen the Central Government. Its main purpose was centralization to the extreme limit of popular acceptance in that period. The States, hitherto substantially independent in fact, were constitutionally subdued, but vestiges of their original sovereignty survived in the Constitution of 1787. This compact clause, however, served no purpose whatever for considerably more than a century, and its renascence in recent times is largely due to the limitations placed by the

Federal courts upon the expansion of the jurisdiction of the Central Government.

Its feebleness, if not its futility, as a substitute for a national power equal to the performance of functions overreaching State lines, must in time be demonstrated if it is experimented with on a broad scale in matters vitally affecting the life and economic interests of the people.

Eleven interstate compacts, the majority dealing with the distribution of river waters, were made and approved by Congress between 1919 and 1930.[26] Previous to that, compact was used chiefly for state boundary settlements. The problems solved by this system had little of the profit motive about them and were of a fairly stable nature. Unlike electric power agreements they were not changing continuously. More recently, with emphasis on planning and regionalism, resort to the compact has become more popular. In 1938 the National Resources Committee referred to approximately sixty compacts made and approved by Congress.[27] As of 1950, the number is more than one hundred.

In March, 1949, the six New England governors met in Boston and drafted an interstate compact for a New England Development Authority to plan and develop for ten years the common economic interests of the region.[28] The proposed compact authorized the Authority to survey the natural and economic resources of New England together with the resources of adjacent areas which affect the economy of New England. The study was to include the utilization and control of water resources, especially in regard to achieving low-cost electric power, lessening flood damage, removing sources of water pollution, and obtaining uniform or competitively fair rates for power and light throughout New England, without prejudice to the agricultural or industrial economy of the area. This survey of the natural and economic resources was further to include (but not be limited to) an investigation and a comprehensive report upon the importation of natural gas into the area by pipe line; the establishment of a steel industry in New England; the promotion and development of textile, electrical, brass, and shoe industries; and the conservation and expansion of marine fisheries, agriculture, and timber and mineral production. The Authority was directed to inquire into and determine the availability of federal grants-in-aid for developing projects recommended by the Authority, and to take steps to procure the necessary funds. Each governor was to appoint one of the six commissioners in the Authority to serve at his pleasure for ten years, the duration of the compact. The functions of the Authority were purely administrative, fact-finding, planning, and advisory. Recommendations were to be made to the New England states, and the findings of the Authority publicized. Additional powers could be delegated to the Authority only by concurrence of all six state legislatures or by acts of Congress. Failure of one state to ratify would invalidate the compact.

The Rhode Island legislature unanimously ratified the compact, but Vermont rejected it so early in the year that Massachusetts did not press for ratification. Although introduced in New Hampshire, it was not enacted. In Maine an unfavorable committee report was accepted by the legislature without debate. The governors planned to reactivate the proposal in 1951, but did not do so.

Certain staunch prejudices must be eliminated, however, before conservative northern New England will agree. Such stereotypes as a ten-year plan by the "planners," and alleged executive usurpation of legislative prerogatives are unpopular there. Although the power of the Authority at first would be advisory only, it would be the entering wedge for a regional economic parliament superimposed on the states. Its instruction to procure federal funds for execution of its projects would simply be an invitation for the national government to encroach further on the reserved powers of the states. And although power is merely one of the several subjects of the proposal, some Maine Solons see an Ethiopian in the kindling, a means for them to be maneuvered out of the Fernald law.

Maine wants neither the national government nor the New England states to control the transmission of its power. Many people believe that they own the power and therefore must control it. So long as this idea persists and the federal government does not extend its jurisdiction, the compact plan will not satisfy the people of Maine. If, however, the climate of opinion becomes less particularistic, if the people of Maine ever arrive at the conclusion that their prosperity and welfare are closely tied in with that of the New England region, and if they decide that the problems of the states having markets to offer are complementary to those of states having surplus power to sell, then a compact deserves further exploration.

# CHAPTER XII

## The Passamaquoddy Tidal Power Project

In his treatise on Maine water power in 1869, Walter Wells predicted that large tidal power sites in Maine would be harnessed. With a mean height of the tide at Eastport at 18.1 feet, and that of other coastal areas ranging from 8.5 to 16 feet, he stated that if anywhere in the world it could be done it was in Maine because of favorable physical conditions.[1]

Wells considered this power valuable even without development for certain forms of manufacturing—sawing lumber and marble, grinding grain and slate—where much power and few attendants are required. Although the unseasonable and constantly changing hours of its availability are disadvantageous, with suitable wheels tidal power could be operated to advantage sixteen out of twenty-four hours. The supply of water never fails, its fluctuations are small, little trouble comes from ice, and the privileges are accessible to market by the cheapest form of transportation. The firm foundations of the rock-bound coast of Maine are excellent for dams and mill structures. Wells, of course, referred to the use of this power in tide mills, an idea which was not at all like the Passamaquoddy tidal power project. The advantages of tide water mills, however, were still valid half a century later.

The late Dexter P. Cooper, well-known engineer, conceived the Passamaquoddy tidal power project some thirty years ago while convalescing at his summer home at Campobello, where he saw the tremendous power of the tides daily. He and the late Franklin D. Roosevelt, then Assistant Secretary of the Navy with a summer home at Campobello, are reported to have discussed the possibilities of a tidal power project. Mr. Roosevelt, while campaigning for the vice-presidency in 1920, hinted in an Eastport address that such plans were being formulated.[2] The Eastport *Sentinel* carried the first public announcement of the Cooper plan.[3]

Cooper, fresh from the construction of the Wilson dam at Muscle Shoals, went to Campbello in the summer of 1924 to make preliminary surveys. The project as originally conceived was international, requiring the coöperation of the United States and Canada. It consisted of two pools: the upper, Passamaquoddy Bay, with a low water area of about one hundred square miles, mostly in Canadian waters; and the lower pool, Cobscook Bay, with a low water area of about twenty-seven square miles, on the American side of the boundary line. Each pool was to be cut off from the ocean by a series of dams connecting the headlands and islands across its entrances. Each basin was to be equipped with sluice gates. In the high level pool, water from the ocean would be allowed to enter at high tide. The two pools would be separated by a powerhouse. Water from the high pool would flow through the powerhouse to the low pool, supplying power at all times. In the low level pool, the gates would be open near the time of low tide, allowing the pool to empty to the lowest tide level.[4] Thus the upper pool would be filled every twelve hours and the lower pool drained every twelve hours. The difference in the level of the water in the two pools would give a normal fall or head of from 8 to 20 feet. In the area of about one hundred square miles, the tide rises and falls from 20 to 25 feet every twelve hours, and four times a day about two billion tons of water boil through the narrow passages at the mouth of the bay.

The operation of the system would require three phases.[5] In the neutral phase the two storage basins, one higher than the other, are entirely cut off from any influence of the tides. Water is simply flowing from the upper to the lower basin, passing through the powerhouse and generating power. Second, when the tide has just reached a level with the water of the upper pool or storage basin, the upper control gates are opened. These are adequate in number and size to permit the upper storage basin to rise and completely fill, along with the tide. At the moment the tide turns and starts to recede, these gates are closed, leaving a new high level and a full supply in the upper storage basin. Third, at the final phase, when the falling tide descends to the level of the water in the lower basin, the lower control gates are opened and the lower storage basin drains out with the falling tide. When the tide turns again and starts to rise, these gates are closed, leaving in the lower pool a newly emptied space to receive water from the powerhouse. Throughout this phase the upper control gates are closed.

Cooper estimated that the project would produce more than 600,000 hp., which would run into several billion kilowatt-hours. The cost of the project was estimated at from $75,000,000 to $100,000,000, and electricity could be produced there for three-quarters of a cent per kilowatt-hour. He believed that this money would be available from private sources.[6] Other estimates were that from eleven to twenty billion kilowatt-hours were theoretically available from the international project, but practical considerations would limit it to three billion kilowatt-hours, or nearly one-half million horsepower each year.[7]

Governor Owen Brewster at first did not favor the proposed Cooper charter.[8] He said that its passage was being facilitated by a belief that the project would never be constructed, and that legislators were willing to vote for the charter only because they were sure that the project would not materialize. He urged the legislature to estimate the value of the project on the assumption that it would be completed. His greatest objection was that by its passage the legislature would violate the pledge of the Republican Party of Maine in allowing exportation of power from the greatest power development ever proposed within the state. It was also unwise, he thought, to give a ten-year option on a valuable piece of property, when the securing of responsible financial backing for the corporation depended upon the grant of the charter by the legislature.

Senator Charles B. Carter opposed the Cooper project in the Maine Senate in 1925, calling it a vision and a phantom, existing only in the imagination of one man.[9] He also expressed doubts of its engineering feasibility. His greatest objection was to the provision of the charter enabling the corporation to transmit surplus power to other states at the discretion of the Public Utilities Commission. Senator Carter saw no difference between salt-water and fresh-water electricity. He argued that to vote for its transmission would be revoking a state policy and repudiating the Republican platform. If

Cooper were allowed to transmit power, all power companies should be treated likewise.

Senator Frederick W. Hinckley undoubtedly expressed the opinion of many Maine people when he asked,[10] "Why not give him [Cooper] a chance to try it? What objection is there?" Hinckley asserted that the Republican platform referred to power from the Maine rivers and streams, and when that platform was adopted, nobody considered tidal power. Consequently, this was a new proposition, outside the range of the platform. On the crucial question of a market for the power in the state it was asserted that the project would revolutionize Maine, bringing great industries into the Lubec and Eastport area, the electrification of every railroad with cheap power, and possibly the heating of every home.

The charter permitted the transmission of power generated from tides to other states as determined by the Public Utilities Commission to be in excess of the demands within Maine itself.[11] The capital stock and the bond issues were subject to the approval of the Public Utilities Commission. Unless the corporation completed the initial construction of its works within ten years, the charter became null and void. The Cooper Corporation was empowered to engage in manufacturing to use its power, but the charter recognized the cardinal principle of no competition in territory already assigned to power companies by expressly forbidding the sale of this power in areas served by other concerns unless approved by the Public Utilities Commission. Power could, however, be sold to public utilities under general law.

The Cooper charter was passed in the legislature subject to approval by the voters of the state at a referendum. A committee to conduct a campaign in preparation for the referendum was organized in Washington County, where the project was to be located. On September 14, 1925, the electorate voted 53,000 to 7,000 in favor of the charter. A proportionally large share of the votes were cast in Washington County: 9,855 for the charter and only 119 against it.[12]

This favorable vote on the exportation of Quoddy power was caused by a combination of several factors. Probably the most important were the willingness to give the project a chance, and a wistful hope in the area affected that the expenditure of thousands of dollars of private capital would bring prosperity. Likewise, there was no reason to fear out-of-state capitalists and power companies in this undertaking. Furthermore, the false notion which was prevalent among many Maine people that they owned the power in the rivers and streams was never applied to Quoddy. This project was a new idea, conceived long after the Fernald law was passed.

The Federal Power Commission issued a preliminary permit to Dexter P. Cooper, Inc., on May 28, 1926. On October 22, 1928, an application for a licence was filed, contemplating initial and ultimate power installations of 464,000 hp. and 1,087,000 hp., respectively.

Canadian federalism required two separate and complementary Quoddy charters because construction would affect not only tidal waters which come under national jurisdiction but also the provincial prerogatives of property and civil rights. The Canadian Dexter P. Cooper Company was incorporated at Ottawa in 1926, and in 1928 the New Brunswick legislature passed a charter bill with many amendments. This charter stipulated that active construction must be started within three years and the project be completed by 1932. On April 16, 1929, the Dominion Parliament rejected Cooper's petition for an extension of the charter because of opposition by fisheries interests and the Canadian Pacific Railroad.[13] Cooper's attempt to secure reversal of parliamentary action through the State Department failed. Thus, although it had been supported by four great electrical concerns with $400,000, the project collapsed because of Canadian opposition and the depression.[14]

On September 16, 1929, Dexter P. Cooper, Inc., filed a revised application, the all-American plan, for a two-pool project entirely within the United States with initial and ultimate installations of 80,000 and 240,000 hp., and contemplating the eventual construction of a pumped-storage plant at Haycock Harbor, twelve miles away, as an auxiliary to the tidal power plant.[15] While still referred to as the Passamaquoddy development, this two-pool all-American plan was actually confined to Cobscook Bay of the United States. The project was generally considered merely the initial step in the consummation of the international project. Since the major installations would be on the American side, the smaller project involved about two-thirds the cost for about half of the power expected from the larger. For this reason the all-American project was vulnerable to attack on the score of power cost. But, on the other hand, it was not intended to function permanently as an independent power-producing unit. Many of its proponents believed that if it were built the Canadians could be induced to grant a charter, and that with little expense the two-pool all-American development could be incorporated into the international Quoddy project. Yet it was difficult to explain the long-range plan.

Quoddy is an example of a project planned by private capital and supported by pressure groups, which could not, however, be financed without public aid. When the P.W.A. was seeking relief projects, Quoddy supporters immediately proposed their plan. There was no assurance that the Quoddy project would be self-liquidating within a specified number of years, but it could be started as a relief measure and in the meantime be given an opportunity to prove its economic worth. No other plans were available to solve the acute relief problem in the area, and the cheapest form of relief, the dole, was generally unacceptable. Hence it was logical for those who were ready with a plan to get a hearing.

Dexter P. Cooper, accompanied by Moses B. Pike, went to Washington in July, 1933, to discuss with President Roosevelt the inclusion of the Quoddy project in the P.W.A. program. His brother, Colonel Hugh Cooper, is reported to have stated, "Quoddy could produce power at a cost that would permit its sale anywhere in New England as far south as Hartford, Connecticut, under present load conditions, at a price less than any existing hydroelectric or any modern steam station in the New England area."[16] With an amended plan and supplementary data, Cooper applied on September 11, 1933, to the P.W.A. for a loan of $43,000,000 with which to construct the project.

Without debate the Maine legislature in its special session of December, 1933, extended the Cooper charter twenty years from 1925. Other amendments were made to facilitate construction if federal funds were forthcoming. The time limit would not be applicable if the United States government through the P.W.A. or other agency lent money or otherwise financed, in whole or in part, initial construction. It was also amended for a project concerning waters entirely within the jurisdiction of the United States but with sufficient latitude to include the international project if it were ever revived.[17]

On January 3, 1934, the Federal Power Commission reported, in reply to the request of the P.W.A., that the tidal power project at Passamaquoddy was unsound and unjustified for these reasons: (1) it would cost approximately $40,000,000, whereas a comparable steam-generating plant would cost only $16,000,000; (2) the steam-electric power would be cheaper at the higher-load factors; (3) Passamaquoddy power could not compete with steam-power rates in export; and (4) there was then no market or prospective market for Passamaquoddy power at any price. As a supplement to this report the commission transmitted to the P.W.A. a letter, dated February 21, 1934, admonishing that agency that "contingencies might cause the costs greatly to exceed the estimates."[18]

Senator Hale and Senator White of Maine arranged with Colonel H. M. Waite, assistant administrator of the P.W.A., for a hearing for Cooper by the P.W.A. Technical Board of Review on March 30. Cooper stated that 60 per cent of the power produced would be used in the manufacture of aluminum, 8 per cent in the manufacture of stainless steel, and the remainder, minus 10 per cent for reserve, would be consumed by six northern and eastern counties of Maine.[19] On May 1 the board reported unfavorably on the project, whereupon the Maine delegation in Congress decided to appeal to President Roosevelt. Congressman E. Carl Moran (D.) charged that the board had surrendered to the aluminum trust, and challenged the board's figures on the comparative cost of steam and Quoddy power. On June 7 the P.W.A. "finally and formally" rejected the Cooper petition.

After its rejection by the P.W.A., Quoddy supporters decided to try to make it a federal project, to be built by the War Department and operated by a Quoddy Authority created by the Maine legislature. Governor Louis J. Brann, Democrat and anti–New Dealer, successfully campaigned for reëlection in 1934 and became Maine's first two-term Democratic governor since the Civil War, on a platform calling for the establishment of the Quoddy project, which would "bring some fifty million dollars into the state, to be expended in a section where it is as much needed as anywhere."[20]

On July 15 Congressman J. G. Utterback of Maine released a

letter from President Roosevelt assuring Utterback of his interest in Quoddy and his belief in its engineering practicability. Said the President:[21]

> The principal stumbling block to a Federal appropriation . . . is that there is no definite assurance for the use of the power when developed. I am not suggesting that the full power development should be contracted for in advance, but in other Federal projects we have had reasonable and definite assurance that the bulk of the power could be sold and a large portion of the receipts applied to the interest and amortization of the actual cost of construction. I think it is very decidedly possible for the good people of Maine to undertake to get a definite distribution use for the power when it is developed.

Governor Brann, in a radio address on July 23, quoted from a message received from President Roosevelt.[22]

> With my summer home so near Eastport for so many years, I have been interested in what is known as the "Quoddy project" for a long time, and it has been my hope that eventually the State of Maine would become not only a great industrial center of the nation but that its agricultural population would be among the first to enjoy the manifest advantages of cheap electrical power on the farm as well.

The President then stated that a study ought to be made of the ways in which this power might be put to work in the shortest possible time, and that government funds were available for such public works projects if it should be found that the creation of the power was practical and economical, could be made available for definite uses, and would not lie idle for many years.

In answer to President Roosevelt's request for a committee of Maine citizens to study possible uses for Quoddy power, Governor Brann appointed the following: Kenneth C. M. Sills, president of Bowdoin College (soon thereafter chosen as chairman of the committee); E. S. French, head of the Maine Central and Boston and Maine railroads; H. B. Crawford, Master of the State Grange; Wingate F. Cram, treasurer of the Bangor and Aroostook Railroad; and William N. Campbell, of the Goodall Mills.

The unanimous conclusions of this committee, the Quoddy Hydro-Electric Commission, were, first, that the Quoddy project could be constructed at this time only as a federal project; and second, as a federal project it should be undertaken at once and carried to completion as promptly as efficiency in construction would permit.[23] It was stated that in the depression era no private capital was available for the project, and that the government had denied a loan to a private corporation because a sufficiently certain market for the power was not shown. The committee suggested numerous possibilities for the sale of the power, and pointed out that many Maine people felt that the state should receive a share of the money available for such projects. The state of Maine could not finance Quoddy even if it desired, because, for constitutional reasons, it could not borrow so large a sum of money. Federal support of the project was argued on the grounds of "social desirability." The committee felt that the project came properly under a program of public works because it would employ a large number of people on the relief rolls for many months, and would bring lasting benefit to the state.

Secretary of the Interior Harold Ickes, after conferences with President Roosevelt, Governor Brann, and F. Harold Dubord, announced that he was reconsidering the rejection of Quoddy and reviewing the evidence. On August 21, 1934, Secretary Ickes inspected the site with Governor Brann, Congressman Utterback, Major Philip B. Fleming, and all the members of the Quoddy Hydro-Electric Commission. At a public meeting attended by several thousand people at Eastport, Secretary Ickes said he couldn't get away from the Quoddy project and advised its friends to keep on fighting for it. A few days later he named Major Fleming, P. M. Benton, and K. S. Wingfield as advisers to the Quoddy Commission. Subsequently, on October 22, the Maine Quoddy Association was formed to conduct the campaign. When it was learned that the Quoddy Commission could not complete its work for lack of funds, the Governor and council appropriated $5,000 for its expenses.

In November, a new Quoddy Commission was named by Secretary Ickes, consisting of Dexter P. Cooper, Moses B. Pike (ardent supporter of the project and assistant to Cooper), Henry T. Hunt, legal adviser of the P.W.A., and H. T. Corey, Reclamation Service expert.[24] The members went to Eastport and later to Augusta, where the Maine State Planning Board began a survey of markets for Quoddy power. For two weeks in December the staff of the Maine State Planning Board made studies at Eastport to report to the Quoddy Commission.

The reports of the Maine Quoddy Commission and Maine State Planning Board on possible markets for Quoddy power were, of necessity, indefinite. Attention was called to the fact that electric power would not be available for over two and a half years and that industrial plants could probably be constructed and ready for operation within six months after the completion of plans and selection of equipment. "Accordingly, it is difficult to anticipate the improvements that may be made in the manufacture of products, now assumed, or the markets for them two or three years hence and we can only base our information in the present and past operations."[25] As possible markets for this power the board pointed to the limited supply available in Aroostook County and in southeastern Maine, a demand for power at reasonable rates by the present electric utilities, many communities without service, and the paper mill at Woodland. With a high-tension transmission line about 110 miles from Quoddy to Houlton, interconnecting with the lines of the Maine Public Service Company and supplying power at low cost, the possibility of a market of twenty to thirty million kilowatt-hours was seen in the near future. Another suggested source of market was the electrification of railroads.

The board also made the suggestion that in a development of this magnitude it might be wise to develop several smaller industries distributed among outlying communities; the current consumption of each community would be comparatively small, but the total amount would be substantial. Except for Governor Joshua L. Chamberlain's plea for this idea in a diversified economy half a century ago, altogether too little attention had been devoted to this possibility.

The board pointed to the growth of Maine's industrial cities of a century ago, resulting from cheap power, inferring that a supply at Eastport in 1936 would be sufficient to induce industries to locate there. Unfortunately, however, the report did not give sufficient attention to the relative importance of power as compared with other factors in determining the location of industry. Its thesis was that development at Eastport would attract industries which required large amounts of cheap power and which, because they dealt in light products, did not have high transportation costs. The fact that some important raw materials existed in eastern Maine would further reduce transportation costs. Consideration was given also to the fact that Eastport has one of the best harbors on the Atlantic coast, 283 miles nearer Gibraltar and 425 miles nearer Liverpool than is New York City. It is ice-free throughout the year, and in exceptionally cold weather is one of the few harbors on the North Atlantic coast that are not closed by ice.[26]

Governor Louis J. Brann, in his contest for United States senator, in an Eastport address suggested that since Eastport is the nearest United States port to Europe, the completion of the project would pave the way for the establishment of the largest naval base in the world.[27]

The Maine State Planning Board attested that the Eastport region is one of the most beautiful parts of the Maine coast, very close to the summer home of President Roosevelt, who was quoted as having felt that it had high possibilities for recreational development,[28] including good hunting and stream fishing, deep-sea fishing, canoeing, and boating. The area has the coolest summers in the state and is free from hay fever. Recreational development should net $10,000,000 annually in ten years. It was estimated that the new industry would use $300,000 worth of electricity a year.

On the basis of available material the board estimated that an initial investment of $8,000,000 would be required to construct the manufacturing plants necessary to utilize the power developed at Quoddy. The approximate cost of the individual plants was given as follows: aluminum, $2,500,000; stainless steel, $2,000,000; nitrogen fixation, $2,100,000; other metallurgical and industrial plants, $1,400,000. The initial investment was to cover the cost of constructing the plants, including such carrying items as fixed charges, depreciation, maintenance, and operation. Thus the report considered possible uses of the power for a few large industries in addition to a larger number of smaller enterprises. It should be remembered that Dexter P. Cooper, Inc., the only Quoddy corporation in existence when the report was issued, was empowered by its charter to engage in manufacturing to use its power.

The report included a table of the estimated costs of various hydroelectric plants in Maine and the country compared with the preliminary estimated costs of the Quoddy development. It indicated that the cost of producing electric power would be very nearly comparable and that Quoddy power might be cheaper than that of some of the other plants in operation or under construction. Others listed were the Wyman plant, all plants of the Central Maine Power Company, Muscle Shoals, Boulder Dam, Grand Coulee Dam, and Bonneville Dam. The fallacy of this contention was that the information of the board was confined to the preliminary estimated cost of the development, which was placed at $42,000,000. On the basis of recent data, obtained after more thorough investigations, the Federal Power Commission estimated the cost at more than twice this amount.

The Quoddy Hydro-Electric Commission and the State Planning Board insisted that, although many of the large federal power developments were undertaken without a definite power market in sight, there was a reasonable possibility of attracting several new major industries to eastern Maine which would not come without Quoddy.[29]

A list of industries which could use Quoddy power, with facts to show that each of the industries could be developed, follows:[30]

1. Stainless steel, nickel alloys, industrial plant and master alloys
2. The aluminum industry, applications, and its alloys
3. Electrochemical industrial plant
4. Sulfuric acid from pyrite
5. Iodine
6. Products of the ceramic industries
7. Potash from feldspar
8. Fertilizer industry (nitrogen and cyanamide processes)
9. Caustic soda—liquid chlorine
10. Wood manufacturing industries
11. Fisheries

Other possible industries, suggested but not described in the report, which might profitably be established in eastern Maine to use Quoddy power were:

1. Explosives—celluloid and plastics, photographic chemicals—artificial leather
2. Lacquers—alcohol—wood chemicals
3. Dyes
4. Calcium carbide—acetylene (oxygen—nitrogen and rare gases)
5. Electrical welding and small-parts plant
6. Commercial refrigeration plant
7. The paint industry

The board considered also the raw materials locally available for these industries, especially feldspar and clay. Its conclusions were:

1. Nickel alloy steel may be profitably manufactured at Eastport.
2. In all probability aluminum silicate can be commercially reduced by the acid process from Eastport clays.
3. Bauxite, the standard material for the manufacture of aluminum oxide, can be shipped to Maine from the Southern states or from foreign countries.
4. Many electrochemical products using Maine minerals may be manufactured by the use of Quoddy power.
5. Iodine, although difficult and expensive to produce, may be manufactured at Eastport.
6. The development of Quoddy would permit local use of feldspars and clays in the preparation and manufacture of many ceramic articles. Most of these natural resources of Maine have been shipped to other states.

From the commission appointed by Secretary Ickes emerged the so-called Hunt Report, which was probably the most favorable that has been made on the Quoddy project. Largely on the basis of this report the administration decided to construct Quoddy on its "social value," as a federal project, by War Department engineers. The report was kept in deepest secrecy, and the P.W.A. persistently refused to give it to reporters or to members of Congress.[31] Regardless of the validity of the charge that this was a "packed" committee, note should be made that it was a report to an administrative agency, not to Congress. Although Congress appropriated the relief money, it was nevertheless mostly on the basis of administrative action that construction work at Quoddy was started and stopped.

On January 17, 1935, the P.W.A. special commission submitted a recommendation to the administration that $30,000,000 be allotted to the War Department to finance the construction, and that a State Power Authority be created to lease and operate the project. The recommendation was for the construction of an "immediate project consisting of a single basin, tidal power installation, utilizing Cobscook Bay; a power storage plant near Haycock Harbor; and a sixteen-mile electric transmission line connecting the two, all within the state of Maine, near Lubec and Eastport," at an estimated cost of $30,125,000; and stated that the ultimate plan as contemplated would constitute an international project.

The single-pool, all-American plan, smaller and less expensive than either the international or the two-pool, all-American projects, called for the construction of a dam across the mouth of Cobscook Bay similar to that in Cooper's original plan. But the contemplated two-mile dam across Cobscook Bay to provide both an upper and lower pool within the bay was omitted.[32] This would have meant less control of the water flow, with the use of all of Cobscook Bay as the lower pool and the ocean as the upper pool. On January 21, favorable reports by both Quoddy commissions, with memorials signed by the Governor and the council and nearly all members of the legislature, were laid before President Roosevelt by Governor Brann.

Governor Brann and the Maine delegation in Washington were reported to have agreed that the Maine legislature would consider the enactment of a law safeguarding the federal government's rights, affording reasonable opportunity for the tidal dams at Quoddy to earn sufficient money to make the project at least partly self-liquidating without doing injustice to the utilities of the state.

A Quoddy bill was drafted in Washington, reputedly by Thomas Corcoran, at that time attorney for the Reconstruction Finance Corporation, who was acting as the government's adviser on Quoddy. Governor Brann sent Attorney General Clyde R. Chapman of Maine to Washington to assist in drafting the proposed law.[33] He and Governor Brann brought the bill to Maine on February 12, and it was introduced into the Senate by Senator Homer Worcester. This bill attempted to set up a board with broad powers, but was so contrary to Maine policies that it had little chance of passage.

The bill set up a corporation consisting of five directors appointed by the governor for five years, serving without compensation until the financial condition of the corporation warranted it. No provision was made for an issue of stock and no limitation was set on capital, which was to be provided by borrowing money, issuing negotiable notes, bonds, and other evidences of indebtedness, which might be taken by individuals, banks, or any federal governmental agency. The corporation was empowered to determine its own rates, which did not depend on the value of its property. Like the coöperative enabling act five years later which emanated from

Washington, this corporation was to have perpetual existence, with the power of eminent domain, together with authority to "acquire, purchase, hold, use, lease, mortgage, sell, transfer and dispose of any property," without limitation. It was authorized to build,

> acquire, construct, and maintain power houses, hydro-electric and other plants and any and all structures, ways and means, necessary, useful or customarily used and employed in the manufacture, generation and distribution of power, including, but without limitation, water power, steam electric power, hydro-electric power, tidal electric power, and any and all other kinds of power, including power transmission lines, poles, telephone lines, sub-stations, transformers, conduits, and generally all things used or useful in the manufacture, distribution, purchase and sale of power generated by tides, water, steam or otherwise. . . . [also] to manufacture, produce, generate, transmit, distribute and sell water power, steam electric power, hydro-electric power, tidal electric power or mechanical power without the State of Maine and within the State of Maine in any manner not in violation of the general law.

The Authority could have entered into contracts with cities and towns to supply them with light and power in spite of existing laws, which afford protection from such competition to light and power companies engaged in business. Some Maine people saw in this an attempt of the "brain-trusters" to set up an instrument which might be used as a yardstick to establish electric light and power rates in Maine destructive to private industry.

Chief Justice William J. Pattangall of the Supreme Judicial Court of Maine was one of the first to attack the bill. He admitted the importance of the project to Maine and especially to Washington County, but contended that the price asked by the passage of such a bill was too great to pay.[34]

> Summarized, this corporation is given the authority to take over any property in the State of Maine, and more especially the property of any existing power company. It is not dependent upon the Public Utilities Commission for its rate schedule. It is not bound by the limitations of the Fernald Act with regard to the exportation of power. It contains not a single word that indicates any intention on the part of anybody to build Quoddy Dam. It places under the control of government every resource of this state, and the authority thus given is without limit as to time or amount of money involved so long as the capital may be furnished by either private agencies or Federal agencies.

Some felt that it was not fitting for the Chief Justice of the Supreme Judicial Court of the state to attack the proposed Quoddy Authority Act. The resulting exchange of letters in the press between Chief Justice Pattangall and the Honorable Roscoe C. Emery of Eastport attracted state-wide attention. The bill was so drastic that the derogation of judicial dignity was tolerated, a sure sign of its impending defeat.

Somewhere between Washington, D.C., and Augusta, Maine, one clause in the original bill was deleted: "The state will not limit or alter the rights vested in the Authority until said obligations [to the federal government] with interest are fully met and discharged." This provision was designed to maintain the law in its original form until the loans had been repaid with interest, and would have acted as a limitation on the authority of the state legislature to alter corporation charters. Although the bill was introduced in the legislature and printed, no hearing was granted.[35] Its introduction was regarded as an attempt to satisfy some people in Washington.

In March, 1935, Congress passed the relief bill in which Quoddy funds were included. Senator Hale, who had voted against the $4,000,000,000 works appropriation, expressed his appreciation that Maine was not to be left out in its distribution:[36]

> The government having adopted a policy of developing water power projects and a very large sum of money having been appropriated over my vote for such developments, I am glad indeed that Maine was not to be left out and that it has been decided to go ahead with the Quoddy project.
>
> The money to be spent in its development will be of great help to the state as a whole and more especially to the people of Washington County, who, through no fault of their own, are in a position where they badly need help. The project has my very best wishes for a successful future.

The investigatory commission in Maine and some of the newspapers and political leaders likewise stressed the pork-barrel aspects.[37]

> Your Commission, however, desires to base its main contention on the fact that the Quoddy project would be of great benefit to the people of the State of Maine. Maine people have always been independent, hardworking, frugal, self-reliant; their philosophy is based on the idea that every man should produce the wealth of which he was capable by industry and ingenuity; that he should live frugally and keep out of

debt; that he should be self-supporting and independent. That attitude still prevails; but the people of Maine realize that conditions in the economic world have greatly changed and that Maine alone cannot prosper cut off from the central energizing power of the government. Maine has always been in an eddy of the national stream little affected by the tides of adversity and prosperity until the past few years. Since 1929 Maine has been watching other parts of the country receive very large sums from the federal government for flood control, irrigation control, power projects, and other purposes in the West and South. Today, perhaps with typical Yankee shrewdness, Maine feels that it is about time that she receive a modest portion of the vast sums that seem to be available, to be expended within her borders on a project that the majority of the people of the state believe will give great renewal to the industrial and agricultural life of Maine and will rehabilitate one of the most hard hit regions of the whole country.

On May 16 the P.W.A. formally recommended allocation of $10,000,000 to Quoddy. On May 28 President Roosevelt signed the initial allocation of $10,000,000 to the project, and Comptroller General J. R. McCarl approved it on June 5. Owen Brewster, who as governor in 1925 had spoken unfavorably on the Cooper charter to the legislature, gave a Quoddy victory dinner at Washington on May 23. He was one of the speakers, along with Mr. Cooper and Major Fleming, at a huge demonstration at Eastport on June 28. As Republican candidate for Congress, Brewster voiced a strong demand for Quoddy.

Congressman Brewster claimed that Thomas Corcoran (R.F.C. attorney) had threatened to hold up the Quoddy project if Brewster voted against the holding company "death sentence" as desired by President Roosevelt. According to Brewster, Corcoran said: "Let me speak with brutal bluntness. If you do not vote for the death sentence I shall find it necessary to stop construction on the Passamaquoddy dam." At the House of Representatives investigation Corcoran denied the charge, maintaining that he had no power to stop the Quoddy project. Ernest Gruening quoted Corcoran as having said, "I have got to speak with brutal frankness and say that as far as I am concerned, if you are going to run out like this, if your political situation in Maine is so delicate and you must depend on power company support, how can we trust you to carry through your commitments on Quoddy?"[38] Although it is impossible to ascertain precisely what was said, from the evidence it appears that Corcoran was zealous that Brewster should vote with the administration on the holding-company act and that he at least inferred that if Brewster voted against the act it would have some effect on Quoddy, or at least remove Brewster from all legal or representative connection with the project.[39]

Late in October, 1935, $5,000,000 was taken away from the original Quoddy allocation of $10,000,000. The press reported that the government had ordered suspension of work on the Quoddy project unless the Maine legislature enacted proper enabling legislation.[40] It was also reported that Secretary Ickes had filed with the President a memorandum advising suspension of Quoddy unless a special session of the legislature were called to create a state authority.[41] Despite denials of this story from Washington, rumors persisted of a demand of the "brain trust" that the Maine legislature enact a law creating a commission with broad powers to control and operate Quoddy's tidal dams.[42] With the Army Engineers in charge of construction, the War Department desired action by the Maine legislature before proceeding with the heavy obligations for Quoddy. In November, army legal experts began to work on a new draft of a Quoddy Authority bill, a simpler and narrower proposal than that of the previous winter.[43]

An editorial in the Lewiston *Evening Journal* mirrored state opinion of the bill when it asserted (an exaggerated half-truth) that the bill was a copy of the T.V.A. to all intents and purposes.[44] "The limitation of all authority to Quoddy itself should be a part of any establishment of Authority. The measure sent to Maine by the Administration at Washington was general and opened the way to a conscription of all water-power in Maine. . . . Be certain, O Ye People, what is asked and what is the price to be paid. . . . Any Authority to be set up should be Maine-made, not made by Tugwell." The writer was willing to accept the Quoddy yardstick only if it apportioned its costs fairly, and set up its books on a basis prescribed by and subject to the Maine Public Utilities Commission.

In December, War Department engineers estimated the cost of a single-basin project, resembling the "immediate project" recommended by the Passamaquoddy Bay Tidal Power Commission, at $61,500,000, exclusive of interest during construction. A review board consisting of three consulting engineers sent to Eastport by the Bureau of Reclamation, Department of the Interior, estimated the cost of the same project at $68,158,000, exclusive of interest during construction.[45] According to Ernest R. Abrams,[46]

Army Engineers . . . , coincident with the start of construction, began extensive explorations, surveys and research studies, which led them to report a revised estimate of cost of $62,000,000 for the project, if the original scheme of having tidal power do all the work was pursued, or of $37,000,000 if the high level pumped basin was eliminated and a modern steam or Diesel plant was substituted. This report was not released to the public but, instead, a commission of experienced hydraulic engineers composed of Charles H. Paul and Joseph Jacobs, members of the American Society of Civil Engineers, and Professor William F. Durand of Leland Stanford University, was appointed to make a new study. Their report raised the estimate of cost of the project above the figures set by the Army Engineers so it, too, was suppressed and the Bureau of Reclamation Engineers were asked to study and report on the undertaking. And when these government engineers again raised the probable cost of the project to $68,000,000, their report was pigeonholed, far from public view.

On January 10, 1936, on recommendation of the Army Engineers, and after appeals from Eastport, Lubec, and Calais, President Roosevelt restored $2,000,000 of the Quoddy allocation, and the intended 40 per cent reduction of force was changed to a 15 per cent layoff.[47]

Actual construction of the Quoddy project was assigned to the Army Engineers, not because Quoddy was classified as a war or national defense measure, but because the Army Engineer Corps traditionally has been the engineering department of the national government. Major Fleming was named director, assisted by Lieutenant Lord and Lieutenant Leehey; Dexter P. Cooper was consulting engineer.

One of the questions which arose when the government took over the tidal power development was to determine its relationship with Cooper. He had started the project and unquestionably had rights in it. It was sometimes alleged that the administration wanted to get rid of him, but the War Department purchased the rights, titles, franchises, engineering plans, and privileges of Dexter P. Cooper, Inc., for $60,000. As adviser to the government, Cooper was delegated to find a market for the electricity Quoddy would generate, and was given $25,000 and a year's time to make a comprehensive study.[48]

The Army Engineers presumably found themselves on the defensive when it was charged that, instead of erecting dams, they were building swanky Quoddy Village at a cost of about $2,172,000.[49] (This, by the way, was indeed in contrast to Cooper's original plan to anchor obsolete ships at Eastport to house the workers.) Nine permanent residences for the officers in charge, on so-called "Snob Hill," at a cost reported to run anywhere from $150,000 to $300,000, a twenty-bed hospital at $55,000, luxurious dormitory furnishings including love seats, grandfather clocks, and old masterpieces for pictures, and wasteful administration of the mess hall caused periodic uproar in the press.[50] Some sixty of the staff were reputed to be supplied with automobiles, many with chauffeurs assigned to them personally.

Further opposition to the War Department construction centered about the use of some eight hundred white-collar workers as compared with fifty used by the Cooper brothers when they built the dam across the Mississippi at Keokuk and the Muscle Shoals dam. At the peak of construction, the project employed five thousand workers, skilled and unskilled, with a weekly payroll of about $140,000. Attempts were made to abide by work-relief regulations, to have no major migration of labor, and to take 90 per cent of the personnel from local relief rolls.[51]

Numerous Quoddy supporters contended that Army Engineers "gummed up" work at Passamaquoddy dam.[52] It was suggested that Army Engineers were less practical than engineers who handle projects for industrial concerns, because the former are not trained to handle commercial jobs "where dollars and cents count, both in the original cost and in the eventual earning power of the project. Theirs is a military training. You might say they are trained to destruction and not to construction."

The Cooper plan was to make Cobscook Bay, not Passamaquoddy, the low-tide pool. This was a concession to Calais, St. Stephen, St. Andrews, and St. George, all on the latter bay or on rivers emptying into it, so that they would not be left high and nearly dry. The Army Engineers went ahead with the single-pool project, but experimented with the idea of departing radically from the Cooper plan by making Quoddy the low-tide pool, intending to keep Cobscook full of water at all times. The reasons given for this change were that it would be an advantage to Lubec, aid river conditions as far up as Whiting, and improve harbor conditions at Eastport. Supporters of the Cooper plan believed that this revision would have spoiled the whole long-range plan by creating a condition strongly discouraging the eventual coöperation of Canada, if not definitely ending all hope for it.

Despite the major differences between Quoddy and the T.V.A., Quoddy supporters showed much interest in the approaching T.V.A. decisions. It was rumored that President Roosevelt wanted to find out what the Court did to the T.V.A. before going any farther with Quoddy,[53] but this theory was weak, for the only common ground between the two was that both were power plants. Whereas the T.V.A. went into the business of generating and selling power, Quoddy was a construction project of the United States Army, presumably to be managed when completed by a state Authority.[54] Lieutenant Colonel Philip B. Fleming, Army Engineer in charge of construction work, explained that the T.V.A. decision did not affect Quoddy because it was never intended that the federal government should operate the Quoddy generating plant or compete with private industry in selling power in Maine.[55]

There were, however, some implications from the T.V.A. decision which did concern Quoddy. In the first place, it indicated that the United States government undoubtedly had the right to operate the power project when completed, and to sell the power wherever markets existed. This decision opened wide the door for federal sale of Quoddy power to other states and possibly for the project to become self-liquidating. If Maine did not create an Authority for its operation, the alternative, if the project had been completed, might have been federal operation. To avoid this alternative and provide for state operation was undoubtedly one of the motivating forces behind the passage of the Quoddy Authority Act the next time the project was revived in 1939.

Another implication of the T.V.A. decision was that it was a "go-ahead" signal for federal power programs, and Quoddy supporters expressed the hope that the reluctance which Congress had shown to provide funds for the completion of the project might be overcome.[56] An outgrowth of this implication, though without specific reference to Quoddy, was a belief that states with large amounts of undeveloped power such as Maine would have to wait for its development under federal auspices, since private capital would, after the decision, hesitate to incur the risk of these developments until the federal government's policy of promoting such enterprises with public funds was determined.

Before the T.V.A. decision, officials in Washington were reported to have expressed concern about the likely effect on Quoddy of an adverse decision. The answer, entirely in the realm of speculation, would depend upon the legal basis for an adverse decision. Had it been that surplus power could not be sold as government property, such a ruling would not necessarily affect a project controlled by a state Authority. Had it been that the construction of the Tennessee Valley project was illegal, its effect on Quoddy would depend upon the reasons for invalidating the Tennessee project.

When President Roosevelt submitted his budget in January, 1936, he recommended to Congress that $29,000,000 be given in the rivers and harbors section of the War Department bill for Quoddy, the Florida ship canal, and three small projects.[57] None of the five projects was examined by the House Committee on Rivers and Harbors, or authorized by Congress to undergo investigation by War Department engineers. They were simply dropped from the War Department bill by the House Appropriations Committee. The Maine delegation in Washington, realizing the hostility to Quoddy in Congress, decided that if they avoided debate on the floor the President would be enabled to continue the project with work-relief funds. But the President said at a press conference that unless Congress gave him authority for Quoddy, he would not give the project any more money from that source.[58] Congress refused this authority, and he did not.

After the Florida ship canal project had been specifically rejected in the United States Senate, Senator Robinson introduced a resolution authorizing engineers to report on both Quoddy and the canal projects. This was referred to the Commerce Committee. At the hearing on the two projects, Governor Brann maintained that it would be expedient to spend relief money on a project already started, and that Quoddy would carry itself after completion.[59] Part of its construction costs ought to be charged to relief.[60] In response to Governor Brann's statement that Quoddy was the most helpful and popular thing in Maine, Senator Vandenberg replied, "Well, $42,000,000 is popular and helpful. That is the answer."

Senator Vandenberg's opposition was based on the contention that an uneconomic project should not be supported simply as a relief measure, and that no markets existed for the power. He objected to spending $36,000,000 to produce power that could be produced for $16,000,000 by steam. Representative Brewster's reply to Senator Vandenberg was that "sea water is cheaper than oil in Maine." He pleaded for work for those on relief, saying that, although doles are cheapest, work relief is best.

Congressman Brewster, Senator White, and Governor Brann insisted that, according to Dexter P. Cooper, there was a market for Quoddy power, although he had not disclosed it. He had arranged for the sale of "all the power Quoddy could produce under the present plans."[61] It was implied that the sale was to concerns of national standing which would establish factories at or near Eastport and employ at least two thousand workers. Would Cooper be willing to testify before the committee to that effect? Representative Brewster replied that Quoddy power was in competition with that of Canada and of western projects, and to divulge these markets might mean their loss.[62]

One question never satisfactorily answered was what would be done with the tidal power if it were made available. One suggested outlet was to transmit Quoddy power by radio for consumption in distant cities![63] Most of the results of Cooper's study were in his head, and he died without putting them on paper. "There was a Cooper report which was never divulged and rumors of a still more secret report, with names and places and amounts of the market but this is one of those Washington mysteries."[64] Senator Vandenberg and other opponents of the project stressed that no specific facts were ever publicly given to support the contention that markets existed for most of the power. However, very few industries could prudently contract with Quoddy for power when its availability in time, amount, and price was so vague and indefinite.

The Robinson resolution was approved by the Commerce Committtee 12 to 5. Senator Hale offered a motion in the Senate to divide the two projects. This division was to allow the Maine group to vote for Quoddy without supporting the canal, and was the basis for Governor Brann's charge, while campaigning for senator, that the Republicans killed the measure. The Senate rejected Quoddy 39 to 28, and approved the canal 35 to 30.

President Roosevelt, speaking from his cottage porch on Campobello Island during the campaign in the summer of 1936, told seven hundred Washington County folk that Quoddy would be completed eventually. First, however, the rest of America—where Quoddy is not well understood—would have to be educated to an appreciation of its possibilities. At an afternoon press conference he called Quoddy a "laboratory" for what might in time become a great hydroelectric development by the United States and Canada.[65] Harry L. Hopkins, National Relief Administrator, speaking in Portland on July 29, 1936, said he had talked about Quoddy to the President at Campobello during the previous week. "If more people, particularly the critics, could see the place as I did, I am sure that much of the opposition would be minimized." He reiterated that the final word on the project must be spoken by President Roosevelt.

A gradual shut-down on Quoddy construction was ordered by Colonel Fleming, and Army Engineers and equipment were transferred elsewhere. In September, 1936, the National Youth Administration took over Quoddy Village. The assertion was sometimes made that work on Quoddy was stopped because it could no longer be considered a relief project. At the outset, to be sure, the construction involved the use of a relatively high proportion of labor in relation to materials. According to Captain Leehey, however, it could not be assumed "that the work yet remaining would logically fit into the Relief Program, and I hope that any resumption of the project may be handled as a direct and definite approved federal project."[66]

The degree to which expensive power projects can be justified on the basis of relief is largely a matter of opinion. Sometimes, however, projects which ordinarily would be uneconomical are justified as work-relief projects because the country would be better off with the development and jobs than with unemployment and its resultant demoralization. Bauer and Gold[67] concluded that if a project can be developed completely and produce power at 6 mills or less per kw-h, it may be regarded as a financially justified undertaking. Beyond 6 mills it becomes dubious except under special circumstances. The two-pool, all-American Quoddy project under federal or state financing was estimated to provide power at 6.65 mills per kw-h, which would put it just beyond the limit of justified projects on this standard. The authors suggested, however, that no hard and fast rules could be laid down.

After construction on Quoddy was stopped and Maine and Vermont were the only two states to vote Republican in 1936, the citizens and Republican leaders of both states were subject to much teasing by New Dealers throughout the country. When one of the Republican leaders of Maine was told that his state no longer belonged to the Union and that they were going to sell Maine, he is purported to have replied, "Well, you can sell us, but you can't buy us." The Republicans had refused to incorporate a Quoddy plan in their platform, and, as a party, did not actively support the project in Maine. However, senators, congressmen, governors—Barrows, Sewall, Hildreth, and Payne,—and many members of the state legislature have given their support to it.

There was much speculation in Maine on the political motives behind Quoddy. Some of these motives, as outlined by Mrs. May Craig, were as follows:[68]

> They say the President started Quoddy for political reasons—to get votes in Maine. They say that practical politicians are telling him that Maine is gone Republican anyway and that besides that Quoddy only makes votes right in Washington County.
>
> While Governor Brann has been regarded as privately cold to Quoddy, especially in view of his refusal to call a special session of the Legislature for the Quoddy Authority, yet he dashed . . . [to Washington] when Quoddy was gasping and is said to have told the President that he, Brann, couldn't get elected to the Senate [1936], without Quoddy. Harold Dubord, Democratic candidate for Governor, who is reported to have filed with the Administration an unfavorable report on Quoddy, was . . . [in Washington] and said he urged Quoddy on Democratic leaders. . . . People suspect some obscure political strategy, but they do not know what it is. Maybe he [Roosevelt] wants to make Maine and Republicans sit up and beg for Quoddy and then he will give it to Brann as a Democratic card to use in the Maine campaign.

A few months later the Portland *Press Herald* editorially commented: "The Quoddy project was originally conceived by the President and his advisers in the hope of influencing the voters of Maine to support the New Deal. He evidently believed that the State of Maine could be bribed. When he found that the people of this state could not be bought, he simply tossed Quoddy on the scrap heap so that he could have the millions to use where they would produce more satisfactory results." And a significant comment by the incisive observer Sam E. Conner was: "When it became evident that Maine voters weren't endorsing the present administration the lid was clamped down tight and securely locked on Quoddy."[69]

It would, of course, be an unwarranted oversimplification to conclude that the Quoddy proposals were merely part of a move to build up party strength. That was important, but by no means exclusive. There is always the necessity of determining whether a public works proposal should be undertaken, and under what conditions, through the process of policy making which at some point in the democratic process includes popular consent. Congress is forced to seek guidance from special sources—independent regulatory commissions, investigatory commission, presidential staff agencies, and political and pressure groups; or else to grant wide discretionary power to administrative agencies. In this case, to date, Congress has followed the lead of the Federal Power Commission, and has been unimpressed with the activities of state pressure groups and presidential staff agencies which have tended to stress pork-barrel aspects.

Undoubtedly, political motives were behind the Quoddy project—for it and against it. Yet the project was more than a political football. Before the 1936 and 1940 elections the administration made gestures toward giving Maine the Quoddy project. To what extent these gestures were motivated by politics is impossible to discover. On the other side, the staunch opposition to this and other administration projects by Senator Vandenberg undoubtedly had political tinges to them. Governor Brann tried to wrest the United States senatorship from Wallace H. White, Jr., partly with a contention that White and the Republicans in the Maine delegation at Washington had managed the Quoddy campaign poorly. President

Roosevelt, regardless of his political aspirations in Maine, unquestionably had a personal interest in the project, especially as an international undertaking. Although he could have completed it with relief funds, he insisted upon the sanction of Congress. It is difficult to determine whether his suggestion for a small experimental plant there was motivated by political aspirations in Maine or a desire to see a concept which had interested him from its origin materialize as an experiment. By 1939 it must have been clear to the President and the Democratic political strategists that Quoddy was not a vote-getter outside Washington County. In January of that year, however, the President asked for a revival of Quoddy:[70]

> Money has been spent at the Passamaquoddy Bay tidal power project. It is my belief that the time will come when there will be a joint agreement between Canada and the United States for joint development of the larger project which would utilize all tidal power in that bay on both sides of the international line. It is a fact that in Eastern Maine the economic situation is, today, at its worst—for the forests have been cut off and the fisheries have greatly declined. In the case of this project, existing surveys are insufficient and it is my thought that an appropriation for the completion of test borings and a determination of the advisability of putting in a small experimental plant on the American side of the border would be justified.

Congressman Brewster introduced a resolution to authorize the Secretary of War to cause a completion of surveys, test borings, and investigation to determine the advisability and cost of a small experimental plant, and to report the results to Congress.[71] The cost of the investigation was estimated at $25,000 out of general appropriations for such purposes, and Brewster indicated that any construction would have to be authorized by Congress later. The resolution was adopted by the Senate and the House Committee on Rivers and Harbors. But a much more significant resolution was introduced by Senator Vandenberg and passed in the Senate earlier in February, asking the Federal Power Commission to review its previous reports on the project, to bring them down to date, and to report to the Senate on the relative costs of power to the consumer, and again on the vital question of markets for power.

Some opposition was registered to Quoddy in Maine. It was a New Deal, Democratic measure, hostile to private enterprise, and was frequently revived before state elections. Quoddy was sometimes attacked for political reasons, sometimes because of skepticism, and probably more often because of a belief that power markets were lacking. Some arguments seemed highly plausible, others merely rationalization; many were steeped in the emotion often inherent in the private and public power controversy.[72]

Many of Quoddy's staunchest adherents believed that its completion would bring an influx of capital to a needy area. A vociferous pressure group eventually won over a large number of skeptics—people who doubted the economic validity of the project but who felt that Maine should obtain its share of the grants from the administration in Washington. The attitude of State Senator Gail Laughlin was typical of the group:[73] "Fundamentally I'm not in favor of government competition with private industry, but if the Government is to go into silly money-spending projects like the finding out of how often folks have chicken for dinner—as they have done—they might as well spend it on something with a chance of success, like the Quoddy project." Many were willing to give passive support to the project if it would cost Maine nothing and would not be nationally controlled.

For a long time Maine had refused to create a state Authority to operate the project, but finally did so. Meanwhile some people had wondered or even feared that, in the absence of state enabling legislation, the national government might attempt to circumvent the state government by constructing and administering Quoddy from Washington. A suggested alternative was for the Bangor Hydro-Electric Company to operate Quoddy as a corporation subsidiary to the state or federal government, thus attempting to combine both public and private power interests.[74] The possibility of creating a Washington County Authority to construct and administer the project was also considered.[75] These suggestions represented "grass-roots" planning in an attempt to fill a vacuum created by conflicting state and national, and public and private power interests. The bill which did pass was drafted at the instance of the Eastport Chamber of Commerce, with the assistance of federal officials and representatives of private companies whose coöperation was sought by sponsors of the bill.[76] It passed both houses without debate, although the legislature refused to send a memorial to Congress for the completion of the project.[77] Early in April, 1939, Governor Barrows signed the legislative act creating the Passamaquoddy District Authority, enabling a state agency to direct construction of the project from federal funds and to have jurisdiction over the power. A five-man Quoddy Authority Board was given power to construct and administer the project without involving state credit. The personnel of the board was appointed by the governor with the advice and consent of the executive council.[78] The area was outlined roughly by drawing a line from Roque Bluffs to Princeton, the most easterly corner of Maine, and including Calais, Lubec, Cutler, Whiting, Trescott, Marion, Edmunds, Pembroke, Cooper, Alexander, Perry, East Machias, Whitneyville, Eastport, Robbinston, Charlotte, Baring, Meddybemps, and Baileyville.

In this Quoddy area the board was allowed to sell electricity for "industrial uses" (defined by the act to mean and include users with a demand in excess of 100 kw.) at its own rates. The Authority would not be permitted to compete with existing utilities by selling electricity for nonindustrial uses within the district until so authorized by the Public Utilities Commission after a public hearing had shown that the public convenience and necessity required competition. The Authority could, however, purchase the plant, property, and franchise of existing companies in the area, subject to approval of the Public Utilities Commission. All sales by the Quoddy Authority outside its district served by any public utility or where such utility was authorized to sell were prohibited unless the Public Utilities Commission gave permission after a public hearing. The rates charged for such sales were to be established by the commission, based on the fair value of all used or useful property of the Authority with a fair return thereon; consideration was to be given to the rights and plant as a going concern, business risk, and depreciation. In other words, no yardstick could be created. The arrangement of permitting the Quoddy Authority Board to sell electricity for industrial uses within a specified area with restrictions on sales outside was not unlike the plan advocated by Wendell L. Willkie but rejected by the T.V.A. for a "ceded area" between the T.V.A. and Commonwealth and Southern.[79]

The board was authorized to act as a quasi Port Authority, controlling wharfage and storage facilities, as it was anticipated that many industries attracted to the completed project would rely on heavy water-borne traffic. Also, believing that the cellulose industry, which requires a tremendous supply of fresh water, might enter into the project, the board was empowered to act as a water district in bringing fresh water from the lake region a few miles away.

Limited rights of eminent domain were provided in the bill. The Authority had no such rights outside its district, but within it could take property to be used for piers, docks, or warehouses at the discretion of the Public Utilities Commission. Likewise, the taking of the plant, property, and franchise of any existing electric or water company in the district was controlled by the Public Utilities Commission, but the Supreme Judicial Court of Maine was to appoint three disinterested appraisers, and the law regulated in detail such appraisal. The Authority had no right to develop electricity from any source other than that of tides except as auxiliary to tidal power, and the amount of the auxiliary power could not exceed the capacity of the tidal power plant. Outside the district it could acquire no power sites or storage dams or reservoirs other than tidal plants or tidal dams in part of the district.

Maine made some concessions, however, in granting the Authority the right of perpetual succession as a corporation and exempting it from taxation. No attempt was made to limit interstate transmission of surplus power, no provision to recall power shipped outside the state, and the Public Utilities Commission had no jurisdiction over the power destined to become subject to interstate transmission. Equally important was the specific guaranty in the law: "This exemption [from taxation] shall not be abridged by any special act, nor shall the state of Maine limit in any way the powers and rights herein conferred unless and until the obligations, as hereinbefore defined, of the authority, with interest, are fully met and discharged."

But this corporation was never used. The construction actually undertaken at the site was carried on several years before the Passamaquoddy District Authority was created, by the federal government direct as the result of a subsequent allocation of federal funds for use through other channels.

Since Quoddy was not approved by specific statute, the legal basis for construction work came from the law creating the Federal Emergency Administration of Public Works, Title 2 of the National

Recovery Act. By this the administrator was charged with the duty of preparing a comprehensive program of public works, to include development of water power, transmission of electrical energy, and construction of river and harbors, provided that no river or harbor improvements be carried out unless adopted by the Congress or recommended by the chief engineers of the United States Army.

The Maine State Planning Board asserted that the federal right to construct the project was based on the government's power to establish corporations, such as the Bank of the United States, and confirmed by the Supreme Court in *McCulloch v. Maryland.*[80] But no federal corporation was ever created to construct Quoddy. The board also maintained that under the N.R.A. all proposed factories could function legally under federal control "providing they were operated for the welfare of the public," a vague and indefinite assertion. The conclusions of the board on the legal aspects of Quoddy were based on a meager and nonincisive report. They were that the United States government was well within its right in constructing the project because:

1. It may establish corporations.
2. It is within its right in the development of water power in any state and transmission of power under state rules and regulations.
3. It has authority to develop power by exercise of the right of eminent domain or to coöperate with any private corporation in so far as its purpose is for the public welfare.

When Quoddy was included in the War Department bill to be approved by Congress, its legal status was more vulnerable. Congress has no specific authority for power projects, except as incidental to the purposes of navigation, flood control, and national defense. The project included the incidental development of Eastport harbor, which gave it a quasi-navigational standing. But the massive power project could not be sustained on the basis of incidental harbor development which might be necessitated as a result of the completed power project. A tidal project does not qualify as a flood-control measure. Quoddy might have been called national defense, but the Work Relief Act forbade the use of its funds for military purposes. This helps to explain the reluctance of Quoddy supporters to allow it to come up before Congress. It qualified as a relief measure, however. Congress gave the President four billion dollars, and authorized him to undertake relief projects at his discretion.

The permission of the Maine legislature in 1939 for Quoddy power to be sold in other states was, of course, in complete harmony with the Fernald law, which permits electric current generated from water power to be transmitted with legislative consent. It is important, however, to consider why the legislature in 1939 was willing to give this consent without a popular referendum and without subjecting such transmission to the Public Utilities Commission as was done in the Quoddy Act passed in 1925. Of course, since the 1939 law was not debated in the legislature, the answer can merely be suggested from inferences. Permission for interstate transmission of Quoddy power in 1925 was based partly on the belief that the Fernald law was not intended to apply to tidal power and that the novel project should be given a chance. In 1939 this idea was more acute, especially when there was a chance for it to be constructed with federal funds as a relief project in an area where relief was needed. Or it may have been that many legislators seriously doubted that the federal government would consider the project again. In that case they could pass the law to satisfy the Washington County group without altering the state's public power policy at all. Actually, too, the transmission issue was a dead one in Maine in 1939. Interest in it had subsided in the interval of ten years between the great controversies of 1927 and 1929. It is possible that in 1939, thirty years after the passage of the Fernald law, some people were beginning to realize that more than cheap power is necessary to attract new industries to remote localities. Could this indicate a tendency toward a change of opinion in the Maine legislature? At least the legislature was willing to take responsibility for the passage of the law without a popular referendum.

Certainly the 1939 law, if based on the assumption that there would be power at Quoddy, was at cross purposes with the *policy* of the Fernald law of 1909. The original idea—to attract new industries to Maine by means of cheap power—had to depend somewhat on a scarcity of power in other areas. The 1939 law made it possible for power from the largest development in Maine, assuming its completion, to be sold in other areas, and in this way would not try to force them to come to Maine. It should be added, however, that Quoddy supporters hoped that little or none of the power from the project would have to be transmitted, and that its completion would make the Eastport area one of the great industrial regions of New England.

Professor Warren B. Catlin, chairman of the Department of Economics at Bowdoin College, has suggested that synthetic rubber plants might profitably be located near Eastport. Synthetic rubber, like aluminum, requires much processing and consequently great quantities of power. It is light in weight, and the transportation costs would be small in spite of the distance between Maine and the market centers. If, however, one gives credence to the statement of the technical committee on regional planning of the National Resources Committee that because of the vulnerability of certain parts of the United States to foreign attack, the War Department desires to place its contracts for military production in inland manufacturing regions, war industries in the Eastport area would not be expected to flourish, in view of the opposition of the Federal Power Commission to a huge project on the seacoast in 1942.[81]

More recent data on Maine's natural resources indicate that this one state produces 25 per cent of the feldspar used in the United States, but exports it to four states for the manufacture of porcelain and pottery. Aroostook County has one of the largest deposits of low-grade manganese iron ore in North America.[82] Labrador's iron-ore deposits may motivate construction of a large steel mill in New England, possibly at Quoddy.

In 1941 another study of possible markets for Quoddy power was made by the Bureau of Engineering of the Federal Power Commission in response to Senate Resolution 62, adopted on February 2, 1939, mainly through the efforts of Senator Vandenberg.[80] Markets were considered in two areas: markets in Maine, and those in New Hampshire, Vermont, central and eastern Massachusetts, and Rhode Island. In the Quoddy area the country is sparsely settled and the population has been declining since about 1900, although the report indicated that the decline seemed to have been checked: the population of Washington County decreased 16.5 per cent from 1900 to 1940, but there had been virtually no decrease during the last decade. High rates for domestic and rural service had resulted in low per capita consumption in Maine. With lower rates, it was predicted that the people of Maine would use at least 50 per cent more energy for domestic purposes. The report likewise noted the accelerated rate of increase in the industrial and commercial demands, chiefly because of the national defense program.

A statistical analysis of Maine's power needs indicated that during 1940 the production of electricity in the state amounted to 1,096,546,000 kw-h, 93.8 per cent of which was generated by hydroelectric plants. The firm potential energy from two-pool, all-American Quoddy was estimated at 578,000,000 kw-h, or 52.7 per cent of Maine's 1940 production. The average annual increase in energy requirements through 1948 was expected to range between 44,000,000 and 59,000,000 kw-h, depending upon the effect and duration of the national defense program. This report was made in April, 1941, before drought conditions on the Maine rivers curtailed the amount of hydroelectric power available; so the need for power was even greater than the report predicted. The report concluded that the growth of the power load reasonably expected would justify a progressive and orderly development of the admirable water-power resources of the state, but that no market was seen in the immediate future for the more expensive tidal power. For the same reason—great cost of tidal power—the report rejected the proposal of using the tidal power in electrometallurgical industries in the Eastport area, as Cooper and the Maine Quoddy Commission had suggested.

The cost of power used in the electrolytic production of aluminum was given as between two and three mills per kilowatt-hour. Although an aluminum plant would utilize power at a high load factor, perhaps about 85 per cent, the costs of Quoddy power at the higher load factors would not be materially different from the 60 per cent load-factor market on which Quoddy costs were based. In conclusion: "It seems obvious that, with knowledge of the high cost of producing tidal power at Passamaquoddy, responsible interests would not seriously consider locating an industry for the production of aluminum at or near Eastport, Maine, with a view to using such power." The report continued that electrometallurgical and electrochemical industries requiring large amounts of low-cost power might be attracted to the area on the Penobscot River below Bangor, where they could take advantage of cheap river hydroelectric power and where they could be reached by ocean-going vessels. The estimated cost of this river hydroelectric power was two and a half to four mills per kilowatt-hour, depending upon the interest rate on capital investment and other factors.

About two-thirds of the energy requirements of the second area were supplied by the Boston Edison Company and the New England Power Association from large steam-electric plants in Boston and Providence and from hydroelectric plants on the Connecticut and Deerfield rivers. The total energy requirement of this area for 1939 was 4,789,000,000 kw-h, of which 69.9 per cent was supplied by steam-electric plants. The report estimated the growth of the power load in this area to absorb energy in excess of the potential output of the Quoddy project every three years in the immediate future. Hence this power could be marketed in the area provided it could be delivered there at a cost equal to or below the cost of obtaining dependable power from other sources. But the Quoddy power would be too expensive to compete with the regular supply.

By the use of a 220,000-volt transmission line, designed for high efficiency, power could be transmitted about 300 miles, from the Passamaquoddy site to the large receiving and switching center at Tewksbury, Mass., near Boston, with energy losses estimated at 9 per cent. Thus, 526,000,000 kilowatt-hours, or 91 per cent of the Passamaquoddy project output, could be delivered annually at Tewksbury. The transmission cost, on the basis of Federal or State financing (3 per cent money and no allowance for taxes), is estimated at 1.56 mills per kilowatt-hour of delivered energy. Adjustment of the switchboard cost, estimated at 6.65 mills per kilowatt-hour, to take account of energy losses, together with the addition of the unit transmission cost, gives 8.87 mills per kilowatt-hour as the cost of 60 per cent load-factor Passamaquoddy energy at Tewksbury.

With private financing at 5 per cent interest and taxes, the corresponding transmission cost was estimated at 2.3 mills per kw-h. Adjusting the estimated switchboard cost of 10.47 mills to take account of energy losses and adding transmission costs, we reach the figure of 13.8 mills per kw-h for 60 per cent load-factor power delivered at Tewksbury. The report stated that the cost of power produced from new steam-electric plants in the vicinity of Boston or Providence would be somewhat less than the corresponding cost at Eastport. At Eastport it was estimated at 5.57 mills per kw-h, and at

Boston or Providence at slightly in excess of 5 mills. Therefore, this area had no market for Quoddy power. The study took the logical position that the cost of the Quoddy power must be determined as well as the cost of power from competitive sources before its market potentialities could be ascertained.[84] The early estimates of the American two-pool project were likewise based on inaccurate data.

On the basis of additional information obtained from construction work by the Army Engineers, the cost of the American two-pool project was estimated at $89,357,000, or, subtracting the work already done by the War Department, at $83,472,000. Including interest at 3 per cent during the three and one-half years' estimated construction period with federal or state financing it would be $87,854,000. With private financing at 5 per cent it would be $90,776,000.

The project as conceived in 1941 was to serve a 60 per cent load-factor market, and an installation of 100,000 kw. in a pumped-storage plant was planned; otherwise the resulting power would not be continuous. This modified combination would deliver 578,000,000 kw-h annually to the load. Thus, about 92 per cent of the output from the tidal plant would eventually be used as firm energy. The remainder would be lost in the pumping and reconversion cycle.

*Unit cost of firm energy.*—The annual charges, including both fixed charges and expense for operation and maintenance, on the combination two-pool tidal and pumped-storage project, as modified herein, in the interest of economy, are estimated at $3,884,000 on the basis of 3 per cent financing, with no allowance for taxes or insurance; the estimated unit cost of the 578,000,000 kilowatt-hours of firm energy being 6.65 mills per kilowatt-hour. On the basis of an interest rate of 5 per cent on the capital investment, and making an allowance of $303,000 annually for taxes and insurance (the equivalent of the estimated annual expense for these items for a substitute steam-electric unit switchboard) cost of firm energy becomes 10.47 mills per kilowatt-hour.

The 1941 report was in accord with that of the Federal Power Commission of 1934 to the effect that steam-electric power would be cheaper than Quoddy power. A steam-electric plant at Eastport capable of performing, with the same degree of dependability, the exact service of the contemplated Quoddy plan could produce power with federal or state financing at 4.49 mills per kw-h, or with private financing at 5.57 per kw-h. While the 1934 report had suggested that the potential water powers of the Maine rivers might be developed and transmitted to Eastport cheaper than Quoddy power could be developed, the 1941 report stated that this power would cost substantially less than either steam or Quoddy power.

The Panama Canal was once abandoned as impractical and impossible; and, although Quoddy was temporarily shelved, it is again a live issue. Since the publication of the Federal Power Commission report, other factors in Maine have revived Quoddy. The conclusions of the commission in 1941 and the future possibilities of Quoddy were stated thus:[85]

> Passamaquoddy tidal power cannot compete successfully at this time with river hydroelectric power potentially available in the State of Maine, or with power from modern, efficient steam-electric plants.
>
> Tidal power, while not economically feasible of development at this time, possesses certain distinct advantages over other sources of power, the water supply being thoroughly dependable and always definitely predictable, with head limitations definitely known. Unaffected by droughts, floods, or ice jams, the tides provide the most dependable and most permanent known source of power. As high-grade fuel prices increase concurrently with expanding power markets in the northeastern States and contiguous Canadian territory, the development of tidal power will, at some time in the future, become economically feasible and desirable.
>
> The fact that development and utilization of tidal power is contraindicated at this time should not preclude thorough exploration of the possibilities of a large international tidal power project at Passamaquoddy by the Governments of the United States and Canada.
>
> The undeveloped water powers of Maine are clearly indicated as the source within that State from which large blocks of additional power should be obtained, as needed, in the immediate future. The cost of steam-electric power does not compare favorably with the estimated cost of power obtainable from the more desirable undeveloped water-power sites in the basins of the Penobscot and Kennebec Rivers.

In spite of the adverse report of the Federal Power Commission, the Maine congressional delegation continued its agitation for the project. In October, 1941, these strategists decided not to put Quoddy in the Rivers and Harbors bill but to consider a separate Senate resolution for a Federal Power Commission study of the international project. The time was believed peculiarly ripe for pushing Quoddy because of the circumstances, namely, shortage of river power caused by drought,[86] unusual demand for power for national defense, and shortage of fuel for other forms of power. Whereas the lack of a market for power used to be the prime argument against Quoddy, Representative Brewster told of a conference in Boston that week with the aim of importing power from Connecticut. The conference had been called by the Federal Power Commission with special reference to Maine. On December 19 Senator White sent a letter to President Roosevelt signed by all members of the Maine delegation asking him for these reasons to take up the international project with Canadian authorities. President Roosevelt's reply, made public by Senator White on April 3, 1942, read in part as follows:[87]

> The Federal Power Commission advises me that extensive laboratory and engineering field studies would be required to determine with any reliability the economic soundness of such a project and that for the purposes of a supreme war effort the two countries must look to projects already more thoroughly investigated. The commission also points out that the location of a power project on the seacoast raises serious questions from a military point of view.
>
> As you know, I have always been interested in the possibility of developing power from the tides at Passamaquoddy. But, considering all the circumstances, it would appear that a joint United States–Canadian investigation of the matter should be postponed until after the war.

The national shortage of electrical power focused attention on the Passamaquoddy project at Eastport again in the summer of 1947. Although it had long since been rejected as an impractical dream, implications that high government officials felt a revived interest in Maine's tidal power encouraged Maine political leaders and Quoddy supporters. The occasion which brought Quoddy to the headlines in 1947 was a controversy over the use of the 232-acre industrial and residential village. One plan was to establish a tractor assembly plant at the site, where displaced persons bound for South America might be given technical training. The other was to transfer Baltic University from Hamburg, Germany, to Quoddy Village. But the White House was reported to have let it be known that "President Truman favors revival and completion of the Quoddy power project."[88] Governor Horace A. Hildreth of Maine stated that plans for the establishment of a gigantic laboratory for future scientific air development were under consideration, "with Maine definitely in the picture as a possible location."[89] He quoted General O'Donnell, director of information of the United States Air Force, as saying, "The plan is so gigantic that we will take a close look at every possible location."

Representative (now Senator) Margaret Chase Smith of Maine suggested to President Truman, the Secretary of the Army, and the Secretary of the Navy that the Quoddy site be made an international military base, an international power development, or both. In reply, Secretary of the Navy James Forrestal said that Passamaquoddy "has not been considered heretofore for use as an international military base. However, all such areas will naturally be scrutinized with a view toward possible use for hemispheric defense in any studies in the future. This consideration applies, of course, to all such locations throughout the entire country and not exclusively to Passamaquoddy."[90]

At the request of the Washington County Chamber of Commerce, Congresswoman Margaret Chase Smith introduced in the Eightieth Congress a bill to authorize construction of Quoddy.[91] The bill authorized and directed the President and the State Department to negotiate with Canada, and appropriated $100,000 for the project. No legislative action was taken.

President Truman requested a budget bureau study of the cost of the investigation, and negotiations were carried on between the State Department and Canada's Department of External Affairs about the scope of the reference. Canada suggested that preliminary inquiries be made by a joint committee of government officials in the interest of speed,[92] but the matter was referred to the International Joint Commission, which has jurisdiction over territorial waters. Each government supplied $30,000 to make possible the hearings which were held at St. Andrews, N.B., and Eastport, Maine, in August, 1949. The International Joint Commission[93] created a Passamaquoddy Engineering Board to report on the scope and estimated cost of a thorough investigation to determine the economic desirability of international Quoddy. In March, 1950, the board reported to the International Joint Commission that approximately eighteen months of field work at a cost of about $3,600,000 exclusive of the fisheries investigation, $3,900,000 and three years fisheries included, would be necesary to study the various construction plans and determine the economic feasibility of the best plan.[94] No recommendation of the apportionment of investigation costs was made, but the board suggested that such costs might be related to the proportional benefits, equal or otherwise, to each country as indicated when and if a project were built. In the interim, the countries, separately or jointly, might make the investigation, leaving to the time of construction of a project any apportionment of costs to each of the two countries. It may well be that President Truman's more recent New England–New York Inter-Agency Committee will include Quoddy on its agenda.

Quoddy's future rests almost entirely on its international aspect, whether the United States and Canada jointly can produce power inexpensively. In spite of the lack of data on which to base an accurate estimate of the cost per unit of power on an international tidal power project, President Roosevelt, Dexter P. Cooper, and Colonel Fleming had long maintained that this would produce much low-cost energy.[95] A report that the New Brunswick fishing industries have declined in recent years was interpreted by State Senator Clarence B. Beckett to mean that opposition to Quoddy by fishing interests would probably be withdrawn if a treaty between the United States and the Dominion of Canada were broached.[96] Whether this might be done as part of a greater St. Lawrence project or whether both countries would hesitate to invest in a huge project at a spot so vulnerable as Passamaquoddy Bay would be in time of war is unpredictable.

Social scientists and engineers who support economic and administrative planning stress the importance of factual information and the use of organized intelligence before wise national or regional policy can be determined. A thorough study of Quoddy costs is merely a step in the consummation of intelligent power policy for the United States and Canada. It would be folly to sink huge sums of money into Bay of Fundy dams if the resulting power costs would be high. If Quoddy power is cheap, then the project has future possibilities. If, on the contrary, Quoddy power is not worth while economically, the knowledge would be well worth the cost of investigation so that Quoddy could be abandoned and the power magnates made free to consider other sources of power.[97] The subject of power is so dynamic and its conditioning factors so interchangeable that detailed knowledge of international Quoddy would be valuable for present or future planners and national and international policy makers. The marginal power projects of today may become the highly desirable ones for future generations.

To date, the commissions which have studied Quoddy have made unfavorable reports or only mildly enthusiastic recommendations. The Federal Power Commission has consistently opposed the all-American project (the only one it has investigated) on the basis of economic infeasibility, but seems to be interested in the international dams. In 1949 the commission censured the Fernald law and stated, in almost complaining language, that the government could do nothing toward further development of New England's potential water power until the people in the region were willing to permit development of multiple-purpose projects.[98] Although Quoddy could not qualify as a multiple-purpose dam, it is perhaps an exception to these contentions of the commission. Washington County groups and the United States senators and representatives from Maine have been begging Congress and the administration for Quoddy for almost twenty years; and that power could be transmitted interstate.

# CHAPTER XIII

## Conclusions

Institutional development in early New England helps to account for the localism and isolationism which prevail north of Boston. In the Massachusetts Bay Colony the town meeting took root and grew from the town. It was also an extension of the idea of family government. A governor's council was established to protect localism—to put a "home-town" check on the state. This mental attitude was carried up to the state level, from which emerged the doctrine, "Maine power for Maine people," and the insistence that power should not go beyond the borders of the state.

Another root from which the concept emerged was the Puritan theocracy of the early settlers. Their belief in Calvinism, the doctrine that a few people were set apart by destiny for eternal salvation and the rest for eternal damnation, gave rise to dogmatism in nonreligious matters also. James T. Adams maintains that because of the close-knit communities in New England this dogmatism became a group unity more than merely an emphasis on individual character.[1] Thus arose work, thrift, and snobbishness as New England traits, "and these were greatly accentuated by the physiographic nature of the region which was a hard taskmaster, in agriculture, hunting, fishing, forestry, and communication."[2] Particularism, furthermore, fitted the ecological setting in Maine's colonial era—long distances, poor transportation, and Indian attacks.

Power has played a major role in the Maine economy from a very early date. Since water power could not be transmitted any distance, the location of industry was determined primarily by the location of power sites. In the frontier period, manufacturing was or a small scale, but a large number of small enterprises amounted to a considerable manufacturing total in the state. Power, together with vast stretches of virgin forest and easy transportation, combined to make Maine a great lumbering state. Manufacturing of textiles by water power encouraged the growth of other industries by the 1850's, and this manufacturing increased as the lumber supply diminished.

Much of New England accomplished the transition from an agricultural to an industrial economy before the nation was settled, and water power gave it a head start. In the last half of the nineteenth century, conscious efforts were made to diversify Maine's economy, and to change from a Jeffersonian to a Hamiltonian economy. Although hampered by conservative concepts of political institutions and the proper function of the state which enabled a more progressive Massachusetts to become industrialized earlier, Maine's abundant water power was paramount in the growth of manufacturing, railroads, and mill cities. Efforts to make the public aware of power resources met earlier with only mediocre success, but by 1875 many people began to realize that Maine could have an economy based on agriculture, manufacturing, and the tourist trade. In some degree these three conflicted and were rivals, yet all three grew.

The shift from direct application of water power to the production of hydroelectricity in the last decade of the nineteenth century brought major changes in power policy. One result was the formation of the power utility company. Transmission lines eventually enabled power to be sent some distance from the points of generation to the points of ultimate consumption, thus lessening the importance of power in the location of industry. When the South became industrialized and began to compete with New England textiles,[3] New England diversified its industry. James M. Langley, chairman of the New Hampshire State Planning and Development Commission, stated that New England had accomplished decentralization of industry to a greater extent, perhaps, than any other region.[4]

The principal tenets of Maine's power policy today may be summarized in the following six points:

1. *Great ponds.*—All lakes or ponds of ten or more acres, important as sources of water for rivers and storage, are owned by the state and controlled by the state legislature.

2. *The Mill Act.*—The riparian proprietor may, to store water for mills, flow land belonging to another by paying just compensation. The 1713 statute originated in environmental determinism in colonial Massachusetts and Maine. At that time the erection of mills was considered a great public use, and came under eminent domain. In Maine the benefits of this act were extended in their application to include upstream reservoirs as well as milldams. Although it is now difficult to sustain this law under eminent domain, its validity has been upheld by state and national courts on the basis of its venerable age. More recently its significance is declining; the new definition of navigable streams may obliterate it. The present tendency is for power companies to buy up the property involved rather than to obtain flowage rights under the statute. It is not possible at this time to evaluate the importance, if any, of the threat of this statute to the bargaining power of those owning land overflowed by utilities. The Mill Act in various forms has been in effect in at least twenty-nine states,[5] thereby making a more nearly uniform national watershed policy than one might suspect.

The first two items of the six-point policy represent a decidedly liberal attitude. Public ownership of great ponds may well be branded "socialistic." The Mill Act, which sacrificed the rights of colonial landowners to fulfill a greater need for mills, was extended in scope despite growls from the courts and legislature.

3. *Power as private property.*—Despite a popular misconception that water power in Maine was once owned by the public,[6] the Maine water-power law is based on the fundamental principle of private ownership of the bed of the river and the flow of the water. The great sources of hydroelectric power on rivers and streams have consistently been regarded by the Maine courts as private property, subject to the law of contract. In this conservative state the right to private property has been recognized as basic, to the extent that individual owners could contract for the sale of their power and even transmit it to other states, since the nonexport law refers to corporations only. Utility companies control most of the power, and their property rights have been protected under regulation. The concept prevails in Maine that private property rights in water power are for the benefit of the owner, and he can control his rights under contract for his own advantage.

This concept is the complete antithesis of a more recent liberal notion that water rights must be interpreted with limitations on the rights of owners. On this point the late Mary P. Follett said,[7] "The idea is becoming accepted that running water is an asset of society which is not capable of private appropriation or ownership except under regulations that protect the general interest. This tendency is changing the whole water law of the western states." As a corollary to this concept goes Roscoe Pound's notion of the decreased influence of contract; he argues that law must have more of the idea of social justification, serving not individuals alone but the community and individuals through the community.[8] The best examples are the T.V.A. and other great public power projects.

4. *Private development.*—Closely akin to the principle of power as private property is the favored policy that the development and distribution of power should generally be under private initiative. To date, private capital has developed about half of Maine's potential power to satisfy the local market. This statement is made, of course, on the assumption that the estimates of several existing studies have some validity.

The Honorable Gifford Pinchot told the Maine legislature, in 1926, that the measure of material civilization is the amount of power used per capita. On this basis the American people have an extremely high standard of living.[9] His plea was that this vital energy should not be monopolized by private companies who charged high rates to users of small amounts and low rates for the sale of mass quantities. But Maine still adheres to regulated monopoly and opposes public power. Power companies, whether privately or publicly owned natural monopolies, are under the Public Utilities Commission. By 1936, three Maine power companies were supplying 95 per cent of the electric power distributed by the public utilities of the state[10] (two of the three companies have since merged), and domestic electric-light rates were high.

Despite geographic difficulties, steady progress has been made in rural electrification under private development. Consumers of power seem to prefer private companies to the Rural Electrification Administration. Some of the hostility in Maine to the national agency must be attributed to objections of the R.E.A. to submit to the regulatory policies of the state.

5. *The Fernald law.*—For more than forty years the most significant tenet of the Maine power policy has been that power shall be kept at home to industrialize Maine. When it began to be realized that this embargo might well be unconstitutional, the policy was adopted, thirty years ago, of writing a nontransmission provision into the charters of corporations in order that the same policy might be in effect maintained even if the Fernald law should be declared unconstitutional. A large majority of the lawyers believe that the Fernald law is constitutionally void, and, with a liberal court personnel, such a pronouncement would be almost a foregone conclusion. But the law has not yet been so declared.

The concept of the power embargo dates from the Kentucky and Virginia Resolutions, and the idea had emerged in Maine long before it was separated from Massachusetts in 1820. Nor is this concept confined to Maine. Studies by Professor F. E. Melder reveal that in numerous ways states have erected trade walls and other barriers to interstate commerce.[11] The Fernald law, a prominent example of state particularism, constitutes an unnatural and isolationist power "Balkanization," a policy which can no longer aid Maine and which discriminates against industrial New England.

6. *Maine power controlled by Maine.*—This tenet includes marked hostility to attempts of foreign corporations to "bore from within" and thereby control the power companies. The Fernald law in 1909 was in part an outgrowth of hostility to foreign corporations, which reached its climax after the Insulls got into Maine in 1925. But more especially it includes open hostility to federal regulation of Maine power or, for that matter, regional control. The great amounts of power in the state are to be controlled by and kept within the state. This has been shown many times—original purpose of the Fernald law, protest against the Federal Water Power Act, hostility to regional power compact, reluctance to coöperate with the federal government in the eventual passage of the Quoddy Authority Act, and distrust of that government in relation to such an act. Home rule is considered the best protection against the emergence of an irresponsible electric-power agency, public or private, which would, if it had near-monopolistic control, wield tremendous influence over the local economy.

In their insistence on maintaining state control over hydroelectric power, Maine voters now see the Fernald law as their bulwark of defense against federal construction and control of multiple-purpose dams and public power. In this view the power companies naturally concur; furthermore, the power embargo law keeps Maine power companies outside the jurisdiction of the Federal Power Commission.

In its most important aspects this six-point policy represents a conservative and home-rule point of view. Although it lacks unanimous approval, the six-point policy has general acceptance within the state. Some malcontents, it is true, oppose the power companies and the regulatory commission, and would like to see the Rural Electrification Administration becoming more prominent in Maine. This is typical of an anticorporation attitude which has existed in Maine for more than a century. But the majority even in this group would probably agree that the power should be kept for local communities.

The most significant of these points center on the *politics* and *economics* of the Fernald law, which is significant not only because of regional and national implications but also because it is an accepted maxim with the people of Maine. It is probably as sacred to them as are the Monroe Doctrine and Lincoln's Gettysburg Address. The political leaders in Maine early capitalized on emotional appeals to the electorate to keep the power at home. Governor Bert M. Fernald (R.) in 1909 was followed by Governor Frederick W. Plaisted (D.) in 1911, and both ardently supported the Fernald law. The Republican governors Milliken, Baxter, and Brewster were prominent in the leadership against transmission of power, although Baxter came out for transmission of surplus in 1929, when the Republicans, supported by corporate interests, straddled the issue by calling for an investigation and for legislation according to the facts obtained.

Public opinion was aroused for retention of power partly because of the erroneous notion that the public has some sort of proprietary interest in water power. The people of Maine became obsessed with the mistaken idea that the abundant power in the state belonged to them exclusively. A corollary to this notion gradually emerged—the voters became intensely "commodity-conscious" of hydroelectricity. This concept, which dates from the last century, has been static and has not kept pace with modern technology.

In 1929 the power companies were willing to bring much outside capital into Maine and invest it in great power developments if they were allowed to transmit surplus power. They were probably on solid ground when they contended that the transmission privilege would benefit the state as well as themselves. Some political leaders in the Republican Party played with the idea, but the voters of Maine decided that their traditional power embargo must not be changed. A negative vote was registered at the 1929 referendum—antitransmission, anticorporation, anticoöperation.

Governor Frederick G. Payne's interest in an interstate power compact and minor agitation in the 1950 elections to repeal or amend the Fernald law gained little momentum. The arguments for retaining the power are easily grasped, but to show that they are fallacious requires a multitude of dull statistics and a new line of reasoning.

Numerous Maine studies of water-power resources have been made since 1867, but more probing should be done on the possible future uses of power. An economic and social survey of Maine, as contemplated by Professor Warren B. Catlin, chairman of the Department of Economics and Sociology at Bowdoin College, would gather data on existing plants, industries, and institutions, and investigate the resources still to be developed. The study would include consideration of the degree to which industries have been attracted to Maine by timber and water-power resources; by the absence of high statutory labor standards and, until recently, of strong labor organizations; and by the presence of readily available and more or less stationary workers, especially women, who could be used by parasitic or low-paid enterprises.[12] This study should continue where the study by the Maine Development Commission left off, and consider additional uses of power. Much more account should be taken of the suggestion of the commission that a concentrated effort be made to encourage many small industries in Maine, the sum total of which could be substantial.

It may be possible to combine power and forest policies in a program of manufacturing from wood such articles as spools, toys, and household appliances.[13] This type of manufacturing requires very small amounts of power, but if a hundred or more Maine communities ventured into such enterprises, the total would provide a steady, varied income production base for thousands of families. Despite the contention that small industries are the first to fail in depression, such a program would be sound. So long as small industries are well diversified and agriculture continues to hold an important position in the economy, less danger of serious disruption prevails than if Maine were dependent upon a few highly specialized industries.

It must be recognized that power is no longer the attraction for drawing industries to a state that it was a century ago. Maine's climate, raw materials, and particularly the abundant and energetic labor supply, not its available power, will be the chief attraction. Nevertheless, further attempts should be made to induce large industry, of the type requiring great amounts of cheap power, to take advantage of low-cost transportation and power in Maine.

Recreation will contribute a large share of the future income of New England, especially in Maine. Electricity is an important element in this industry, because it is an important factor in the standard of living. The summer tourist business is concentrated in the coastal, mountain, and inland lake regions. Recreational services represent the most profitable social and economic activities possible in many of these areas,[14] since tourists are usually in the higher income group.

Recreational assets are somewhat threatened by failure to prevent water pollution. Corrective measures are necessary on some lakes and streams, especially on the Androscoggin. Attention is called to the increasing pollution from untreated domestic sewage and industrial wastes. Because of the growing density of population in industrial centers, objectionable conditions are rapidly developing. Since the Androscoggin is an interstate stream, it was suggested that Maine and New Hampshire coöperate in working out a control program. The New England Regional Planning Commission advised a technical survey to determine how much can be done within reasonable economic limitations, and, on the basis of this survey, a program of treating domestic sewage and industrial wastes.

Maine's strictly internal power problems are limited to water power and hydroelectric power because the state does not have additional energy resources. In fact, it has been suggested that Maine does not want other sources of power and prefers to depend on its own particular type of power.[15] Likewise, it is claimed, Maine's isolationism includes an unwillingness to assist coal and oil producers. However, Congressman Robert Hale of Maine and others have been concentrating efforts recently on natural gas pipe-line service to New England. In a national economy it is recognized that each source of energy affects all the others. They are interdependent variables, and in the final analysis sound power policy is determined only by the relation of these variables to each other. On this point the National Resources Committee said,[16] "Bituminous coal, petroleum, natural gas, anthracite coal, and water power—in descending order of relative contribution to the nation's energy supply—these are the energy foundations of our industrial civilization. A policy for any one of these resources is bound to affect its relative position with respect to the others." With conservation defined as "the efficient use of our energy resources in the interest of the national welfare,"[17] Maine's surplus hydroelectric power and the embargo on its transmission has a direct bearing on the regional and national aspects of conservation of energy resources.

Maine apparently has much hydroelectric power undeveloped—undeveloped for lack of local markets and because it cannot be transmitted where it is needed. Consequently, other states engaged in war production must consume oil and coal, and Maine itself had to obtain emergency quantities of fuel oil to generate power.

In a war economy, state isolationism cannot be sustained. Coöperation, coördination, and integration are essential so that each unit—town, city, county, state, and region—can perform its special task and make its best contribution to the national whole. Modern wars are largely contests between or among opposing national forces of production. In this modern era, industry depends mainly upon power, as do agriculture and transportation.

Even in peacetime it is important to obtain maximum efficiency by coöperation among states, by specialization and division of labor. Such a program requires the states to have access to one another's raw materials, natural resources, power, and markets. One of the major reasons for substituting the Constitution for the Articles of Confederation was to give Congress, instead of the states, control of interstate and foreign commerce in order to create a national economy.[18]

It has been suggested that the dependence of the Army and the Navy on petroleum and its products is so great as to reinforce the general peacetime demand for a federal policy to protect this resource.[19] Such a plan logically requires the use of water power in industry to save petroleum for more specialized contributions. The Power Survey Committee of the New England Council estimated that every kilowatt of energy produced by water power saves approximately 0.9 pound of coal or 0.09 gallon of fuel oil when the estimate is based on new, large, efficient steam plants, appreciably more when it rests on inefficient types.[20] The committee further estimated that the economically feasible undeveloped water-power plants and storage reservoirs in New England could contribute an additional annual saving of about 860,000 tons of coal or 4,100,000 barrels of fuel oil. Water-power plants spare man power because few people are required to operate them; also, they save transportation of fuel and other vital war commodities.

After the disastrous floods of 1936 the National Resources Committee set up a nation-wide power and flood-control program[21] which had no affinity with Maine's policy. Its advocacy of multiple-purpose drainage basins virtually excluded such undertakings by states, municipalities, or private initiative, and required the participation of the national government.[22] The power combination and flood-control programs were integrated. Power development was to cover the entire country through a series of regional conservation authorities.

President Roosevelt was reported as opposing interstate compacts for flood and power control because they were slow and cumbersome and did not fit into his nation-wide plan.[23] His National Power Policy Commission suggested in 1937 that the country be divided into seven districts for systematic flood control.[24] The late Senator George W. Norris had a somewhat similar plan.[25] It was a multiple-purpose program, involving prevention of soil erosion, regional improvements, irrigation, and power. The latter would be mostly a by-product made available from the dams and turned over to public use. Bauer and Gold advocated the coördination of the principal power resources of each state, with interstate and intersectional transmission lines where very low-cost hydroelectric power is available.[26] The public power bloc called for the development of power production from the flood program, under federal control, in order to obtain lower rates to consumers.

The report of the Hoover Commission shows the controversial nature of the subject. Although five separate extensions of views were filed, five commissioners recommended that Congress define the priority in use of multiple-purpose reservoirs in this order: (1) domestic water, (2) irrigation, (3) flood control, and (4) navigation. They recommended that the generation of electrical power should be regarded as a by-product, and be subordinate to all other uses.[27]

The New England Regional Planning Commission argues, however, that Maine does not need federally financed flood-control projects:[28]

> Flood control presents no State-wide major water resource problems in Maine. . . . Damages on the Penobscot estimated at $55,000 annually, are too small to justify extensive protective construction, but such local measures as removal of chemical obstructions and barriers to ice are desirable. . . . There has been more flood damage on the Androscoggin than on any other Maine river, but even there and likewise on the Saco, where damages have been fairly high, the construction of flood control reservoirs would entail expenditure quite out of proportion to the benefits that would accrue.

This conclusion is indicative of strong and vigorous local feeling and the traditional desire of New Englanders to do things for themselves rather than to depend upon federal authority and money.[29]

With 65 per cent of New England's latent water power in Maine, the nonexport law of the state "constitutes an obstacle to the widespread distribution and use of the potential resources of New England," according to the report of the Federal Power Commission.[30] The commission also observed that New Englanders are unwilling to permit federal development of multiple-purpose reservoir projects, and suggested that the national government is not interested in single-purpose individual projects. The commission envisioned full development and integration of a New England power program through little T.V.A.'s dotted over five New England states, with Maine headquarters for more than half of the power supply.[31]

This report shows that the commission is now interested in Maine's undeveloped power, that it seems "cold" toward the Fernald law, and that only superior financial resources can bring about multiple-purpose projects. The implications of this report raise several basic questions. Could the Fernald law prevent transmission of federally developed Maine power? Can the national government undertake regional power projects regardless of local sentiment? Would Maine's concept of power isolationism change with the advent of large national developments?

In the final analysis, Congress and not the Federal Power Commission determines national policy on multiple-purpose dams. The commission may act as a staff agency or even a pressure group, but the broad lines of policy are determined and funds are voted by elected representatives. No one can predict how far Congress will go in accepting the commission's blueprints. If Congress should authorize more multiple-purpose dams where power production will be paramount, Maine's other relatively unimportant river problems would also be alleviated.

President Truman, who as Senator voted for Quoddy, is focusing attention on public power development in New England and New York. Tacked onto the rivers and harbors bill of 1950 was an amendment to set up a seven-man committee to study plans for a gigantic power pool from Niagara Falls to Eastport, between which are to be all the undeveloped power sites of New England, most of which are in Maine. In October, 1950, without congressional action, President Truman set up the New England–New York Inter-Agency Committee, which hopes to complete the survey by July 1, 1954. The committee consists of one member from the departments of the Army (chairman), Interior, Agriculture, and Commerce, the Federal Power Commission, and the Federal Security Agency. The President's letter, dated October 9, 1950, calls for state participation in the survey, though the degree of this state activity seems vague. He wrote:

> Each agency and the committee as a whole should coördinate its plans and activities with those of interested State and local agencies. The State and local agencies have a direct and vital interest in the conduct of this investigation and the report that will result. Many of the existing activities of State and local agencies in the resources field should fit into the projected investigation. I am sure that State and local agencies will be anxious to coöperate. In order that they be afforded every opportunity and encouragement to participate in the work of the committee, I am asking the Governors of the seven states concerned to designate official

representatives to act as liaison between the committee and the various State agencies concerned with resource development. In addition, I want the committee to invite the ideas and help of local governments and private groups and individuals to the extent possible. It is essential that the Federal agencies draw upon the experience and ideas of the people of the region to the fullest extent and that the final report carry the concurrence or comments of each affected state.

In Maine the objective has been called a northeastern T.V.A., and opposition is developing. It will involve basic cleavages: Republican versus Democrat, public power versus private power, and strong national government versus state rights. The issues will not be entirely clear cut. Maine's Republican Party will oppose multiple-purpose developments, public power, and national "encroachment," but some Republicans will want an exception made for Quoddy, and a very few will welcome an opportunity to strike at corporate interests. How far Maine Democrats will follow national leadership is doubtful, but of minor significance. They can try to subject the power companies to another regulatory stratum, but the consequence may be to renounce state control of power resources. This administrative survey may well cause that sector of the Maine electorate which considers the power embargo outmoded—and in this the author includes himself—to subordinate the Fernald law to the newer and greater issues involved in the survey.

The agency is holding a series of meetings and hearings in the seven states, and apparently a large part of the field work will be done by Army Engineers. Meanwhile New York and Vermont have warned that they are "watchful" of a plan to federalize the resources of the Northeast; Maine and New Hampshire insist that this survey be made without any "preconceived notions" and that it must recognize the rights of the people.

Aside from the matter of public power, however, much constructive work needs to be done on the New England regional power situation which transcends state and regional lines. The new commission has an opportunity to make a positive contribution to regional and national natural resources policy. The international Quoddy project can be investigated only as a joint enterprise of the United States with the Dominion of Canada. Even though these governments may have no immediate interest in its development, a thorough and impartial investigation of the amount of power available and its cost per unit are important facts for both governments to know for future reference. A planning agency should have this information available for emergency or an opportune occasion for development. Furthermore, the wide variation in, and almost complete misunderstanding of, the estimates of undeveloped power in New England show the need for a more scientific study based on actual field work, and objective but skillful public reporting of the results. Full and free discussion based on substantiated data would permit the people to decide broad issues intelligently.

In order to carry the necessary weight and prestige to have any internal effect on Maine policy, such a survey will have to be nonpolitical and must be conducted with substantial local participation. The reaction to a study made by outlanders on either a regional or a national level, advising changes in Maine power policy, would be regarded with suspicion. When change is to come, Maine voters prefer to find it out for themselves.

It is obvious that the people of Maine do not like to participate in great collective efforts; the state will not serve as entrepreneur in them, and cannot do so without constitutional amendment. Probably the only way by which Maine's power can ever be sold elsewhere will be, not through the initiative of the Maine electorate, but on the assumption of jurisdiction by the federal government. Federal control could be asserted by the invalidation of the Fernald law through Supreme Court decision. Or construction of large federal projects in Maine would precipitate a decision on the legality of the law—a decision which will not be forthcoming on the initiative of Maine people. Eventually, however, Congress by law, or the Federal Power Commission, in demanding that the power companies apply for license under the new definition of "navigable rivers," may force the issue, with the Supreme Court as final arbiter in this national, state, and regional issue. The majority of the Maine people would oppose loss of control, and would oppose the administration responsible for it. But the days of the Hartford Convention are over in New England, and the citizens of Maine would acquiesce. Their patriotism and nationalism are more important than their localism.

The Supreme Court's interpretation of the Federal Power Act of

1935 is highly significant in showing the determination of Congress to have the long-idle water-power resources of the nation utilized. Counteraction in the suggestion for state aid to stimulate private power development might forestall the invasion of federal power in Maine. If change is inevitable, transmission of surplus power at the discretion of the Maine Public Utilities Commission, with recognition for a reasonable margin of local preference, may be the most effective legislation for giving Maine the greatest amount of influence in future regional power policy.

This writer favors a state conservation measure in the form of a modification of the Fernald law which would recognize the right to make reasonable provision for local needs and at the same time not of itself prevent interstate commerce in hydroelectric power. Excerpts from some court decisions could be construed more favorably toward what might be an indirect rather than a direct burden on interstate commerce. At least, such a law would permit some flexibility and would recognize that a regulatory commission in a quasi-judicial capacity could attempt to reconcile state and regional power requirements in the transaction of interstate commerce. In the light of the decision in *Cities Service Gas Company v. Peerless Oil and Gas Company*, 340 U.S. 179 (1950), it appears that a distinction has been made between absolute prohibition of interstate commerce and a state conservation measure which gives preference to home consumers but also sees the problem in a broader perspective.

Regionalism offers a middle course between control by the nation and control by the state in helping to solve power problems. The fact that Maine has developed perhaps half of its power, and is in ordinary times allowing secondary power to run to waste when other states are using more expensive sources which ought to be diverted to higher and more specialized tasks, indicates lack of administrative and economic integration when viewed as an interstate problem. Very few Maine people concede that the "have-not" states possess any right to Maine power or to formulate in any way the principles of Maine's power policy, as was shown when compacts were considered in the late 'twenties; yet from the point of view of public administration the power problems of New England are regional. This suggestion is not a new contribution to thought; it is only unusual that it should emanate from Maine. When Professor Felix Frankfurter urged Maine to enter a regional power compact in 1927, the idea was ridiculed, even though Governor Brewster gave it some support.

Judge Benjamin F. Cleaves, sometime chairman of the Maine Public Utilities Commission and former secretary of the Associated Industries of Maine, advocated transmission of surplus power in 1925. His interest in regionalism and his belief that power no longer attracts industry is in complete accord with the theses developed in this study. Judge Cleaves wrote that surplus power should be sold to other states:[82]

> regardless of those imaginary lines between states which are necessary only for governmental purposes and ought never to be recognized economically or commercially.
>
> The cost of power in the ordinary industry is very small as compared with other elements of cost; and so I feel that if we are to attract, as we hope we are, new industries, we have many other things in the State of Maine about which we can make a selling talk before we get to the matter of power.
>
> I further believe that the present law and the existing policy not only partially strangle our own hydroelectric companies, but prevent outside interests from coming in and joining us. However much we may feel pride in our state of Maine, and however much we may feel that we are set apart from the rest of New England, we must realize that the entire outside world looks upon New England as a unit.
>
> We must think and act more often in terms of New England if we would protect New England interests. If this be true, then Maine would be foolish to undertake to set up any kind of wall between itself and the rest of its family. The power need in New England is a New England need. If Maine makes its reasonable contribution outward, it will find in the rest of New England a spirit and an ability to feed inward to Maine, if we ever need this contribution.
>
> Maine cannot afford in any of its activities, including the development and distribution of hydroelectric energy, to be unduly provincial.

And Dr. Hugh L. Elsbree, in his study on the interstate transmission of power, concluded that the problem is neither national nor intrastate, but usually affects two and not more than three states. He wrote:[83] "It is perhaps unfortunate that there are no political or administrative units between the state and the federal government. In the absence of such intermediary units, economic situations which have outgrown the boundaries of individual states will have, sooner or later, to be dealt with by an administrative system which can regulate them as entities, and not break them up artificially into particularized problems." He gave great weight to the article by Professor Frankfurter and Professor Landis on compacts.[34]

The approach to Maine's power problems in a New England regional area is in accord with several advanced ideas.[35] One school of thought holds that the United States Supreme Court has been liberal in allowing Congress to coöperate with the states through acts passed under the commerce clause.[36] However, when a state withholds a great potential supply of hydroelectric power from interstate commerce it is not an intrastate problem. The Fernald law isolationism is an antithesis to uniform state action as a possible substitute for centralization, as expounded by Professor W. Brooke Graves.[37]

Some attention should be devoted to the degree to which the Fernald law stands in the way of enabling Maine to fit into a regional power program for the New England area. The answer depends upon the importance of hydroelectric power in future with respect to alternative sources of power. One trend points to a decline in the importance of water power. Although steam power is more expensive under some conditions, it is becoming much more efficient. Until recently, steam was so much cheaper that it sometimes could undersell hydroelectric power; and presently, if scientists develop and control atomic power inexpensively for industrial uses, even steam power may be outmoded, leaving water power a bad third. While water-power costs tend to remain static, the cheapest sites are first developed and, as more power is required, it is necessary to resort to more expensive and marginal sources, with a resultant tendency to raise the cost per unit.[38] If we set aside for the moment the desirability of conserving coal and oil, in future the alternative sources of power may be so much cheaper than hydroelectric power that near-by states will no longer be interested in Maine's potential supply, which consequently will remain undeveloped.

Hydroelectric transmission, nevertheless, may become more important as science promotes greater efficiency in long transmission lines and thus lowers cost. Longer and cheaper transmission, the exigency of wise use of coal and oil, and the recent high prices and uncertainty of these fuels caused by strikes may put a premium on Maine's undeveloped power in the immediate or not distant future. Since a time lag is likely until science perfects the alternative sources of supply, Maine's restrictive policy will continue to hamper industrial efficiency in New England as long as hydroelectric power remains cheapest.

Professor Roland B. Greeley, formerly with the New England Regional Planning Commission, summarized the effects of the Maine power embargo on the general situation in New England:[89]

> 1, Secondary power in Maine is, practically speaking, wasted at the same time that similar power is being generated by coal in nearby New Hampshire and Massachusetts cities; 2, potential power sites in Maine remain undeveloped at the same time that less economical sites in other New England states have been and are being developed. Though these effects will become increasingly marked as the efficiency of power transmission increases, the effects are already significant if studied from the point of view of a completely integrated system for Maine and the other New England states.

Technological improvements now make Maine a natural power area. The rest of New England is interconnected, but the transmission embargo has prevented Maine power companies from making export interconnections with New Hampshire and Massachusetts. Thus Maine cannot participate actively in a regional network; in emergencies this has come back on Maine like a boomerang.

Maine need not enter a regional power pact with the five New England states, for some of them are too far away to make transmission pay. The acute need is in Massachusetts. The Maine power companies prefer to sell power near its source unless more remote markets can afford to pay a higher price. Even at that, they may still prefer to supply the local market more cheaply than distant ones, because the prosperity of power companies depends upon the prosperity of mills and inhabitants of the area served by them.

If or when Maine's power particularism is relaxed, it will not necessarily mean that Maine's power is gone forever. On the contrary, for federalism or regionalism to succeed, workers, thinkers, and planners are as necessary on the lower levels as on the high. The state selling power has as much to say about its sale as does the state buying it, and the surplus could be sold on terms mutually agreeable to buyer and seller. In this as in most conflicts of centralization versus decentralization, the important point is that national or state control should be merely a means, not an end in itself. The real problem is not so much one of authority but of administration, because central or regional concentration of authority, when properly and conscientiously administered, has actually strengthened local units of government.

One of the major postulates of this study is that power alone will not industrialize any state. That Massachusetts needs cheap power in a regional and national economy is now axiomatic. Despite protests that Maine should not become a power station for New England, the business of generating and transmitting power, properly safeguarded, would mean large investments, taxable property, and more employment. To be sure, Maine would obtain greater benefit if industries settled at power sites, but they have not done so and need not do so. Rather than let power development slowly proceed, full development of a great power industry might prove a valuable asset to the Maine economy, thereby providing employment in power development and transmission, the cultivation of the tourist trade and summer-home communities, and the creation of a broader tax base for public schools and roads.

This author does not like the Fernald law and public power, but recognizes that private capital cannot undertake some multiple-purpose projects essential both to the national economy and grass-roots welfare. Maybe public and private power are not necessarily incompatible.[40] He would like more information on New England's natural resources—scientific data, not propaganda,—and more probing on the possibilities of mixed enterprise; he thinks that a state will not suffer by sharing the resources it does not need. In the end, feasible improvements for the *summum bonum* of the state, region, and nation must go forward according to legislative and judicial standards—personal prejudice or purely local custom to the contrary notwithstanding.

# NOTES

# NOTES TO CHAPTER I

## The Great-Pond Ordinance

[1] William H. Whitmore (ed.), *The Colonial Laws of Massachusetts. Reprinted from the Edition of 1660. Containing also the Body of Liberties of 1641* (Boston, 1889), p. 37.

[2] *Fay v. Salem & Danvers Aqueduct Co.*, 111 Mass. 27 (1872); see also 147 Mass. 548 (1888).

[3] 7 Cushing 53, 68 (1851).

[4] Max Farrand, *The Laws and Liberties of Massachusetts* (Cambridge, Mass., 1929), p. vi. Reprinted from copy of 1648 edition in Henry E. Huntington Library.

[5] John Winthrop, *Winthrop's Journal: History of New England, 1630–1649* (ed. by J. K. Hosmer; New York, 1908), Vol. 2, p. 49.

[6] *Conant v. Jordan*, 107 Maine 229, 236 (1910).

[7] John J. Whittlesey, *Law of the Seashore, Tidewaters and Great Ponds in Massachusetts and Maine* (Boston, 1932), p. xxxix.

[8] *Ibid.*, pp. xxviii–xxix.

[9] *Ibid.*, pp. xxix–xxx.

[10] John M. Gould, *Law of Waters* (3d ed.; Chicago, 1900), p. 154.

[11] *Ibid.*, pp. 154–156. Henry P. Farnham, *The Law of Waters and Water Rights* (Rochester, N.Y., 1904), Vol. 1, pp. 265–267. Whittlesey, *op. cit.*, p. xxx.

[12] Quoted in Gould, *op. cit.*, pp. 155–156.

[13] *Ibid.*, p. 156.

[14] W. S. Holdsworth, *A History of English Law* (Boston, 1926), Vol. 7, p. 338.

[15] Lucilius A. Emery, "The Legal Phase of the Water Power Investigation," Maine Public Utilities Commission, *Special Water Power Investigation* (Lewiston, Maine, 1918), pp. 11–12.

[16] Edward P. Ricker, "The Rights of the People in the Great Lakes of Maine," Lewiston *Evening Journal*, February 21, 1907.

[17] Holdsworth, *op. cit.*, Vol. 4, pp. 505–506.

[18] *Ibid.*, Vol. 2, p. 358.

[19] *Ibid.*, Vol. 4, p. 506.

[20] Personal letters from the Hon. Harvey D. Eaton, Waterville, Maine, August 23, 1944; and William L. Macintosh, Assistant Attorney General for Massachusetts, Boston, Mass., October 5, 1944. Eaton wrote, "Our forefathers came here and found great forests and great ponds galore. They did not propose to be hung for shooting a partridge or catching a trout." And from Macintosh: "It is my understanding that the ordinance was originally enacted because the extensive royal forests and privately owned hunting preserves in England had deprived the general public of the privilege of hunting and fishing."

[21] 7 Cushing 53, 68 (1851).

[22] Stated in *Conant v. Jordan*. See Robert H. Gardiner, "History of the Kennebec Purchase," *Collections of the Maine Historical Society*, Series 1 (Portland, Maine, 1847), Vol. 2, pp. 269–271.

[23] Herbert L. Osgood, *The American Colonies in the Seventeenth Century* (New York, 1904), Vol. 1, p. 426; Oscar Handlin and Mary F. Handlin, *Commonwealth* (New York, 1947), p. 100.

[24] Osgood, *op. cit.*, pp. 439–440, 451.

[25] *Ibid.*, p. 454. There were, however, common fields in England also. See Roy H. Akagi, *The Town Proprietors of the New England Colonies* (Philadelphia, 1924), p. 110.

[26] Clive Day, "Capitalistic and Socialistic Tendencies in the Puritan Colonies," American Historical Association, *Annual Report, 1920* (Washington, D.C., 1925), pp. 233–234.

[27] *West Roxbury v. Stoddard,* 89 Mass. 158, 169–170 (1863).

[28] Osgood, *op. cit.*, pp. 440–442, 459.

[29] Frederick J. Turner, *The Frontier in American History* (New York, 1935), p. 63.

[30] Gardiner, *op. cit.*, p. 272.

[31] Robert P. T. Coffin, *Kennebec, Cradle of Americans* (New York, 1937), p. 225.

[32] Day, *op. cit.*, p. 235.

[33] Winthrop, *op. cit.*, Vol. 1, pp. 315–317.

[34] Hamilton Basso, *Mainstream* (New York, 1943), p. 11.

[35] *Conant v. Jordan,* 107 Maine 227, 238 (1910).

[36] Winthrop, *op. cit.*, p. 323.

[37] These may be seen in Whittlesey, *op. cit.*, pp. xxxvi–xxxix.

[38] Whitmore, *op. cit.*, p. 170. Until recently it was frequently assumed in the United States that the jurisdiction of the state extended under the open sea to the three-mile limit. The impact of the decision in the tideland oil case, however, forces a revision of prior views. The court ruled that the federal government rather than the state has paramount rights in and jurisdiction over the three-mile marginal belt along the coast. The implications of this decision on the proposed Quoddy tidal power project will be considered later. *United States v. California,* 332 U.S. 19 (1947).

[39] *Conant v. Jordan,* 107 Maine 227, 234 (1910).

[40] *Litchfield v. Scituate,* 136 Mass. 39, 47 (1883).

[41] *Conant v. Jordan,* 107 Maine 227, 234–235 (1910)

[42] *Conant v. Jordan,* 107 Maine 227, 241–242 (1910). The authority quoted by the court was *Records of Plymouth Colony,* Vols. 3 and 4, pp. 58, 60. See also Joseph Sewall, "History of Bath," *Collections of the Maine Historical Society,* Series 1 (Portland, Maine, 1847), Vol. 2, p. 195.

[43] *Barrows v. McDermott,* 73 Maine 441, 448 (1882).

[44] William Willis, *History of Portland,* quoted in *Conant v. Jordan,* 107 Maine 227, 239 (1910).

[45] "All laws now in force in this State, and not repugnant to this Constitution shall remain, and be in force, until altered or repealed by the Legislature, or shall expire by their own limitation." *Constitution of Maine,* Art. X, sec. 3.

[46] *West Roxbury v. Stoddard,* 89 Mass. 158, 159–160 (1863).

[47] *Ibid.*, p. 161.

[48] *Barker v. Bates,* 13 Pickering 255, 258 (1832).

[49] *Conant v. Jordan,* 107 Maine 227, 240–241 (1910). See also Gould, *op. cit.,* p. 162.

[50] Farnham, *op. cit.,* p. 270

[51] Whittlesey, *op. cit.,* p. 45.

[52] *West Roxbury v. Stoddard,* 89 Mass. 158, 167, 171 (1863). "With the growth of the community, and its progress in the arts, these public reservations, at first set apart with reference to certain special uses only, become capable of many others which are within the design and intent of the original appropriation. The devotion to public use is sufficiently broad to include them all, as they arise."

[53] *Ibid.,* p. 171.

[54] *Fay v. Salem & Danvers Aqueduct Co.,* 111 Mass. 27 (1872).

[55] *Watuppa Reservoir Co. v. Fall River,* 147 Mass. 548 (1888).

[56] *Barrows v. McDermott,* 73 Maine 441, 449 (1882).

[57] *Brastow v. Rockport Ice Co.,* 77 Maine 100 (1885).

[58] 90 Maine 576 (1897).

[59] 118 Maine 503 (1919).

[60] Questions put by the Maine legislature to the Supreme Judicial Court in seeking advisory opinions on water power, February 20, 1919. 118 Maine 503 (1919).

[61] For the status of advisory opinions see *Sawyer v. Gilmore,* 109 Maine 169, 175 (1912), and *Laughlin v. City of Portland,* 111 Maine 486, 497 (1914).

[62] 118 Maine 535 (1919).

[63] *Ibid.,* pp. 503, 530.

[64] 147 Mass. 557 (1888).

[65] 118 Maine 503, 531 (1919).

[66] 90 Maine 576 (1897).

[67] *Scott v. Sanford,* 19 Howard 393 (1856).

[68] Frederick C. Hicks, *Materials and Methods of Legal Research* (Rochester, N.Y., 1942), p. 106.

[69] *Cummings v. Barrett,* 10 Cushing 186, 188 (1852).

[70] *Fay v. Salem & Danvers Aqueduct Co.,* 111 Mass. 27 (1872).

[71] 147 Mass. 548, 564 (1888).

[72] *Ibid.,* p. 565.

[73] *Commonwealth v. Roxbury,* 75 Mass. 451, 492 (1857).

[74] Walter Wells, *The Water Power of Maine* (Augusta, Maine, 1869), p. 29.

[75] Felix Frankfurter and James M. Landis, "The Compact Clause of the Constitution—A Study in Interstate Adjustments," *Yale Law Journal,* Vol. 34, No. 7 (May, 1925), p. 716 n.

[76] Portland *Sunday Telegram,* December 28, 1947.

[77] All factual information on this controversy was obtained in the Maine *Legislative Record,* 1907, pp. 472–489; also files of the Lewiston *Evening Journal,* February 9–March 6, 1907.

[78] 82 Maine 48 (1889).

[79] *Ibid.,* p. 56.

[80] *Ibid.,* pp. 56–57.

[81] 152 Mass. 444 (1890).

[82] Maine *Legislative Record,* 1907, p. 482. The case and citation were incorrect.

[83] 142 U.S. 254 (1891).
[84] *Commonwealth v. Vincent,* 108 Mass. 441 (1871).
[85] *Fay v. Salem & Danvers Aqueduct Co.,* 111 Mass. 27 (1872).
[86] 147 Mass. 548, 557 (1888). Italics mine.
[87] Two were later chief justices and one of these was Governor of Massachusetts; one, United States Attorney General; and Holmes, a United States Supreme Court Justice. 102 Maine 153, 156 (1906).
[88] 90 Maine 576 (1897). See also *McFadden v. Ice Co.,* 86 Maine 319 (1894).
[89] Maine *Private and Special Laws,* 1891, c. 82.
[90] 90 Maine 576, 587 (1897).
[91] 102 Maine 153 (1906). Decided eight months after the legislature defeated the lake bill.
[92] Maine *Private and Special Laws,* 1891, c. 60.
[93] Maine *Acts and Resolves,* 1893, c. 399.
[94] Maine *Legislative Record,* 1907, p. 479.
[95] 118 Maine 503, 504–505 (1919). Italics mine.
[96] 102 Maine 153 (1906).
[97] *Sixteenth Annual Report of the Power Authority of the State of New York, 1946* (Albany, 1947), p. 46.
[98] *Potter v. Howe,* 141 Mass. 357 (1868).
[99] *Fernald v. Knox Woolen Co.,* 82 Maine 48, 56 (1889).
[100] 118 Maine 503, 506 (1919).
[101] Maine *Laws,* 1909, c. 147.
[102] Arthur G. Staples, "Maine Water Powers," *Sprague's Journal of Maine History,* Vol. 12, No. 2 (April–June, 1924), p. 134.
[103] Lincoln Smith, "The Great Pond Ordinance—Collectivism in Northern New England," *Boston University Law Review,* April, 1950.

# NOTES TO CHAPTER II

## The Mill Act

[1] Edward Johnson, *Johnson's Wonder-Working Providence, 1628–1651* (ed. by J. Franklin Jameson; New York, 1910), Book 2, chap. 22.
[2] William D. Williamson, *The History of Maine from Its First Discovery, A.D. 1602, to the Separation, A.D. 1820, Inclusive* (Hallowell, Maine, 1832), Vol. 1, *passim.*
[3] James P. Baxter (ed.), *Sir Ferdinando Gorges and His Province of Maine* (Boston, 1890), Vol. 2, p. 58.
[4] Richard G. Wood, *A History of Lumbering in Maine, 1820–1861* (Orono, Maine, 1935), p. 27.
[5] G. T. Ridlon, *Saco Valley Settlements and Families* (Portland, Maine, 1895), p. 191.

[6] *Ibid.*

[7] *Ibid.*, p. 190.

[8] Clive Day, "Capitalistic and Socialistic Tendencies in the Puritan Colonies," American Historical Association, *Annual Report, 1920* (Washington, D.C., 1925), p. 234. Oscar Handlin and Mary F. Handlin, in *Commonwealth* (New York, 1947), p. 110, show that "manufacturing had always borne a public aspect from the necessity of utilizing millsites for power." Later, however, the Massachusetts courts began to make a distinction between public and private corporations (pp. 144–172), and to impose more stringent regulations on the former. Although the lines of demarcation were not always consistent, the tendency was to classify private corporations as those whose stock was owned by private persons, or those which competed with one another. The weight of evidence indicates, for example, that eminent domain was granted to railroads because they were public corporations. But insurance companies, hotels, stagecoach companies, and mills belonged in the category of private corporations.

[9] Abner C. Goodell and Ellis Ames (eds.), *The Acts and Resolves, Public and Private, of the Province of the Massachusetts Bay* (Boston, 1869), Vol. 8, p. 306. Additional examples are given in Roy H. Akagi, *The Town Proprietors of the New England Colonies* (Philadelphia, 1924), pp. 88–92.

[10] *York Deeds* (Portland, Maine, 1887), Book 3, fol. 125.

[11] Ridlon, *op. cit.*, p. 191.

[12] Herbert L. Osgood, *The American Colonies in the Eighteenth Century* (New York, 1924), Vol. 3, p. 565.

[13] Williamson, *op. cit.*, Vol. 1, p. 574.

[14] George C. Wing, Jr., Lewiston *Evening Journal*, January 27, 1926; Akagi, *op. cit.*, pp. 31–32.

[15] *York Deeds*, Book 1, fols. 12, 15.

[16] Goodell and Ames, *op. cit.*, Vol. 21 (1793), pp. 668–669; Vol. 9 (1708), p. 18.

[17] Benjamin P. Poor, *The Federal and State Constitutions, Colonial Charters, and Other Organic Laws of the United States* (Washington, D.C., 1877), Part 1, p. 954. See also Robert G. Albion, *Forests and Sea Power* (Cambridge, Mass., 1926), esp. pp. 231–280; Williamson, *op. cit.*, Vol. 2, pp. 188–189.

[18] Goodell and Ames, *op. cit.*, Vol. 1, p. 130.

[19] *Acts and Laws of the Province of Massachusetts Bay, May, 1709* (Boston, 1726), p. 202.

[20] Goodell and Ames, *op. cit.*, Vol. 2, p. 497.

[21] *Ibid.*, Vol. 11, p. 425.

[22] Edward Russell, "History of North Yarmouth," *Collections of the Maine Historical Society*, Series 1 (Portland, Maine, 1847), Vol. 2, p. 160.

[23] Robert H. Gardiner, "History of the Kennebec Purchase," *ibid.*, p. 281.

[24] *Tinkham v. Arnold*, 3 Maine 120 (1824).

[25] Goodell and Ames, *op. cit.*, Vol. 16, p. 761.

[26] W. R. French, *A History of Turner, Maine* (Portland, Maine, 1887), pp. 7, 11, 13–21.

[27] Williamson, *op. cit.*, p. 332.

[28] *Ibid.*, p. 202.

[29] Gardiner, *op. cit.*, pp. 274–279.

[30] *Ibid.*, pp. 269–294. The economic interest of absentee proprietors and men of political influence with the government is also stated in Frederick J. Turner,

*The Frontier in American History* (New York, 1935), p. 55; and Akagi, *op. cit.,* pp. 44–45, 48, 210.

[31] Williamson, *op. cit.,* pp. 513–514.

[32] Henry P. Farnham, *The Law of Waters and Water Rights* (Rochester, N.Y., 1904), Vol. 3, pp. 2134–2135.

[33] *Bean and Bingham Land Co. v. Central Maine Power Co.,* 133 Maine 9, 27 (1934).

[34] Goodell and Ames, *op. cit.,* Vol. 1, pp. 729–730.

[35] Massachusetts *Acts of 1795* (Boston, 1896), pp. 443–446.

[36] Massachusetts *Acts and Resolves,* 1809, p. 229.

[37] Massachusetts *Statutes,* 1808, c. 65.

[38] Maine *Revised Statutes,* 1841, c. 126, sec. 1.

[39] *National Fibre Board Co. v. Lewiston & Auburn Electric Co.,* 95 Maine 320 (1901).

[40] Maine *Revised Statutes,* 1857, c. 92, sec. 1.

[41] *Wolcott Woolen Manufacturing Co. v. Upham,* 5 Pickering 292 (1827), in 123 Maine 535, 546 (1924).

[42] Maine State Water Storage Commission, *Third Annual Report, 1912,* pp. 86–87.

[43] Maine *Revised Statutes,* 1930, c. 106, sec. 10. *Norris v. Pillsbury,* 74 Maine 67 (1882); 123 Maine 535, 547 (1924).

[44] Maine *Revised Statutes,* 1930, c. 106.

[45] Goodell and Ames, *op. cit.,* Vol. 10 (1722), pp. 228–229; Vol. 13 (1743), pp. 272–273.

[46] *Ibid.,* Vol. 19 (1776), pp. 578–579.

[47] Williamson, *op. cit.,* p. 571.

[48] Lucilius A. Emery, "The Legal Phase of the Water Power Investigation," Maine Public Utilities Commission, *Special Water Power Investigation* (Lewiston, Maine, 1918), p. 15.

[49] Farnham, *op. cit.,* p. 2135.

[50] *Ibid.,* p. 2136.

[51] *Brown v. Gerald,* 100 Maine 351, 370 (1905).

[52] *Newcomb v. Smith,* 1 Chand. 71 (1849).

[53] *Olmstead v. Camp,* 33 Conn. 532 (1866).

[54] *Venard v. Cross,* 8 Kansas 248 (1871).

[55] 113 U.S. 9, 18 (1885).

[56] John M. Gould, *Law of Waters* (3d ed.; Chicago, 1900), p. 516.

[57] *Ryerson v. Brown,* 35 Mich. 333 (1877).

[58] *Newell v. Smith,* 15 Wis. 101 (1862).

[59] *Harding v. Goodlett,* 3 Yerg. 41 (1832).

[60] *Loughbridge v. Harris,* 42 Georgia 501 (1871); *Tyler v. Beacher,* 44 Vermont 648 (1871).

[61] 1 Mass. 422, 429 (1805).

[62] 16 Gray 187, 188 (1860).

[63] *Talbot v. Hudson,* 16 Gray 417, 426–427 (1860).

[64] *Fisk v. Framingham Manufacturing Co.,* 12 Pickering 68, 70–71 (1831).

[65] *Bates v. Weymouth Iron Co.,* 8 Cushing 548, 553 (1851).

[66] 113 U.S. 9, 21 (1885).

[67] 75 Vermont 235, 242 (1903).

[133] *Bean and Bingham Land Co. v. Central Maine Power Co.,* 133 Maine 9 (1934).

[134] *Ibid.,* p. 22. *Hatch v. Dwight,* 17 Mass. 289 (1821).

# NOTES TO CHAPTER III

## The Increasing Complexity of the Economy

[1] Maine *Public Acts,* 1824, c. 280, pp. 993–997.

[2] 118 Maine 503, 521–522 (1919).

[3] Van Wyck Brooks, *The Flowering of New England* (New York, 1936), p. 4.

[4] E. W. Morehouse, "Some Problems of Power," *New England's Prospect,* American Geographical Society, Special Publication no. 16 (New York, 1933), p. 279.

[5] Silas Adams, *The History of the Town of Bowdoinham* (Fairfield, Maine, 1912), p. 29.

[6] Richard G. Wood, *A History of Lumbering in Maine, 1820–1861* (Orono, Maine, 1935), p. 28.

[7] *Ibid.*

[8] Edward C. Kirkland, *A History of American Economic Life* (New York, 1932), p. 136.

[9] Maine *Legislative Record,* 1919, p. 712.

[10] Edward P. Ricker, *Let Maine Keep Her Birthright* (Lewiston, Maine, 1921), esp. p. 9; *The Water Power Resolve* (Lewiston, Maine, 1921), pp. 3–8

[11] Percival P. Baxter, *Maine's Water Powers—Our Natural Inheritance* (Lewiston, Maine, 1918), p. 8.

[12] G. W. Stephens, "The Industrial Development of Maine," *Maine, A History* (ed. by Louis C. Hatch; New York, 1919), pp. 664–670.

[13] Kirkland, *op. cit.,* p. 331.

[14] *Maine, A Guide "Down East"* (Boston, 1937), p. 57.

[15] Gilbert Verney, president of a New England chain of mills, has stated (Brunswick *Record,* October 28, 1948) that certain primary costs now give the South an advantage over New England textiles—freight, fuel, light and power, wages and salaries, and state and local taxes. He declared that wages are 10 per cent lower in the South, that some southern communities offer as much as ten years of freedom from taxes, and that tax-free generating units under government control help to lower power costs in the South. If New England is to withstand this competition, it is necessary to produce as efficiently and cheaply as possible. One could add that although power is usually only 2 to 4 per cent of the cost of production, even that small percentage may mean the difference be-

tween success and failure for competitive industries in competitive sections of the country.

[16] Sam E. Conner, Lewiston *Evening Journal* (feature article), December 16, 1925.

[17] Charles B. Carter, Lewiston *Evening Journal,* January 6, 1926.

[18] Frederick J. Turner, *The Frontier in American History* (New York, 1935), esp. "The First Official Frontier of the Massachusetts Bay," pp. 52–53.

[19] Joshua L. Chamberlain, *Maine: Her Place in History* (Augusta, Maine, 1877), p. 97. This statement is entirely consistent with the extreme ease with which corporations could organize under the Maine law. Acts of incorporation were granted under general laws in an attempt to induce foreign corporations to take out their papers in Maine in order that the state might obtain a revenue from the fees charged. Their *activity* in Maine was an entirely different matter.

[20] *Constitution of Maine,* Art. IX, sec. 14.

[21] Edward E. Chase, *Maine Railroads* (Portland, Maine, 1926), p. 22.

[22] *Ibid.,* p. 46.

[23] Edward C. Kirkland, *Men, Cities, and Transportation* (Cambridge, Mass., 1948), Vol. 1, p. 469.

[24] *Ibid.,* p. 491.

[25]

| | | | | | |
|---|---|---|---|---|---|
| 1790 | 96,540 | 1850 | 583,169 | 1900 | 694,466 |
| 1810 | 228,705 | 1860 | 628,279 | 1910 | 742,371 |
| 1820 | 298,269 | 1870 | 626,915 | 1920 | 768,014 |
| 1830 | 399,455 | 1880 | 648,936 | 1930 | 797,423 |
| 1840 | 501,793 | 1890 | 661,086 | 1940 | 847,226 |

[26] Maine *Acts and Resolves,* 1851, pp. 359–363.

[27] *Ibid.,* 1856, p. 393.

[28] Chamberlain, *op. cit.,* p. 96.

[29] *Ibid.,* p. 93.

[30] Maine *House Journal,* 1878, pp. 36–37.

[31] *Ibid.,* 1881, p. 44.

[32] *Ibid.,* 1891, p. 38.

[33] *Ibid.,* 1893, pp. 21–22; 1895, p. 26.

[34] A special study of this topic in an industrial survey of Maine would be a real contribution to Maine history.

[35] Charles E. Artman, "New England's Industrial Prospects," *New England's Prospect,* American Geographical Society, Special Publication no. 6 (New York, 1933), pp. 51–52.

[36] Robert P. T. Coffin, *Kennebec, Cradle of Americans* (New York, 1937), pp. 190–198.

[37] Arthur M. Schlesinger, *The Rise of the City* (New York, 1933), p. 74.

[38] Maine *House Journal,* 1893, p. 27; 1895, p. 30.

[39] Laura E. Poor (ed.), *The First International Railway and the Colonization of New England: Life and Writings of John Alfred Poor* (New York, 1892), pp. 91–92.

[40] Maine *Acts and Resolves,* 1851, pp. 359–360.

[41] Poor, *op. cit.,* p. 92.

[42] *Ibid.,* p. 93.

[43] Maine *Acts and Resolves,* 1887, c. 69, pp. 52–53.

[44] Walter Wells, *The Water Power of Maine* (Augusta, Maine, 1869), p. 156.

[45] *Ibid.*, p. 8. Cf. citations in notes 46 and 58 below. The inconsistencies of the horsepower and manpower conversions may be attributed to dissimilar bases of computation and to differences in opinion.

[46] Chamberlain, *op. cit.*, pp. 98–99.

[47] Arthur G. Staples, "Maine Water Powers," *Sprague's Journal of Maine History*, Vol. 12, No. 2 (April–June, 1924), p. 131.

[48] Wells, *op. cit.*, p. 65.

[49] Act of March 8, 1864, c. 234, sec. 1.

[50] Wells, *op. cit.*, pp. 67, 157.

[51] *Ibid.*, p. 157.

[52] Chamberlain, *op. cit.*, p. 96.

[53] *Ibid.*, p. 97.

[54] Maine *Senate Journal*, 1867, esp. pp. 38–46.

[55] Maine *Acts and Resolves*, 1870, pp. 164–165.

[56] Chamberlain, *op. cit.*, p. 100.

[57] Maine *Acts and Resolves*, 1871, pp. 232–234.

[58] *Ibid.*, 1874, p. 234.

[59] 58 Maine 590 (1871).

[60] 60 Maine 124, 133 (1872).

[61] 62 Maine 62, 72 (1873).

[62] *Ibid.*, pp. 74–75.

[63] Charles Eliot, *Charles Eliot, Landscape Architect* (Boston and New York, 1902), pp. 308–315.

[64] Lewiston *Evening Journal*, March 1, 1907.

[65] Governor Nelson Dingley, Jr., message, Maine *Laws*, 1874, p. 233; Maine *House Journal*, 1891, p. 38; *ibid.*, 1895, p. 37.

[66] Eliot, *op. cit.*, pp. 313–315.

[67] Maine State Water Storage Commission, *First Annual Report, 1910*, p. 25.

[68] *Report of the New England Regional Planning Commission for the New England Basins* (Washington, D.C., 1937), p. 6. As of 1948, the highest figure this business ever reached was $115,000,000 in 1947.

[69] Maine *Laws*, 1929, c. 181. It must be cleared five feet below the mean water level.

[70] Portland *Evening Express*, January 2, 1948.

[71] Lawrence H. Alline, president, Maine Public Service Company, Hearing before Maine Public Utilities Commission, Presque Isle, Maine, January 8, 1948, mimeo. MS, pp. 13–14.

[72] *Report of the New England Regional Planning Commission for the New England Basins*, pp. 5–6.

[73] Portland *Press Herald*, August 21, 1946.

# NOTES TO CHAPTER IV

## New Technologies

[1] Edward C. Kirkland, *A History of American Economic Life* (New York, 1932), p. 318.
[2] Richard G. Wood, *A History of Lumbering in Maine, 1820–1861* (Orono, Maine, 1935), p. 167.
[3] John Bauer and Nathaniel Gold, *The Electric Power Industry* (New York, 1939), p. 46–47.
[4] Amasa Loring, *History of Piscataquis County, Maine* (Portland, Maine, 1880), p. 219.
[5] George O. Smith, "Industry and Business," *Skowhegan on the Kennebec* (ed. by Louise H. Coburn; Skowhegan, Maine, 1941), Vol. 2, pp. 961–962.
[6] C. Herman Pritchett, *The Tennessee Valley Authority* (Chapel Hill, N.C., 1943), p. 79 n.
[7] National Resources Committee, *Our Energy Resources* (Washington, D.C., 1939), pp. 20–21.
[8] *National Fibre Board Co. v. Lewiston & Auburn Electric Co.,* 95 Maine 318, 323 (1901).
[9] 95 Maine 318, 327 (1901).
[10] *Report of the Power Survey Committee of the New England Council* (Boston, 1948), p. 33.
[11] *Saturday Evening Post,* Vol. 201, Part 3, p. 126. Also National Resources Committee, *Our Energy Resources,* p. 4.
[12] *Electric Power and Government Policy* (Twentieth Century Fund, New York, 1948), p. 11.
[13] "The Electric Light and Power Industry in the United States," *Statistical Bulletin* (Edison Electric Institute, New York, 1948), p. 25.
[14] *Report of the Power Survey Committee of the New England Council,* chap. 6, p. 36.
[15] Personal letter from Harold L. Gerrish, electrical engineer, Maine Public Utilities Commission, Augusta, Maine, September 22, 1948.
[16] *Electric Power and Government Policy,* p. 16.
[17] Personal letters from President William B. Skelton, Augusta, Maine, October 17, 1945; Lewiston, Maine, January 11, 1946.
[18] Portland *Sunday Telegram,* January 4, 1948.
[19] *Federal Power Commission v. Hope Natural Gas Co.,* 320 U.S. 591, 659 (1944).
[20] Edward F. Merrill, attorney for Central Maine Power Company (now a Justice of the Maine Supreme Court), speech on rural electrification bill at Hearing on Coöperative Enabling Act, Legislative Committee, Maine Legislature, 1941, MS, p. 2.

[21] Maine *Laws,* 1895, c. 102.

[22] *Ibid.,* 1901, c. 273.

[23] Orren C. Hormell, *Maine Public Utilities* (Brunswick, Maine, 1927), pp. 30–31.

[24] *Electric Power and Government Policy,* p. 42.

[25] *Report of the Power Survey Committee of the New England Council,* chap. 4, p. 17.

[26] *Ibid.,* p. 63.

[27] The report of the New England Council suggests the desirability of interconnections between Maine and New Hampshire, which would integrate all New England. *Ibid.,* p. 64.

[28] "History of the Central Maine Power Company." Unsigned MS in State Library, Augusta, Maine. Checked for details by Harvey D. Eaton, a founder and former president of the company.

[29] *Electrical World* (Boston), Vol. 95 (1930), p. 380.

[30] Statement of Lawrence H. Alline, president, Maine Public Service Company, at hearing before Maine Public Utilities Commission, Presque Isle, Maine, January 8, 1948, MS, pp. 17, 23.

[31] *Report of the Power Survey Committee of the New England Council,* chap. 9, p. 64.

[32] Hormell, *op. cit.,* p. 31.

[33] *Ibid.,* pp. 31–32.

[34] Maine *Private and Special Laws,* 1917, c. 203.

[35] *Prospectus,* Maine Public Service Company to New York Curb Exchange, April 2, 1947, pp. 5–6, 19.

[36] Portland *Sunday Telegram,* January 4, 1948.

[37] Personal letter from Roy M. Somers, clerk, Public Utilities Commission, Augusta, Maine, March 30, 1948.

[38] Personal letter from Eugene M. Dole, treasurer, Bangor Hydro-Electric Company, Bangor, Maine, March 11, 1948.

[39] *Official Report of Proceedings before the Securities and Exchange Commission,* Docket Section, file 59-15-1-1. Original: Utilities Section 11*B* (2), Northern New England Company and New England Public Service Company, November 7–December 17, 1940, p. 145. Cited as *Official Report.*

[40] Hearing before Federal Trade Commission on Investigation of Public Utility Corporations, Washington, D.C., March 16, 1932. *Utility Corporations Report* no. 42, 70th Cong., 1st sess., S. Doc. 92 (1932), Part 42, pp. 70–71.

[41] Securities and Exchange Commission, *Notice of Filing of Amended Plan of Reorganizing and Order Reconvening Hearing re Northern New England Company and New England Public Service Company* (Philadelphia, 1944), December 5, 1944, p. 2.

[42] *Official Report,* pp. 145–146.

[43] *Ibid.,* pp. 279–280.

[44] Stephen J. Kennedy, *Profits and Losses in Textiles* (New York, 1936), p. 106.

[45] *Official Report,* pp. 281–282.

[46] Kennedy, *op. cit.,* pp. 106–108.

[47] *Official Report,* pp. 279–280.

[48] New York *Times,* December 13, 1931, sec. 2, pp. 9, 11.

[49] *Official Report,* p. 285.

[50] Kennedy, *op. cit.*, p. 110.
[51] *Official Report*, pp. 285–288.
[52] Kennedy, *op. cit.*, p. 110.
[53] Lewiston *Evening Journal*, June 25, 1945.
[54] Kennedy, *op. cit.*, p. 113.
[55] Lincoln Smith, "The Regulation of Some New England Holding Companies," *Land Economics*, August, 1949.

# NOTES TO CHAPTER V

## The Fernald Law: Quantitative Analysis

[1] Edward P. Ricker, *Let Maine Keep Her Birthright* (Lewiston, Maine, 1921), pp. 6–7.
[2] Charles B. Carter, address to Lions' Club, Lewiston, March 16, 1926. MS in State Library, Augusta, Maine.
[3] Fernald was a resident of Poland and a neighbor of Ricker.
[4] Governor Bert M. Fernald, address, Maine *Senate Journal*, 1909, p. 28.
[5] Maine *Legislative Record*, 1909, p. 1114.
[6] *Ibid.*, p. 1116.
[7] Ricker, *op. cit.*, p. 5.
[8] Maine *Laws*, 1909, c. 224.
[9] *Official Report of Proceedings before the Securities and Exchange Commission*, Docket Section, file 59-15-1-2. Original: Utilities Section 11*B* (2), Northern New England Company and New England Public Service Company, November 7–December 17, 1940, pp. 532–534.
[10] It has been maintained that this exception was made through the efforts of a powerful lobby. The New Haven Railroad had taken over the Boston and Maine and the Maine Central, and was attempting to control all electric railroads in the territory served. Maine *Legislative Record*, 1917, pp. 1325–1326. A more logical explanation is that this exception was to make it legal for the Maine Central Railroad to electrify its mountain division, which runs into New Hampshire. *Ibid.*, 1927, p. 1053.
[11] Ricker, *op. cit.*, p. 8.
[12] William E. Mosher (ed.), *Electrical Utilities* (New York, 1929), p. 132.
[13] Maine Public Utilities Commission, *Twelfth Biennial Report, 1945–1946*, p. 106.
[14] Personal letter from Paul L. Bean, Lewiston, Maine, April 24, 1934. The Androscoggin River, although it is not navigable to Bethel and Berlin Falls, is nevertheless floatable. *Gerrish v. Brown*, 51 Maine 256 (1863).

[15] Robert D. Baum, *The Federal Power Commission and State Utility Regulation* (Washington, D.C., 1942), pp. 44, 48.

[16] Personal letter from Charles V. Shannon, Federal Power Commission, Washington, D.C., June 28, 1945.

[17] Maine *Laws,* Special Session, 1933, c. 90.

[18] 332 U.S. 19 (1947).

[19] United States Supreme Court, Order and decree, October 27, 1947, p. 2.

[20] The dissent of Mr. Justice Reed was based on original state sovereignty and ownership of the land. Mr. Justice Frankfurter's dissent drew a distinction between the power of the national government to regulate interstate and foreign commerce and ownership of the soil beneath the sea belt.

[21] Portland *Sunday Telegram,* December 28, 1947.

[22] Maine Development Commission, *Report on Water Power Resources of the State of Maine* (Augusta, Maine, 1929), pp. 20–52.

[23] *Report to the Associated Industries of Massachusetts of Its Power Investigating Committee* (Boston, 1924), pp. 26–27.

[24] E. W. Morehouse, "Some Problems of Power," *New England's Prospect,* p. 281. As of 1948, New England, exclusive of Maine, was 80 per cent dependent upon steam power. *Report of the Power Survey Committee of the New England Council* (Boston, 1948), p. 67.

[25] Mosher, *op. cit.,* p. 132. Likewise, some was exported.

[26] Personal letter from William J. Keefe, chief engineer, Massachusetts Department of Public Utilities, Boston, February 28, 1945.

[27] Hugh L. Elsbree, *Interstate Transmission of Electric Power* (Cambridge, Mass., 1931), p. 21. *Report to the Associated Industries of Massachusetts of Its Power Investigating Committee,* pp. 28–29.

[28] Maine Development Commission, *Report on Water Power Resources of the State of Maine,* pp. 26–27.

[29] *New England's Prospect,* American Geographical Society, Special Publication no. 6 (New York, 1933), p. 283.

[30] Maine Public Utilities Commission, *Ninth Biennial Report, 1939–1940,* p. 140.

[31] Passamaquoddy Tidal Power Project, 77th Cong., 1st sess., S. Doc. 41 (1941), pp. 18–24.

[32] U. S. Department of Commerce, Bureau of the Census, *Statistical Abstract of the United States, 1947* (68th ed.; Washington, D.C., 1947), p. 489. The *Interim Report* of the Federal Power Commission's "National Power Survey" indicated that most of this potential water power was on the Penobscot and Kennebec rivers. For the largest sources the estimated average annual output of undeveloped power was 1,082,000,000 kw-h for the Kennebec; 742,000,000 kw-h for the Penobscot; and 734,000,000 kw-h for the Androscoggin. See *Interim Report* (Washington, D.C., 1935), p. 35. This huge potentiality was again substantiated with an estimate of approximately 2,500,000 kw.: Federal Power Commission, *Twenty-seventh Annual Report, 1947* (Washington, D.C., 1948), p. 64. The estimated undeveloped power for the other states was: New Hampshire, 266,000 kw.; Vermont, 430,000 kw.; Massachusetts, 110,000 kw.; Rhode Island, none; Connecticut, 94,000 kw. See *Statistical Abstract . . . ,* p. 489.

[33] Letter from D. J. Wait, regional engineer, Federal Power Commission, New York, August 24, 1948, to Frank E. Southard, chairman, Public Utilities Commission, Augusta, Maine.

[34] Personal letter from Leon M. Fuquay, secretary, Federal Power Commission, Washington, D.C., June 23, 1948.

[35] *Report of the Power Survey Committee of the New England Council*, chap. 8, p. 47.

[36] *Ibid.*, p. 62.

[37] Federal Power Commission, "Memorandum on Information Requested by Senator Leverett Saltonstall," February 17, 1949. Made public July 10, 1949. Mimeo. MS.

[38] Maine Public Utilities Commission, *Twelfth Biennial Report, 1945–1946*, p. 17.

[39] George H. Arris, *New England Power—Myth or Fact?* (Providence, R.I., 1949).

# NOTES TO CHAPTER VI

## The Fernald Law: Opposition, Evaluation

[1] The National Resources Planning Board divided the factors into transportation and nontransportation categories, with subtopics not dissimilar to the analysis given in this text. Lincoln Gordon, *Industrial Location and National Resources* (Washington, D.C., 1943), pp. 329–330. See also *Report of the Power Survey Committee of the New England Council* (Boston, 1948), p. 68; *Report to the Associated Industries of Massachusetts of Its Power Investigating Committee* (Boston, 1924), p. 99.

[2] The aluminum industry, with its great dependence upon an abundance of cheap power, appears to be the one most likely to be attracted to Maine if power is capable of attracting any. The research staff of the Twentieth Century Fund says that power accounts for 18 per cent of the total operating costs in the aluminum industry. In other electrochemical industries it is from 12.5 to 35 per cent. *Electric Power and Government Policy* (New York, 1948), p. 24.

[3] Stenographic report on power bills, February 24 and 25, 1927, p. 4.

[4] Portland *Evening Express*, July 27, 1948.

[5] Personal letter from George D. Bearce, Bucksport, Maine, September 22, 1944.

[6] These figures are based on a speech by Representative Edward E. Chase, who contributed some of the most incisive ideas in the debates. Maine *Legislative Record*, 1929, p. 858.

[7] *Sixteenth Census, Manufactures, 1939*, Vol. 2, Part 1, pp. 22 ff. Professor Gordon (*op. cit.*) estimated power costs at 2.5 per cent in 1943. On the basis of data for 1947, J. A. Whitlow concludes that the average proportion of electricity in cost of industrial production for 103 industries is little more than 0.5 per cent. *Electrical World*, November 6, 1950, pp. 84–85. Power costs are greater in

relation to *net earnings.* However, transportation and labor costs are more significant here, too.

[8] Maine Development Commission, *Report on Water Power Resources of the State of Maine* (Augusta, Maine, 1929), p. 19.

[9] Manager Hamlin of the American Thread Company of Milo stated at the power hearing in 1929 that, without exaggeration, his company paid the Bangor and Aroostook Railroad Company more freight in thirty days than it cost to pay for power in his mill for ten years. Hearing on power measures, March 7, 1929, p. 69.

[10] *Report of the Power Survey Committee of the New England Council,* chap. 10, p. 68; also chap. 3.

[11] Gordon, *op. cit.,* p. 180.

[12] Hearing on power measures, March 7, 1929, p. 45.

[13] Maine *Legislative Record,* 1929, p. 845; Francis H. Farnum, "Water Power Situation in Maine" (n.d.), MS in State Library, Augusta, Maine.

[14] Portland *Press Herald,* December 31, 1946.

[15] Dr. Alfred C. Neal, director of research, Federal Reserve Bank of Boston, address at twenty-fifth New England Conference, Boston, November 17, 1949.

[16] Maine *Legislative Record,* 1909, pp. 1115–1116.

[17] Maine *Senate Journal,* pp. 35–36.

[18] Maine *Legislative Record,* 1911, p. 81.

[19] Louis C. Hatch (ed.), *Maine, A History* (New York, 1919), Vol. 3, p. 656.

[20] Maine *Legislative Record,* 1911, pp. 473, 672.

[21] *Ibid.,* 1913, p. 117.

[22] Hearing on power measures, March 7, 1929, pp. 110–112.

[23] Maine *Legislative Record,* 1911, pp. 991, 1073.

[24] Maine *Senate Documents,* S. Doc. 431 (1915).

[25] Maine *Legislative Record,* 1915, pp. 1169–1175, 1199.

[26] *Ibid.,* 1917, pp. 1323–1335.

[27] Clarence C. Stetson, "One Phase of Our Water Power Problem: Shall Maine Progress or Retrogress?" address to Bangor Chamber of Commerce, November 22, 1923. Press release MS in State Library, Augusta, Maine. See also Lewiston *Evening Journal,* November 22, 1923; December 5, 1925.

[28] Percival P. Baxter, *Maine Water Powers . . . ,* address at annual Grange Conference, Augusta, Maine, January 30, 1924, p. 6.

[29] Governor Owen Brewster, address to Maine members of New England Council, Portland, Maine, January 31, 1925. MS in State Library, Augusta, Maine.

[30] Hearing on power bills, February 24 and 25, 1927, p. 65.

[31] Maine *Legislative Record,* 1927, p. 1389.

[32] *Ibid.,* 1929, p. 689.

[33] Maine Development Commission, *Report on Water Power Resources of the State of Maine.*

[34] Maine *Legislative Record,* 1929, pp. 144–146, 176–178, 199–201, 910, 912.

[35] *Ibid.,* p. 851.

[36] Hearing on power bills, February 24 and 25, 1927, p. 14; Percival P. Baxter, address to Federated Women's Clubs of Piscataquis County, Willimantic, Maine, June 4, 1929.

[37] *Ibid.* Two years earlier, Baxter attributed this statement to Walter S.

Wyman. See Percival P. Baxter, *Maine Politics and Water Powers,* radio addresses over WCSH, Portland, Maine, February 1, 8, 15, 1927, p. 7.

[38] Maine *Legislative Record,* 1929, p. 683; Hearing on power measures, March 7, 1929, pp. 30–31.

[39] For testimony given at this hearing, on March 16, 1932, see *Utility Corporations Report* no. 42, 70th Cong., 1st sess., S. Doc. 92 (1932), Part 42, pp. 52–87.

[40] *Ibid.,* p. 53. The money was provided through the use of part of the profit realized by this company from the sale in the open market of 3,000 shares of the common stock of the Central and Southwest Utilities Company. This stock was acquired in 1926 at $35 a share. It was sold at an average price of $138.88 a share, leaving a profit after income tax of $277,359.60.

[41] Portland *Evening News,* September 9, 1929.

[42] Ernest Gruening, *The Public Pays* (New York, 1931).

[43] Portland *Evening News,* June 7, 8, August 20, 27, 28, September 4, 5, 6, 7, 10, 1929.

[44] The argument to retain power for rural consumption is weak, however. The fact that all the cities and towns, half of the population, and all the large industries demanded less than one-half of the potential power clearly showed that the unsupplied rural families alone could not use the other half of the future supply. See chap. ix.

[45] Maine *Legislative Record,* 1929, pp. 856, 862.

[46] Considered in chap. ix.

[47] Referendum question, voted upon September 9, 1929: "Shall the act to provide for the exportation of surplus power, as defined and restricted in said act, permitting the sale outside of Maine of hydroelectric power not needed in Maine, be accepted?"

| County | Yes | No | County | Yes | No |
|---|---|---|---|---|---|
| Androscoggin | 4,423 | 8,134 | Penobscot | 3,313 | 10,542 |
| Aroostook | 3,009 | 3,476 | Piscataquis | 1,038 | 1,862 |
| Cumberland | 12,089 | 11,409 | Sagadahoc | 1,622 | 1,330 |
| Franklin | 1,045 | 1,629 | Somerset | 2,960 | 3,350 |
| Hancock | 1,971 | 2,200 | Waldo | 1,402 | 1,818 |
| Kennebec | 7,367 | 5,923 | Washington | 2,384 | 1,693 |
| Knox | 1,959 | 1,276 | York | 5,942 | 4,795 |
| Lincoln | 1,766 | 948 | | | |
| Oxford | 1,782 | 3,659 | Totals | 54,070 | 64,044 |

[48] Baltimore *Evening Sun,* February 28, 1945.

[49] *Legislative Documents,* nos. 1221, 1222, 1223.

[50] The quotations are from the Portland *Press Herald,* March 19, 1947, and the *Kennebec Journal,* March 20, 1947.

[51] Maine *Legislative Record,* 1947, p. 577; also *Kennebec Journal,* March 27, 1947.

# NOTES TO CHAPTER VII

## The Constitutional Issue

[1] This refers to state, not federal, legislation for "general welfare." The Fernald law was passed as a measure for the conservation of natural resources.

[2] *Constitution of Maine,* Art. IV, part 3, sec. 14.

[3] 9 Wheat. 1 (1824). J. A. C. Grant, "State Power to Prohibit Interstate Commerce," *California Law Review,* Vol. 26, No. 1 (November, 1937). Hugh E. Willis, "Gibbons v. Ogden Then and Now," *Kentucky Law Journal,* Vol. 28, No. 3 (March, 1940), pp. 280–305. J. C. Phillips, "The Growth and Development of the Federal Commerce Power," *Temple Law Quarterly,* Vol. 11, No. 4 (July, 1937), pp. 517–537.

[4] Some states permit transmission only when approved by the Public Utilities Commission. A Wisconsin statute gives preference to local consumers, leaving for export what is not required by such customers, but there are no special provisions requiring extension of lines in rural areas. Wisconsin *Statutes,* 1943, c. 31, sec. 27.

[5] Hugh L. Elsbree, *Interstate Transmission of Electric Power* (Cambridge, Mass., 1931), pp. 23–24 and note.

[6] Maine *Legislative Record,* 1927, p. 842.

[7] 116 U.S. 517; see also *The Daniel Ball,* 10 Wallace 557 (1870).

[8] *United States v. E. C. Knight Co.,* 156 U.S. 1, 13 (1895).

[9] 247 U.S. 251 (1918).

[10] 259 U.S. 20 (1922).

[11] 295 U.S. 330 (1935).

[12] 298 U.S. 238 (1936).

[13] 286 U.S. 165 (1932).

[14] 10 Wallace 557, 565 (1870).

[15] 262 U.S. 553, 600–601 (1923)

[16] 161 U.S. 519, 533 (1896).

[17] *Ibid.,* p. 534.

[18] *Ibid.,* p. 538.

[19] 263 U.S. 545 (1924).

[20] *Hudson County Water Co. v. McCarter,* 209 U.S. 349, 356–357 (1908).

[21] For example, Mr. Justice Holmes's dissent in *Pennsylvania v. West Virginia,* 262 U.S. 553, 602–603 (1923).

[22] 237 U.S. 52 (1915).

[23] 90 Nebraska 627, 631 (1912).

[24] 177 U.S. 190 (1900).

[25] 262 U.S. 553, 602–603 (1923)

[26] 278 U.S. 1, 15 (1928).

[27] *Hood v. Du Mond,* U.S. Sup. Ct. (Law ed.), *Advance Opinions, 1949,* Vol. 93, No. 12 (April, 1949), p. 709.

[28] *Ibid.,* p. 698. After this was written, the Court sustained, as a conservation measure, state price fixing of natural gas sold in interstate commerce, because nondiscriminatory rate orders do not clearly harm national interest. *Cities Service Gas Co. v. Peerless Oil & Gas Co.,* 340 U.S. 179 (December 11, 1950).

[29] For example, in *Cooley v. Board of Wardens,* 12 Howard 297 (1851): "To these precise questions [state regulation of pilots] which are all we are called on to decide, this must be understood to be confined. It does not extend to the question what other subjects, under the commercial power, are within the exclusive control, of Congress, or may be regulated by the states in the absence of all congressional legislation; nor to the general question, how far any regulation of a subject by Congress, may be deemed to operate as an exclusion of all legislation by the states upon the same subject. We decide the precise question before us . . . We go no further . . ."

Then again in *Hall v. Decuir,* 95 U.S. 495 (1878): "The line which separates the powers of the States from this exclusive power of Congress is not always distinctly marked, and oftentimes it is not easy to determine on which side a particular case belongs. Judges not unfrequently differ in their reasons for a decision in which they concur. Under such circumstances it would be a useless task to undertake to fix an arbitrary rule by which the line must in all cases be located. It is far better to leave a matter of such delicacy to be settled in each case upon a view of the particular rights involved."

[30] 242 U.S. 311 (1917).

[31] *Kentucky Whip and Collar Co. v. Illinois Central Railroad Co.,* 299 U.S. 334 (1937).

[32] *Prudential Insurance Co. v. Benjamin,* 328 U.S. 408 (1946).

[33] 95 U.S. 485 (1878).

[34] *Wabash, St. Louis and Pacific Railway Co. v. Illinois,* 118 U.S. 557 (1886).

[35] 244 U.S. 205 (1917).

[36] 12 Howard 299 (1851).

[37] 234 U.S. 317 (1914).

[38] Edward F. Dow, "Public Utility Regulation in Maine" (unpublished doctoral dissertation, Harvard University, 1932), pp. 31–32.

[39] *South Pacific Co. v. Arizona,* 325 U.S. 761 (1945).

[40] 234 U.S. 317, 332 (1914).

[41] 113 U.S. 27, 31 (1885).

[42] Owen Brewster, *Maine and Its Water Resources,* address to Androscoggin Pomona Grange, Danville Junction, Maine, May 7, 1924.

[43] Lewiston *Evening Journal,* March 21–24, 28, 1928; Roy L. Fernald, "The Fernald Law" (unpublished LL.M. thesis, Boston University Law School, 1928). F. Eugene Melder is of the opinion that Fisher oversimplified the legal problems. *State and Local Barriers to Interstate Commerce in the United States* (Orono, Maine, 1937), p. 163.

[44] Edward S. Corwin, "Social Planning under the Constitution," *American Political Science Review,* February, 1932, pp. 1–24.

[45] *Addyston Pipe and Steel Co. v. United States,* 175 U.S. 211, 246 (1899).

[46] *Swift and Co. v. United States,* 196 U.S. 375 (1905).

[47] *Houston, East and West Texas Railway Co. v. United States,* 234 U.S. 342 (1914).

[48] 257 U.S. 563, 588 (1922).

[49] 258 U.S. 50 (1922).

[50] 301 U.S. 1 (1937).

[51] 307 U.S. 38, 47 (1939).

[52] 312 U.S. 100, 118 (1941).

[53] *United States v. South-Eastern Underwriters Assn.,* 322 U.S. 533 (1944).

[54] *United States v. Wrightwood Dairy Co.,* 315 U.S. 110 (1942).

[55] *Consolidated Edison Co. v. National Labor Relations Board,* 305 U.S. 197 (1938).

[56] Federal Power Commission, *In re Hartford Electric Co.,* Opinion no. 58, Docket IT-5560, 1941.

[57] Robert D. Baum, *The Federal Power Commission and State Utility Regulation* (Washington, D.C., 1942), pp. 58–60.

[58] *State ex rel. Corwin v. Indiana & Ohio Oil, Gas, and Mining Co.,* 120 Ind. 575 (1900).

[59] 117 U.S. 190, 205–206 (1900).

[60] 221 U.S. 229 (1911).

[61] *Ibid.,* p. 257.

[62] 177 U.S. 190 (1900).

[63] 172 Fed. 545 (1909).

[64] 221 U.S. 229, 255 (1911).

[65] *Ibid.,* p. 261.

[66] 262 U.S. 553, 596–597 (1923).

[67] Felix Frankfurter and James M. Landis, "The Compact Clause of the Constitution—A Study in Interstate Adjustments," *Yale Law Journal,* Vol. 34, No. 7 (May, 1925), p. 718. The core of this article was that states could postpone federal jurisdiction over hydroelectric power by entering into regional compacts.

[68] *Public Utilities Commission v. Attleboro Steam & Electric Co.,* 273 U.S. 83 (1927).

[69] *Attleboro Steam & Electric Co. v. Public Utilities Commission,* 46 R.I. 496 (1925).

[70] 273 U.S. 83, 88 (1927).

[71] *Ibid.,* p. 90.

[72] Orren C. Hormell, *Maine Public Utilities* (Brunswick, Maine, 1927), p. 67.

[73] *Foster-Fountain Packing Co. v. Haydel,* 278 U.S. 1, 10 (1928).

[74] Elsbree, *op. cit.,* p. 42.

[75] *Pennsylvania v. West Virginia,* 262 U.S. 553 (1923).

[76] 294 U.S. 511, 525–527 (1935).

[77] *Hood v. Du Mond,* U.S. Sup. Ct. (Law ed.), *Advance Opinions, 1949,* Vol. 93, No. 12 (April, 1949), p. 688. Italics mine.

[78] *Crawford Electric Co. v. Power Co. and Shaw,* 110 Maine 285, 293 (1913). Yet Percival P. Baxter, five years later, said, "If electricity is a *commodity,* once it is shipped out of Maine, the Maine Legislature loses all control over it." *Maine's Water Power—Our Natural Inheritance* (Lewiston, Maine, 1918), p. 5. He was arguing for control by charter, and undoubtedly felt the need for a ruling on this point by the United States Supreme Court.

[79] "The electricity is in a way the subject of possession as it flows from the gen-

erator onto the distribution system. Of course it cannot be taken off the system and carried away as can gas or tangible personal property, but I should say it could be reduced to possession in that it can be controlled while upon the system." Personal letter from Mr. Justice Merrill, March 25, 1935.

[80] *Gibbons v. Ogden,* 9 Wheat. 1, 196 (1824). "And if the trading intercourse be between two states remote from each other, must it not commence in one, terminate in the other, and probably pass through a third?"

[81] 221 U.S. 229, 260 (1911).

[82] Lewiston *Evening Journal,* March 12, 1929.

[83] *Sprout v. City of South Bend,* 277 U.S. 163, 171 (1928); 221 U.S. 229, 261 (1911).

[84] Robert L. Stern, "That Commerce Which Concerns More States Than One," *Harvard Law Review,* June, 1934, p. 1351.

[85] Homer C. Hockett, *The Constitutional History of the United States* (New York, 1939), Vol. 1, p. 217.

[86] Maine Water Power Commission, *First Annual Report, 1920,* pp. 86–87.

[87] 262 U.S. 553, 590–591 (1923).

[88] Melvin G. DeChazeau, *Southern Economic Journal,* Vol. 7, No. 4 (April, 1941), p. 497.

[89] Elsbree, *op. cit.,* p. 25; see also John Bauer and Nathaniel Gold, *The Electric Power Industry* (New York, 1939), p. 35.

[90] Personal letter from Edward F. Merrill, Skowhegan, Maine, March 25, 1935.

[91] Edward F. Dow, "Public Utility Regulation in Maine" (unpublished doctoral dissertation, Harvard University, 1932). See also Lucilius A. Emery, "The Legal Phase of the Water Power Investigation," Maine Public Utilities Commission, *Special Water Power Investigation* (Lewiston, Maine, 1918), pp. 11–22.

[92] 286 U.S. 165, 179–180 (1932). That John Locke would consider that there are property rights in electricity and that it is not a natural resource is clear from this famous passage: "The 'labour' of his [man's] body and the 'work' of his hands, we may say, are properly his. Whatsoever, then, he removes out of the state that Nature hath provided and left it in, he hath mixed his labour with it, and joined to it something that is his own, and thereby makes it his property." John Locke, *Of Civil Government* (Everyman's Library ed.; New York and London, 1936), p. 130. The *Encyclopaedia Britannica,* in listing physical resources, includes water power but not electric current.

[93] *Great Falls Manufacturing Co. v. Fernald,* 47 N.H. 444 (1867). Quoted in *Brown v. Gerald,* 100 Maine 351, 377 (1905).

[94] National Resources Committee, *Our Energy Resources* (Washington, D.C., 1939), p. 1.

[95] In the opinion of Professor F. Eugene Melder of Clark University, "There appears to be little doubt that the Court would consider such state export restriction laws to be burdens on manufactured goods in interstate commerce, even though the source of the energy is a state-owned natural resource." Melder, *op. cit.,* p. 164.

[96] Orren C. Hormell, "Governmental Control of Power Utilities in the New England States," *New England's Prospect,* American Geographical Society, Special Publication no. 6 (New York, 1933), p. 312.

[97] Henry Rottschaeffer, *The Constitution and Socio-Economic Change* (Ann Arbor, Mich., 1948), p. 75.

[98] Merle Fainsod and Lincoln Gordon, *Government and the American Economy* (New York, 1941), p. 325.

[99] William E. Mosher, "Public Utility Regulation," *Regulatory Administration* (ed. by George A. Graham and Henry Reining, Jr.; New York, 1943), p. 163.

[100] Nelson Lee Smith, "Rate Regulation by the Federal Power Commission," *American Economic Review*, Proceedings, Vol. 36, No. 2 (May, 1946), p. 411.

[101] Fainsod and Gordon, *op. cit.*, pp. 333–334.

[102] Nine recommendations and (or) orders were issued by the Federal Power Commission on June 27, 1941. They are Docket IT-5703–5711 incl.

[103] 311 U.S. 377 (1940). Forty-one states, including Maine, filed briefs opposing Federal Power Commission jurisdiction.

[104] *Ibid.*, pp. 377, 426–427.

[105] *Oklahoma v. Atkinson Co.*, 313 U.S. 508, 523 (1941). Former Attorney General Lawrence C. Jones of Vermont, reluctantly admitting that Congress has plenary flood-control power on navigable streams and their nonnavigable tributaries, suggested that the remedy is for the states to launch their attack in Congress rather than in the courts. *Biennial Report of the Attorney General of the State of Vermont, 1940*, pp. 207–231.

[106] *Fox River Paper Co. v. Railroad Commission*, 274 U.S. 651, 657 (1927).

[107] *Oklahoma v. Atkinson Co.*, 313 U.S. 508 (1941).

[108] *Ibid.*, pp. 533–534.

[109] 152 Fed. 2d 909 (1946).

[110] Control might be asserted, likewise, on the basis of national authority over admiralty and maritime jurisdiction. *In re Garnett*, 141 U.S. 1 (1891). In *Lord v. Goodall Steamship Co.*, 192 U.S. 14 (1881), an American ship traveling between two California ports was declared subject to federal maritime law. Almost a century ago, Maine rivers were widely used in interstate and foreign commerce, but with the advent of railroads the rivers have become relatively unimportant as transportation channels.

[111] "Any person, association, corporation, State, or municipality intending to construct a dam or other project works across, along, over, *or in any stream or part thereof, other than those defined in this chapter as navigable waters,* and over which Congress has jurisdiction under its authority to regulate commerce with foreign nations and among the several States shall before such construction file declaration of such intention with the Commission, whereupon the Commission shall cause immediate investigation of such proposed construction to be made, and if upon investigation it shall find that the interests of interstate or foreign commerce would be affected by such proposed construction, such person, association, corporation, State, or municipality shall not construct, maintain, or operate such dam or other project works until it shall have applied for and shall have received a license under the provisions of this Act . . ."

[112] 152 Fed. 2d 909 (1946).

[113] Although ex post facto laws are unconstitutional, retroactive laws frequently are valid.

[114] Portland *Sunday Telegram*, March 3, 1946; Portland *Press Herald*, August 14, 1948.

[115] Federal Power Commission, *Reports, 1941*, Vol. 2, p. 381.

[116] "It shall be unlawful for any person, State, or municipality, for the purpose of developing electric power, to construct, operate, or maintain any dam, water

conduit, reservoir, power house, or other works incidental thereto across, along, or in any of the navigable waters of the United States, or upon any part of the public lands or reservations of the United States (including the Territories), or utilize the surplus water or water power from any Government dam, except under and in accordance with the terms of a permit or valid existing right-of-way granted prior to June 10, 1920, or a license granted pursuant to this Act." Federal Power Act, sec. 23*B*.

[117] Federal Power Commission, *Reports, 1941*, Vol. 2, p. 8.

[118] Federal Power Commission, *In the Matter of Bellows Falls Hydro-Electric Corporation, Connecticut River Power Company, and New England Power Company*, Project no. 1855, August 18, 1942, pp. 3, 5.

[119] Federal Power Commission, *In the Matter of Connecticut River Power Company and New England Power Company*, Project no. 1904, August 1, 1944.

[120] 328 U.S. 152 (1946).

[121] *First Iowa Hydro-Electric Coöperative v. Federal Power Commission*, 328 U.S. 152, 164 (1946).

[122] *Ibid.*, p. 171.

[123] 2 F.P.C. 61, 31 P.U.R. (N.S.), 1.

[124] 315 U.S. 806 (1942). See also *Niagara Falls Power Co. v. Federal Power Commission*, 137 Fed. 2d 787; cert. denied, 320 U.S. 815 (1943).

[125] 3 F.P.C. 495, 50 P.U.R. (N.S.), 305; 147 Fed. 2d 743; cert. denied, 325 U.S. 880 (1945); 3 F.P.C. 449, 50 P.U.R. (N.S.), 297; Docket nos. IT-5696–98, September 29, 1947.

[126] Montana Power Company, F.P.C. release no. 3102, November 18, 1946; St. Anthony Falls Water Power Company and Minneapolis Mill Company, F.P.C. release no. 3151, January 16, 1947.

[127] *Prospectus*, Maine Public Service Company to New York Curb Exchange, April 2, 1947, p. 20.

[128] Federal Power Act, as amended August 26, 1935, sec. 4*E*.

[129] *Oklahoma v. Atkinson Co.*, 313 U.S. 508, 534–535 (1941).

[130] 297 U.S. 288 (1936).

## NOTES TO CHAPTER VIII

### Planning, Public Ownership, and State Development

[1] *Tenth United States Census, 1880*, Vol. 16, pp. 70–112; U.S. Geological Survey, *Nineteenth Annual Report, 1899*, Part 4, pp. 34–111.

[2] Maine *Laws*, 1899, c. 99.

[3] Henry A. Pressey, U.S. Geological Survey, *Water-Supply and Irrigation Papers* no. 69 (Washington, D.C., 1902).

[4] Maine *Legislative Record,* 1917, pp. 1141, 1249, 1251.

[5] Maine *Laws,* 1909, c. 212, pp. 280–282.

[6] State Water Storage Commission, *First Annual Report, 1910,* pp. 1–2.

[7] Maine *Legislative Record,* 1911, p. 1071.

[8] State Water Storage Commission, *Second Annual Report, 1911,* pp. 3–16.

[9] State Water Storage Commission, *Third Annual Report, 1913,* p. 3.

[10] Maine *Legislative Record,* 1917, p. 1255.

[11] *Ibid.,* 1919, p. 717.

[12] *Ibid.,* 1913, pp. 847–848.

[13] *Ibid.,* 1917, p. 1252.

[14] *Ibid.,* 1919, p. 718.

[15] Maine Public Utilities Commission, *First Annual Report, 1915,* Vol. 2, pp. 27–141; *Second Annual Report, 1916,* Vol. 2, pp. 106–207.

[16] Maine Public Utilities Commission, *Special Water Power Investigation* (Lewiston, Maine, 1918), p. 6.

[17] *Ibid.,* p. 7. The commission expressed its gratitude that the corporations gave it access to data collected by the private investigations, thereby avoiding duplication of effort.

[18] Maine *Legislative Record,* 1917, pp. 1249–1255.

[19] *Ibid.,* p. 1372.

[20] *Ibid.,* pp. 1282–1285, 1467–1472.

[21] Maine *Laws,* 1917, c. 203, sec. 9.

[22] *Ibid.,* 1919, c. 132.

[23] Maine Water Power Commission, *First Annual Report, 1920,* p. 16.

[24] Maine *Legislative Record,* 1921, p. 250.

[25] *Ibid.,* pp. 170, 175.

[26] *Ibid.,* p. 46.

[27] Maine Water Power Commission, *Second Annual Report, 1921–1922,* p. 6.

[28] Maine *Legislative Record,* 1923, pp. 1297–1298.

[29] The Maine Constitution provides that unless such a bill is returned by the governor within three days after the next session of the legislature it becomes law. Maine *Legislative Record,* 1925, pp. 71–72.

[30] Arthur G. Staples, "Maine Water Powers," *Sprague's Journal of Maine History,* Vol. 12, No. 2 (April–June, 1924), p. 135.

[31] Maine *Senate Journal,* 1909, p. 27.

[32] *Ibid.,* 1911, p. 35.

[33] *Ibid.,* 1919, p. 41.

[34] Harvey D. Eaton, Lewiston *Evening Journal* (feature article), February 28, 1929. Maine *Legislative Record,* 1915, p. 480.

[35] For example, *Water Power Cases,* 148 Wis. 124 (1912).

[36] William R. Pattangall, *The Meddybemps Letters* (Lewiston, Maine, 1924), pp. 105–111, 214–216, 238–256. See also *Sprague's Journal of Maine History,* Vol. 12, No. 2 (April–June, 1924), p. 134.

[37] Percival P. Baxter, *Maine Water Powers: The Prophecy of Theodore Roosevelt in 1909 Applied to the State of Maine in 1924,* address at annual Grange Conference, Augusta, Maine, January 30, 1924, pp. 22–24.

[38] Maine *Legislative Record,* 1917, pp. 171, 893.

[39] Lewiston *Evening Journal,* February 12, 1918.

[40] Percival P. Baxter, *Maine's Water Powers—Our Natural Inheritance* (Lewiston, Maine, 1918), pp. 7–8.

[41] *Fletcher v. Peck,* 6 Cranch 87 (1810).

[42] Owen Brewster, *Maine and Its Water Resources,* address to Androscoggin Pomona Grange, Danville Junction, Maine, May 7, 1924.

[43] Lucilius A. Emery, "The Legal Phase of the Water Power Investigation," Maine Public Utilities Commission, *Special Water Power Investigation* (Lewiston, Maine, 1918).

[44] 118 Maine 503, 512 (1919).

[45] Emery, *op. cit.,* p. 22.

[46] *Constitution of Maine,* Art. I, sec. 21. 118 Maine 503, 513 (1919).

[47] 118 Maine 503, 514 (1919).

[48] Emery, *op. cit.,* pp. 16–17.

[49] 40 Maine 317, 323–324 (1855).

[50] *State v. Edwards,* 86 Maine 102, 105 (1893).

[51] *Brown v. Gerald,* 100 Maine 351, 365, 373–377 (1905). That this decision was out of line with that of the United States Supreme Court is obvious from the following judgment by Mr. Justice Holmes: "In the organic relations of modern society it may sometimes be hard to draw the line that is supposed to limit the authority of the legislature to exercise or delegate the power of eminent domain. But to gather the streams from waste and to draw from them energy, labor without brains, and so to save mankind from toil that it can be spared, is to supply what, next to intellect, is the very foundation of all our achievements and all our welfare. If that purpose is not public we should be at a loss to say what is." *Mt. Vernon-Woodberry Cotton Duck Co. v. Alabama Interstate Power Co.,* 240 U.S. 30, 32 (1916).

[52] To distinguish between police power and eminent domain would be a study in itself. But, generally, the police power is legislative authority to protect the people by regulating private property for public health, safety, convenience, and regulation of public callings. Eminent domain is the right of a government to appropriate private property to a public use, whenever the public exigency requires it, provided that just compensation is paid.

[53] 118 Maine 503, 517–518 (1919).

[54] *Union Water Power Co. v. Auburn,* 90 Maine 60 (1897); 118 Maine 503, 518–520 (1919).

[55] Emery, *op. cit.,* pp. 21–22.

[56] Governor Percival P. Baxter, address to Portland Kiwanis Club, Lewiston *Evening Journal,* February 12, 1918.

[57] Governor Frederic H. Parkhurst, inaugural address, Maine *Senate Journal,* 1921, p. 29.

[58] Percival P. Baxter, *Water Powers: A Communication Embodying Constitutional Amendment to the 80th Legislature,* March 17, 1921, p. 4.

[59] *Maine's Water Power Policy as Defined by Governor Percival P. Baxter and Endorsed by Hon. John A. Peters,* Augusta, Maine, November 8, 1921.

[60] Baxter, *Water Powers,* pp. 5–6. Maine *Legislative Record,* 1921, p. 1257.

[61] Baxter, *Water Powers,* pp. 6–7.

[62] Edward P. Ricker, *The Water Power Resolve* (Lewiston, Maine, 1921), pp. 3–12; *Let Maine Keep Her Birthright* (Lewiston, Maine, 1921), pp. 9–12.

[63] For example, letter from the Hon. Benjamin F. Cleaves to Congressman John A. Peters, October 17, 1921. See *supra,* n. 59.

[64] Ricker, *Let Maine Keep Her Birthright,* p. 11.

[65] Letter from Congressman John A. Peters to the Hon. Benjamin F. Cleaves, October 20, 1921. See *supra*, n. 59.

[66] Maine *Legislative Record*, 1921, pp. 1278–1279, 1303.

[67] Baxter, inaugural address, Maine *Senate Journal*, 1923, p. 21.

[68] Maine *Legislative Record*, 1923, pp. 733–735.

[69] Maine Water Power Commission, *Second Annual Report, 1921–1922*, p. 18.

[70] Baxter, *Maine Water Powers*, Grange address, Augusta, Maine, January 30, 1924, p. 20.

[71] Owen Brewster, *Maine and Its Water Resources*, address to Androscoggin Pomona Grange, Danville Junction, Maine, May 7, 1924.

[72] Baxter, *Maine Water Powers*, Grange address, p. 12.

[73] Actually, the grant was for fifty years, but Governor Baxter claimed that this was perpetual, since the state could not take the property at that time without amending the Constitution, and he charged that this valuable right would induce the power companies to prevent the passage of such an amendment. Maine *Legislative Record*, 1923, p. 549. It would be difficult to reconcile this with his later proposal to lease the site for forty years.

[74] *Ibid.*, pp. 573, 637.

[75] Baxter, *The Dead River Reservoir Company and the Kennebec Reservoir Company*, message to 81st Legislature, State of Maine, April 5, 1923, p. 3.

[76] Maine *Legislative Record*, 1923, pp. 797–803, 896–901.

[77] Baxter, *The Inside History of the Kennebec–Dead River Storage Charters. A Message to the People of Maine*, 1923, p. 4.

[78] *Ibid.*, and Maine *Legislative Record*, 1923, pp. 1134–1137.

[79] Maine *Legislative Record*, 1923, pp. 1164, 1261.

[80] Baxter, *The Dead River Reservoir Company and the Kennebec Reservoir Company*, p. 7.

[81] Maine *Legislative Record*, 1923, pp. 1135–1136.

[82] Baxter, *The Repudiation of the Act Incorporating the Dead River Reservoir Company*, message to 81st Legislature, State of Maine, April 6, 1923; *The Inside History of the Kennebec–Dead River Storage Charters.*

[83] Maine *Legislative Record*, 1923, pp. 1266–1269.

[84] Baxter, *The Inside History of the Kennebec–Dead River Storage Charters*, p. 10.

[85] Letter quoted in Governor Baxter's Grange address, January 30, 1924, pp. 16–18.

[86] Maine *Legislative Record*, 1925, pp. 1091–1092.

[87] Maine *Senate Journal*, 1925, p. 111.

[88] 100 Maine 351 (1905).

[89] 125 Maine 238 (1926).

[90] *Ibid.*, p. 241.

[91] Maine *Legislative Record*, 1927, pp. 814, 882, 889.

[92] Maine *Private and Special Laws*, 1927, c. 113

[93] Baxter, *Maine Politics and Water Powers*, radio addresses over WCSH, Portland, Maine, February 1, 8, 15, 1927, pp. 21–22.

[94] Maine *Private and Special Laws*, 1929, c. 96; 1931, c. 64; 1933, c. 74; 1935, c. 37; 1937, c. 62; 1939, c. 14.

[95] Lewiston *Daily Sun*, February 21, 1950.

[96] Orren C. Hormell, *Maine Public Utilities* (Brunswick, Maine, 1927), pp. 33–34.

[97] Personal letter from George E. Hill, commissioner, Public Utilities Commission, Augusta, Maine, July 15, 1949.

[98] Federal Power Commission, *Typical Residential Bills, 1947* (Washington, D.C., 1947), p. 21.

# NOTES TO CHAPTER IX

## Rural Electrification; War Problems

[1] Maine *Public Laws,* 1913, c. 129, secs. 27, 28. This prohibition applies to corporations, but not to private individuals. In *Crawford Electric Co. v. Power Co. and Shaw,* 110 Maine 285 (1913), the Supreme Judicial Court permitted an individual to supply electricity to territory assigned by a franchise to a corporation which had never installed apparatus for that purpose.

[2] Maine *Revised Statutes,* 1944, c. 46, sec. 6.

[3] Maine *Legislative Record,* 1931, pp. 580–582. Maine Public Utilities Commission, *Fourth Biennial Report, 1929–1930,* p. 10. All biennial reports below are from the same commission.

[4] *Facts about Rural Electrification* (Central Maine Power Co., 1929), p. 3. The average cost of $1,400 a mile in 1936 dropped within a year to $1,200, a decline of almost 20 per cent. Some lines were constructed for $600 a mile (Wilson, Herring, and Eutsler, *Public Utility Regulation,* pp. 469, 477). With the consequent rise in prices, however, President William B. Skelton says that present costs compare with those of 1929. Personal letter, Lewiston, Maine, January 18, 1945. For an itemized account of the cost of rural lines see Maine Development Commission, *Report on Water Power Resources of the State of Maine* (Augusta, Maine, 1929), pp. 46–49.

[5] Stated in James C. Bonbright, *Public Utilities and the National Power Policies* (New York, 1940), p. 52.

[6] The R.E.A. objects to this, maintaining that there are few remote farms and that the remote farms are large and have more use for electric power.

[7] *Fifth Biennial Report, 1931–1932,* pp. 14–15.

[8] Personal letter from Allyn A. Walters, chief, Information Services Division, Rural Electrification Administration, Washington, D.C., April 28, 1948.

[9] Maine *Legislative Record,* 1929, p. 848. These percentages oversimplify but illustrate the point. Roughly one-third of the cost today is frequently assigned to generation and two-thirds to distribution, but this varies with areas and what is included in each category. R.E.A. expenses for power purchased at wholesale in Maine in 1949 amounted to almost exactly 50 per cent of its total operating expenses (depreciation not included).

[10] *Kennebec Journal,* Augusta, Maine, September 9, 1929. Since then the capacity of this dam has been increased from 48,000 to 72,000 kw.

[11] *Fourth Biennial Report, 1929–1930,* pp. 12–13.

[12] Maine *Legislative Record,* 1931, pp. 579–585, 831

[13] Maine *Laws,* 1931, c. 230.

[14] *Rural Electrification News,* Vol. 6, No. 10 (June, 1941), p. 14.

[15] Edward F. Merrill, Hearing on Coöperative Enabling Act, Maine Legislature, 1941, pp. 12–13. Merrill's statements were made in his capacity as attorney for the power company, and were in no way official pronouncements of a member of the court on which he now sits.

[16] *Fifth Biennial Report, 1931–1932,* p. 11.

[17] Merrill, Hearing on Coöperative Enabling Act, 1941, pp. 13–16.

[18] *Eighth Biennial Report, 1937–1938,* pp. 22–23.

[19] *Ninth Biennial Report, 1939–1940,* p. 17.

[20] A significant survey of rural electrification in Maine by the Central Maine Power Company since 1920, including the Cumberland County Power and Light Company, 1927 to 1942 inclusive, throws light on rural progress in the southern and central parts of the state. (Source: letter from President William B. Skelton to the Hon. Leon R. Williams, House of Representatives, March 23, 1945.)

[21] *Tenth Biennial Report, 1941–1942,* p. 14.

[22] *Fifth Biennial Report, 1931–1932,* pp. 10–11

[23] Rural Electrification Administration, *Comparison of Rank, Percentage and Number of Farms Electrified with Central Station Service by States, 1935, 1945, 1946, and 1947* (Washington, D.C., 1947).

[24] *Report of the Power Survey Committee of the New England Council* (Boston, 1948), p. 22. Percentages for the other New England states were: New Hampshire, 92.1; Vermont, 97.0; Massachusetts, 95.1; Rhode Island, 94.4; Connecticut, 97.1. See also *Fourteenth Biennial Report, 1949–1950,* p. 8.

[25] Federal Power Commission, *Typical Residential Bills, 1947: Cities of 2,500 Population and More* (Washington, D.C., 1947), pp. iv, vi. This writer precludes attention to the reasons for high rates in Maine. Even with the assistance of economists, engineers, and cost accountants, any conclusion would be relative and would have to rest on many value judgments and not on objective measurement. Rates depend on such variables as weak or strong commissions, density of population, presence or threat of municipal plants, alternative sources of supply, high quality of service or service risks, degree and stability of firm and secondary power demands, quantity and dependability of water flow, presence of anchor ice in cold climates, cost and damages in erecting new dams, proximity of natural resources, and transportation distances.

[26] Federal Power Commission, ... *Cities of 50,000 Population and More,* p. viii.

[27] *Ibid.,* p. 11. Low power consumption per farm in Maine can be explained by a combination of factors—the climate, the nature of the country, the small number of dairy farms, and the situation of the people, which prevents expensive use of power. Refrigeration is less of a necessity, for example; firewood is still plentiful, and frontier conditions have not yet disappeared in some areas. Farm consumption is, however, increasing. The Rural Electrification Administration reports an increase from 49 kw-h per farm in Maine in 1941 to 59 kw-h in December, 1946. The Public Utilities Commission points out that the average

residential cost in Maine in 1937 was 5.11 cents per kw-h and in 1945, 4.07 cents. The average for farm service was 5.01 cents per kw-h in 1937, and in 1945, 3.56 cents per kw-h. See *Twelfth Biennial Report, 1945–1946,* p. 17.

[28] Personal letter from Allyn A. Walters, April 28, 1948.

[29] John M. Carmody, "Rural Electrification in the United States," *Ownership and Regulation of Public Utilities* (ed. by G. Lloyd Wilson), American Academy of Political and Social Science, *Annals,* Vol. 201 (January, 1939), pp. 85–86.

[30] *Tennessee Electric Power Co. v. Tennessee Valley Authority,* 306 U.S. 118, 141 (1939).

[31] Personal letter from Allyn A. Walters, April 28, 1948.

[32] Maine *Legislative Record,* 1941, p. 845.

[33] Bonbright, *op. cit.,* pp. 54–55.

[34] Merrill, Hearing on Coöperative Enabling Act, 1941, p. 23*a*.

[35] *Ibid.;* Maine *Legislative Record,* 1941, pp. 844–845.

[36] Personal letter from Allyn A. Walters, March 2, 1948.

[37] Maine *Legislative Record,* 1931, p. 584.

[38] Merrill, Hearing on Coöperative Enabling Act, 1941, p. 18*a*.

[39] Information supplied by Allyn A. Walters, chief, Information Services Division, U.S. Department of Agriculture, R.E.A., April 25, 1945.

[40] *Ninth Biennial Report, 1939–1940,* pp. 18, 133; *Tenth Biennial Report, 1941–1942,* p. 137.

[41] Maine *Legislative Record,* 1941, p. 844.

[42] To quote Chairman Southard on this point: "As I view the matter at the present time these coöperatives are not public utilities—are not subject to the Commission's jurisdiction as to rates, securities, etc., and the Commission's sole function is to grant or deny authority to render service in a territory where a public utility is now authorized to render service. The question as to the status of a coöperative is not free from doubt but the decisions of the Courts, so far as I am informed, are to the effect that they are not public utilities. What our own Court may say, one cannot determine in advance." Maine *Legislative Record,* 1941, pp. 836–837.

[43] *Ibid.,* p. 845.

[44] *Tenth Biennial Report, 1941–1942,* p. 137; *Twelfth Biennial Report, 1945–1946,* p. 3.

[45] Maine *Legislative Record,* 1941, p. 850.

[46] *Ibid.,* p. 833.

[47] Merrill, Hearing on Coöperative Enabling Act, 1941, pp. 12*a*–21*a*.

[48] Maine *Legislative Record,* 1941, pp. 836–838.

[49] Maine *Revised Statutes,* 1944, c. 47.

[50] William J. Neal, address at annual meeting of State Grange, Bangor, Maine, December 7, 1944, p. 3.

[51] Portland *Press Herald,* March 2, 1945.

[52] Information supplied by Allyn A. Walters, chief, Information Services Division, U.S. Department of Agriculture, R.E.A., Washington, D.C., March 2, 1948.

[53] *Tenth Biennial Report, 1941–1942,* p. 14.

[54] Circular letter to stockholders of Central Maine Power Company, October 2, 1944, signed by President William B. Skelton.

[55] *Eleventh Biennial Report, 1943–1944,* p. 16.

[56] *U.S. Government Manual,* Fall, 1940, p. 104.

[57] Brunswick *Record,* April 5, 1945.
[58] *Twelfth Biennial Report, 1945–1946,* p. 17.
[59] Portland *Press Herald,* January 3, 1947; Brunswick *Record,* April 17, 1947.
[60] Leonard J. Cohen, Portland *Sunday Telegram,* January 4, 1948.
[61] Portland *Press Herald,* January 9, 1948.
[62] *Twelfth Biennial Report, 1945–1946,* p. 18.

# NOTES TO CHAPTER X

## Charter Control

[1] *Utah Power and Light Co. v. Pfost,* 286 U.S. 165, 181–182 (1932).
[2] 278 U.S. 300 (1929).
[3] *The Slaughter House Cases,* 16 Wallace 36 (1873).
[4] *Bangor, Oldtown and Milford Railroad Co. v. Smith,* 47 Maine 34, 48 (1859). Charters "are liable to be amended, altered or repealed by the Legislature, as if express provision therefor were made in them, unless they contain an express limitation." In this case the court held that a general law relating to railroad corporations amounted to a modification of a charter. The United States Supreme Court has ruled that a general statute which in effect alters or amends a charter is to be construed as an amendment thereof even if not in terms so designated. *Berea College v. Kentucky,* 211 U.S. 45 (1908).
[5] 4 Wheat. 518 (1819).
[6] 13 Peters 519 (1839).
[7] 9 Howard 172, 184 (1850).
[8] 8 Wallace 168 (1868).
[9] 21 Wallace 456 (1874).
[10] 130 U.S. 1 (1888).
[11] 143 U.S. 305 (1892).
[12] 153 U.S. 436, 440–444 (1894).
[13] 211 U.S. 45, 54 (1908).
[14] Edward F. Merrill, Proceedings of Hearing on power bills, February 24 and 25, 1927, p. 47.
[15] Maine *Legislative Record,* 1927, pp. 1053–1059.
[16] Advisory opinions in 97 Maine 590 (1903); also Lewiston *Evening Journal,* March 12, 1929.
[17] 141 U.S. 47, 57 (1891).
[18] *Addyston Pipe and Steel Co. v. United States,* 175 U.S. 211 (1899).
[19] *West v. Kansas Natural Gas Co.,* 221 U.S. 229, 260 (1911).
[20] 262 U.S. 553, 559 (1923).
[21] 257 U.S. 529, 532–533 (1922).
[22] 271 U.S. 583, 593–594 (1926).

[23] 247 U.S. 105, 114 (1918).

[24] 90 Nebraska 627 (1912).

[25] 274 U.S. 651 (1927).

[26] Hugh L. Elsbree, *Interstate Transmission of Electric Power* (Cambridge, Mass., 1931), pp. 50–53.

[27] Letter to George C. Danforth, hydraulic engineer, Augusta, Maine, dated at Washington, D.C., March 12, 1927. MS in State Library, Augusta, Maine.

[28] Portland *Evening News,* June 13, 1929. Justice Edward F. Merrill of Maine, the principal author of the bill, expressed his belief that it was constitutional, but showed some doubt. "This is one of those questions which is on so close a line that a careful attorney would be justified in expressing an opinion either way. With the Supreme Court of the United States dividing time after time on these questions, one can never tell just what the court might do." Personal letter to Roy L. Fernald, November 7, 1927. Quoted in Fernald, "The Fernald Law" (unpublished LL.M. thesis, Boston University Law School, 1928), p. 76.

[29] Portland *Evening News,* June 27, August 5, 13, 1929.

[30] Maine *Legislative Record,* 1929, p. 855.

[31] Copy of opinion lent by the Hon. Charles Evans Hughes, Jr., on February 19, 1946.

[32] Proceedings of Hearing on power measures, March 7, 1929, p. 58. See also Maine *Legislative Record,* 1929, p. 674.

[33] Proceedings of Hearing on power measures, pp. 58–59.

[34] Personal letter from the Hon. Charles Evans Hughes, Jr., New York, February 7, 1946.

[35] Augustus L. Richards, after reading the manuscript of this chapter, wrote to me on February 1, 1949, as follows: "From the faded remnants of my recollection of the discussions I had with the Judge on this subject, I think it quite likely that Mr. Wyman's 'business associates' have quoted Mr. Wyman correctly as reporting to them 'that Judge Hughes said the Fernald Law as it stood was probably unconstitutional'; and, after refreshing my mind from the excerpt you quote from my letter to Mr. Maxcy of May 22, 1928, I am certain that the Judge suggested the possibility of more effective legislation."

[36] In June, 1946, Judge Hughes had no sufficient recollection to be of assistance in the matter. Personal letter from Charles Evans Hughes, Jr., New York, June 21, 1946.

[37] Personal letter from Augustus L. Richards to E. H. Maxcy, New York, May 22, 1928.

[38] *Cyclopedia of American Government* (New York, 1914), Vol. 3, pp. 228–229.

[39] See chap. i, "The Great-Pond Ordinance." This principle may, of course, have to be modified since the California tidewater oil decisions.

[40] *Montgomery v. Reed,* 69 Maine 510 (1879). See also *Proctor v. Maine Central Railroad Co.,* 96 Maine 458 (1902), and *Abbott v. Treat,* 78 Maine 121 (1886).

[41] Percival P. Baxter, *Maine Politics and Water Powers,* radio addresses over WCSH, Portland, Maine, February 1, 8, 15, 1927, p. 21.

[42] Personal letter from the Hon. Harvey D. Eaton, Waterville, Maine, April 10, 1945.

[43] 229 U.S. 53, 54, 66 (1913).

[44] 311 U.S. 377, 424 (1940).

[45] Maine *House Documents*, H. Doc. 812 (1929).

[46] *Hope Natural Gas Co. v. Hall*, 274 U.S. 284 (1927).

[47] *Pullman's Palace Car Co. v. Pennsylvania*, 141 U.S. 18 (1891).

[48] *Wisconsin and Michigan Railway Co. v. Powers*, 191 U.S. 379 (1903).

[49] *Pullman Co. v. Richardson*, 261 U.S. 330 (1923). See also *American Manufacturing Co. v. St. Louis*, 250 U.S. 459 (1919).

[50] *Maine v. Grand Trunk Railway Co.*, 142 U.S. 217 (1891).

[51] 210 U.S. 217 (1908). See also *Philadelphia and Southern Steamship Co. v. Pennsylvania*, 122 U.S. 326 (1886); *Fisher's Blend Station v. State Tax Commission*, 297 U.S. 860 (1936); *Adams Co. v. Storen*, 304 U.S. 307 (1938).

[52] 120 U.S. 489 (1887).

[53] 136 U.S. 104 (1890).

[54] 127 U.S. 1 (1888).

[55] *Ibid.*, p. 640.

[56] Portland *Evening News*, September 6, 1929.

[57] *Ex parte Levitt*, 302 U.S. 633 (1937).

[58] *Official Report of Proceedings before the Securities and Exchange Commission*, Docket Section, file 59-15, pp. 533–534.

[59] Securities and Exchange Commission, *Decisions and Reports* 2 (1937), pp. 118–123.

[60] *Official Report of Proceedings before the Securities and Exchange Commission*, pp. 607–608.

# NOTES TO CHAPTER XI

## The Compact Plan

[1] The fact that the amount of power crossing state lines has increased since 1926 may signify greater reason for federal control. Of the total quantity generated by all privately owned companies in 1929, 14.7 per cent crossed state lines. The percentage was 15.3 in 1930; and 13.4 per cent of the quantity generated by both privately and publicly owned plants in 1929, and 14.4 per cent in 1930. *Utility Corporations Report* no. 42, 70th Cong., 1st sess., S. Doc. 92 (1932), Part 72*A*, p. 43. Or, stated in another way, outward and inward movement of electric energy across state boundaries for the United States in 1929 was as follows: ratio of outward movement to amount generated, 15:18; inward movement to amount consumed, 19:65. Despite the Fernald law, these ratios were considerably higher for the New England area, the outward ratio being 27:94, and the inward ratio 34:61. In 1929 Maine's export ratio to the amount generated was 0:51 and the import ratio to the amount consumed was 2:30. Federal Trade Commission, *Interstate Movement of Electric Energy*, 71st Cong., 3d sess., S. Doc. 238 (1931), pp. 5, 58. It should be noted in passing that one of

the bases for federal regulation of public utility holding companies was that their subsidiaries often sell and transmit gas and electricity in interstate commerce. Public Utility Holding Company Act of 1935, sec. 1*A*.

[2] Hearing on power bills, February 24 and 25, 1927, p. 88.

[3] William E. Mosher and Finla G. Crawford, *Public Utility Regulation* (New York, 1933), p. 405.

[4] Howard S. Knowlton, Boston, January 14, 1927, to Carl F. Morrison, secretary to Governor Brewster.

[5] "It is indicated that the so-called Compact Clause of the Constitution offers the surest refuge for protection from annulment of our regulation by the action of a Federal court with the additional protection that is proposed by certain pending bills. No method can be guaranteed, but the best legal opinion indicates that the regulations and limitations specified in a compact between the states and ratified by Congress would leave the situation in our control, at least, until Congress should deem it necessary to act. As a practical matter, it seems doubtful if Congress would enter the field if a reasonably workable arrangement was being carried on between the states and the citizens in this section had no reason to complain that an important public utility was outside their control." Maine *Legislative Record,* 1927, p. 535.

[6] S.P. 177, S. Doc. 75 (1927).

[7] Lewiston *Evening Journal,* March 9, 1927.

[8] Felix Frankfurter and James M. Landis, "The Compact Clause of the Constitution—A Study in Interstate Adjustments," *Yale Law Journal,* Vol. 34, No. 7 (May, 1925), p. 727.

[9] Lewiston *Evening Journal,* March 9, 15, 1927.

[10] Maine *Legislative Record,* 1927, pp. 1059–1060.

[11] *Ibid.,* p. 711.

[12] Lewiston *Evening Journal,* March 24, 1928. Wyman estimated that such a line carrying about 130,000 kw. as a maximum load would cost $26,000 a mile, or $5,200,000, including fixtures and equipment; and the expense of transmission 2.40 or 2.45 mills. Hearing on power measures, March 7, 1929, p. 57. This estimated cost seems low, particularly for the more densely settled areas near Boston.

[13] Maine *Legislative Record,* 1929, pp. 110, 971, 1021.

[14] Lewiston *Evening Journal,* March 12, 1929.

[15] William E. Mosher (ed.), *Electric Utilities* (New York, 1929), p. 141.

[16] Hearing on power measures, March 7, 1929, p. 121.

[17] National Resources Committee, *Regional Factors in National Planning and Development* (Washington, D.C., 1935), pp. 50–52.

[18] W. Brooke Graves, *Uniform State Action* (Chapel Hill, N.C., 1934), p. 24.

[19] Hugh L. Elsbree, *Interstate Transmission of Electric Power* (Cambridge, Mass., 1931), p. 178.

[20] Letter from O. C. Merrill, Washington, D.C., March 12, 1927. MS in State Library, Augusta, Maine.

[21] 8 Wheat. 1 (1823).

[22] "This [blanket authority] is hardly feasible; and it is all but inconceivable that Congress would so divest itself of its authority in interstate commerce. It would be contrary to all precedent. Moreover, a serious question might be raised as to the constitutionality of the action." Mosher and Crawford, *op. cit.,* pp. 427–428.

[23] 18 Howard 421, 433 (1855).

[24] Elsbree, *op. cit.*, p. 180.

[25] National Resources Committee, *Regional Factors in National Planning and Development*, p. 48.

[26] Mosher and Crawford, *op. cit.*, pp. 424–425.

[27] National Resources Committee, *Regional Planning* (Washington, D.C., 1938), p. 7.

[28] Lincoln Smith, "The Proposed Development Authority Compact for New England," *Political Science Quarterly*, March, 1951, pp. 37–64.

# NOTES TO CHAPTER XII

## The Passamaquoddy Tidal Power Project

[1] Walter Wells, *The Water Power of Maine* (Augusta, Maine, 1869), pp. 33–34. According to Representative Brewster, the mean change in tide is 18 feet, but sometimes it runs as high as 30 feet. Hearings on H.R. 6264, rivers and harbors bill, House Committee on Rivers and Harbors, 76th Cong., 1st sess., January–May, 1939, p. 84.

[2] Eastport *Sentinel*, March 16, 1938.

[3] *Ibid.*, October 29, 1924.

[4] John W. Roche, Portland *Sunday Telegram*, September 7, 1947. See also A. G. Huntsman, *The Passamaquoddy Bay Power Project and Its Effect on the Fisheries* (Atlantic Biological Station, St. Andrews, N.B., *ca.* 1928). There is a short but good description of the project in the report of the Maine State Planning Board to the Quoddy Hydro-Electric Commission, January, 1935, pp. 155–156.

[5] Brief of P. E. McLaughlin presented to the International Joint Commission at St. Andrews, N.B., August 19, 1949, for the St. Stephen–Milltown Board of Trade.

[6] Maine *Legislative Record*, 1925, pp. 975–979.

[7] *Principles and Facts Underlying Quoddy Tidal Power Project*, pamphlet issued by Eastport District, U.S. Engineer Office (n.d.), p. 3.

[8] Governor Owen Brewster, "New Brunswick Water Power Development," message to 82d Legislature, State of Maine, Maine *Legislative Record*, 1925, pp. 735–737.

[9] Maine *Legislative Record*, 1925, pp. 976, 978.

[10] *Ibid.*, p. 979.

[11] Maine *Private and Special Laws*, 1925, c. 111, pp. 437–441.

[12] Referendum question, voted upon September 14, 1925: "Shall the act pro-

viding for the incorporation of Dexter P. Cooper, Incorporated, for the purpose of developing and utilizing the power of the tides in the Bay of Fundy and waters adjacent thereto, including the right to transmit outside the state electric power generated by the tides under restrictions provided for therein, be accepted?"

[13] It was maintained that the construction of the project would greatly reduce the sardine, clam, cod, and haddock fisheries in Passamaquoddy Bay and along the coast of Charlotte County. See Huntsman, *op. cit.*, pp. 44–45. Early in 1930

| County | Yes | No | County | Yes | No |
|---|---|---|---|---|---|
| Androscoggin | 1,957 | 518 | Penobscot | 5,216 | 378 |
| Aroostook | 1,848 | 381 | Piscataquis | 797 | 110 |
| Cumberland | 8,424 | 1,258 | Sagadahoc | 3,332 | 365 |
| Franklin | 574 | 210 | Somerset | 1,234 | 387 |
| Hancock | 1,385 | 154 | Waldo | 1,287 | 279 |
| Kennebec | 3,626 | 1,052 | Washington | 9,855 | 119 |
| Knox | 5,405 | 333 | York | 3,562 | 895 |
| Lincoln | 3,821 | 426 | | | |
| Oxford | 1,224 | 355 | Totals | 53,547 | 7,220 |

President Hoover announced the allocation of $45,000 as the share of our country in a joint investigation by the United States and Canada of the effect of dams on the fisheries in the area. After four years of investigation an international commission reported that it would hurt the fishing business. The opposition of the Canadian Pacific was based on the contention that the project would ruin the resort business of the locality. Ernest R. Abrams, *Power in Transition* (New York, 1940), p. 262. Subsequent engineering changes have, however, eliminated the latter defect. See also Lincoln Smith, article in *Queen's Quarterly,* Vol. 57, No. 3 (1950).

[14] Walter S. Wyman, president of the Central Maine Power Company, one of the backers of Cooper's first investigations, maintained in 1940 that the private companies gave up the project when studies revealed that tidal power would be uneconomical; it could not produce power cheap enough and firm enough to compete with other forms of production of energy. See May Craig, Portland *Sunday Telegram,* December 22, 1940.

[15] Passamaquoddy Tidal Power Project, 77th Cong., 1st sess., S. Doc. 41 (1941), pp. 2–3.

[16] Eastport *Sentinel,* March 16, 1938.

[17] Maine *Acts and Resolves,* April 1, 1933—April 6, 1935, c. 90, pp. 66–69.

[18] Passamaquoddy Tidal Power Project, S. Doc. 41, pp. 1, 3.

[19] However, Cooper's plan submitted to the P.W.A. included a transmission line from the generating station to Tewksbury, Mass., about 20 miles northwest of Boston. He gave the length of this line as 287 miles, but the P.W.A. estimated it at more than 300. The application indicated that this line would not be necessary if the power could be sold to new industries in the vicinity of Eastport. Passamaquoddy Tidal Power Project, S. Doc. 41, p. 3. The transcript of the hearing before the Board of Review is Docket 1641, March 30, 1934.

[20] Abrams, *op. cit.,* p. 263.

[21] Portland *Press Herald,* July 16, 1934.

[22] Letter dated at the White House, Washington, D.C., July 1, 1934, published in Fort Fairfield *Review,* July 25, 1934.

[23] "Report on Passamaquoddy Tidal Power Project by the Quoddy Hydro-Electric Commission," January, 1935, MS, p. 2.

[24] Senator Arthur H. Vandenberg (R.) of Michigan, an ardent opponent of Quoddy, called this a "packed" committee because the original backer of the project and his assistant were members. "It was about like a bank referring an application for a loan to the applicant himself." *Christian Science Monitor,* March 10, 1936.

[25] "Report . . . by the Quoddy Hydro-Electric Commission," January, 1935, MS, pp. 3–4; Maine State Planning Board, "Report on Passamaquoddy Tidal Power Project," January, 1935, MS, p. 159.

[26] The facilities of the area and its proximity to Europe were factors advanced by John A. Poor in his railroad plans for Maine and the European and North American Railroad almost a century ago.

[27] Portland *Press Herald,* August 13, 1936.

[28] Maine State Planning Board, "Report," pp. 241–255.

[29] "Report . . . by the Quoddy Hydro-Electric Commission," p. 4; Maine State Planning Board, "Report," p. 159. Once the T.V.A. was attacked because of the fantastic amounts of power which it was proposing to generate for which no immediate demand was seen, yet the planned capacity of the T.V.A. proved to be inadequate for national defense and had to be supplemented by hastily authorized additional projects and steam auxiliaries. But opponents of T.V.A. say that part of this market was obtained by absorbing private power companies and by putting "practically every city in Tennessee, as well as many in adjacent states, in the power business." C. Herman Pritchett, *The Tennessee Valley Authority* (Chapel Hill, N.C., 1943), pp. 56, 73.

[30] Maine State Planning Board, "Report," pp. 33 ff.

[31] May Craig, Portland *Press Herald,* March 8, 1935.

[32] Portland *Press Herald,* May 18, 1935.

[33] *Ibid.,* October 3, 1935.

[34] Bangor *Daily News,* February 18, 1935.

[35] *Legislative Document* no. 515, S.P. 423 (1935); Lewiston *Evening Journal,* February 22, 26, 1935.

[36] *Kennebec Journal,* May 18, 1935.

[37] "Report . . . by the Quoddy Hydro-Electric Commission," p. 5.

[38] Lewiston *Evening Journal,* July 9, 10, 11, 1935.

[39] *Ibid.,* September 12, 1935.

[40] Portland *Press Herald,* October 3, 1935.

[41] *Ibid.,* November 9, 1935.

[42] *Ibid.* For a parallel case, South Carolina was not only required to create a state authority before any federal money was allocated to the power project on the Santee-Cooper rivers, but also the State Supreme Court had to declare that the state legislature had the right, under the state constitution, to create such an authority.

[43] *Ibid.*

[44] Lewiston *Evening Journal,* December 30, 1935.

[45] Passamaquoddy Tidal Power Project, S. Doc. 41, p. 4.

[46] Abrams, *op. cit.,* p. 263.

[47] Eastport *Sentinel,* January 15, 1936.

[48] Lewiston *Daily Sun,* March 6, 1936; Portland *Press Herald,* January 18, 1939.

[49] Kenneth Roberts, *Trending into Maine* (Boston, 1938), p. 382.

[50] Portland *Press Herald,* January 16, 1936; Eastport *Sentinel,* March 16, 1938. The War Department replied to the charges of extravagance in fitting up dormitory and apartment houses "to counteract and correct the false impressions given." Eastport *Sentinel,* February 19, 1936.

[51] *Principles and Facts Underlying Quoddy Tidal Power Project,* pamphlet issued by Eastport District, U. S. Engineer Office, p. 8. Kenneth Roberts criticised the relief aspects of Quoddy because jobs were given to paupers and the improvident when Washington County had many deserving citizens who needed employment but who did not qualify under the W.P.A. Roberts, *op. cit.,* pp. 382–383.

[52] Lewiston *Evening Journal,* July 17, 1937; also Lewiston *Daily Sun,* January 4, 1936.

[53] Portland *Sunday Telegram,* January 19, 1936.

[54] The Lewiston *Daily Sun* (January 1; May 30, 1936) was unique in its editorial assertions that Quoddy was illegal, but it was unable to support its contention. Much of the argument was based on the false assumption that the United States government would operate the project after its completion, that it would be in violation of the Fourteenth Amendment, and involve interference with intrastate commerce, illegal price-fixing, and competition of the federal government with private industry.

[55] *Ibid.,* February 18, 1936.

[56] Portland *Press Herald,* February 18, 1936.

[57] *Ibid.,* April 4, 1936.

[58] May Craig, *ibid.,* April 24, 1936.

[59] Florida Ship Canal and Passamaquoddy Tidal Power Projects, Hearing on S.J. Res. 266, Part 1, Senate Committee on Commerce, 74th Cong., 2d sess., May 20, 1936, pp. 3–7.

[60] Portland *Press Herald,* May 21, 1936.

[61] Lewiston *Daily Sun,* March 6, 1936; Eastport *Sentinel,* March 11, 1936; Portland *Press Herald,* August 13, 1936. This announcement came when the financial future of the project was before Congress. Cooper estimated the output to be 260,000,000 kw-h annually from the single-pool, all-American project, and declared that he could sell more power if the project were constructed on a larger scale. Federal Power Commission estimates of the output of the single-pool project varied from 175,000,000 to 340,000,000 kw-h, depending upon the number of generating units installed. See Passamaquoddy Tidal Power Project, S. Doc. 41, p. 15.

[62] Florida Ship Canal and Passamaquoddy Tidal Power Project, Hearing on S.J. Res. 266, Part 1, Senate Committee on Commerce, 74th Cong., 2d sess., May 20, 1936, pp. 4–11. State Senator Clarence B. Beckett of Calais, a member of the Washington County Chamber of Commerce committee on Quoddy, stated that Cooper "was unable to publish the list of those industries for fear of embarrassing them in the communities where they are now located." Portland *Press Herald,* February 1, 1939.

[63] Portland *Press Herald,* February 15, 1936.

[64] *Ibid.,* January 18, 1939.

[65] *Ibid.,* July 30, 1936.

[66] Eastport *Sentinel,* October 28, 1936.

[67] John Bauer and Nathaniel Gold, *The Electric Power Industry* (New York, 1939), p. 38.

[68] May Craig, Portland *Press Herald,* April 24, 26, June 1, 1936.

[69] Lewiston *Evening Journal,* July 17, 1937.

[70] Portland *Press Herald,* January 18, 1939.

[71] Hearings on H.R. 6264, rivers and harbors bill, House Committee on Rivers and Harbors, 76th Cong., 1st sess., January–May, 1939, pp. 80–87.

[72] Yet the power companies now do not oppose an international investigation. Eastport *Sentinel,* August 25, 1949.

[73] Lewiston *Daily Sun,* January 18, 1939.

[74] Portland *Press Herald,* January 18, 1939.

[75] *Ibid.,* January 22, 1938.

[76] *Ibid.,* February 1, 1939. Quoddy supporters maintained that the only means for securing passage of the Authority bill was to present one agreed to, in effect, by the power companies.

[77] Maine *Legislative Record,* 1939, pp. 64–65.

[78] Maine *Private and Special Laws,* 1939, c. 71.

[79] Pritchett, *op. cit.,* pp. 69–70.

[80] 4 Wheat. 316 (1819).

[81] National Resources Committee, *Regional Factors in National Planning and Development* (Washington, D.C., 1935), p. 75.

[82] Maine Development Commission, *Facts about Maine* (Augusta, Maine, 1948), pp. 13, 50; *Report of the State Geologist, 1947–1948,* pp. 8–10. The value of Maine's manganese, except in the emergency of war, is controversial.

[83] Passamaquoddy Tidal Power Project, S. Doc. 41, esp. pp. 9–35.

[84] There is no accurate determination of the costs of power from the international project. Extensive and expensive field investigations would be necessary to ascertain the cost and the amount of power obtainable. Passamaquoddy Tidal Power Project, S. Doc. 41, p. 34.

[85] *Ibid.,* p. 37.

[86] Under conditions of long-continued drought, hydroelectric power developed on the rivers of Maine may become so unreliable that resort is necessary to the most dependable and permanent source of power known—tidal power.

[87] Portland *Press Herald,* April 4, 1942.

[88] *Ibid.,* August 30, 1947.

[89] *Ibid.,* September 6, 1947.

[90] *Ibid.,* September 11, 1947.

[91] H.R. 5821. There is a valuable chronology of Quoddy by C. Frank Keyser, Legislative Reference Service, Library of Congress, May 10, 1948.

[92] Portland *Press Herald,* August 28, 1949.

[93] The International Joint Commission has jurisdiction over territorial waters and other matters between the United States and Canada. Its administrative jurisdiction is well analyzed by C. J. Chacko, *The International Joint Commission between the United States of America and the Dominion of Canada* (New York, 1932).

[94] International Passamaquoddy Engineering Board, *Report to International Joint Commission on Scope and Cost of an Investigation of Passamaquoddy Tidal Power Project* (Washington, D.C., 1950), p. 4.

[95] Colonel Fleming estimated that the international project could produce power at 2 mills per kw-h. Eastport *Sentinel,* March 16, 1938.

[96] Portland *Press Herald,* February 1, 1939.

[97] Lincoln Smith, "Quoddy Tidal Power for New England and New Brunswick?" *Public Utilities Fortnightly,* March 16, 1950.

[98] Federal Power Commission, "Memorandum on Information Requested by Senator Leverett Saltonstall," February 17, 1949, MS, p. 9.

# NOTES TO CHAPTER XIII

## Conclusions

[1] James T. Adams (ed.), *New England's Prospect,* American Geographical Society, Special Publication no. 16 (New York, 1933), p. 3.

[2] Howard W. Odum and Harry E. Moore, *American Regionalism* (New York, 1938), p. 509. There is little justification for the contention that New England people are snobbish. The term "stolid" or even "self-contained" is more nearly correct. Much of the traditional New England "reserve" does not arise from any notion that New Englanders consider themselves better than the people of other areas or that they are unsocial as a group. Rather it is that New Englanders respect the rights of others and do not wish to impose their views on others.

[3] It would be interesting to speculate on the extent to which, if any, the transmission of cheap power from Maine to near-by states would have stayed the southern trend of industry from New England. Since Maine lost some industries also, the effect probably would have been negligible. On the other hand, however, it is maintained that Maine has attracted some industries from southern New England, mainly because of the labor factor.

[4] Harlean James (ed.), *American Planning and Civic Annual* (Washington, D.C., 1937), p. 152.

[5] *Head v. Amoskeag Manufacturing Co.,* 113 U.S. 9, 16–17 (1885).

[6] Two suggestions can be made for the basis of this incorrect idea. It is sometimes confused with the law that great ponds are owned by the public. Then again there is a general belief, coming from the Roman law, that property beyond what a man has created by his own hands is designed for public benefit. The *water* of a river, for example, cannot be privately owned. But in Maine the courts say that the *flow* of the water and the power resulting from it are private property.

[7] M. P. Follett, *The New State* (New York, 1926), p. 127.

[8] *Ibid.,* pp. 122, 125, 126.

[9] Gifford Pinchot, *Giant Power,* address to joint convention of houses of 83d Legislature, State of Maine, February 16, 1926, Augusta, Maine, p. 4. "Giant power" was defined as a great national network of electric wires for the interest of the people and the profit of the companies, but with the interest of the people coming first. "Super-power" consisted of the extension of wires and service only as the profits of the companies dictate.

On the basis of the most recent figures available, the per capita consumption of power in Norway far exceeded that of the United States; also, Canada and Switzerland had better averages than the United States. U. S. Department of Commerce, *Electrical Foreign Trade Notes* no. 362 (Washington, D.C., 1935), pp. 7–10. The per capita consumption in the United States is high, however—50 per cent higher than that of Great Britain, more than twice that of Germany, more than 10 times that of Japan, and 150 times that of China. National Resources Committee, *Our Energy Resources* (Washington, D.C., 1939), p. 2.

[10] Maine State Planning Board, "Report on Passamaquoddy Tidal Power Project," January, 1935, MS, p. 95.

[11] F. Eugene Melder, *State and Local Barriers to Interstate Commerce in the United States* (Orono, Maine, 1937). Also, by the same author, "State Trade Walls," *Public Affairs Pamphlets* no. 37 (New York, 1939).

[12] Personal letter from Warren B. Catlin, Brunswick, Maine, June 23, 1945.

[13] The S. D. Warren Company recently announced a special pulp product to be made into blankets which can be discarded after a single use. Portland *Sunday Telegram,* September 1, 1946.

[14] *Report of the New England Regional Planning Commission for the New England Basins* (Washington, D.C., 1937), p. 6.

[15] Joseph F. Preston, "Every Knock a Boost," Eastport *Sentinel,* December 11, 1935.

[16] National Resources Committee, *Our Energy Resources,* p. 30. The proportion of electric energy for public use derived from water power has ranged from 32 to 40 per cent since 1920. *Ibid.,* p. 4.

[17] *Ibid.*

[18] James T. Young, *The New American Government and Its Work* (4th ed.; New York, 1941), p. 301; Frederic A. Ogg and P. Orman Ray, *Introduction to American Government* (8th ed.; New York, 1945), p. 525.

[19] National Resources Committee, *Our Energy Resources,* p. 23.

[20] *Report of the Power Survey Committee of the New England Council* (Boston, 1948), p. 45.

[21] May Craig, Portland *Sunday Telegram,* April 11, 1937; *Report of the New England Regional Planning Commission for the New England Basins.*

[22] National Resources Committee, *Our Energy Resources,* p. 22.

[23] May Craig, Portland *Sunday Telegram,* April 11, 1937.

[24] *Electric Power and Government Policy* (Twentieth Century Fund, New York, 1948), pp. 711–712.

[25] John Bauer and Nathaniel Gold, *The Electric Power Industry* (New York, 1939), p. 44.

[26] *Ibid.,* p. 53.

[27] *The Hoover Commission Report* (New York, 1949), p. 415.

[28] *Report of the New England Regional Planning Commission for the New England Basins,* p. 7.

[29] National Resources Committee, *Regional Factors in National Planning and Development* (Washington, D.C., 1935), p. 13. This idea was stated by the late Roy L. Fernald as follows: "Real improvement, to be a powerful community force, must come from within. Leave us with ourselves. There's almost nothing the Federal Government does that private enterprises in this or any other state can't do better and cheaper." Editorial, Portland *Press Herald,* February 13, 1951.

[30] Federal Power Commission, "Memorandum on Information Requested by Senator Leverett Saltonstall," February 17, 1949, MS, p. 9.

[31] *Ibid.;* also Portland *Sunday Telegram,* July 10, 1949.

[32] Lewiston *Evening Journal,* December 5, 1925.

[33] Hugh L. Elsbree, *Interstate Transmission of Electric Power* (Cambridge, Mass., 1931), p. 173.

[34] Felix Frankfurter and James M. Landis, "The Compact Clause of the Constitution—A Study in Interstate Adjustments," *Yale Law Journal,* Vol. 34, No. 7 (May, 1925).

[35] William Y. Elliott, *The Need for Constitutional Reform* (New York, 1935), pp. 191 ff.; Odum and Moore, *op. cit.;* National Resources Committee, *Regional Factors in National Planning and Development.*

[36] Joseph E. Kallenbach, *Federal Co-operation with the States* (Ann Arbor, Mich., 1942).

[37] W. Brooke Graves, *Uniform State Action* (Chapel Hill, N.C., 1934), p. 24.

[38] Bauer and Gold, *op. cit.,* p. 38.

[39] Personal letter from Roland B. Greeley, Cambridge, Mass., April 26, 1945.

[40] William F. Wyman, now president of the Central Maine Power Company, recently warned against a complacent attitude toward the entrance of government into any field of business. "There is a limit to which compromises with socialism can be made without arriving there in fact, if not in name."

# SELECTED BIBLIOGRAPHY

A fulsome bibliography of this study would be both purposeless and valueless. The specialized reader will obtain more precise sources in the notes and citations. In selecting bibliographical materials for general readers, numerous volumes on the periphery of the subject are omitted.

## GUIDES


ABRAMS, ERNEST R. *Power in Transition* (New York, 1940).

ADAMS, JAMES T. (ed.). *New England's Prospect,* American Geographical Society, Special Publication no. 16 (New York, 1933).

AKAGI, ROY H. *The Town Proprietors of the New England Colonies* (Philadelphia, 1924).

ARRIS, GEORGE H. *New England Water Power—Myth or Fact?* (Providence, R.I., 1949).

BAUER, JOHN, and NATHANIEL GOLD. *The Electric Power Industry* (New York, 1939).

BAUM, ROBERT D. *The Federal Power Commission and State Utility Regulation* (Washington, D.C., 1942).

CHAMBERLAIN, JOSHUA L. *Maine: Her Place in History* (Augusta, Maine, 1877).

COBURN, LOUISE H. (ed.). *Skowhegan on the Kennebec* (Skowhegan, Maine, 1941).

*Electric Power and Government Policy* (Twentieth Century Fund, New York, 1948).

ELSBREE, HUGH L. *Interstate Transmission of Electric Power* (Cambridge, Mass., 1931).

FARNHAM, HENRY P. *The Law of Waters and Water Rights* (Rochester, N.Y., 1904).

FARRAND, MAX. *The Laws and Liberties of Massachusetts* (Cambridge, Mass., 1929).

FRENCH, W. R. *A History of Turner, Maine* (Portland, Maine, 1887).

GOULD, JOHN M. *Law of Waters* (3d ed.; Chicago, 1900).

HANDLIN, OSCAR, and MARY F. HANDLIN. *Commonwealth* (New York, 1947).

HASSE, ADELAIDE R. *Index of Economic Material in Documents of the States of the United States. Maine, 1820–1904* (Washington, D.C., 1907).

HATCH, LOUIS C. (ed.). *Maine, A History* (New York, 1919).

HORMELL, ORREN C. *Maine Public Utilities* (Brunswick, Maine, 1927).

MELDER, F. EUGENE. *State and Local Barriers to Interstate Commerce in the United States* (Orono, Maine, 1937).

PATTANGALL, WILLIAM R. *The Meddybemps Letters* (Lewiston, Maine, 1924).

*Power in New England,* Report of the Power Survey Committee of the New England Council (Boston, 1948).

*Report of the Special Commission Relative to the Textile Industry and to Prevent the Removal Thereof from the Commonwealth* (Boston, 1950).

RIDLON, G. T. *Saco Valley Settlements and Families* (Portland, Maine, 1895).

WELLS, WALTER. *The Water Power of Maine* (Augusta, Maine, 1869).

WHITMORE, WILLIAM H. (ed.). *The Colonial Laws of Massachusetts* (Boston, 1889).

WHITTLESEY, JOHN J. *Law of the Seashore, Tidewaters and Great Ponds in Massachusetts and Maine* (Boston, 1932).

WILLIAMSON, WILLIAM D. *The History of Maine from Its First Discovery, A.D. 1602, to the Separation, A.D. 1820, Inclusive* (Hallowell, Maine, 1832), 2 vols.

WINTHROP, JOHN. *Winthrop's Journal: History of New England, 1630–1649* (ed. by J. K. Hosmer; New York, 1908).

WOOD, RICHARD G. *A History of Lumbering in Maine, 1820–1861* (Orono, Maine, 1935).

## MANUSCRIPTS

ALLINE, LAWRENCE H. Speech at hearing before Maine Public Utilities Commission, Presque Isle, Maine, January 8, 1948. Mimeo. MS.

BREWSTER, OWEN. Address to Maine members of New England Council, Portland, Maine, January 31, 1925. MS in State Library, Augusta, Maine.

CARTER, CHARLES B. Address to Lions' Club, Lewiston, Maine, March 16, 1926. MS in State Library, Augusta, Maine.

DOW, EDWARD F. "Public Utility Regulation in Maine" (unpublished Ph.D. thesis, Harvard University, 1932).

FERNALD, ROY L. "The Fernald Law" (unpublished LL.M. thesis, Boston University Law School, 1928).

MERRILL, EDWARD F. Speech on rural electrification bill, at legislative committee hearing, Augusta, Maine, 1941.

NEAL, WILLIAM J. Address at annual meeting of State Grange, Bangor, Maine, December 7, 1944.

THAXTER, SIDNEY. "The State of Maine and Electric Power Development." MS. in State Library (undated).

## PERIODICALS

*Electrical World* (Boston), January 17, 1927.

FRANKFURTER, FELIX, and JAMES M. LANDIS. "The Compact Clause of the Constitution—A Study in Interstate Adjustments," *Yale Law Journal,* Vol. 34, No. 7 (May, 1925).

*Rural Electrification News,* Vol. 6, No. 10 (June, 1941).

SMITH, LINCOLN. "Maine's Power Embargo—How It May Be Terminated," *Cornell Law Quarterly,* Winter, 1951; "The Proposed Development Authority Compact for New England," *Political Science Quarterly,* March, 1951.

SMITH, NELSON LEE. "Rate Regulation by the Federal Power Commission," *American Economic Review,* Proceedings, May, 1946.

STAPLES, ARTHUR G. Series of articles on Maine's water powers in *Sprague's Journal of Maine History,* Vol. 12 (January–September, 1924).

## PAMPHLETS

BAXTER, PERCIVAL P. *The Inside History of the Kennebec–Dead River Storage Charters. A Message to the People of Maine,* 1923; *Maine's Water Powers—*

*Our Natural Inheritance* (Lewiston, Maine, 1918); *Maine Water Powers: The Prophecy of Theodore Roosevelt in 1909 Applied to the State of Maine in 1924,* address at annual Grange Conference, Augusta, January 30, 1924; *Maine's Water Power Policy as Defined by Governor Percival P. Baxter and Endorsed by Hon. John A. Peters,* Augusta, Maine, November 8, 1921; address to Portland Kiwanis Club, Lewiston *Evening Journal,* February 12, 1918; *Maine Politics and Water Powers,* radio addresses over WCSH, Portland, Maine, February 1, 8, 15, 1927.

BREWSTER, OWEN. *Maine and Its Water Resources,* address to Androscoggin Pomona Grange, Danville Junction, Maine, May 7, 1924.

Central Maine Power Company (1929). *Facts about Rural Electrification; The Facts about Surplus Power; Information on the Smith Bill; Surplus Power Export Law.*

HUNTSMAN, A. G. *The Passamaquoddy Bay Power Project and Its Effect on the Fisheries* (Atlantic Biological Station, St. Andrews, N.B., *ca.* 1928).

Maine Public Service Company. *Prospectus* to New York Curb Exchange, April 2, 1947.

MELDER, F. EUGENE. *State Trade Walls,* Public Affairs Pamphlet no. 37 (New York, 1939).

RICKER, EDWARD P. *Let Maine Keep Her Birthright* (Lewiston, Maine, 1921); *The Water Power Resolve* (Lewiston, Maine, 1921).

STETSON, CLARENCE C. *One Phase of Our Water Power Problem: Shall Maine Progress or Retrogress?* address to Chamber of Commerce, Bangor, Maine, November 22, 1923.

## DOCUMENTS AND PUBLIC PAPERS

Florida Ship Canal and Passamaquoddy Tidal Power Projects, Hearing on S.J. Res. 266, Part 1, Senate Committee on Commerce, 74th Cong., 2d sess., May 20, 1936.

Hearings on H.R. 6264, rivers and harbors bill, House Committee on Rivers and Harbors, 76th Cong., 1st sess., January–May, 1939.

KEYSER, C. FRANK. *Passamaquoddy Tidal Power Project,* Legislative Reference Service, Library of Congress, May 10, 1948.

Passamaquoddy Tidal Power Project, 77th Cong., 1st sess., S. Doc. 41 (1941).

Public Works Administration, Board of Review. "Application of Dexter P. Cooper, Inc., for a Loan of $43,000,000 for Tidewater Power Development—Passamaquoddy Bay," Docket 1641, March 30, 1934.

### FEDERAL POWER COMMISSION

In addition to numerous annual reports and releases, the following documents deserve to be listed:

"Memorandum on Information Requested by Senator Leverett Saltonstall," February 17, 1949. Mimeo. MS.

"National Power Survey," *Interim Report,* Power Series no. 1, 1935.

"Power Market Survey," Bureau of Power, New York Regional Office, August, 1949.

*Typical Residential Bills, 1947: Cities of 2,500 Population and More; . . . Cities of 50,000 Population and More* (Washington, D.C., 1947).

FEDERAL TRADE COMMISSION

Hearing before F.T.C. on Investigation of Public Utility Corporations, Washington, D.C., March 16, 1932. *Utility Corporations Report* no. 42, 70th Cong., 1st sess., S. Doc. 92 (1932), Part 42; see also S. Doc. 92, Part 72*A*.

*Interstate Movement of Electric Energy*, 71st Cong., 3d sess., S. Doc. 238 (1931).

SECURITIES AND EXCHANGE COMMISSION

*Decisions and Reports*, 2 (1937).

*Notice of Filing of Amended Plan of Reorganization and Order Reconvening Hearing re Northern New England Company and New England Public Service Company* (Philadelphia, 1944), December 5, 1944.

*Official Report of Proceedings before the Securities and Exchange Commission*, Docket Section, file 59-15. Northern New England Company and New England Public Service Company, 1940.

NATIONAL RESOURCES COMMITTEE

*Our Energy Resources* (Washington, D.C., 1939); *Regional Factors in National Planning and Development* (1935); *Regional Planning* (1938). See also *Industrial Location and National Resources*, National Resources Planning Board (1943).

NEW ENGLAND

*Report of the New England Regional Planning Commission for the New England Basins* (Washington, D.C., 1937).

*Water Resources of New England*, Publ. no. 51, New England Regional Planning Commission (Boston, 1937).

MAINE

Numerous documents dating from more than a century ago include, at various times, the following: Maine *Acts and Resolves, House Documents, House Journal, Laws, Legislative Documents, Legislative Record, Private and Special Laws, Revised Statutes, Senate Documents, Senate Journal;* annual reports of the Maine State Water Storage Commission, Maine Water Power Commission, and Maine Public Utilities Commission.

Hearings in the Maine House of Representatives: on power bills, February 24 and 25, 1927; on power measures, March 7, 1929; on an Act to Amend the Mill Act, March 18, 1927; on an Act to Incorporate Fish River Power and Storage Company, March 18, 1927.

Maine Development Commission. *Report on Water Power Resources of the State of Maine* (Augusta, Maine, 1929); *Industrial Maine* (n.d.); *Facts about Maine* (1948).

Maine Public Utilities Commission. *Special Water Power Investigation* (Lewiston, Maine, 1918).

"Report on Passamaquoddy Tidal Power Project by the Quoddy Hydro-Electric Commission," January, 1935. One of the few available copies of this manuscript is in the Bowdoin College Library, Brunswick, Maine.

# INDEX

CPSIA information can be obtained
at www.ICGtesting.com
Printed in the USA
BVHW042157210922
647713BV00003B/79

9 780520 347922